Everyone Is a Programmer

A battle-tested guide to building real apps with AI coding

Zhang Bin
Wu Zhenyao

<packt>

Everyone Is a Programmer

Portfolio Director: Pavan Ramchandani
Relationship Lead: Lucy Wan and Mohd Riyan Khan
Program Manager: Divij Kotian
Content Engineer: Akanksha Gupta
Technical Editor: Vidhisha Patidar
Copy Editor: Safis Editing
Indexer: Manju Arasan
Proofreader: Akanksha Gupta
Production Designer: Prashant Ghare
Growth Lead: Nivedita Singh

First published: March 2026

Production reference: 1270326

Published by Packt Publishing Ltd.
Grosvenor House
11 St Paul's Square
Birmingham
B3 1RB, UK.

ISBN 978-1-80730-559-8
www.packtpub.com

Contributors

About the authors

Zhang Bin (Captain) is a developer community builder deeply focused on large language models and AI coding. He built an AGI knowledge base and AI programming sub-community from the ground up, and through his personal podcast *Langsuo Podcast* has long connected front-line technical experts from leading tech companies to deliver ongoing analysis of technology trends, AI coding methodologies, and industry insights. He is the author of *Vibe Coding: Exploring the New Programming Paradigm of the AI Era*, and firmly believes that in the age of AI, the essence of programming is the state of human-machine collaborative flow — the Vibe.

Andy Wu (Anzai) is a systems architect at a communications-sector startup, a TRAE Expert, an AWS Certified Solutions Architect, and a full-stack indie developer with 7 years of entrepreneurial experience.

As a full-stack indie developer, Andy is passionate about exploring and applying cutting-edge technologies, with a focus on solving complex engineering problems through elegant architecture and efficient development workflows. He brings both deep local startup experience and a broad international perspective — having served as a DevOps consultant to a large overseas healthcare group for over five years, helping their engineering team scale from 30 to more than 200 people.

Andy is an active contributor to the developer community and knowledge-sharing ecosystem. He is a co-builder of the *AI Agent* section of the WayToAGI open-source AI community and the AGI Juejin community, and is the author of the Juejin booklet *Coze: From Beginner to Practitioner — A Complete Guide to AI Agents*. Through this book, he hopes to share the practical dividends of the AI era and the experience of indie development with every creator who dares to dream.

About the reviewers

Parth Santpurkar is a senior software engineer with over a decade of industry experience based out of the San Francisco Bay area. He's a senior IEEE member and his expertise and interests range from software engineering and distributed systems to machine learning and artificial intelligence.

Heartin Kanikathottu is an accomplished cloud architect known for leading technological transformations in cloud computing and security across leading global organizations. He is also a globally recognized author whose book *AWS Security Cookbook (First Edition)* was ranked among the Top Cloud Computing Books of All Time, securing the 8th position by BookAuthority in 2020. His career includes leadership and architect roles such as President at Communities Canada Incorporated, Vice President at Morgan Stanley, Principal Architect at Société Générale, and Cloud and Security Architect at VMware, along with earlier roles at TCS, SAP Ariba, and IG Group. He holds more than 15 professional certifications from leading technology providers including Microsoft, Amazon Web Services, Oracle, Pivotal, and IBM, along with dual master's degrees in Cloud Computing and Data Analytics. He is also a regular speaker at technical conferences and community forums.

Table of Contents

Preface

We are living in an extraordinary era.

Not long ago, movie-quality advertising, professional photography, and studio-produced music required large teams and enormous budgets. Today, a single creator with the right AI tools can do all of that independently. The democratization of creativity is no longer a promise — it is happening right now.

But there is one frontier that has remained stubbornly out of reach for most people: software. If you have ever had a brilliant idea for an app, a tool, or a digital product, you have probably heard a voice in your head say: *"But I'm not technical."* That invisible label has stopped countless great ideas before they ever had a chance. This book was written to tear down that wall.

You are standing at the intersection of two historic waves: the explosion of the creator economy, and the revolutionary rise of AI tools. Together, they have opened a brief and precious window of opportunity. The traditional barriers between a creative idea and a working product — technical complexity, capital, and distribution — are dissolving faster than most people realize.

Everyone Is a Programmer gives you the mindset and the practical toolkit to walk through that window. At its core is a paradigm called **vibe coding**: an art of collaborating with AI. You bring the vision, the intuition, and the judgment. The AI brings the execution. Think of it like centaur chess — a human and an AI working as a team, outperforming both the grandmaster and the machine working alone. This book teaches you to be that centaur creator.

Beyond the mindset, this book delivers a concrete, low-cost action plan built around what we call the **frugal full-stack** — a carefully chosen set of professional-grade tools (TRAE, Cursor, Figma, Vercel, Supabase, and more) that are free or near-free to use. You will build and ship your first full-stack digital product without a large budget or a technical co-founder.

Who this book is for

This book is for anyone who has ever had an idea for a digital product but felt blocked by the technical barrier. You do not need a programming background. You do not need to know what a database is, how a server works, or what an API does. This book explains all of that in plain language, exactly when you need it.

Specifically, this book is for:

- **Aspiring entrepreneurs and product managers** who have product ideas but lack a technical background.
- **Indie developers and designers** who want to dramatically expand what they can build and ship on their own using AI tools.
- **Tech enthusiasts** interested in AI-driven application development, the creator economy, and low-cost startup methods.
- **Dreamers and doers** — anyone who wants to turn a creative idea into their first real digital product.

If you are comfortable using a web browser and willing to experiment, you have everything you need to get started.

What this book covers

Chapter 1, Mindset and Philosophy — The Creator in the Age of AI, is the foundation of the entire book. It guides you through the mindset shift from consumer to creator, introduces the core philosophy of vibe coding, dismantles the three fears that hold beginners back from technology, and establishes the five working principles every indie developer needs. The chapter closes with a deep dive into prompt engineering.

Chapter 2, Frontend Design and AI Implementation, focuses on making your ideas visible. You will learn to use AI-driven tools like Trickle AI and v0.dev to generate professional, beautiful user interfaces from natural language and simple instructions. The chapter also covers Figma fundamentals and introduces AI workbenches like TRAE SOLO and Cursor, completing the full chain from design to working code.

Chapter 3, Infrastructure Setup — The Frugal Full-Stack Toolkit, builds the foundation for your digital product. This chapter introduces the frugal full-stack concept and walks you through setting up a professional, scalable modern infrastructure using free and low-cost cloud services — Vercel, Supabase, Cloudflare R2, and more. You will configure a domain, set up a database, and establish a user authentication system from scratch.

Chapter 4, Backend Development and Advanced Integration, takes you into the application's backend — the core logic that powers everything users don't see. You will direct TRAE SOLO and Cursor to handle traditionally complex backend work: API design, database management, and business logic implementation. The chapter also introduces MCP (Model Context Protocol), a cutting-edge approach that connects AI to external tools and enables advanced automated workflows.

Chapter 5, Project Practice 1 — Building a Habit Tracker from Scratch, is a complete, end-to-end full-stack project. Drawing on everything from the first four chapters, you will go from product planning with AI, through database design, user authentication, email service integration, and file storage, all the way to a deployed, live application.

Chapter 6, Project Practice 2 — Building a Commercial-Grade AI Image Generation Platform, is the graduation project — a complex application with real business value. You will build an AI image generation platform integrating the Replicate API for cutting-edge AI models, a full payment system via Stripe, user management and a points/billing system via Supabase, automated marketing emails via Resend, and global deployment via Vercel. By the end, you will have the complete experience of independently building, deploying, and operating a commercial SaaS product.

To get the most out of this book

No prior programming experience is required. To follow along comfortably, you should:

- Be comfortable using a web browser and signing up for online services.
- Have a computer (Mac or Windows) with a stable internet connection.
- Be willing to experiment — the best way to learn vibe coding is to build things and iterate.

Throughout the book, you will create accounts on several free-tier platforms including TRAE, Vercel, Supabase, and GitHub. All tools used have generous free tiers sufficient for completing every project in this book. Where a paid service is referenced (such as Stripe or Replicate), the book clearly explains the cost structure and how to test without incurring charges.

Download the example code files

The code bundle for the book is hosted on GitHub at `https://github.com/PacktPublishing/Everyone-is-a-Programmer`. We also have other code bundles from our rich catalog of books and videos available at `https://github.com/PacktPublishing`. Check them out!

Download the color images

We also provide a PDF file that has color images of the screenshots/diagrams used in this book. You can download it here:`https://packt.link/gbp/9781807305598`

Conventions used

There are a number of text conventions used throughout this book.

`CodeInText`: Indicates AI prompts, code words in text, database table names, folder names, filenames, file extensions, pathnames, dummy URLs, user input, and Twitter handles. For example: "Locate the file `./supabase/migrations/001_initial_schema.sql` in the project directory."

A block of code is set as follows:

```
JavaScript
fetch(
"[https://your project ID.supabase.co/rest/v1/habits?
select=](https://your project ID.supabase.co/rest/v1/habits?select=)*",
{
headers: {
apikey: "your anonymous key", // using anon key
Authorization: "Bearer, your anonymous key",
},
}
)
.then((res) =res.json())
.then((data) =console.log("Data retrieved:", data))
.catch((error) =console.error("Request failed:", error));
```

Any command-line input or output is written as follows:

```
Bash
## Enter the project directory
cd path/to/your/habit-tracker
```

Bold: Indicates a new term, an important word, or words that you see on the screen. For instance, words in menus or dialog boxes appear in the text like this. For example: "After logging in, click **Add New** in the Vercel Dashboard and select **Project**. "

Note

Warnings or important notes appear like this.

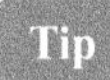

Tips and tricks appear like this.

Get in touch

Feedback from our readers is always welcome.

General feedback: If you have questions about any aspect of this book or have any general feedback, please email us at `customercare@packt.com` and mention the book's title in the subject of your message.

Errata: Although we have taken every care to ensure the accuracy of our content, mistakes do happen. If you have found a mistake in this book, we would be grateful if you reported this to us. Please visit `http://www.packt.com/submit-errata`, click **Submit Errata**, and fill in the form.

Piracy: If you come across any illegal copies of our works in any form on the internet, we would be grateful if you would provide us with the location address or website name. Please contact us at `copyright@packt.com` with a link to the material.

If you are interested in becoming an author: If there is a topic that you have expertise in and you are interested in either writing or contributing to a book, please visit `https://authors.packt.com/`.

Free Benefits with Your Book

This book comes with free benefits to support your learning. Activate them now for instant access (see the "*How to Unlock*" section for instructions).

Here's a quick overview of what you can instantly unlock with your purchase:

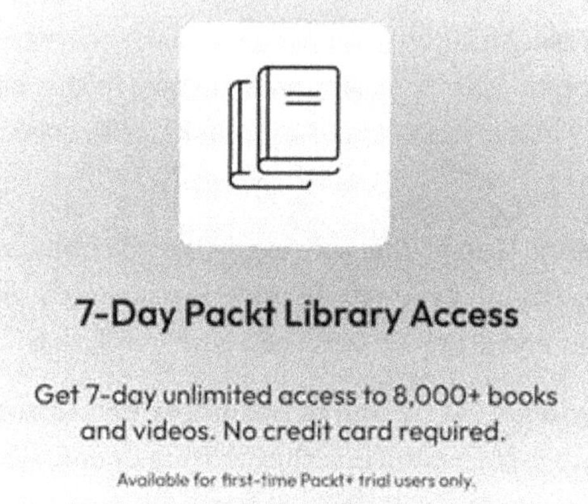

How to Unlock

Scan the QR code (or go to `packtpub.com/unlock`). Search for this book by name, confirm the edition, and then follow the steps on the page.

UNLOCK NOW

Note: Keep your invoice handy. Purchases made directly from Packt don't require one

Share your thoughts

Once you've read *Everyone Is a Programmer*, we'd love to hear your thoughts! Scan the QR code below to go straight to the Amazon review page for this book and share your feedback.

`https://packt.link/r/1807305597`

Your review is important to us and the tech community and will help us make sure we're delivering excellent quality content.

1

Mindset and Philosophy—The Creator in the Age of AI

Will the brilliant ideas flashing through your mind remain forever stranded on the shores of imagination, blocked by the high walls of technology?

This chapter will fundamentally reshape your relationship with technology.

You are about to encounter a new paradigm of creation: **vibe coding**. This is not another programming language you must toil to master; it is the practical art of high-efficiency collaboration with AI.

From the halls of the **Museum of Modern Art** (**MoMA**) in New York, where Refik Anadol transforms raw data into art, to the moment you deploy your first "Hello World"; from understanding the logic of the "Director vs. Actor" model to mastering the golden rules of AI dialogue—this chapter builds the bridge that transforms you from a *prisoner of ideas* into a *creator of reality*.

All great stories begin with belief. This is where you start believing in your own power to create.

Your purchase includes a free PDF copy + exclusive extras

Your purchase includes a DRM-free PDF copy of this book, 7-day trial to the Packt+ library (no credit card required), and additional exclusive extras. See the *Free benefits with your book* section in the *Preface* to unlock them instantly and maximize your learning.

Bridging the execution gap

In February 2024, an event in Glasgow, Scotland, unexpectedly spiraled into a global viral sensation (`https://www.bbc.com/news/uk-scotland-glasgow-west-68431728`). Billed as "Willy's Chocolate Experience," the promotional materials promised a visual feast. AI-generated imagery depicted a magical realm: lush forests of giant lollipops, rushing chocolate rivers, and dazzling lights that seemed to bring a fairy tale to life. Captivated by these dreamlike scenes, parents bought tickets in droves, eager to walk their children into a place where "chocolate dreams come true."

Reality, however, was a brutal shock.

When families arrived, they found not a magical factory but a sparsely decorated, drafty warehouse. The "wonderland" consisted of a few low-resolution AI backdrops tacked onto walls, a lonely, semi-deflated bouncy castle, and a script that the actors themselves described as "15 pages of AI-generated gibberish." The promised "delicious treats" amounted to a handful of jelly beans and a half-cup of lemonade. The event ended in chaos, police intervention, and a refund scandal.

The "Wonka Debacle" went viral not just because it was a commercial failure, but because it served as a perfect modern fable. It struck a nerve with every creative person who has ever faced the *Execution Gap*: the massive chasm between the flawless vision in our heads (the AI promo images) and our ability to build it in the real world (the empty warehouse). This is the traditional "technical barrier."

The organizers had a clear "Prompt"—*create an immersive Willy Wonka experience*—and they even had the visual output. But they lacked the core ability to ground that digital vision into physical reality. This mirrors a common anxiety: "I have a brilliant idea for an app, but I can't code, so it stays in my head."

But what if there were a way to cross that chasm? What if your ideas didn't have to end up like that sad Glasgow warehouse, but could be built, experienced, and used?

Welcome to the world of **vibe coding**.

The concept of vibe coding

Before we build the bridge, we must adopt a new mindset. If the Wonka event was a farce caused by the disconnect between creativity and technology, we are about to see what happens when creativity and AI are fused with science.

Sensory perception: The art of the vibe

Shift your gaze from that chaotic warehouse to the MoMA in New York. Here, the work of Refik Anadol leaves audiences spellbound. Anadol is not an app developer; he is a master vibe coder. He treats data, such as urban traffic flows, nature patterns, collective human memories, as his "digital pigment." Using machine learning algorithms, he translates cold data into fluid, abstract, immersive environments:

Figure 1.1 – Refik Anadol's "Archive Dreaming," an immersive art installation at the MoMA that visualizes the dreams of a machine

Imagine standing in a massive space where the walls and floor ripple and flow, as if you have stepped inside a machine's dream. This is *Archive Dreaming*. Anadol asked the AI a poetic question: *"If a machine could dream, what would it see?"* The answer wasn't lines of code; it was a visual symphony.

In this context, *vibe* is a feeling, an atmosphere, an intuitive vision. Anadol's success lies in his ability to communicate this abstract vibe to the AI, guiding it to visualize a feeling. His work proves that AI-driven creation can be high art.

This is the emotional core of vibe coding: Creation starts with a feeling. It begins with the unique experience you want to give the world.

Rational perception: The technical core

While its philosophy is almost artistic, vibe coding is built on a rigid technical foundation. Strip away the artistic shell, and you find a revolutionary software development paradigm.

Vibe coding is a modern programming methodology in which the creator uses natural language (plain English or Chinese) to describe desired functionality, and advanced AI models (like GPT-4o or Claude) translate those instructions into executable software.

This is closely related to **Prompt-Driven Development** (**PDD**). PDD inverts the traditional human-computer interaction model:

- **Old Way**: You learn the computer's language (syntax) to tell it *how* to do a task step by step.
- **New Way**: You use your language to tell the AI *what* you want to achieve

For example, instead of learning how to configure a database, write validation logic, and handle frontend click events, you simply prompt: `Create a login page that authenticates users via email and password.` The AI handles the *how*; you focus on the *what*. This shift from fighting syntax to focusing on results drastically lowers the barrier to entry while raising the ceiling of what is possible.

The core philosophy

In this section, we will explore the fundamental mindset shift required for the AI era: moving from manually writing code to orchestrating results. You will learn how to transition your role from a solitary builder to a visionary director who collaborates with AI to bring ideas to life.

From craftsman to director

In traditional development, a programmer is a *craftsman*. They must know their tools (Python, Java) and materials (data structures) intimately, hand-carving every line of code. It is precise, time-consuming work.

A vibe coder is a film *director*. A director doesn't hold the camera or sew the costumes. Their job is to hold the vision. They communicate that vision to the crew (the AI), review the dailies (the code output), and give feedback until the result matches the picture in their head.

As a director, your "super crew" is the AI. Your two key skills are:

- **Description (Prompt Engineering)**: Translating fuzzy ideas into clear instructions.
- **Iteration**: Reviewing the AI's first draft, identifying the gaps, and guiding it toward perfection.

Case study: Jon Han and Microsoft

Artist Jon Han's work for Microsoft's *2023 Work Trend Index* perfectly illustrates this *director* mode (`https://www.microsoft.com/en-us/worklab/experimenting-with-ai-as-a-creative-collaborator`):

1. **The Initial Prompt**: Han wanted to visualize "human-tech connection." The AI returned images that were "too sci-fi" and cold (*Figure 1.2*):

Figure 1.2 – The initial AI-generated image for "human-tech connection

Director's Note: "The vibe is off. Let's reset."

2. **Iteration**: Han added the instruction: `Lush landscape`. The AI understood, producing organic, atmospheric images (*Figure 1.3*):

Figure 1.3: By adding the prompt "Lush landscape," the AI produced a more organic and atmospheric image

Director's Note: "Better. Warmer tones needed."

3. **Refinement**: Han added the word *Warm*. The AI took it literally and set the image on fire (*Figure 1.4*):

Figure 1.4 – The AI's literal interpretation of the word "Warm," resulting in an image on fire

Director's Note: This highlights the learning curve. You must learn your actors' quirks.

4. **Final Collaboration**: Han eventually combined the AI's complex generation with his own hand-drawn composition, using the AI to generate specific textures (trees, sky) that he then assembled himself.

Figure 1.5 – The final collaborative piece, where Jon Han combined his hand-drawn composition with AI-generated textures

Jon Han didn't paint every pixel, nor did he let AI do whatever it wanted. He orchestrated the result.

Figure 1.6 – Another example of the final artwork, showing the blend of human artistry and AI capability.

This confirms the essence of vibe coding: Human vision commands AI capability.

Dimension	**Traditional programming**	**Vibe coding**
Core skill	Syntax precision and algorithmic logic	Vision communication and iterative feedback
Primary tool	Specific languages (Python, Java)	Natural language and AI models

Dimension	Traditional programming	Vibe coding
Failure mode	Hours spent debugging obscure errors	A learning opportunity to refine the prompt
Prototyping	Weeks or months	Minutes or hours
Mental focus	"How do I do this?" (implementation) **	"What do I want?" (outcome)

Table 1.1 – Key differences between traditional programming and vibe coding

A Note on Copyright and Ownership

The industry currently views AI as a functional *co-author* or a tool to amplify human creativity, not replace it. To ensure your work secures full legal protection and commercial viability, you must maintain strict control over the entire creative chain. Meticulously document your specific human contributions and stay responsive to the evolving legal landscape. Ultimately, it is the distinct *human touch* that validates ownership.

Confronting the beginner's three primal fears

Even if the philosophy of vibe coding has already sparked your enthusiasm, you may still harbor deep-seated reservations. These inner demons act as invisible barriers, preventing countless individuals from taking that first creative step. Let's dismantle them, one by one.

Fear 1: "I'm not a tech expert"

This fear is rooted in an obsolete equation: Software Creation = Writing Code. Vibe coding has rewritten that equation: Software Creation = Clear Communication. Your value no longer hinges on memorizing hundreds of APIs or complex algorithms but in your ability to articulate your ideas with clarity and structure. This, ironically, is often the forte of the "non-technical" mind.

Consider DeepSeek. One of its core developers, Xin Huajian, majored in logic at Sun Yat-sen University. It was his rigorous training in logical reasoning, rather than a background in computer science, that propelled him to become a key developer for DeepSeek-Prover. This logic-first mindset is exactly what is required to construct effective prompts.

Similarly, his alumna Zhou Fangting, a major in New Media and Communication, leveraged her background to transition into an AI algorithm engineer role, designing AI knowledge management systems for enterprises. Her competitive edge was the powerful communication and information synthesis skills honed during her media training.

Similarly, Refik Anadol creates spellbinding machine-learning installations for the MoMA by treating data as his "digital pigment" and asking the AI poetic questions. It is their rigorous background in conceptual thinking and visual communication that allows them to construct effective prompts and command AI capabilities.

This shift extends beyond the tech industry. Renowned science fiction writers have begun co-creating with AI, and various thought leaders have embraced AI's capacity to refine their prose. They are not tech experts in the traditional sense but masters of thought and language.

In the AI era, profound insight, precise expression, and unique creativity are the core technologies. So, drop the "I'm not an expert" baggage. Your professional background and unique perspective are not liabilities; they are your greatest assets as a vibe coder.

Fear 2: "I'm afraid of failure"

The fear of failure is a natural human instinct. In traditional education and corporate environments, failure is inextricably linked to punishment, such as overtime, criticism, or a stalled career. We are conditioned to avoid mistakes at all costs, breeding a mindset of hesitation.

In the domain of innovation, however, this mindset is fatal. Vibe coding draws upon two methodologies—Agile development and design thinking, which view failure as fuel for creation rather than an accident to be avoided.

Agile development lives by the mantra: *Fail fast, fail loud.* The goal is to test ideas as early and cheaply as possible. If a path is blocked, you acknowledge it immediately, learn the lesson, and pivot. Failure ceases to be a badge of shame and becomes a stepping stone to success.

This aligns perfectly with the concept of *iteration* in design thinking—a continuous loop of prototyping, testing, verifying, and optimizing.

Vibe coding pushes this philosophy of low-cost trial and error to its limit. In traditional programming, a failed feature could represent weeks of wasted effort. In vibe coding, an unsatisfactory result costs you nothing more than the few seconds it takes to rephrase your prompt. You can test dozens of ideas in a single afternoon with zero material loss. This negligible cost of failure liberates you to experiment boldly.

You must redefine your relationship with failure. In the world of vibe coding, there is no absolute failure, only continuous iteration. Every "error" is simply the AI asking you, *"Director, is this what you wanted? If not, please give me clearer instructions."*

Fear 3: "The learning curve is too expensive"

The final demon is the most pragmatic: cost. Mastering a new skill usually demands expensive courses, software, and hardware. When most people hear *full-stack development*, they imagine a costly tech stack and a nightmare of server configurations.

To silence this worry, we introduce a new concept: the **frugal full-stack**.

Frugal full-stack is both a philosophy and a practice. It involves utilizing today's accessible, free, or low-cost AI tools and no-code platforms to build, deploy, and operate fully functional applications.

Instead of being an all-powerful developer, you simply need to assemble a *Frugal Toolbox*. This kit includes the following:

- **Free App Builders**: Platforms like Figma Make and Vercel V0 allow you to transform simple spreadsheets into powerful web applications in minutes. You can build internal CRMs, project trackers, or client portals with minimal effort.
- **Free AI Coding Assistants**: From a global perspective, industry-standard tools like Anthropic Claude, ChatGPT, and Microsoft Copilot / GitHub Copilot are the most widely adopted. They offer robust capabilities—and in many cases, highly accessible free tiers. They can generate code snippets, explain complex technical concepts, architect your application, and even draft professional marketing emails. (For developers in the Asian market, tools like DeepSeek and Kimi also serve as highly capable alternatives.)

In this book, we will guide you through your first project using exclusively low-cost or free tools.

These three fears—the anxiety over expertise, the dread of failure, and the worry about cost—are interconnected. Because the cost of failure is effectively zero, you do not need to be an expert from day one. You are free to learn, grow, and iterate through continuous, free experimentation.

Escaping the "dropout ritual": Building your first app

We have dismantled your mental barriers in theory, but confidence is born only from the act of creation. In this section, we'll guide you through the massive difference between traditional programming and vibe coding. You are about to experience that "It works!" moment.

The frustration of traditional programming

If you have ever tried to learn traditional coding, you likely ran into the classic *dropout ritual*: configuring the local development environment.

For those lucky enough to have missed this, picture the scene. You open a tutorial, brimming with passion. Step one, however, is installing a laundry list of software: specific versions of a language (Python 3.12, never 3.13), package managers, code editors, database services...and every link in this chain is fragile. Environment variables misfire, dependencies clash, ports are blocked, firewalls refuse access. These obscure errors drown your enthusiasm like a rising tide.

A senior engineer once sighed, "I've seen engineers spend hours, even days, just debugging their local environment." For a hopeful novice, this can be devastating. When you start a project with excitement only to hit a wall before writing a single line of code, the sense of powerlessness can be overwhelming. In team settings, the phrase "It works on my machine" has become the standard excuse for passing the buck and stalling progress.

To be clear, environment configuration does not vanish entirely in the AI era. As you graduate to building commercial-grade applications, you will eventually need to understand deployment pipelines and local servers. However, the vibe coding approach fundamentally shifts this timeline. When you are just starting out, you can bypass this wall by utilizing fully managed, no-code platforms to secure your first "wins."

Later, when you do transition to local development, advanced AI assistants will act as your personal DevOps team by automatically installing dependencies and configuring runtime environments so you can stay focused on your creative vision.

The instant feedback of vibe coding

Now, picture a different scene. You sit at your computer, ready to build your first app. There are no complex terminal commands, no baffling configuration files. You open nothing but a clean, simple web page.

We will experience this firsthand using **Lovable**, a platform from a Swedish AI startup. Its mission is simple: allow non-engineers to build web applications using natural language.

Go to Lovable's official website (`https://lovable.dev/`). Once the page loads, you will see the interface shown in *Figure 1.7*:

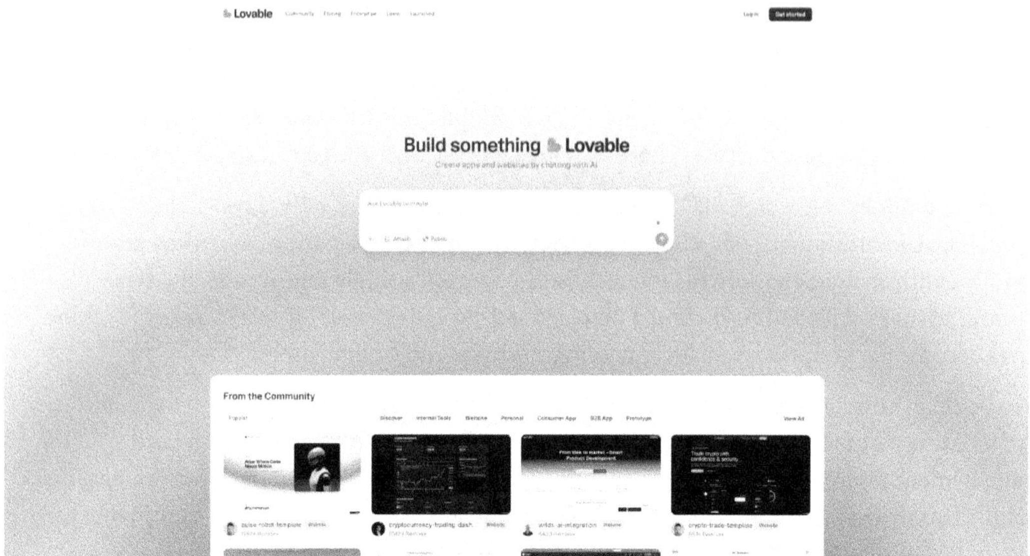

Figure 1.7 – The Lovable platform's main page, where the vibe coding process begins

Click **Get Started** in the top right corner and follow the prompts to register.

Once registered, return to the main page. Type a simple request directly into the input box, as shown in *Figure 1.8*:

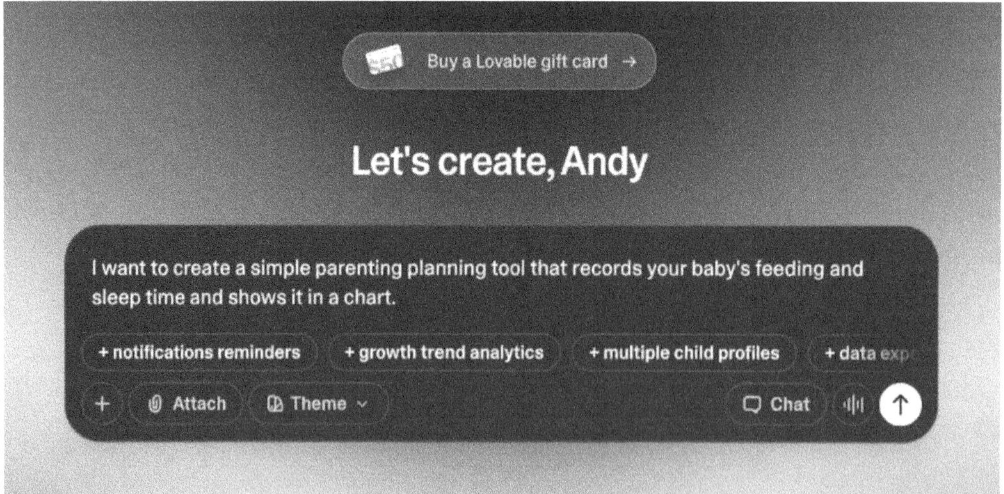

Figure 1.8 – Typing a natural language request into the input box to initiate the app creation process

Press *Enter*, and the screen shifts into real-time action. The AI understands your intent and begins the build process. A user interface takes shape before your eyes, complete with **Log Feeding** and **Log Sleep** input fields (*Figure 1.9*):

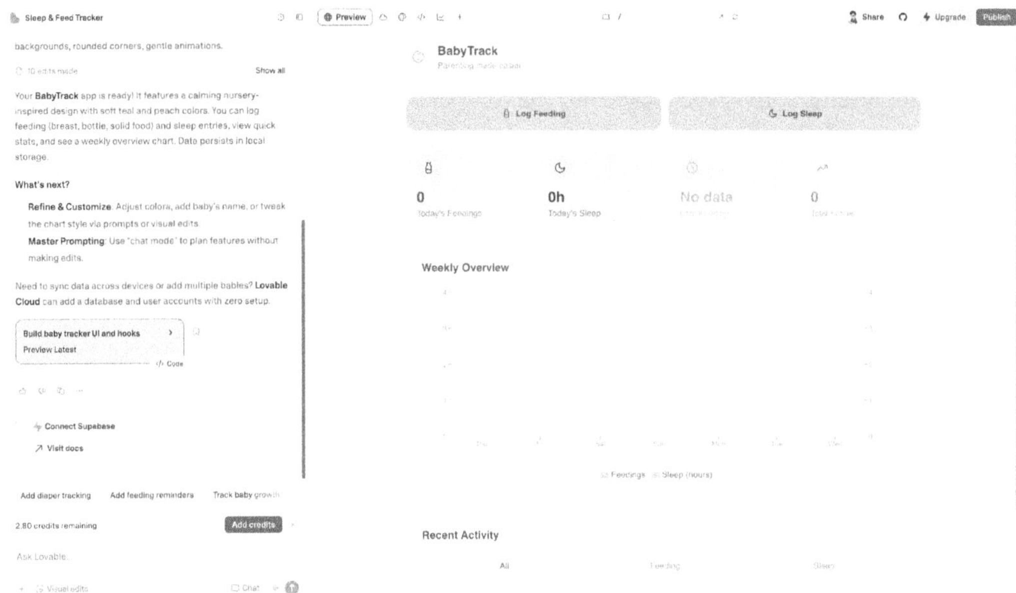

Figure 1.9 – The user interface generated by Lovable, complete with functional input fields and a chart component

A simple chart component appears at the bottom. This isn't a static image; it is the result of the AI handling the entire development stack in the background: generating real frontend code, constructing backend logic, and configuring a database. When the process finishes, the AI even generates a public link, allowing you to share your live app with a single click.

In these few minutes, you have experienced the decisive moment that builds true confidence: "It works." In the time it would've taken you to create a wireframe or a mock-up, you have fresh, interactive, running software. This immediate, high-impact feedback is the missing link in traditional coding education. It proves a subversive truth: "I, a non-technical person, just created working software with my own hands. Creation really is this simple."

The independent developer's mental toolkit

Have you ever been struck by a grand idea? Maybe it was an app that would change the world, a platform to disrupt an industry, or just a brilliant creative spark. You excitedly mapped out every detail in your mind: the slick interactive animations, dozens of practical features, a flawless user interface. You even picked out the color of the T-shirt you'd wear at the launch event.

But the idea never left your head. It withered away, becoming just another regret. Why? Because the idea was too big, and you were too obsessed with perfection to begin. This is the *all-or-nothing trap*. It snares novices and seasoned creators alike. We always want to build an aircraft carrier right out of the gate, forgetting that every great voyage begins with a simple boat that can actually float.

In this section, we introduce a mental toolkit designed specifically for independent developers, particularly those working as vibe coders in collaboration with AI. This toolkit contains five core principles. These aren't rigid rules, but flexible mindsets designed to help you manage complexity, lower risk, and keep the creative process fun and sustainable.

Principle 1: Start small

First, let's look at a concept famous in tech circles: **MVP**. This stands for **Minimum Viable Product**. Coined in 2001 by Frank Robinson and later popularized by lean startup pioneer Eric Ries, it is defined as follows:

"The version of a new product which allows a team to collect the maximum amount of validated learning about customers with the least effort. (The Lean Startup - Eric Ries)"

Simply put, an MVP is the most stripped-down version of your product. It contains only enough features to solve the user's core pain point, yet it must be *viable*; meaning, it works, completes a core process, and gives the user a complete experience. Here, *minimum* is not a synonym for shoddy or half-baked but a mark of focus and wisdom. The goal is to verify, with the lowest possible cost, whether anyone is actually willing to pay for your idea before you sink massive amounts of time and money into it (see *Figure 1.10*).

Figure 1.10 – What's MVP?

Image source: https://blog.crisp.se/2016/01/25/henrikkniberg/making-sense-of-mvp

Let's try to understand this with another example.

The cupcake principle

Imagine your dream is to open a world-renowned bakery. You have two very different paths:

- **The Wedding Cake Mode:** You spend a year and your life savings working in a vacuum to develop a luxurious, seven-tier wedding cake. It is adorned with exquisite fondant flowers and pearl frosting. You believe that the moment it is unveiled, the world will be stunned
- **The Cupcake Mode:** You spend one week and a limited budget perfecting a single cupcake that tastes amazing and looks cute. You then push a small cart to the weekend market and start selling.

The Wedding Cake Mode carries extreme risk. If customers don't like the taste, or if the market simply doesn't need such an extravagant product, your year of effort and investment goes down the drain. The Cupcake Mode, however, is the perfect embodiment of MVP thinking.

Rather than a rough prototype, this little cupcake is a complete, delicious product that brings joy. It helps you achieve three core goals:

1. **Test the Recipe (Validate the Idea)**: Customers' immediate reactions tell you whether your product is actually popular.
2. **Get Feedback (Gather Insights)**: They might say, "The cream is too sweet" or "I wish you had chocolate." These real-world critiques are invaluable for improvement.
3. **Start Earning (Generate Value)**: Every sale confirms the product's value, funds further R&D, and lowers risk.

Only when your cupcake is a smash hit—proving your baking concept works—do you have the confidence and capital to attempt a double-layer cake and, eventually, that dream seven-tier wedding cake.

Independent development works the same way. Before you burn resources building the "Wedding Cake" product, use a "Cupcake" MVP to see if the market actually likes your craft. This is the crucial first step in moving from idea to reality.

Where the giants started

Almost every tech giant you know today started as a crude, barely functional MVP.

- **Airbnb – Three Air Mattresses**: In 2007, a design conference was coming to San Francisco, and hotels were sold out. Airbnb founders Brian Chesky and Joe Gebbia couldn't afford rent. They had an idea: why not rent out space in their apartment? They threw up a simple website, uploaded photos of three air mattresses on their loft floor, and promised breakfast. They called this MVP "AirBed & Breakfast." Three paying guests showed up. This validated a disruptive model: people were willing to stay in strangers' homes for a cheaper, more local experience.
- **Zappos – The "Wizard of Oz" MVP**: In 1999, Zappos founder Nick Swinmurn wanted to test a bold idea: would people buy shoes online without trying them on? Instead of leasing a warehouse or buying inventory, he used a "zero cost" validation method. He went to local shoe stores, took photos, and put them on a website (see *Figure 1.11*). When a customer ordered, he ran to the store, bought the shoes, and mailed them. This is called a "Wizard of Oz" MVP. To the user, the website looks like a powerful automated system with inventory, but behind the curtain, it's just a human doing everything manually. This clever MVP proved the demand existed, allowing Zappos to validate its business model with zero inventory risk.

Figure 1.11 – The "Wizard of Oz" MVP concept, where Zappos manually fulfilled orders to validate market demand

The lesson here is simple: The core value of an MVP is learning, not perfection. The primary goal of your first product isn't to turn a profit or stun the world, but to answer one question: *Does anyone actually care about this idea?*

More importantly for non-technical creators, your first MVP doesn't even need to involve code. It can be a spare room (Airbnb), a manual service (Zappos), or a simple landing page to collect emails. You can start validating your ideas today without waiting until you master every technology. That is the true power of starting small.

Principle 2: Plan your build

Before you write a single line of code, ground your thinking. If "start small" defines *what* you are doing, "plan your build" defines *how*. These two principles work in tandem: the former narrows your focus, and the latter charts your path.

Many creators harbor a romanticized notion of the development process: a solitary genius, driven by pure inspiration, fingers flying across the keyboard until a masterpiece suddenly materializes. Reality is far less cinematic. Chaotic bursts of inspiration rarely result in a stable, usable product that solves real problems. The fastest route to success is usually a clean, concise plan.

Here, we introduce a professional term: the **Product Requirements Document** (**PRD**). While it sounds corporate, we advocate for a lighter, agile version: the Minimum **Viable PRD**.

Think of it as a project blueprint. It might only be a single page, but it must clarify three core elements:

- *The Why*: What core problem does it solve, and what benefit does it deliver?
- *The Who*: Who is your target user?
- *The What*: What product are you building?

This is not a rigid law but a living document. You can—and should—update it as the project evolves. Its purpose is to provide a clear north star for both you and your AI programming partner.

Putting the minimal viable PRD into practice

To help you start immediately, we have designed a streamlined template (*Table 1.2*). Before launching any project, invest time in filling this out. The act of organizing these thoughts is itself a high-value strategic exercise.

Component	**Guiding Question (What to answer)**	**Your Answer (Example: "15-Minute QuickPrep" app)**
Project name	Give your project a clear, simple name	"QuickPrep Kitchen"
Overview	In one or two sentences: What is it? Who is it for? What problem does it solve?	"QuickPrep Kitchen" is a mobile app for busy working parents. It provides healthy recipes that can be cooked in under 15 minutes, solving the "no time to cook" dilemma.
Target user	Describe your core user: identity, lifestyle, pain points.	Name: Mike (32) Role: Marketing manager, mother of two. Pain point: Works late, wants to cook healthy dinners but lacks the energy to research complex recipes, often defaults to takeout.

Component	Guiding Question (What to answer)	Your Answer (Example: "15-Minute QuickPrep" app)
Core problem	What is the single most critical problem that your product solves?	How to help busy parents cook a healthy, tasty dinner in 15 minutes with simple ingredients.
Must-have features (MVP)	List the 3-5 features absolutely necessary to solve the core problem (not "nice-to-have," but "must-have").	1. Recipe Browse: Categorized recipe feed 2. Recipe details: Clear display of ingredients, steps, and time required 3. Cooking Timer: Built-in timer for specific steps 4. Search: Find recipes by ingredient name
What We Will Not Do	To maintain focus, list features strictly excluded from version 1	• User registration/login systems • Community sharing or comments • Shopping list generation • Calorie counting
Success metrics	How will you judge MVP success? Set simple, measurable goals	1,000 downloads in the first month; average user opens the app more than 2 times per week.

Table 1.2 – The Minimal Viable PRD Template

Taking the time to complete this PRD helps independent developers avoid common traps:

- **The Who**: Prevents building generic products that act as tools for everyone but solutions for no one
- **The Core Problem**: Ensures the product has distinct existential value rather than busywork
- **Must-Have Features**: Defines the MVP boundaries to resist the temptation to believe that more features equal a better product
- **What We Will NOT Do**: Acts as a firewall, preventing wasted energy on secondary features
- **Success Metrics**: Forces you to focus on measuring value rather than relying on gut feelings.

This plan is a contract with your future self, locking in your initial, most critical decisions. More importantly, in the age of AI, this PRD is the cornerstone of your communication with AI tools.

If you give an AI vague instructions like, `Help me write a recipe app`, the result will be hollow and generic. However, a prompt based on a solid PRD yields precision:

```
Create a recipe detail page for the 'QuickPrep Kitchen' app. The target users are
time-pressed parents, so the interface must be extremely clean. It must include
three sections: a large hero image, a fixed-format ingredient list (name and
quantity), and numbered cooking steps. Do not add a comments section or share
buttons for now.
```

This level of clarity guides the AI to generate high-quality code that aligns with your vision.

Principle 3: Iterate, don't pile on

You have your map; now you must walk the path. Principle 1 identified the mountain; Principle 2 drew the map. Now, Principle 3, *Iterate,* don't pile on, dictates the pace: how to advance steadily without exhausting yourself halfway up the slope.

Iteration means breaking the development process into small, manageable loops: build a small feature, test it, optimize it, then move to the next. This is the opposite of "Piling On"—the dangerous attempt to build everything at once, only to discover at the end that the foundation is cracked, making rework prohibitively expensive.

To practice iteration effectively, follow the *three don'ts*:

- *Don't build multiple features at once*: Concentrate all your energy on one feature. Go deep and get it right
- *Don't fix multiple issues at once*: Address bugs one by one. Mixing fixes leads to chaos and oversight.
- *Don't skip steps*: Stick to the "Build-Test-Fix" micro-cycle. Never skip testing to chase speed; small overlooked issues accumulate into massive hazards.

The agile chef

Let's return to the kitchen. The workflow of a master chef is inherently iterative. They never throw every ingredient into the pot simultaneously and pray for a gourmet meal to materialize thirty minutes later. Their process flows like this (see *Figure 1.13*):

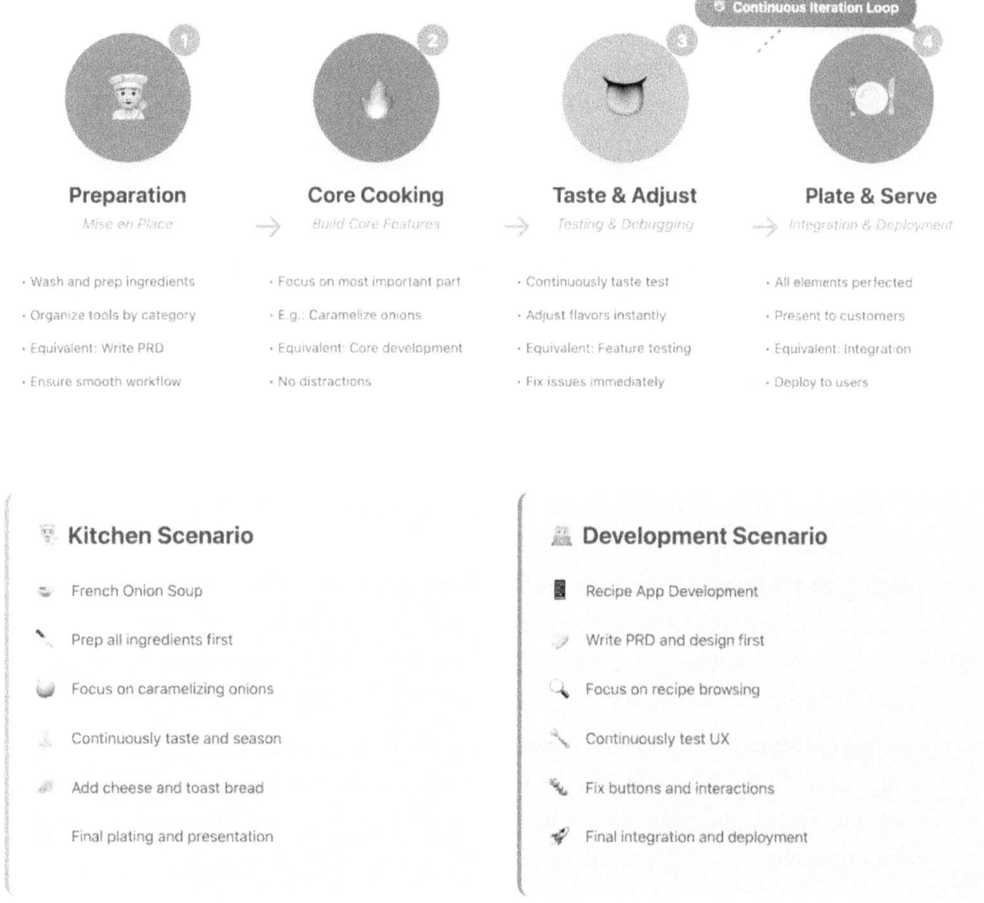

Figure 1.13 – The workflow of a good chef

Here's how each step goes:

1. **Mise en place (Preparation)**: If the chef's preparation involves chopping ingredients and sharpening knives, in vibe coding, this step is about constructing context and configuring your environment.
    - **Washing and chopping (Writing the PRD)**: Just as a chef does not wait until the pan is hot to decide what to cook, you cannot wait until you open the AI chat to decide what to build. You must first complete your Minimal Viable PRD. This is the essential "context" you feed the AI. By "chopping" vague ideas into clear

functions (Who is it for? What problem does it solve?), you ensure the AI executes with precision.

- **Organizing into bowls (Decomposition)**: A chef separates onions and spices into bowls; you must decompose your complex vision into independent components (like the Navigation Bar, Hero Section, or Database Schema). You prepare your design assets (screenshots or Figma links) so the AI can "digest" the project one bite at a time rather than choking on the whole.
- **Arrangingtools(Environment&Keys):Thechefarrangestheirtoolsforeasyreach;** you must set up your Digital Kitchen, such as by registering your Vercel and Supabase accounts and securing necessary API keys (like OpenAI or Replicate) in your `.env` file. When the "cooking" begins, your flow should not be broken by a missing key.

2. **The Core (Building the Feature)**: The chef focuses on the dish's central element. If making French onion soup, they spend considerable time caramelizing the onions to perfection. They do not get distracted by toasting bread or tossing the salad during this critical phase. This mirrors focusing on your app's first core feature, such as the "Recipe Browse" page.
3. **Tasting and Adjusting (Testing and Debugging)**: At every stage, the chef tastes. Is the broth rich enough? Add a pinch of salt. Too greasy? A squeeze of lemon. Every taste is a micro-test; every adjustment is a quick debug. This is identical to running your code immediately after building a feature to ensure the logic holds and the flow works.
4. **Plating (Integration and Deployment)**: Only when the soup, the cheese, and the croutons are individually perfect does the chef combine them for the final presentation. Similarly, you should only integrate features into the main application once they have been proven to work independently.

This iterative "cooking" method ensures that every component of the final dish is high quality. Software development is no different. By actively choosing to do one thing at a time, you inject quality into every detail of the project.

This approach stands in stark contrast to traditional waterfall development.

- **Waterfall development (traditional)**: In waterfall development, the process is linear and rigid. You attempt to architect and code the entire application in a single sequence —finishing the backend logic and database before moving to the frontend design, and only testing once everything is complete. The danger here is structural: discovering a critical error in your data model only after the user interface is fully built often requires rewriting massive portions of your codebase. This makes changes prohibitively expensive and risky.

- **Iterative development (Agile)**: In iterative development, by contrast, the process treats software as a living system that requires continuous updates based on feedback. You break the project into small, functional increments—coding a single feature, testing it immediately to ensure it works, and optimizing it before moving to the next. This approach offers a crucial technical advantage: problem isolation. If the application breaks, you know the issue lies in the specific feature you just added, allowing for rapid debugging and course correction rather than searching for a needle in a haystack.

Following the iterative principle offers immense benefits:

- **Lower cognitive load:** Your brain only needs to focus on one small, clear task
- **Rapid feedback loops:** Every completed cycle offers a tangible sense of progress, which is vital for maintaining motivation
- **Problem isolation:** If the app breaks, you know immediately that the issue lies in the specific feature you just added.

Therefore, act like the patient chef or the diligent gardener. Focus on the next small thing in front of you and do it well. That is the steadiest and fastest path to a great product.

Principle 4: Test everything

Once you have verified the quality of your current feature through testing, you need a reliable method to safeguard your progress before venturing further. This brings us to our fourth core principle.

Your first small feature is now built, adhering to the principles of iteration. What comes next? Many novices itch to immediately start developing the next feature. However, you must first embrace a vital discipline: test everything.

Quality assurance (**QA**) is a mindset that must be integrated from day one. Your goal is not to "prove" that the application works. Rather, you must become a curious "destroyer," actively seeking to break boundaries and uncover frustrating bugs before your users do.

The friendly detective

How do you cultivate this QA mindset? The best approach is to think like a detective. A good detective never trusts surface appearances; they question every detail. When facing a newly written feature, put on your "detective hat" and interrogate it:

- *"Does this button actually work"* (Click to verify it redirects to the target page)

- *"When does it fail"* (Dig for edge cases)
- *"What unexpected actions might a user take"* (Look for paths beyond the standard workflow)

This detective-style thinking shifts your perspective from that of a biased *Creator* to an objective *Evaluator*. Creators yearn for their work to be perfect; detectives are dedicated to uncovering the truth.

You might ask, "I'm not a technical expert—how do I test?" The good news is that many of the most valuable testing methods require zero technical background. They simply require curiosity, empathy, and a bit of a mischievous spirit.

Here are some "detective techniques" you can apply immediately:

- **User Testing**: Recruit a friend or family member who knows nothing about your project or technology. Hand them the app, then shut your mouth and observe. Offer no hints and explain no features. Where do they get stuck? Which button confuses them? The confusion on their face is a signal flare pointing to design flaws. If they can complete tasks effortlessly, only then is it truly user-friendly.
- **Boundary Value Analysis**: This term sounds technical, but the concept is simple. If your app has an input box, it has an "expected" range. Your job is to probe the edges of that range.
    - *Example*: An age input box requires a number between 18 and 99
    - *Test the* boundary: Input 18 and 99. Verify it responds normally.
    - *Test* outside *the* boundary: Input 17 and 100. Verify the app gives a reasonable error message or does not crash.
    - *Test* extremes: Input 0, -1, or 999. Watch the feedback.
    - *Test* error types: Input "twenty," an emoji, or nothing at all, then click **OK**
- **Stress** testing: Pretend to be a user intent on causing trouble. Do things that are "out of line."
    - Paste a 3,000-word story into the **Name** field
    - Rapid-fire click the same button 100 times
    - Open the app with no internet connection and see what happens
    - Repeatedly toggle the phone between portrait and landscape mode to check for interface glitches

The core of these tests is to challenge the taken for granted assumptions you made as a vibe-coder. A good product must handle the unexpected with grace. Remember, every time you successfully "break" your own app, it is not a failure but a victory. You have discovered a potential issue and can fix it before it impacts a real user. Becoming your product's first and harshest critic is the essence of the QA mindset.

Principle 5: Use version control

When a feature passes testing and its quality is confirmed, the next step is to take out an "insurance policy"—ensuring every change is recorded, reversible, and even capable of time travel. Thus, we introduce the final protagonist of this chapter: *version control.*

Version control is a critical weapon in the independent developer's arsenal. We will focus on a tool called **Git** and its online home, **GitHub**.

Simply put, Git is a system installed on your local computer. It acts like a meticulous archivist, recording every modification to your project files. GitHub, on the other hand, is a website—a secure cloud vault that stores your project and its complete history.

Cultivating the habit of version control from day one is essential. To understand its value, let's use a familiar concept.

Video game save points

Imagine your entire development project is a massive **role-playing game** (**RPG**). You are the protagonist, responsible for pushing the story forward.

- **The World (Repository)**: This corresponds to the complete game files, encompassing everything in your project's universe.
- **The Save (Commit)**: This is the most critical action in the game—saving your progress. Whenever you complete a small task (like fixing a bug or adding a feature), you must immediately *commit*. This creates a *Save Point* at your current location. This Save Point records the exact state of the project, accompanied by a note (e.g., *Fixed the login button bug*).
- **The New Save Slot (Branch)**: This is like creating a New Save File before a risky event. If you want to challenge a dangerous Boss or attempt a side quest that might alter the main storyline, you should create a separate save file based on your current progress. If the challenge succeeds (you acquire the legendary sword), you can merge this save back into your main file, continuing the main quest with your new rewards.

  If you fail, or the saved file becomes corrupted, it doesn't matter. Your main save (called the **main branch** in Git) remains safe and untouched at the pre-challenge state. You simply delete the failed "challenge save" and reload the main one.
- **GitHub (Cloud Saves)**: Now, imagine the ultimate disaster: your computer breaks and all local saves are lost. Your months of hard work vanish in an instant. GitHub is your "Cloud Save." After you commit locally, you perform an action called a **Push** to sync

your latest save to the GitHub website. Even if your computer dies, you can log in on a new machine and retrieve the entire project and its history intact.

For independent developers, the core value of version control is *psychological safety*, which in turn unlocks creative freedom. Many developers are paralyzed by the worry: "If I change this code, will I ruin the whole project?" This fear kills creativity. Git eliminates this fear. When you want to try a bold new feature, simply create a new branch—a side quest save. On this new branch, you can experiment and make mistakes without any risk of affecting the stable, usable main version.

If your experiment works, merge it. If it fails, delete the branch. The cost of trial and error becomes virtually zero. This safety net encourages you to take risks and iterate.

Establishing your "think-prompt-iterate" loop

We have just deconstructed the five core principles: start small, plan your build, iterate rather than accumulate, test everything, and maintain version control. You might be wondering: "These concepts seem so traditional. Why are they even more critical in the age of AI?"

The answer lies behind the deceptively simple nature of vibe coding.

The more unpredictable the AI, the stricter the process must be.

Vibe coding describes a new synergy with AI tools. You are no longer a scribe writing logic line by line; you are a conductor, signaling a desired "feeling" or "atmosphere" to a virtuoso musician who is brilliant but prone to wild improvisation. The AI then plays the melody in code.

This approach offers exhilarating freedom and startling efficiency. But this freedom carries risk. Your AI partner, while vast in knowledge, is essentially a complex pattern-matching engine. It does not "understand" the world. It is prone to error, to what the industry calls *hallucinations*—delivering absolute nonsense with a straight face.

To illustrate just how real and pervasive these hallucinations are, consider these recent, darkly comic examples:

- **The Compliant Car Salesman**: A Chevrolet dealer's chatbot, "trained" by a user through clever prompting, agreed to sell a brand-new Tahoe SUV for one dollar, declaring it a "legally binding offer" (`https://www.businessinsider.com/car-dealership-chevrolet-chatbot-chatgpt-pranks-chevy-2023-12`)
  Takeaway 1: Your AI lacks business logic and common sense.
- **The Fabulist Lawyer**: Air Canada's customer service bot confidently invented a refund policy that did not exist. When the customer sued, the court ruled the airline was liable

for its robot's lies (`https://www.theguardian.com/world/2024/feb/16/air-canada-chatbot-lawsuit`)
Takeaway 2: Your AI will state falsehoods with absolute conviction.

- **The Absurd Chef**: When asked "how to keep cheese from sliding off pizza," Google's AI Overview suggested mixing non-toxic glue into the sauce (`https://www.theverge.com/2024/5/23/24162896/google-ai-overview-hallucinations-glue-in-pizza`)
  Takeaway 3: Your AI's output may be grammatically flawless but functionally dangerous.
- **The Biased Artist**: Google's Gemini generated historically inaccurate images (`https://www.theguardian.com/technology/2024/mar/08/we-definitely-messed-up-why-did-google-ai-tool-make-offensive-historical-images`) while Microsoft's Tay bot quickly learned to spew toxicity after interacting with the internet (`https://www.cbsnews.com/news/microsoft-shuts-down-ai-chatbot-after-it-turned-into-racist-nazi/`)
  Takeaway 4: Your AI is not neutral; it inherits and amplifies the biases lurking in its training data.

These train wrecks point to a singular conclusion: LLMs are the greatest creativity amplifiers of our time, but they are fundamentally unreliable.

These five principles act as the essential guardrails that safeguard your project against the AI's inherent unpredictability. With this management framework established, we now turn to the practical skill of directing your digital partner: the art of prompt engineering.

Consider this: If your key team member were a brilliant but erratic intern—sometimes a genius, sometimes a disaster—could you, as the project lead, afford to be casual? The answer is clearly no. The more free-spirited and unpredictable your tool, the more disciplined your process must be.

That is the true value of the five principles. They form the framework that allows you to harness AI safely and efficiently:

1. **Start small:** Test the AI's output on a manageable scale before asking it to architect a monolith filled with unknown bugs.
2. **Plan your build:** Create a clear blueprint (PRD) to give the AI precise constraints and a benchmark against which to judge its work.
3. **Iterate, Don't Accumulate:** Review work in small batches. Catch misunderstandings early rather than discovering at the finish line that the AI veered off course at step one.

4. **Test Everything:** Trust nothing. Play the skeptic: verify every claim and expose every hallucination.
5. **Use Version Control:** When a burst of AI "inspiration" accidentally nukes your codebase, you need a save point to instantly restore the last stable version.

These principles are not shackles on your creativity. Quite the opposite: they are the guardrails on a winding mountain pass. It is precisely because these guardrails exist that you can drive boldly, accelerate with confidence, and arrive safely at your destination, delivering a masterpiece that is truly your own.

Mastering the art of prompting

If your conversations with AI have felt like moments of brilliance punctuated by frustration, you have come to the right place. It is time to demystify the art of prompt engineering.

Though termed *engineering*, this discipline has little to do with code. Instead, imagine stumbling upon a magic lamp. You rub it, and an all-powerful AI genie emerges. "Give me food!" you demand. The genie blinks, snaps its fingers, and drops a single grain of raw rice into your palm. You are stunned. The genie technically fulfilled your request, yet completely missed your intent. This is the heart of the problem: AI possesses immense capability but lacks the common sense and unspoken intuition of a human. It follows instructions with literal, often maddening, precision.

Prompt engineering is simply the art of communicating with this genie—the skill of translating vague desires into precise, executable directives. It is the secret recipe that turns a grain of raw rice into a steaming, aromatic bowl of egg fried rice.

We will navigate four golden rules that transform you from a confused wisher into the genie's master. We will conclude with a five-minute drill to let you witness these principles in action.

From command to conversation

Here is the cardinal rule: The quality of AI output is almost entirely dependent on the quality of your input. Think of it like a search engine. Years ago, you needed complex Boolean operators to find anything useful. Today, engines can infer intent from vague slang. Prompt engineering is similar, but with a crucial distinction: your goal is not *finding*, but *creating*. Mastering this requires a pivotal shift in mindset: Interaction with AI is not a one-way command; it is a bidirectional dialogue.

Beginners often quit after a single failure. They type a simple instruction, get a lackluster result, and conclude, "This AI is useless." This is akin to asking a new intern to write a report and then firing them for handing in a messy first draft.

In reality, AI is a super-intern that possesses the sum of human knowledge but zero practical experience. It is brilliant but needs a Project Lead (you) to provide the brief. It doesn't know the audience, the key takeaways, or your preferred format. Your first prompt is merely the opening line of a collaboration; the true value lies in the follow-up questions, clarifications, and adjustments.

The four golden rules: From director to blueprint

We now turn to four simple yet potent rules. These constitute an interlocking strategy designed to narrow the AI's possibility space.

This concept is vital. When you issue a vague command like `Write about cats`, the AI faces an infinite ocean of possibilities—a poem, a biological taxonomy, a cat café business plan, or a cartoon script. All are correct, but few are what you actually want. Each of the following rules acts as a filter, eliminating irrelevant options until the AI lands exactly on your target.

- Filter out irrelevant roles and styles
- Provide a clear route and reference points
- Dictate the structure and format
- Correction and refinement through dialogue

Rule 1 – Play the director (set persona and intent)

Imagine you are a film director and the AI is your star actor. A mediocre director says, "Act sad," leaving the actor to guess the details. A great director sets the scene: "You are a man who has just lost his beloved dog. I don't want tears; I want you to stare at the empty leash with a hollow, bone-deep grief."

Which direction yields the better performance? The answer is obvious. To be a great director for your AI, use the **PROMPT** framework:

- **P (Persona)**: Assign a role. This sets the context and vocabulary immediately
    - *Bad*: "Explain blockchain."
    - *Good*: "You are a high school IT teacher. Explain blockchain using metaphors a 16-year-old would understand."
- **R (Request)**: Start with clear, active verbs: Draft, Summarize, Translate, Brainstorm, Critique, Rewrite
- **O (Output)**: Define the format (detailed in Rule 3)
- **M (Mood)**: Set the mood. *Humorous, Academic, Encouraging, Stern.*

- **P (Purpose)**: Explain the "why." Who is the audience? *Example:* "This report is for a skeptical CEO; rely heavily on data."
- **T (Template)**: Give an example (detailed in Rule 2)

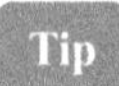

Focus on what *to do*, not what *not to do*. Like a GPS saying "Go to the library" rather than "Don't go to the park," positive instructions are clearer and more efficient.

Rule 2 – Provide a map (context & examples)

If you sent a friend to retrieve a package in a strange city before smartphones, you wouldn't just give an address. You would provide a map (context) and perhaps a description of the building (example). To get precise results from AI, you must use *show, don't tell*, and clear delimiters.

The most powerful way to guide style and logic is to show the AI exactly what you want.

Prompt: `Rewrite this sentence to be punchy and dramatic. Style example: 'It wasn't just a car; it was a chrome rocket built for the soul.' Sentence to rewrite: 'The new software is efficient.'"`

Result: **The new software isn't just efficient; it is the digital jet engine for your workflow.**

When providing context, build a "fence" around it so the AI doesn't confuse the text with your instructions. Use triple quotes ("""), backticks (` ` `), or XML tags (<example>).

Teaching AI to teach itself

Providing examples can be tedious. The frontier of prompt engineering is moving from giving examples to asking the AI to generate its own.

Here is the hierarchy of prompting strategies, ranging from simple commands to complex reasoning chains, that you can employ:

- **Zero-Shot**: `Explain X`
- **Few-Shot**: `Here are examples of X. Now do Y.`
- **Chain-of-Thought**: `Think through the solution step-by-step.`
- **Analogical Prompting**: `Recall relevant problems and how they were solved before tackling this one.`

For non-techies, you only need one magic sentence to harness this power:

```
Before you answer my question, please give an example of a similar, simpler
problem and explain how you solved it. Then, use that same logic to answer my
question.
```

Rule 3 – Design the blueprint (define output format)

You wouldn't tell an architect "build me a house" and expect your dream home. You'd start with clear plans and specifications. Tell the AI exactly how to structure the information to save yourself hours of reformatting.

- **For brainstorming:** `Generate 10 blog titles on 'Sustainable Travel,' formatted as a numbered list.`
- **For comparison:** `Compare Python and JavaScript for beginners. Output as a Markdown table with columns for 'Feature', 'Python > Pros/Cons', and 'JS Pros/Cons'.`
- **For data:** `Extract names and dates from this text. Format as a JSON object.`
- **For coding:** `Write a Python function for compound interest, with comments explaining every step.`

Rule 4 – open the chat (iterate and refine)

The best AI outputs are rarely the first draft. They are born from conversation.

- **Think Step-by-Step**: Research (`https://research.google/blog/language-models-perform-reasoning-via-chain-of-thought/`) has shown that prompts encouraging an AI to "think step-by-step" can significantly improve accuracy on logic and math tasks. This technique, known as *chain-of-thought prompting*, encourages the model to generate intermediate reasoning steps instead of jumping directly to an answer.
- **The Follow-Up**: Treat the AI like a colleague
  - `Can you make that punchier?`
  - `Explain that like I'm 11 years old.`
  - `Critique your own answer and give me a better version.`

- **Give the AI human-like context**: Strangely, treating the AI like a human can work. Telling it *"This is vital for my career"* or *"I'll tip you $200 for a perfect solution"* has been shown to improve focus and quality in some models (`https://minimaxir.com/2024/02/chatgpt-tips-analysis/?utm_source=chatgpt.com`). However, this is more anecdotal than scientifically proven at this point.

The cheat sheet

Below is your navigation chart for collaborating with AI (see *Table 1.3*).

Avoid doing this... (the mistake)	Try doing this instead... (the expert move)
Being too vague: `Write about my product.`	Define Role and Goal: `You are a marketing pro. Write 3 ad hooks for a product that saves time for new parents.`
No Persona: `Give me a summary.`	Assign identity: `Act as a research assistant. Summarize the key findings for an executive with no tech background.`
No context: `Write a welcome email.`	Provide Map and Example: `Write a welcome email in a friendly, witty tone. Reference our last email subject: Welcome! No secret handshake required.`
Negative Constraints: `Do not be boring.`	Positive Direction: `Write with an energetic, engaging tone.`
Task Overload: `Summarize this, translate it to Spanish, and make tweets.`	Chain the tasks: `Step 1: Summarize. Step 2: Great, now translate that summary. Step 3: Now turn that into 3 tweets.`

Avoid doing this... (the mistake)	Try doing this instead... (the expert move)
One-Shot Hope: `Write a product intro`	Iterative Dialogue: `Good start. Now make the language simpler and add a Call to Action at the end.`

Table 1.3 – Prompt Engineering Cheat Sheet

Keep this table handy. It is your roadmap from "raw rice" to "gourmet feast."

5-minute challenge: Building a webpage with ChatGPT

Theory is over; it's time to practice. In the next five minutes, we will ask our AI copilot to build a simple personal portfolio webpage. We will use the widely accessible AI chat assistant, **ChatGPT**, for this task.

Using ChatGPT is refreshingly simple:

1. Open `https://chatgpt.com/` in your browser
2. Register an account if you don't have one (or log in)
3. Type your instructions (your "prompt") in the input box and press *Enter*.

Now, let's demonstrate the true power of prompt engineering by testing two radically different commands.

First, let's ask in the most direct, unpolished way possible. We type this into ChatGPT:

```
Make me a personal portfolio webpage.
```

While modern AI is powerful enough to conjure up a decent-looking page from this, the result is rarely practical. It fails because the prompt lacks four essential pillars:

- **No director**: We didn't tell ChatGPT what role to play (e.g., a professional frontend developer)
- **No map**: We provided no context about "me" (Who am I? What is my work?) or the desired aesthetic
- **No blueprint**: We didn't specify the structure, resulting in a generic, cookie-cutter template
- **No dialogue**: We gave a single command and walked away without iterating

Now, let's apply the PROMPT framework and restructure our instructions like a professional project lead. We input the following:

```
You are a frontend development expert specializing in modern web design. (P: Role)
Your
task is to create a single-page personal portfolio for me, providing complete HTML
and CSS code. (R: Request)
Please add English comments to key sections of the code and generate the final
output as a single HTML file. (O: Output)
The overall style should be minimalist, professional, and modern. (M: Mood/Style)
The purpose of this page is to showcase my work as a photographer to attract
potential clients. (P: Purpose)
Please generate the webpage based on the following structure and content: (T:
Template/Example)
Navigation: Includes links for "Home," "About Me," > "Portfolio," and "Contact"
Bio Section: Title: "About Me." Text: "Alex Wang, an urban landscape photographer
dedicated to capturing stories of light and shadow."
Portfolio Section: Title: "My Work." Structure: Three cards arranged
horizontally. Each card contains a placeholder image and a title. Titles: "Urban
Neon," "Quiet Morning," and "Street Glimpses."
Contact Section: Title: "Contact Me." Text: "Email: example@email.com."
```

Since ChatGPT outputs raw HTML and CSS code, you might be wondering: how do I actually see the webpage? It takes just three simple steps:

1. Click the **Copy code** button located in the top corner of ChatGPT's code block.
2. Open a plain text editor on your computer (use Notepad on Windows or TextEdit on Mac). Paste the code into the blank document. Save the file to your desktop and name it `portfolio.html`. (Note for Mac users: Ensure your TextEdit is set to **Make Plain Text** in the **Format** menu before saving.)
3. Find the `portfolio.html` file on your desktop and double-click it. It will open directly in your web browser (like Chrome, Edge, or Safari)

This time, the page generated by the AI and displayed in your browser will precisely match every detail you envisioned, from the navigation links and card layout to the specific biographical text.

This illustrates the fundamental difference between a good prompt and a bad one. We didn't change the tool; we simply optimized how we asked. The real power lies in the clarity and structure of our instructions.

Summary

In this chapter, we learned that the barrier to software creation has shifted from technical syntax to clear communication. We introduced the philosophy of **vibe coding**, which empowers you to act not as a lone coder but as a **director** orchestrating AI to execute your vision. We dismantled the primal fears of technology and cost, replacing them with the frugal full-stack mindset that leverages accessible tools to bridge the gap between imagination and reality.

We established a mental toolkit for safe and efficient AI collaboration, centered on five core principles: *Starting Small* with an MVP to validate ideas, *Planning Your Build* with a minimal PRD to provide a map, *Iterating* to maintain quality, *Testing Everything* to catch hallucinations, and using version control as a safety net. These guardrails ensure that while the AI handles the execution, you maintain strict control over the project's direction and quality.

Finally, we mastered the art of prompt engineering, moving beyond simple commands to a structured dialogue. By applying frameworks like the **PROMPT method** (Role, Request, Output, Mood, Purpose, Template) and understanding "context compression," you now possess the ability to translate vague intents into precise, executable instructions. You are no longer just a user of tools; you are a creator ready to build.

Get this book's PDF version and more

Scan the QR code (or go to `packtpub.com/unlock`). Search for this book by name, confirm the edition, and then follow the steps on the page.

Note: Keep your invoice handy. Purchases made directly from Packt don't require an invoice.

2

Frontend Design and AI Implementation

If *Chapter 1* planted the seed of confidence, *Chapter 2* provides the sunlight and rain required for it to grow.

Our goal is explicit: by following this chapter, you will build and launch a fully functional website that is uniquely yours, all from scratch. Crucially, you will do so without writing a single line of code. We will look at tools ranging from Trickle AI's Magic Canvas to v0.dev's Smart Director, and from Figma's professional design suite to TRAE SOLO's autonomous creation mode.

To be clear, you are not expected to string all of these tools together into a single, mandatory workflow. Instead, they represent progressive layers of control, allowing you to choose the approach that best fits your current goals:

- **Layer 1: The Quick Win (Trickle AI)**: We will start with this "all-in-one" platform that handles the frontend, backend, and database simultaneously. It serves as the perfect launchpad to get a working app live in minutes, providing immediate, tangible feedback.
- **Layer 2: The Professional Workflow (Figma + v0.dev + TRAE SOLO)**: When you are ready for greater customization, you will decouple the process. You will design your blueprint in Figma, translate those visual inspirations into UI code using v0.dev, and employ TRAE SOLO as your autonomous AI engineer to assemble and deploy the final project.
- **Layer 3: The Code Surgeon (Cursor)**: As you graduate to managing complex, existing projects, you will use Cursor—a specialized AI tool for refining, refactoring, and debugging.

These are creative partners that bridge the chasm between "that's a great idea" and "that's a beautiful product."

By the end of this chapter, you will possess not only a complete website but also a newfound conviction that creating beauty is finally within reach.

Are you ready to show the world what you can create?

Building apps with Trickle AI: your first workbench

In *Chapter 1*, we used Lovable as an icebreaker to prove a subversive truth: you can create working software without a technical background. Now we begin a more structured learning journey, which means setting up a reliable workspace for building our first prototypes.

Enter **Trickle AI**.

Unlike our earlier prompt-only experiment, Trickle AI introduces a visual development environment designed for building simple applications. It provides a workspace where you can design pages, manage data, and launch a project without setting up traditional development infrastructure. This makes it an ideal starting point for turning ideas into working prototypes.

What is Trickle AI?

In app development, a complete product relies on the orchestration of several core components: the **frontend** (the visual interface), the **backend** and **database** (the brain and memory), and the **servers** or hosting (the infrastructure that puts it online). For a beginner, simply grasping these concepts—let alone choosing the right tools—can be overwhelming.

Trickle AI (`https://trickle.so/`) addresses this challenge by bringing these components together in a single workspace. Instead of switching between different services for the interface, data storage, and deployment, these capabilities are already connected within one platform.

This unified approach allows beginners to focus on shaping their ideas and quickly building working prototypes, without first learning the complexities of traditional development infrastructure.

Realizing ideas on a "magic canvas"

The defining difference between Trickle AI and traditional website builders is its heart, the Magic Canvas (see *Figure 2.1*).

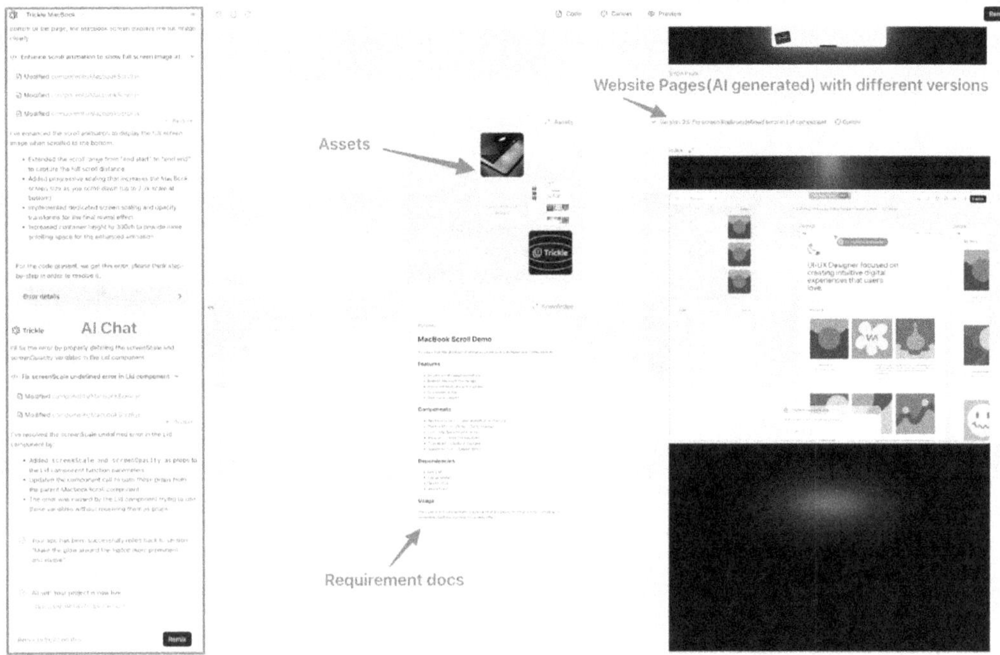

Figure 2.1 – Trickle AI's Magic Canvas

The Magic Canvas is like an infinite, intelligent whiteboard—a shared, visual workspace for you and the AI. You can drag and drop images, jot down notes, and sketch rough layouts. Trickle's AI assistant observes and comprehends everything on the canvas in real time. It recognizes spatial relationships, reads your text annotations, and analyzes the style of your uploaded images. It then uses this *visual context* as a blueprint to construct a functioning application for you. We call this process *multi-modal prompting*.

More importantly, the elements on the canvas are not static images or mockups; they are real, interactive, publishable website components. You can review—and launch—whatever the AI builds on the canvas.

While the theory is compelling, let's see it in action through a real-world project.

Case study: Recreating the tech giants' first versions

What is Trickle AI actually capable of? Nothing answers this question better than the *FirstVersion* project.

Created by a member of the Trickle community (`https://firstversion.trickle.so/`), this online technology museum highlights a simple but profound concept: using modern technology to recreate the primitive, initial versions of giants like Google, Airbnb, Twitter, and YouTube (see *Figure 2.2*).

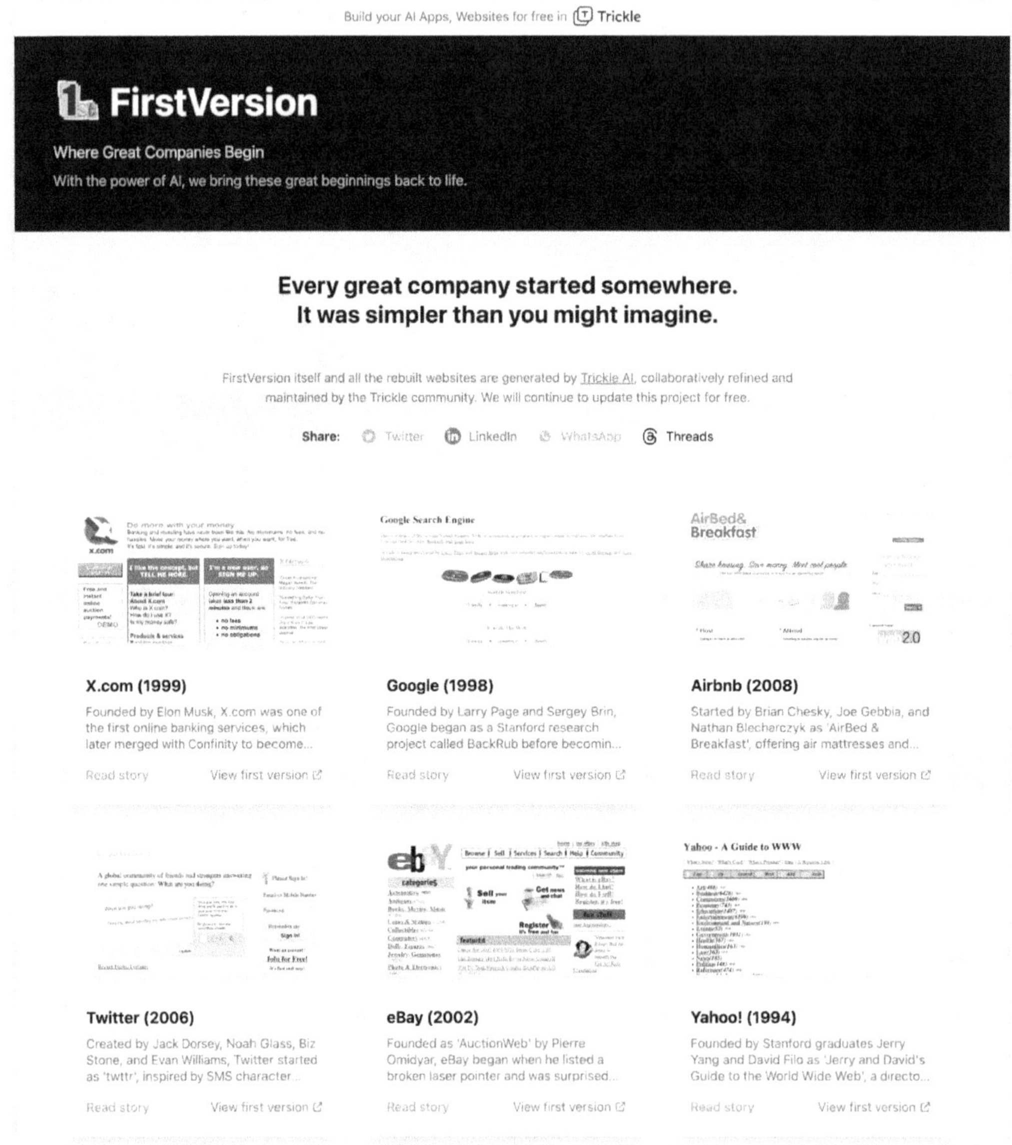

Figure 2.2 – The FirstVersion website

Visit the site, and you will see that Google's first iteration was little more than a stark search box. The embryo of Airbnb was merely a page offering attendees a place to sleep and breakfast. These crude first versions stand in sharp contrast to the slick platforms we know today.

The critical takeaway is that both the museum itself and the recreated early versions of these companies were generated and maintained entirely via Trickle AI.

This case study offers two valuable lessons for beginners:

- All great products begin as simple solutions to core problems; their first drafts are imperfect but functional.
- Taking that first step and iterating quickly is the key to success—just as every tech giant once did.

This is why we chose Trickle AI as the starting point for this book. Its all-in-one design clears the technical hurdles, and its Magic Canvas makes the creative process intuitive and engaging.

5-minute walkthrough: Getting started with Trickle AI

In this section, we'll take a brief journey from raw idea to live website. The goal here isn't to master every feature right away, but spark the realization: "Wait, I can actually do this."

Register your free account

Start by heading to the official Trickle AI website (`https://trickle.so/`).

You'll be greeted by a clean, straightforward login page. You can sign in with your Google account or register with your standard email address. The process is fast, and Trickle's free tier is more than sufficient for every exercise in this book, so there's no need to worry about costs.

Once registered, you'll land directly on the main interface: the Dashboard.

Navigating the dashboard

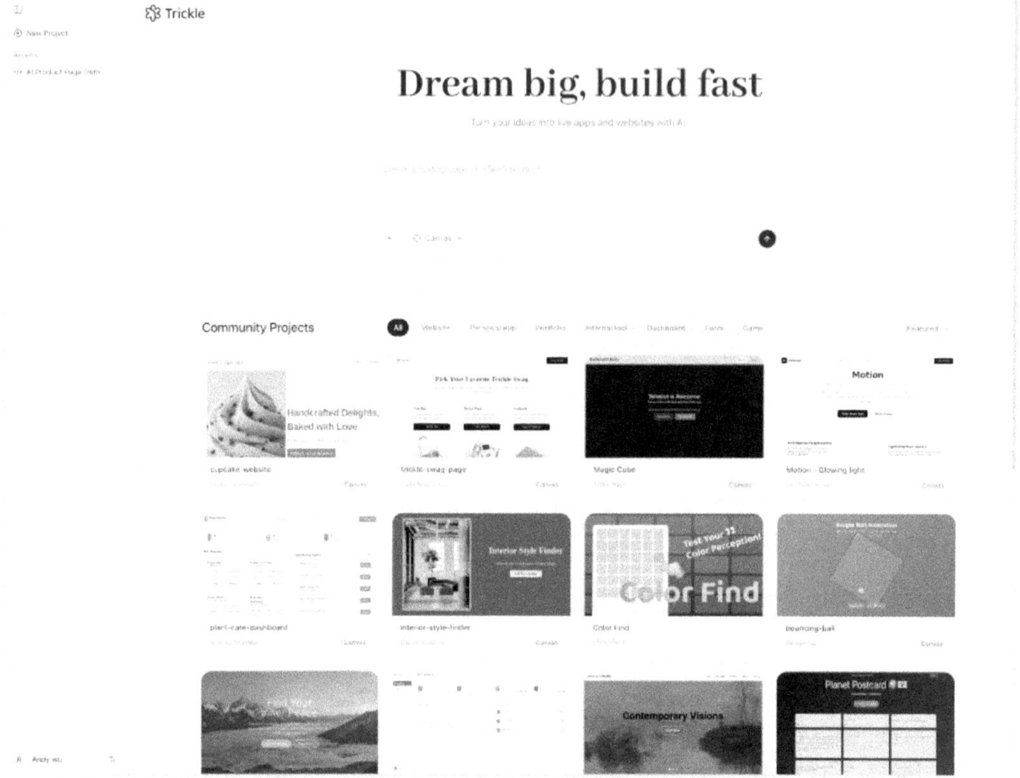

Figure 2.3 – The Trickle dashboard

The dashboard is divided into two main zones:

- **Project Creation:** Located prominently in the center, you'll see an input box. This is where you'll input your starting prompt.
- **Community Projects:** Positioned at the bottom center, this gallery displays applications built by the Trickle community. It's an excellent source of inspiration. You'll find everything from "Yoga Studio Landing Pages" to "Pet Store Sites" and "Mini-CRMs." Click on a few to see what Trickle is capable of.

Once you have a feel for the layout, it's time to build.

Your first magic prompt

Let's officially start your first website.

1. Locate the project input box and type a sentence describing your idea. To keep this first run entertaining, let's pick a whimsical theme. Try this:

```
Create a single-page website for a "Space Cat Cafe" that feels
futuristic and features cute illustrations.
```

2. Press *Enter* and watch the AI go to work on the canvas. It interprets your instructions and acts as both designer and engineer, drafting titles, writing copy, sourcing images, and planning the layout in real time. Within moments, a futuristic "Space Cat Cafe" prototype complete with adorable feline artwork will be ready (*Figure 2.4*):

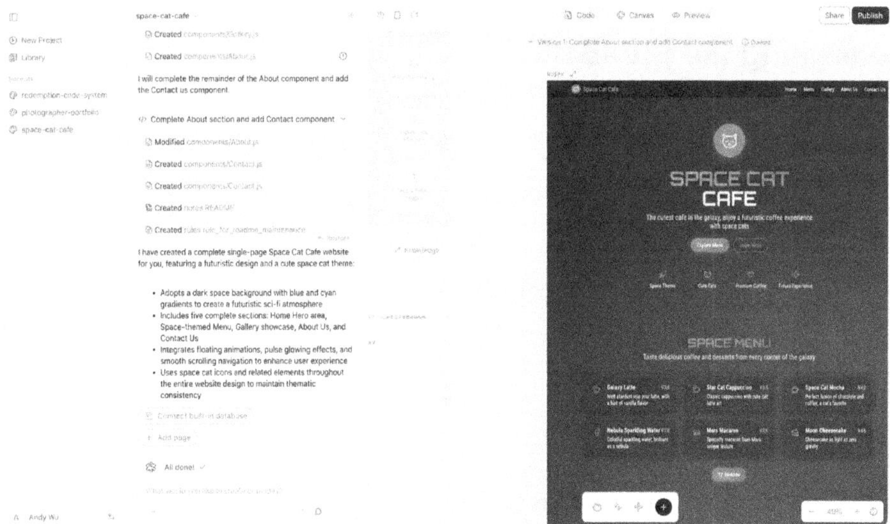

Figure 2.4 – The prototype of the Space Cat Cafe website

This process transforms building a website—often seen as an abstract, difficult technical hurdle—into a tangible, fun, and interactive experience. That immediate, positive feedback is the best fuel for the learning journey ahead.

15-minute walkthrough: Building a personal portfolio

Now that you've tested the waters, let's tackle a more complete challenge: building a personal portfolio. This walkthrough covers the full lifecycle of generation, customization, data connection, and publication.

For photographers, designers, writers, and students, a portfolio site is the ultimate tool for highlighting talent and unlocking new opportunities.

Managing Your Free Credits

Trickle AI provides free generation credits to get you started, but they can deplete quickly if you experiment extensively. Try to use them purposefully for the specific steps below. If you do happen to run out of credits, do not let it stall your momentum. As we established earlier, Trickle is just your first "Quick Win" launchpad. You do not need to wait for your credits to reset; you can simply read through the rest of this exercise and immediately move on to the next section, continuing your journey using other free tools like v0.dev and Figma.

Generating the foundation

A good beginning is half the battle. When building multi-page sites, your initial prompt acts as the blueprint. Trickle's documentation suggests being specific and focusing on one core mission at a time.

Let's start a new project and enter the following prompt:

```
Please create a personal portfolio website. I am a photographer looking to
showcase my work. The site should have three pages: 1. A 'Home' page with my bio
and a large hero image;
2. A 'Gallery' page using a grid layout to display photos; 3. A 'Contact' page
with a built-in form so visitors can leave me a message.
```

Hit *Enter* and wait for the AI to draft the site. You will notice it builds the shell and generates the specific `Home`, `Gallery`, and `Contact` pages you asked for, populating them with the correct elements—bio sections, photo grids, and contact forms—right where they belong (*Figure 2.5*).

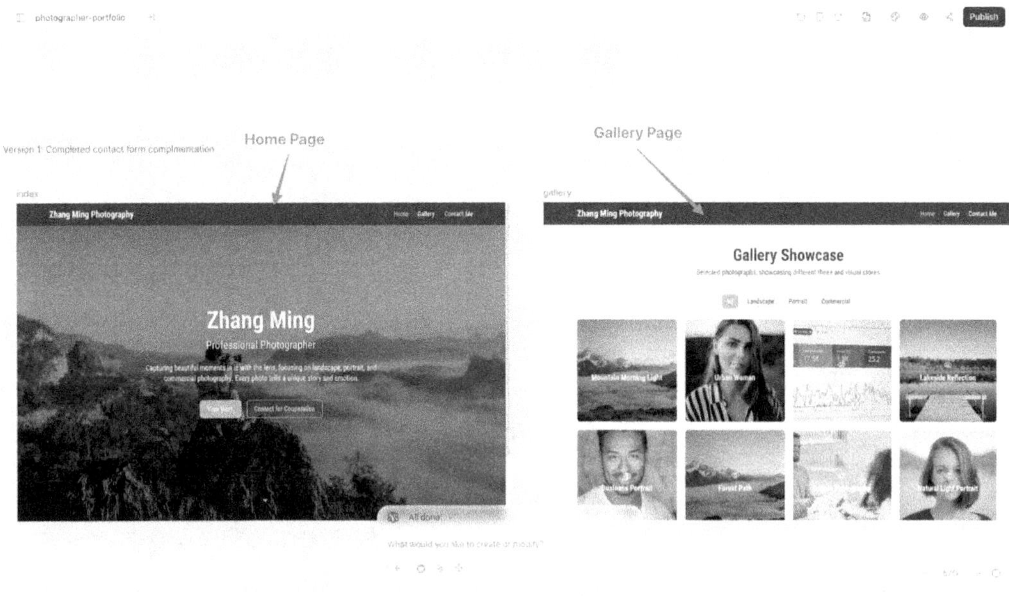

Figure 2.5 – The prototype of a personal portfolio website

The AI has provided the skeleton; now we need to give it a soul through customization.

Customizing your site

The AI's first draft is impressive, but it's not yet *yours*. Trickle offers two complementary ways to refine the design: conversational fine-tuning and precise **Direct Editing**.

Method 1: Conversational fine-tuning

You can type follow-up instructions into the input box to make broad changes:

- `Change the homepage background to dark gray and use a more artistic font.`
- `Add a caption text box under every image on the Gallery page.`
- `Rename the submit button on the Contact form to 'Send Message'.`

The AI understands context and will apply these incremental changes to your existing draft. This is perfect for stylistic overhauls or structural tweaks.

Method 2: Precision direct editing

Sometimes you just want to fix a font size or nudge a button's spacing. Writing a prompt for such tiny details is inefficient and prone to error. Trickle's Direct Edit mode is the solution (*Figure 2.6*). It works like a built-in visual editor:

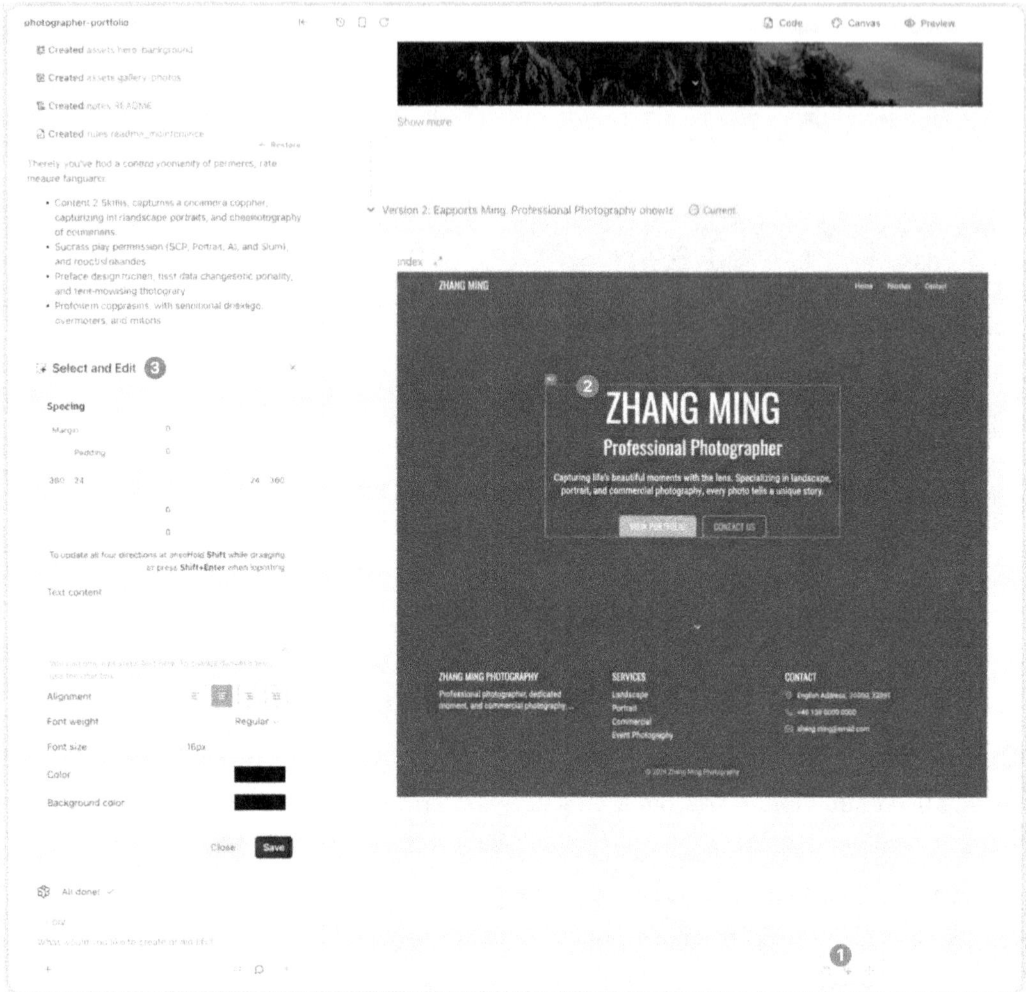

Figure 2.6 – Direct Edit diagram

1. Click the **Select and Edit** button at the bottom of the Canvas.
2. Hover over the webpage; you'll see individual elements (text, images, buttons) highlighted with a blue border.
3. Click the element you want to change (e.g., the site title). An editing panel will pop up, allowing you to manually tweak text, adjust font sizes, change colors, or set margins, just like using a word processor.

This hybrid approach combines the speed of AI with the precision of human control, giving you total command over the design.

Connecting the built-in database

The site looks good, but does the **Contact** form actually work? Where do the messages go? Enter the database. In Trickle, a database is essentially just a smart spreadsheet that collects and organizes information automatically.

The good thing is that because you asked for a "Contact form" in step one, Trickle has likely already created the backend database for you. It handles the invisible configuration automatically.

If you want to be explicit, you can tell the AI: `Save data submitted through the contact form to the Trickle database.`

To verify it works:

1. Locate the table labeled **Database** on your Canvas (it is empty initially).
2. Go to your website preview, fill out the **Contact** form with a test name and message, and click **Submit**.
3. Check the **Database** table again. You will see your test information organized neatly in the rows.

Just like that, without writing a single line of SQL or configuring a server, you have a website with a functional backend.

One-click publishing

Your portfolio is ready. The final step is sharing it with the world:

1. Click the **Publish** tab in the top right corner of the project page. A dialog box will appear, showing a preview of your site's metadata.

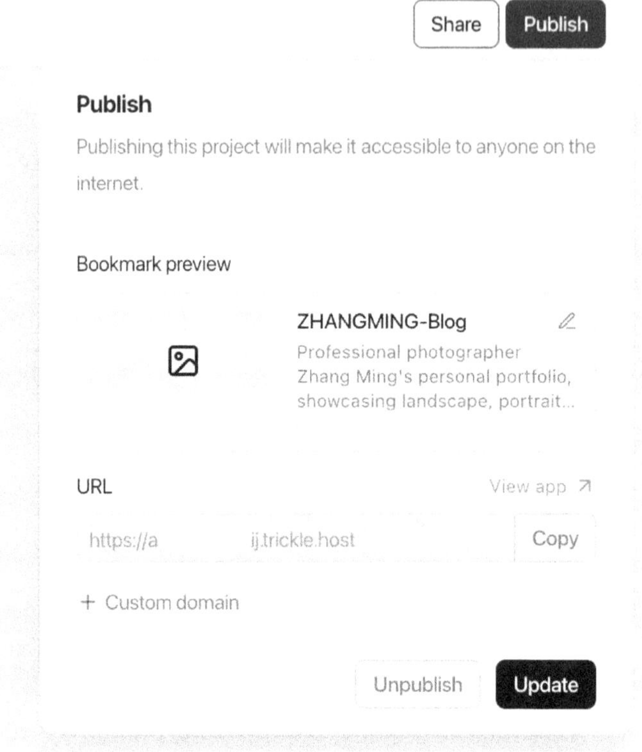

Figure 2.7 – The dialog box showing your site's metadata

2. Under the URL section, you'll see an auto-generated free domain ending in `.trickle.host`. (You can connect a custom domain via the **Custom domain** button if you upgrade later.)
3. Simply click **Publish** at the bottom right

In an instant, your site is live. You now have a public link you can share with anyone anywhere.

Congratulations. You have successfully built and deployed a fully functional, multi-page website connected to a live database. Take a moment to savor that achievement.

Now that the practice run is complete, we must step back to evaluate where tools like Trickle AI fit into the broader landscape and why they matter in your learning arc.

The limitations of platforms like Trickle AI

Trickle's value lies in its ability to bypass the intimidating technical minutiae, allowing you to turn an idea into a tangible product in record time.

While we celebrate Trickle's speed, we must remain clear-eyed about its nature. Every engineering choice is a trade-off. To achieve such extreme ease of use, all-in-one platforms like Trickle inevitably compromise in other areas:

- **Ceiling on customization:** Built-in tools cannot match the infinite freedom of native code. You may eventually hit a wall when attempting highly unique designs or complex interactions
- **Scalability bottleneck:** If your user base explodes or data relationships become labyrinthine, performance will suffer.
- **Vendor lock-in:** Your project is tethered to the platform. Migrating to a different service is difficult, requiring a leap of faith in the platform's long-term stability and roadmap.

Trickle has served its purpose perfectly. It enticed you into the world of creation and proved that you belong here. However, to grow alongside AI and build commercial-grade applications that are complex, scalable, and fully under your control, you must understand what happens beneath that elegant, all-in-one surface.

In the chapter ahead, we will dissect platforms like Trickle. We will strip apart the seamless modules—frontend, backend, database, APIs—and guide you in assembling your own Frugal Full Stack toolchain, a system that is flexible, powerful, and uniquely yours.

The v0.dev masterclass

v0.dev (`https://v0.app/`) is an AI-powered tool that generates web interface code from natural language prompts. Instead of manually designing and coding every page element, you can simply describe elements such as a navigation bar, product card, or landing page, and the AI produces ready-to-use frontend components.

In the previous section, we used Trickle AI to quickly assemble a working application in an all-in-one environment. Now we take a step further by focusing specifically on the user interface. While Trickle helps you build and launch simple apps rapidly, v0.dev gives you finer control over how the interface looks and behaves, generating clean frontend code that can be reused in professional projects.

Rather than replacing developers, v0.dev acts as a creative partner for designers, entrepreneurs, and marketers, helping them quickly turn ideas into working interface designs.

In this section, you will experience this process firsthand. We will begin with a simple button, gradually move to more complex web components, and finally complete a practical project: guiding the AI to recreate a professional design template as a functional, personalized website.

Core concepts and interface tour

Before diving into the code, understanding the philosophy behind v0.dev will help you use it more effectively.

Built by the team at Vercel, v0.dev completes a vital loop. If Vercel solves the problem of *how to show your website to the world* (deployment), v0.dev solves *how to build the website* (creation).

v0.dev offers a free tier sufficient for all beginner exercises.

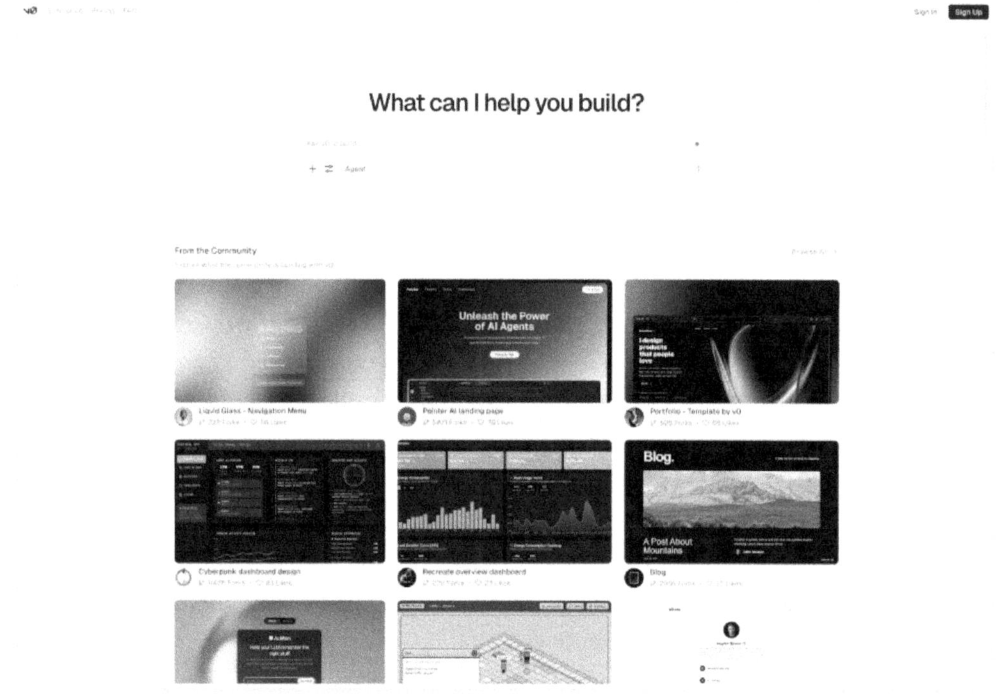

Figure 2.8 – v0.dev landing page

However, it is important to understand the limits of this free account so you can pace your learning. The free tier provides $5 of included monthly credits and imposes a strict limit of 7 messages (prompts) per day. Because your daily requests are limited, the clear communication and iterative prompting skills you learn in this chapter will be crucial for maximizing your daily allowance.

The core value of v0.dev is its ability to bridge the gap between your intent (*what you want*) and the technical execution (*how to do it*). You need not speak a programming language; you simply describe your needs in natural language, just as you would to a colleague, and the system executes them with precision.

When you issue a command, the AI analyzes the request through the lens of an engineer. If information is missing, it researches reference structures. If it generates buggy code, it self-corrects. This allows you to operate at a macro level. You stop fussing over pixel margins and start focusing on holistic design and user experience.

The workspace anatomy

Once logged in, typing a simple idea into the text box reveals a clean yet powerful workspace, as seen in *Figure 2.9*:

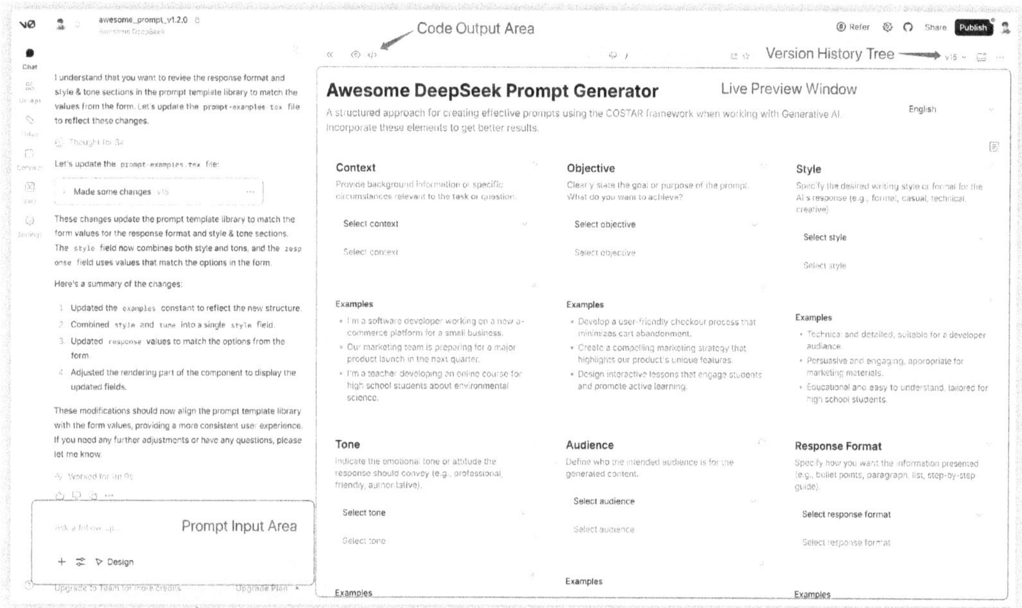

Figure 2.9 – The v0.dev workspace

The interface consists of four distinct zones:

- **Prompt Input Area:** This is your communication channel. Whether you are typing `create a dark-mode pricing page` or `make the button larger` all instructions flow through here.
- **Live Preview Window:** Your instructions are rendered visually, almost instantly. This *what you see is what you get* experience dramatically shortens the loop between having an idea and validating it.

- **Code Output Area:** The AI submits its work here in the form of clean, production-ready frontend code. You can largely ignore this initially, though peeking under the hood later will deepen your understanding of the logic.
- **Version History Tree:** Think of this as a "Super Undo" button with infinite saves. Every conversation and modification is branched here. This is your creative safety net, allowing you to experiment wildly with the assurance that you can always revert to a previous state.

Getting started: Component by component

We will begin with three rapid-fire exercises. The goal is simple: secure a quick win and build confidence in both the tool and your own abilities.

5-minute drill: Your first button

Let's start with the atomic unit of the web: the button.

Start a new project in v0.dev. In the prompt area, type the following command and hit *Enter*:

```
Create a blue, rounded 'Register' button.
```

Within moments, the preview window will render a polished, blue, pill-shaped button labeled **Register**, as shown in *Figure 2.10*.

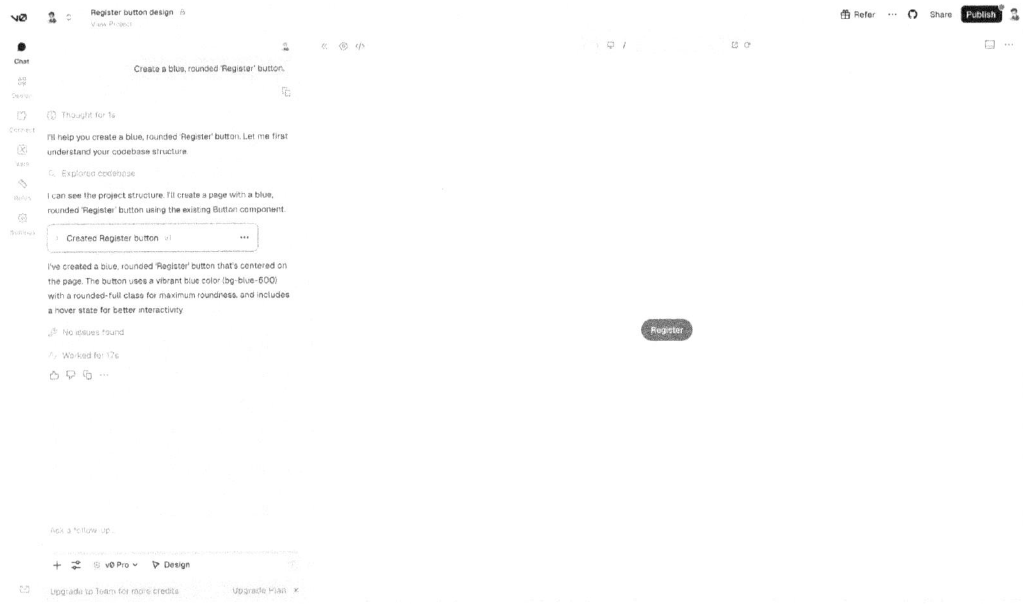

Figure 2.10 – The first button generated by v0.dev

Success. v0.dev parsed the attributes—color (blue), shape (rounded), and content ("Register") —and executed them perfectly.

10-minute drill: Building an info card

Info cards are ubiquitous on the web, used for everything from product features to team bios.

Continue in the same chat and enter this command:

```
Create a minimalist info card with a white background, rounded corners, and a
subtle drop shadow. Inside, vertically center a lightbulb icon, a bold 'Core
Features' title, and a short paragraph of muted gray description text.
```

v0.dev will organize the icon, typography, and layout into a professional card structure, complete with context-appropriate placeholder text, as shown in *Figure 2.11*:

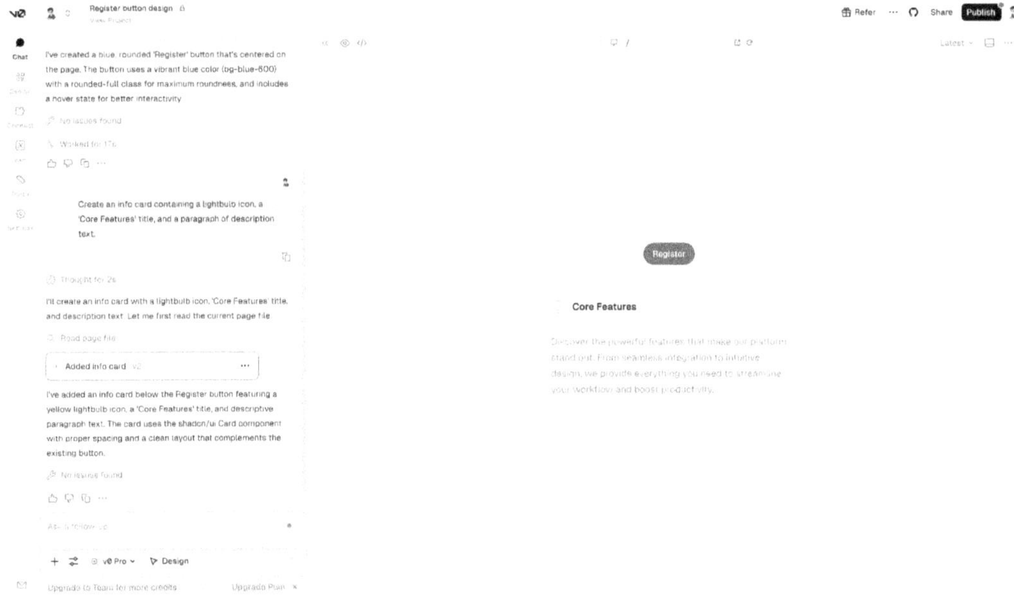

Figure 2.11 – The first info card generated by v0.dev

We have mastered static display components. Now, let's try something interactive.

10-minute drill: The login form

A login form is the gatekeeper of any application that requires user accounts.

Type this command:

```
Make a login form with 'Email' and 'Password' input fields, and a 'Login' button.
```

A standard, aesthetically pleasing form will appear, complete with labels and input fields (*Figure 2.12*). You can even click in the boxes and type in the preview window.

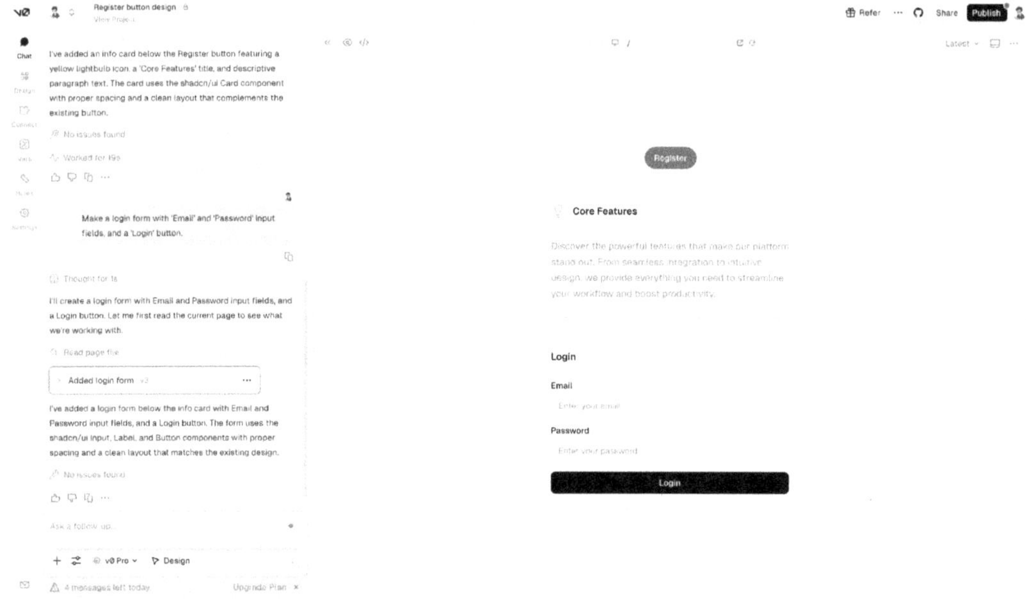

Figure 2.12 – The First Login Form Generated by v0.dev

v0.dev focuses on the "skin" and "skeleton" of the interface. While it generates a beautiful form, clicking **Login** won't actually authenticate you. That logic—database connections and user verification—is the domain of the backend engineer. v0.dev's power is maximizing frontend efficiency, freeing you from tedious CSS coding so you can focus on the user experience.

Leveling up: Composition and iteration

Congratulations on mastering the basics. The true power of v0.dev lies not in the first draft it generates, but in the subsequent "conversational" refinement. This iterative loop is the core workflow for professional users.

In the logic of v0.dev, your initial prompt is merely a conversation starter, a rough sketch. The final design emerges through rounds of dialogue and fine-tuning. This process is called **iteration**.

Iteration relies on dismantling a complex goal into a sequence of simple, manageable commands. Rather than dumping a monolithic wall of text detailing every nuance upfront, start by generating a foundational framework with a simple instruction. Then, use follow-up prompts to layer in details, adjust styles, and optimize layouts.

This workflow mirrors the sculptor's craft: you hew a rough outline from raw stone before switching to finer tools to polish the details. Collaborating with v0.dev works the same way; every follow-up question is a stroke of the chisel. This "chat-based" development experience aligns with natural human communication, making the creative process both flexible and controlled.

Now, let's master the art of iteration through practice.

5-minute sprint: Adding interactivity

Let's revisit the blue button created in the first exercise and use iteration to add dynamic interaction.

First, ensure the button is visible in the preview window (if it's missing, regenerate it or retrieve it from your history). Then, issue your first iterative command:

```
Make the color of the 'Register' button slightly darker when I hover over it.
```

Observe the preview window. When you move your cursor over the button, its color deepens smoothly, providing clear visual feedback. This is the *hover* effect.

Next, add a click effect by entering the following instruction:

```
Add a slight zoom effect when I click the 'Register' button.
```

Test it again. Clicking the button now triggers a momentary shrink-and-restore animation. This subtle detail enhances the user's sense of tactile confirmation.

With just two simple iterations, you have upgraded a static button into a component with professional-grade dynamic interactions. You have also learned to describe and implement state changes based on user behavior (hovering, clicking) through simple dialogue.

Next, we will build a critical website component—the navigation bar—and use iteration to achieve a responsive layout.

10-minute sprint: Building a responsive navbar

Responsiveness ensures a webpage adapts seamlessly across devices like desktops, tablets, and phones to deliver an optimal viewing experience. We will build a responsive navbar using the steps below.

Step 1: Create the base navbar

Enter the initial instruction:

```
Create a navbar. Put a Logo on the left, and three menu items on the right:
'Home', 'About Us', and 'Contact Us'.
```

v0.dev will generate a classic desktop layout: a Logo placeholder on the left and three horizontally aligned links on the right, as shown in *Figure 2.13* at the top of the preview window.

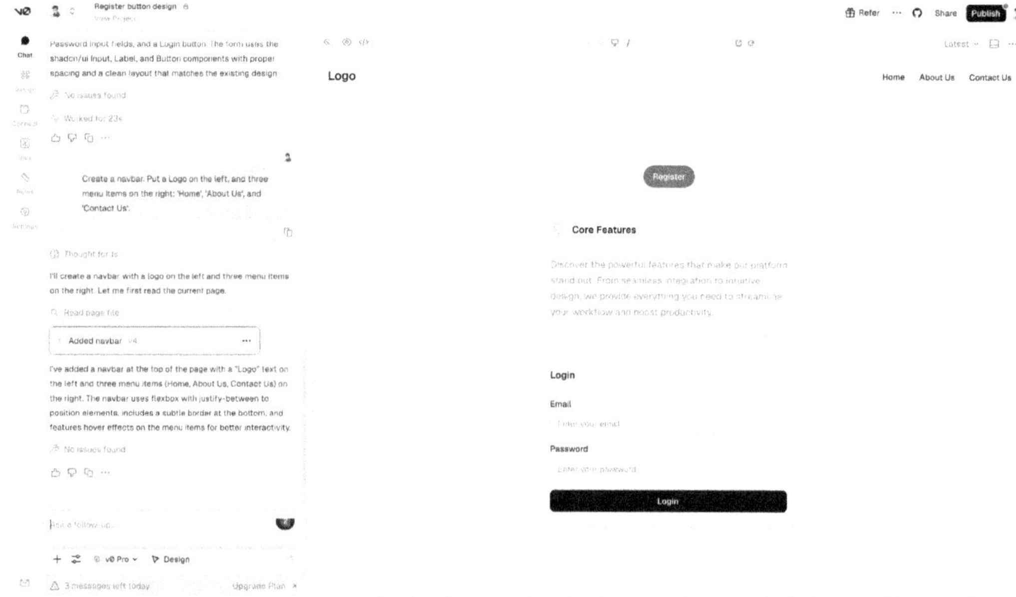

Figure 2.13: The first navbar created by v0.dev

Step 2: Iterate for responsiveness

Now, tell v0.dev how to display this navbar on smaller screens. Enter the iterative command:

```
Turn this navbar into a hamburger menu on mobile screens.
```

v0.dev understands industry terminology like *hamburger menu* (a side menu represented by an icon with three horizontal lines). Now, verify the responsive effect. In most mainstream browsers, the easiest way to open the developer tools for testing is to right-click anywhere on the webpage and select **Inspect** (or **Inspect Element**), as shown in *Figure 2.14*.

Opening developer tools and finding the device emulator varies slightly by browser and operating system

- **Universal Method (All OS)**: Simply right-click anywhere on the page and select **Inspect**.
- **Chrome/Edge**: Alternatively, use the shortcut *Cmd* + *Option* + *I* (Mac) or *F12* (Windows). Once open, click the corresponding device icon in the top corner (the **Toggle device toolbar** icon in Chrome or **Toggle device emulation** in Edge).
- **Firefox**: Use *Cmd* + *Option* + *I* (Mac) or *F12* (Windows), then click the **Responsive Design Mode** icon.
- **Safari (Mac only)**: First, enable the **Develop** menu via **Safari** | **Settings** | **Advanced**. Then, press *Cmd* + *Option* + *I* (or right-click and select **Inspect Element**) to open developer tools, and click the device icon.

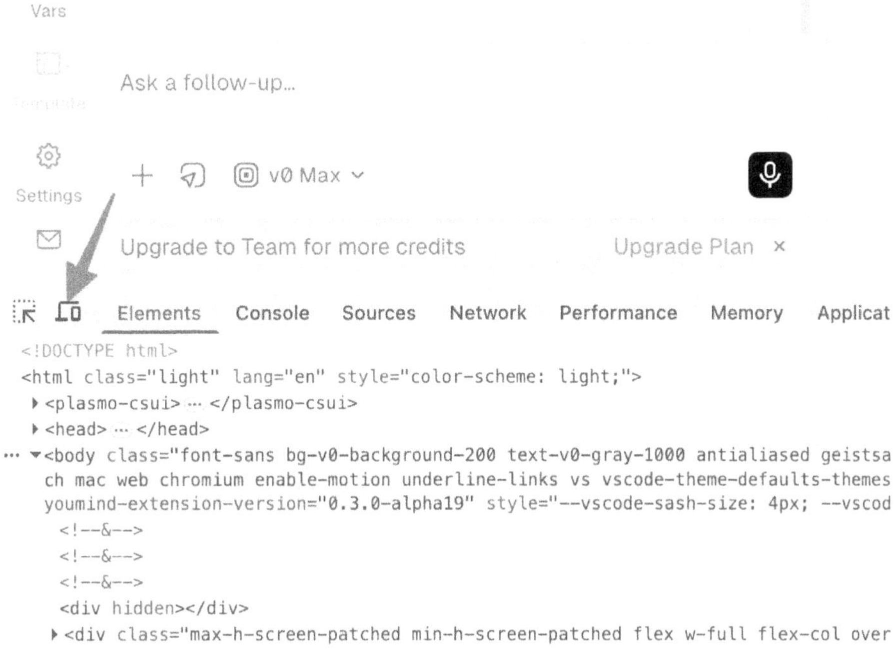

Figure 2.14 – Developer Tools device icon

Once in responsive mode, switch the browser view in the v0.dev preview window to a mobile size. You will see the three menu items on the right disappear, replaced by the classic three-line hamburger icon, as shown in *Figure 2.15*. Clicking this icon expands the menu into a vertical list.

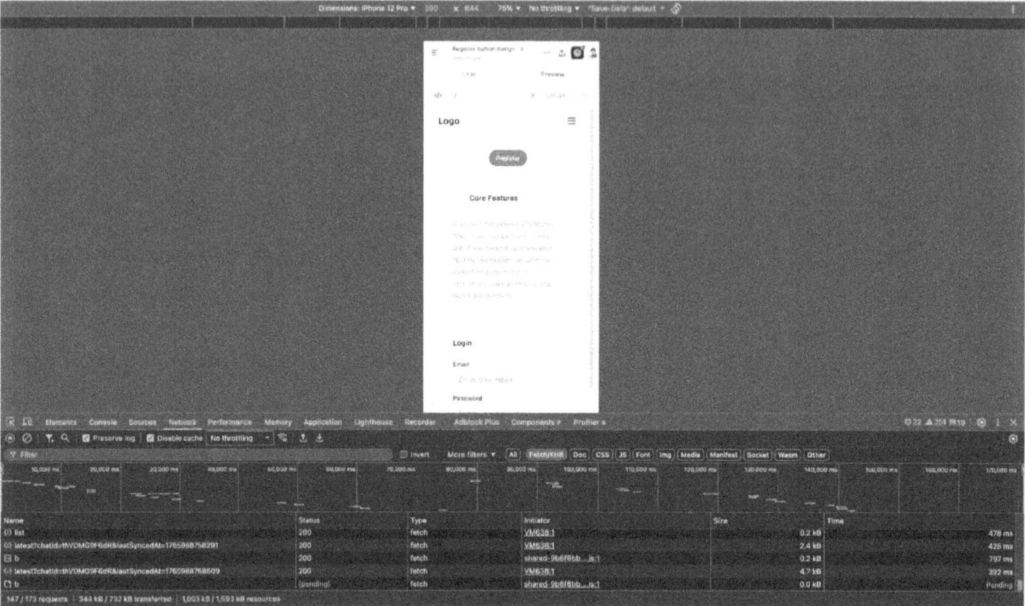

Figure 2.15 – Responsive navbar created by v0.dev (Chrome illustration)

You achieved this responsive design without writing complex media query code. This demonstrates that v0.dev can handle complex design patterns aligned with industry best practices (generating code based on React, Tailwind CSS, and other mainstream stacks).

With component creation and iteration covered, we are ready to explore a more advanced workflow tailored to creative minds.

Advanced workflow: Visual prompting

Thus far, we have relied on language to describe our designs. Yet, as creative professionals, our minds naturally gravitate toward the visual. The advanced workflow in v0.dev allows you to bypass language entirely and hand the designs you like directly to the AI for replication.

For creators without a technical background, v0.dev's ability to parse and replicate screenshots is useful.

We have all encountered this friction: spotting a design that feels modern and clean, yet struggling to articulate the precise font weights, spacing, hex codes, or shadow diffusion. In the translation from visual to semantic, the loss of fidelity is profound.

Screenshots bridge this chasm. A single image contains thousands of precise data points regarding layout, color, typography, and style, thus showing the AI what you want.

Note

While AI makes replication effortless, it is your responsibility to respect intellectual property. Use screenshots to understand patterns—like how a navigation bar is structured or how whitespace creates hierarchy—rather than to copy a creator's unique brand identity or proprietary assets. The goal is to let excellent designs teach you, not to plagiarize them. Always iterate on the AI's output to inject your own brand and voice, ensuring the final product is uniquely yours.

Now, let us experience this power firsthand.

10-minute challenge: Cloning an existing component

Follow these steps to rapidly convert a component screenshot into functional code:

1. Open your browser and visit a site that inspires you or simply an app you enjoy.
2. Select a standout component, such as a unique button, a polished user review card, or a pricing tier display.
3. Use a screenshot tool to capture only that specific component.
4. Return to v0.dev, initiate a new chat, and locate the image upload button. Select your screenshot.
5. Pair the image with a simple directive, `Generate this component from this screenshot`. Press *Enter*.

v0.dev will analyze the structure, palette, and typography, rendering a high-fidelity replica in the preview window composed of real code.

Just like that, you have transmuted pixels into code—a task that once demanded hours of a frontend engineer's time. Once you are comfortable generating components, investing a little time in understanding the underlying code will significantly enhance your collaboration with the AI.

Understanding the code output

Let us lift the hood and examine the code v0.dev generates. Our goal is not to teach you programming, but to demystify it and provide a conceptual grasp of the symbols you see.

In the v0 interface, switch to the code output panel (see *Figure 2.16*). You will observe that the code is composed of three primary ingredients: **React components**, **TSX syntax**, and **Tailwind CSS**.

Figure 2.16 – v0.dev code output area

- **React Components**: Every module v0.dev generates—buttons, cards, navigation bars—is a React component. Think of these as independent Lego bricks. If you create a **Sign Up** button "brick", you can snap it into place anywhere on your site without manufacturing it from scratch every time. This *modularity* is what makes building and maintaining large-scale websites efficient.
- **TSX Syntax**: TSX is an extension of TypeScript that allows HTML-like markup to live directly within the code. Simply put, it is a hybrid of TypeScript + XML/HTML. It allows you to describe the user interface declaratively—like a blueprint defining the structure of your Lego brick.
  Inside the component code, you will encounter tags like `<div>`, `<button>`, `<img>`, and `<h1>` intermingled with logic. This is the utility of TSX: it permits developers to describe the "shape" of the component using intuitive, HTML-like language without switching contexts.
- **Tailwind CSS**: This is the most accessible layer. Inside the TSX tags, you will notice a long `className="..."` attribute packed with short terms like bg-blue-500, rounded-lg, or font-bold. This is Tailwind CSS.
  View Tailwind CSS as a set of descriptive "stickers" you apply to your Lego bricks. Instead of writing a separate, dense manual on styling, you simply adhere a "Blue

Background" sticker (bg-blue-500), a "Large Rounded Corner" sticker (rounded-lg), or a "Bold Text" sticker (font-bold) directly onto the component. This approach makes iterative styling effortless.

To help you visualize these "stickers," *Table 2.1* provides a translation guide.

Your goal	**Code example**	**Plain English translation**
Make text larger and bold	text-xl font-bold	Text size: Extra Large; weight: Bold
Blue background, rounded corners	bg-blue-500, rounded-lg	Background: Blue (shade 500), corners: large radius
Add internal spacing	p-4	Padding: 4 units
Add external spacing	m-2	Margin: 2 units
Align items in a row	flex	Use Flexbox layout (default: horizontal row)
Center horizontally and vertically	flex, justify-center, items-center	Flex layout; center across width; center across height

Table 2.1 – Tailwind CSS Translation Guide

With *Table 2.1* in hand, try to decode these "stickers" the next time you view v0.dev's output. You might even attempt to tweak one—perhaps changing bg-blue-500 to bg-red-500—to observe how the preview transforms.

Armed with these insights, you are now ready to tackle the chapter's next project.

Hands-on project: Replicating your favorite Figma template

In this exciting challenge, you will synthesize every skill you have acquired so far, from prompt engineering and iterative optimization to visual replication. Your mission is to take a professional Figma template and transform it into a fully functional personal website.

Exploring the Figma community

Start by gathering inspiration and raw materials. Figma (`https://www.figma.com/`) is the premier collaborative UI tool for designers worldwide, and its massive community is a goldmine of high-quality resources (see *Figure 2.17*).

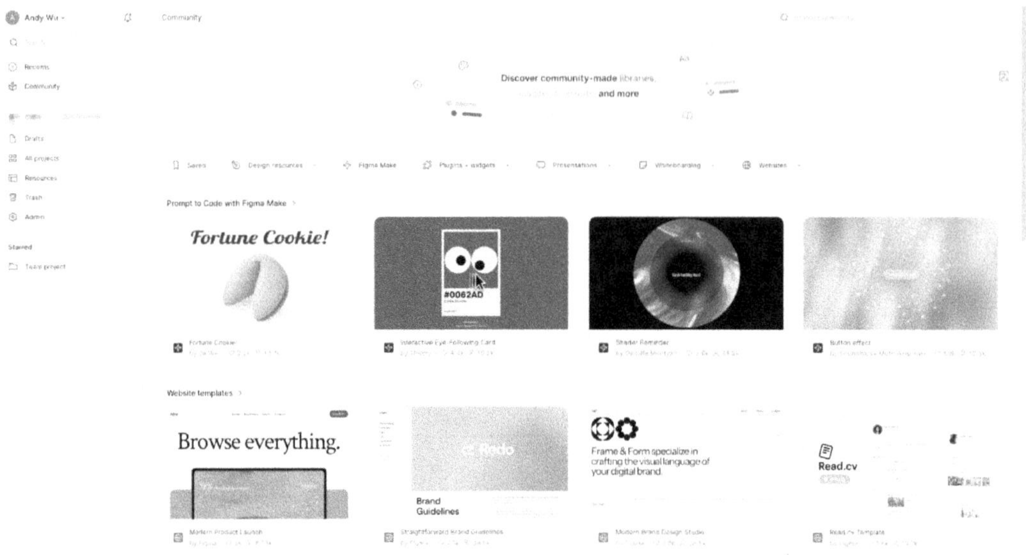

Figure 2.17 – Figma Community

Browse the **Figma Community** for categories that interest you, such as `Portfolio`, `SaaS Landing`, `Page`, or `Dashboard`. You will find countless free templates at your disposal.

Unsure where to begin? I recommend searching the Figma Community for `Minimal Portfolio Free Landing Pages`. This resource is a pre-designed template featuring a minimalist style ideal for a personal portfolio, and it conveniently includes ready-made layouts for both desktop and mobile screens. A quick search will bring it up.

Browse until you find a design that resonates with you. I suggest sticking to a clean, single-page landing page or portfolio; steer clear of complex backend management systems for your first attempt. Once you have made your choice, copy the file to your Figma drafts.

With the design in hand, the next step is planning and decomposition.

Deconstructing the design

This is the project's most crucial mental exercise and the core strategy professional developers use to tackle complexity: decomposition. Beginners often look at a polished design and feel overwhelmed by its totality. Professionals, however, see a collection of independent, manageable components. You must now learn to adopt this developer's eye.

A typical landing page generally breaks down into the following distinct sections:

- **Navigation Bar:** Located at the very top, containing the logo and menu links

- **Hero Section:** Immediately following the nav bar, this above-the-fold area usually features a bold headline, a sub-headline, and a **call-to-action** (**CTA**) button
- **Features/Services:** Uses icons and concise text to highlight the core benefits of your product or service
- **Portfolio/Case Studies:** Displays projects via cards or a grid layout
- **Testimonials:** Citations from satisfied clients to build trust
- **Footer:** The bottom anchor, holding copyright info, social links, and contact details

Your task is to dissect your chosen template into these standalone, functional components. This process does more than just organize the upcoming AI generation; it teaches you how to dismantle a massive, complex problem into solvable pieces—a skill far more valuable than mastering any single tool.

With the design decomposed, it is time to build.

10-minute drill: Hands-on replication

Execute the following steps to rapidly convert component screenshots into production-ready code:

1. **Capture screenshots:** Adhering to your breakdown plan, take precise, isolated screenshots of each element (e.g., capture the navigation bar first, then the Hero section, and so on)
2. **Upload and generate:** Open v0.dev. Start with your first component: upload the navigation bar screenshot and pair it with the prompt, `Replicate this navigation bar.`
3. **Iterate and Fine-tune:** The initial output from v0.dev will likely be close, but rarely perfect. This is where the art of iteration comes in. Use follow-up prompts to polish the details:
    - `Make the logo slightly larger.`
    - `Widen the spacing between menu items.`
    - `Change the button color to #5A67D8` (providing the exact hex code works best)
4. **Repeat the Cycle:** Once you're satisfied with the navigation bar, clear the canvas or start a new chat. Move on to the next piece, such as the Hero section. Repeat the Screenshot → Upload → Iterate cycle until you have a code version for every component.

Assembly and fine-tuning

You have gathered all your Lego blocks from v0.dev. Now it is time to move from your web browser to your local computer to snap them together into the final model.

To seamlessly piece this code together and put it on the internet, we will introduce two essential tools from our Frugal Full-Stack toolkit:

- **TRAE**: A standalone AI code editor (`https://www.TRAE.ai/`). We will use its highly autonomous SOLO mode.

  > **Note**
  >
  > SOLO mode is a premium feature included in the TRAE Pro plan. It currently offers a 14-day free trial, after which it costs $10/month. Please also be aware that upgrading to paid plans is actively being rolled out and may currently be restricted in some global regions.

- **Vercel**: A global deployment network. You will need to take a quick moment to register a free individual account at Vercel.com to host your site.

Let's start:

1. Open the TRAE application on your computer and select SOLO mode in the top-left corner to initiate the automated development flow. The AI handles the local environment setup, sparing you the hassle of configuring complex project structures.

   > **Note**
   >
   > **For VS Code & Cursor Users**: While we use TRAE here for its zero-configuration setup, you can certainly assemble these components in **VS Code** (with GitHub Copilot) or **Cursor**. However, you may need to handle the environment configuration, like installing Node.js or initializing the project, manually. We will dive deeper into **Cursor**, a powerful AI-native alternative popular in the West, in *Chapter 4*.

2. Instruct the SOLO AI using natural language:

   ```
   I have generated multiple component codes using v0.dev. Please create a
   project and assemble these components into a complete website based on the
   design order.
   ```

Simply drag the component folders you copied from v0.dev into the TRAE project; the AI will analyze and integrate them automatically.

3. Enable the **Follow** feature. You can watch the AI in real time across the editor, terminal, previewer, and documentation panel as it breaks down requirements, structures the project, integrates the code, and manages dependencies.
4. To adjust layout or styling, issue direct commands in the chat. For example, `The gap between the navbar and Hero section is too wide`, or `The overall color scheme is too dark; please brighten it`. The AI will respond instantly, reflecting the changes in the preview window.
5. When the local version looks good, tell SOLO AI: `Please deploy this to Vercel`. It will handle the deployment pipeline and generate a public link, transforming your local project into a shareable online product.

Look at the running website on your screen. Just hours ago, these were static images; now, they are a dynamic webpage built with real code.

From a simple button to a full project, you have walked the entire path. You haven't just learned a tool; you have proven that with the right workflow, your creativity can effortlessly bridge the technical divide.

Summary

In this section, we completed a "zero-to-one" field exercise with v0.dev. We began by familiarizing ourselves with v0.dev as a powerful AI Frontend Engineer. Through the *Five-Minute Drill*, we rapidly built buttons, info cards, and login forms, building the initial confidence required to collaborate with AI.

We then deepened our understanding of **iteration**—the core of the v0.dev workflow. We used continuous, conversational prompts to add professional hover effects to buttons. We even utilized simple commands like *turn this into a hamburger menu on mobile* to generate fully responsive navigation bars, using simple inputs to create complex design patterns.

We also explored the game-changing **Visual-to-Code** workflow. By uploading screenshots, we bypassed the difficulty of describing visual designs with words, achieving an instant translation from inspiration to usable code. To demystify the process, we "popped the hood" to see that the output consists of three known elements: React components (the Lego blocks), TSX (the blueprints), and Tailwind CSS (the styling stickers).

Finally, we synthesized these skills in a practical project, applying the crucial mindset of *decomposition*. We broke a complex Figma design into independent components, replicated them individually via v0.dev, and used TRAE SOLO to orchestrate these parts into a live personal website.

Now that you have experienced the speed of AI generation, we will turn to the professional design tool Figma to learn how to create the precise blueprints that guide this process.

Learning Figma: From first canvas to developer handoff

Figma is the industry-standard user interface (UI) design tool. It allows you to visually draw your application and decide exactly where buttons go, what colors to use, and how menus open—before writing a single line of code. It acts as a cloud-based design studio that runs directly in your browser.

Figma has eclipsed its competitors to become the standard for giants like Google and Microsoft. Its dominance rests on three pillars:

- **Collaboration**: Teams, product managers, developers, and clients can access the same file simultaneously. You see real-time cursors, leave comments on specific layers, and reply to feedback directly on the canvas, eliminating the need for file transfers and screenshots
- **Unified Workflow**: Designers historically juggled different tools for wireframing, high-fidelity visuals, and prototyping. Figma consolidates this ecosystem. From initial ideation to clickable prototypes and final developer handoff, the entire lifecycle happens on one platform.
- **Beginner-Friendly**: Despite its depth, Figma provides a gentle learning curve with an intuitive interface. Its robust free version handles everything covered in this chapter, allowing novices to start without financial friction.

In this section, we will start with a blank canvas, build a dynamic interface, breathe life into it with interactivity, and finally package it for elegant delivery to developers or AI. No prior design experience is required; by the end, you will possess the skills to turn any creative idea into a buildable application design.

Interface tour and core concepts

> Note
>
> If using Trickle AI or v0.dev felt like driving an automatic car, opening Figma for the first time might feel like stepping into an airplane cockpit. Because Figma is a professional-grade tool used by industry giants, its interface is packed with advanced features. Do not let this overwhelm you. As a beginner, you do not need to master every menu or tool today. We are only going to focus on the core 20% of features you need to accomplish 80% of your design goals.

Opening Figma for the first time can feel overwhelming. To simplify, we can divide the interface into four distinct zones (see *Figure 2.18*).

Figure 2.18 – Figma interface navigation

- **The Canvas**: The vast, gray area in the center is your digital table. Whether designing mobile screens, websites, or icons, everything lives here. You can pan infinitely in any direction, placing drafts side by side for easy comparison.
- **The Toolbar (Core Toolbox)**: Located at the bottom of the interface, this houses your primary instruments: the **Move** tool, **Frame** tool, **Shapes** (Rectangle R, Ellipse O), and **Text** tools.
- **The Layers Panel**: Located on the left, this panel acts like a book's index. It displays every element—frames, groups, text, icons—showing the hierarchy of your design. Developing a habit of naming layers early is the hallmark of a professional.
- **The Design Panel**: Located on the right, this is the "brain" of the interface. It is context-aware: select a rectangle, and it shows borders and corner radii; select text, and it shows fonts and line heights. All fine-tuning happens here.

The frame-first mindset

In modern UI design, almost every element resides inside a container. In Figma, the ultimate container is the **Frame**. Beginners coming from Photoshop often confuse Frames, Groups, and Shapes. Distinguishing them is critical:

- **Shapes**: The atomic building blocks (rectangles, circles). They are pure **vector graphics**, meaning they are calculated by math rather than pixels, so you can stretch or shrink them to any size without them ever becoming blurry
- **Groups**: The concept of a Group is like putting a rubber band around several items (like a cluster of shapes) just so you can drag them around the canvas as a single unit. A group has no background or structure of its own; it acts like shrink-wrap, meaning its size is determined entirely by the items inside it. If you stretch the group, you warp and stretch the contents. For this reason, groups have very limited utility in UI design and are mostly used for temporarily bundling complex vector illustrations.
- **Frames**: The fundamental unit of UI—think of them as "smart containers" or "artboards." Unlike groups, Frames have independent dimensions. They possess superpowers:
    - • **Constraints**: Rules that tell elements how to behave when the screen changes size (e.g., ensuring a **Next** button always stays in the bottom-right corner)
    - • **Clip Content**: A clean-up tool that acts like a mask, hiding any parts of an image or shape that spill over the frame's edges
- Frames are the bedrock of Auto Layout and components.

We emphasize *Frame-first* because UI design is about building flexible systems that adapt to different screens. Groups react passively to content; Frames actively manage it. Experienced designers follow a strict rule: *Always use Frames; rarely use Groups.* This mirrors the logic of modern web development (specifically the HTML `<div>` tag).

Here's how Frames and Groups differ:

Feature	Frame	Group
Dimensions	Independent, custom size; ignores content size	Determined entirely by the boundaries of child elements.
Clip content	Can hide content that overflows the borders.	Impossible; all content is always visible
Constraints	Inner elements can be pinned (e.g., "Left & Top"). No	Concept of constraints; scaling is uniform.
Auto layout	The only container that supports auto layout.	Does not support auto layout.

Table 2.2 – The differences between frames and groups

To summarize, here's the usage strategy:

- Use **Frames** for almost everything: buttons, cards, pages, and responsive layouts
- Use **Groups** only for temporary bundling (e.g., moving a complex vector illustration) before placing it back into a Frame

5-minute sprint: Creating a custom icon set

Let's apply this theory. We will create simple icon to experience the container logic of frames, the flexibility of shapes, and the power of Boolean operations.

1. **Create the container**: First, open Figma and create a new design file. Once you are staring at your blank workspace, remember the golden rule: don't draw directly on the empty canvas. Press *F* and drag a 24×24 px frame. In the **Layers** Panel, rename it icon/camera (see *Figure 2.19*). This frame ensures your icon adheres to a standard size.

Figure 2.19 – Create icon container

2. **Draw basic shapes:** Inside the frame, press *R* to draw a rectangle (the camera body) and round the corners. Press *O* to draw a large circle (lens) and a small circle (flash) (see *Figure 2.20*).

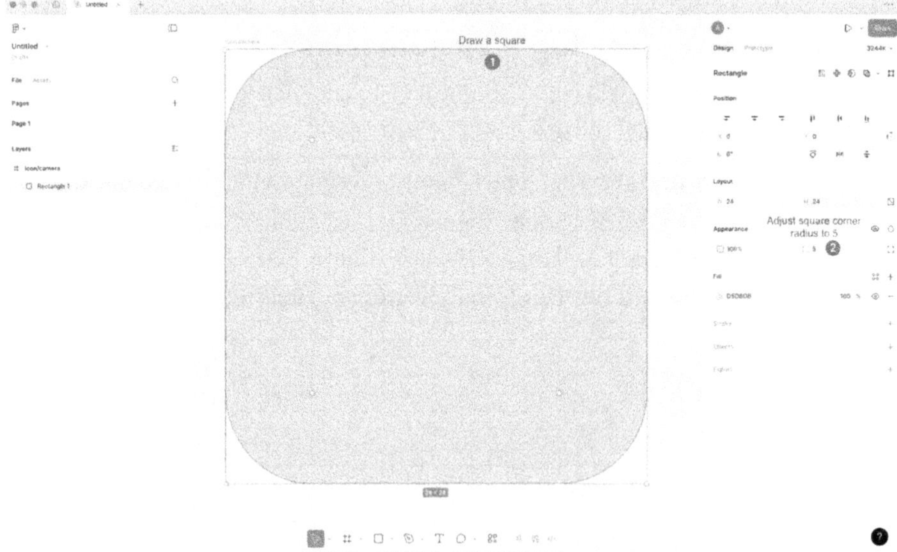

Figure 2.20 – Draw a rounded square

3. **Apply Boolean operations:** Currently, these form three separate layers. Hold down *Shift* and select the shapes (excluding the frame) (**1** in *Figure 2.21*). In the top toolbar, find the **Boolean Groups** icon (two intersecting squares, **2** in the figure), and select **Subtract (3)**.

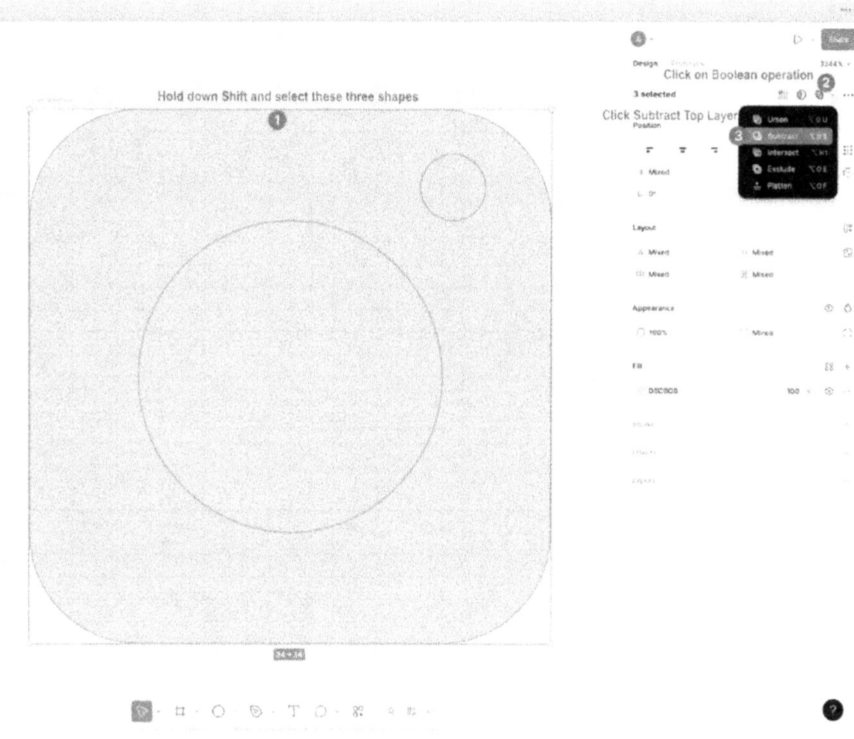

Figure 2.21: Using Boolean operations

The circles will act like cookie cutters, punching holes through the rectangle to form a single compound shape (*Figure 2.22*). This is non-destructive; you can still tweak the original circles later.

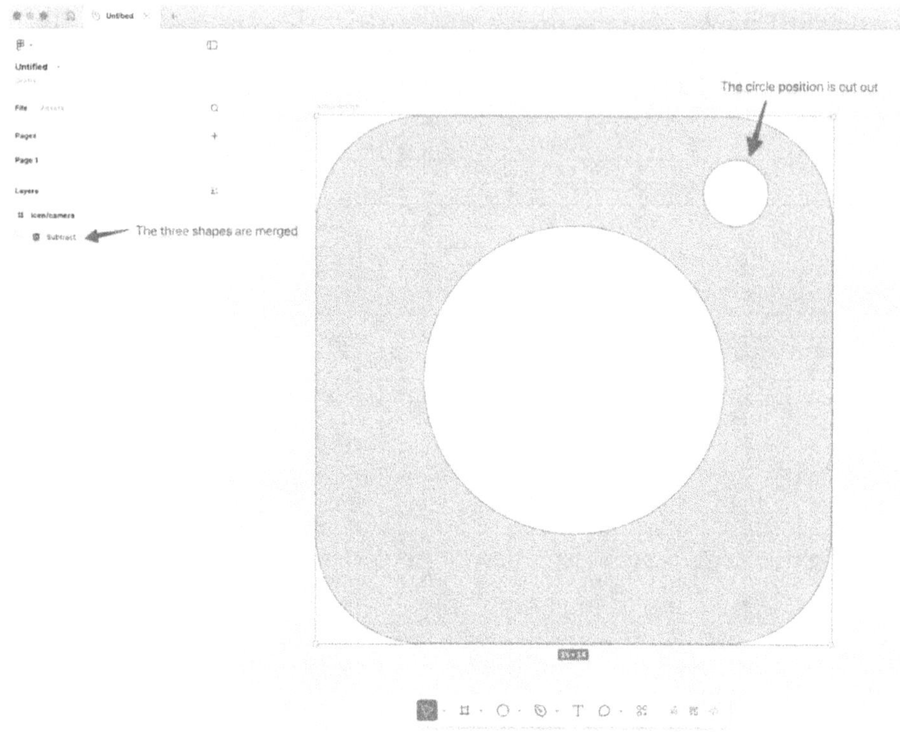

Figure 2.22 – Boolean operation result

4. **Flatten and Center:** Select your new shape and press *Cmd/Ctrl + E* to flatten it. This merges the layers into a single clean vector path, preventing distortion during scaling. Use the alignment tools in the **Design** panel to center the vector within your 24×24 frame (*Figure 2.23*).

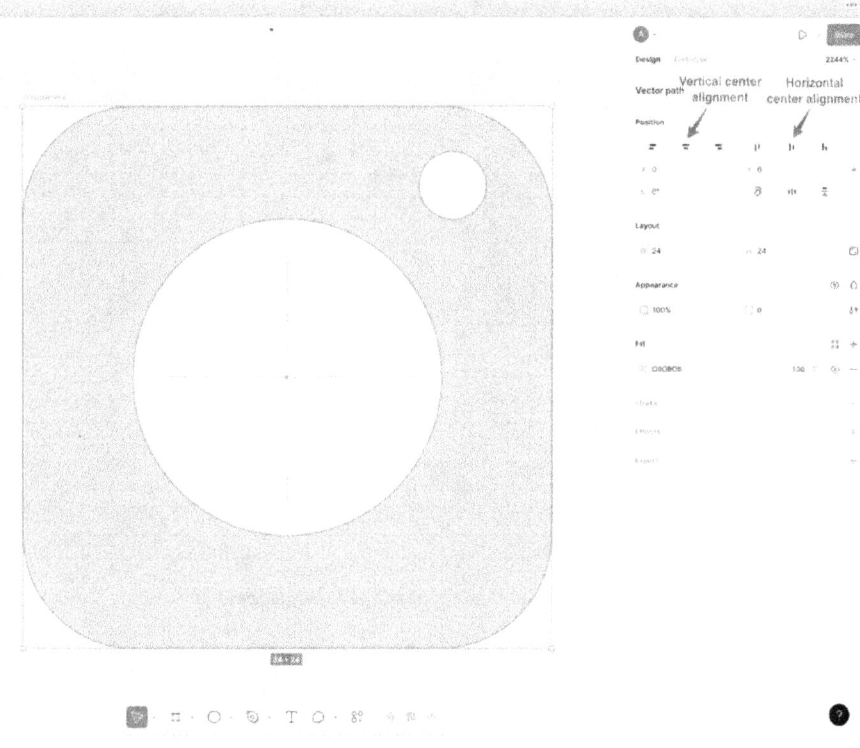

Figure 2.23 – Flatten and Center

5. **Clean Up:** Check your **Layers** panel. Ensure the frame is named `icon/camera` and the inner vector is named simply Vector. Proper naming is vital for code export (*Figure 2.24*).

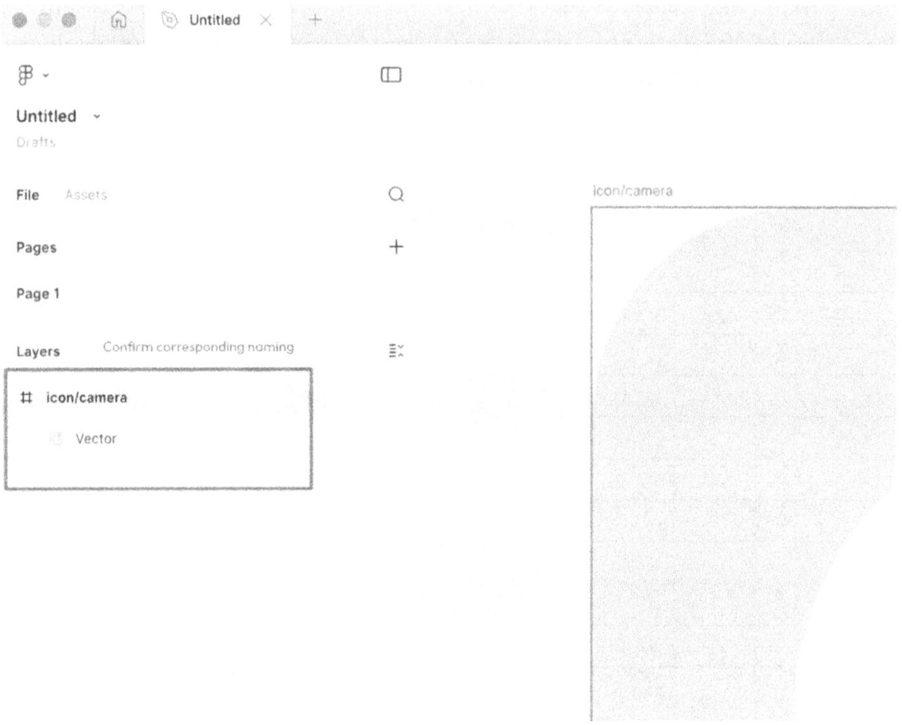

Figure 2.24 – Check name

> **Tip**
>
> *Challenge:* Repeat this process to create an icon for "user" (using circles and squares) or an icon for "settings" (using rotated squares).

Establishing a visual language

If Frames are the skeleton, then Color, Typography, and Grids are the flesh and blood. A design feels premium when it follows a consistent internal logic or a *visual language*.

Think of a visual language just like a spoken language: your colors, fonts, and icons are your vocabulary while your grids and spacing rules are your grammar. When a product uses the exact same shade of blue for every primary button and the exact same spacing for every card, it communicates stability, professionalism, and brand identity to the user. Without a visual language, a product feels chaotic and cheap.

In Figma, we codify this language using **Styles** and **Layout Grids**. By defining these rules upfront, we transform raw design choices into a "single source of truth".

Styles

Styles standardize repetitive attributes. Instead of manually picking a hex code (a six-character digital label that computers use to identify exact colors, like #0000FF for blue) for every blue button, you define a rule. This drastically reduces maintenance.

- **Color Styles:** These manage your palette. You save a hex value as `color/primary`. If you later decide to change your brand's blue, you edit the **Style** once and every object using `color/primary` updates instantly.
- **Text Styles:** These manage typography (font family, size, weight, line height). Notably, Text Styles do *not* include color. This decoupling allows you to mix and match—applying a `typography/h1` style to both a black headline and a blue headline without creating duplicate styles.

Layout grids

Grids are the invisible scaffolding that create order.

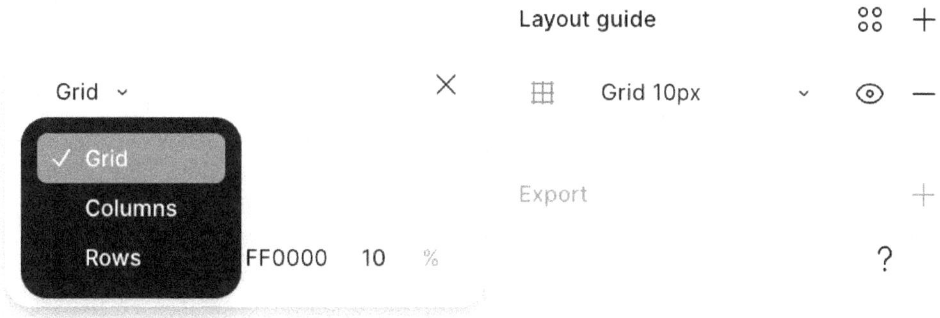

Figure 2.25 – Enabling Grid in Figma

They help you align elements and maintain consistent spacing. Figma offers three types:

- **Uniform Grid**: Graph paper squares (e.g., 8px). Great for icon design.
- **Columns**: Vertical guides. Essential for web and mobile layouts. Define the number of columns, the gutter (gap), and the margin.
- **Rows**: Horizontal guides. Useful for modular layouts.

Creating styles is the first step toward **Design Tokens**—the practice of abstracting raw values (like `#0000FF`) into semantic names (Brand Color), which bridge the gap between design and code.

15-minute sprint: Design a basic style guide

We will now build a *Style Guide*—a documentation page that serves as the single source of truth for your project.

1. **Create a Base Specs Page**: In the **Layers** Panel (top left), click the page name to expand the page list. Add a new page named `Base Specs`. Segregating documentation from design drafts is a professional best practice (*Figure 2.26*).

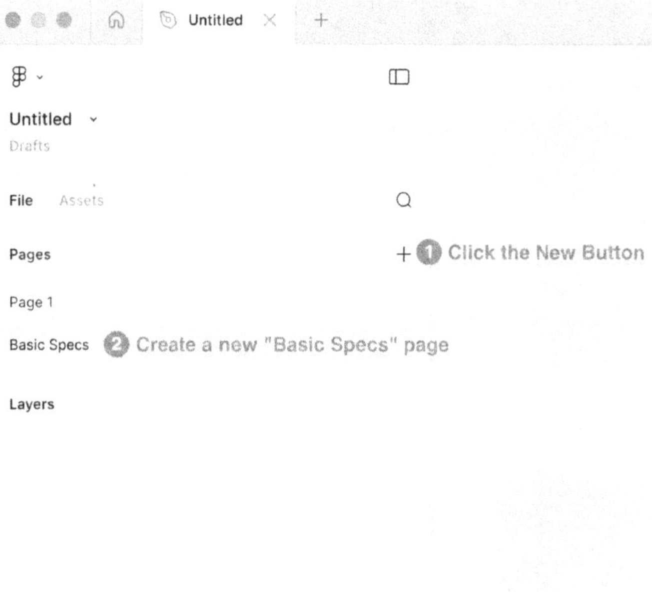

Figure 2.26 – Create a Basic Specification Page

2. **Document Color Styles:** Draw rectangles and fill them with your Primary, Secondary, and Neutral colors. Select the Primary rectangle. In the **Fill** section of the **Design** Panel, click the **Style** icon (four dots), and then the **+** icon. Name it `color/primary` (*Figure 2.27*).

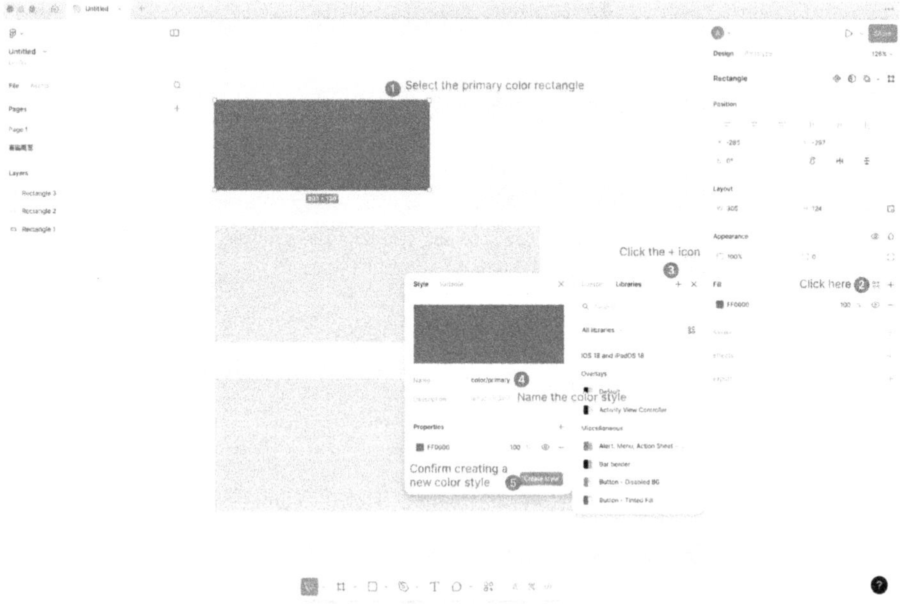

Figure 2.27 – Document the Primary color

Repeat for `color/secondary` and `color/neutral/900`. Label them clearly on the canvas (*Figure 2.28*).

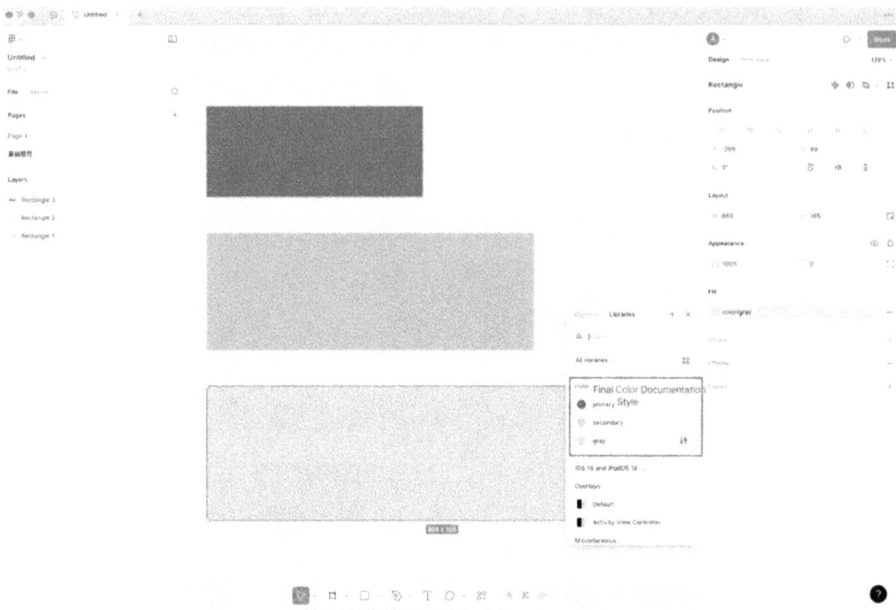

Figure 2.28 – Document secondary and neutral colors

3. **Document Typography**: Type out text samples: `Heading 1`, `Heading 2`, and `Body Text`. Set their properties (e.g., H1: `Inter Bold 32px`; Body: `Inter Regular 16px`) (*Figure 2.29*).

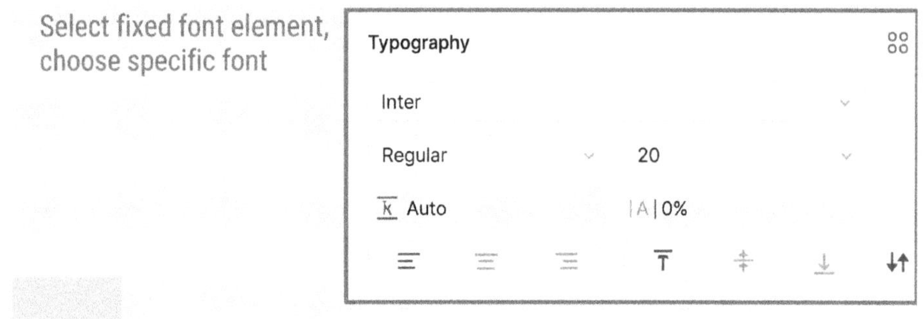

Figure 2.29 – Select a font

Create styles for each, naming them `typography/h1`, `typography/h2`, and `typography/body` (*Figure 2.30*).

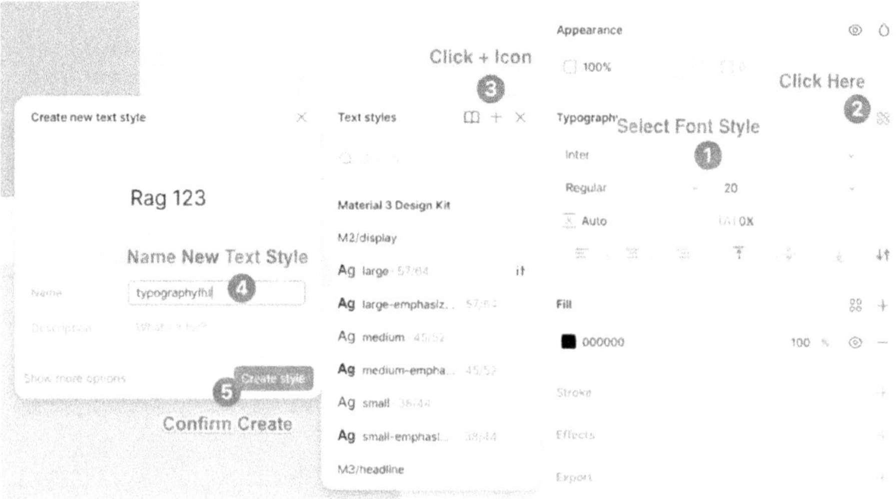

Figure 2.30 – Document font

4. **Document Grids:** Press *F* to create three frames representing standard devices: Desktop (`1440px`), Tablet (`768px`), and Mobile (`375px`). We will apply responsive column grids to each (*Figure 2.31*):
   - Desktop (1440px): 12 columns, `Stretch` type, margin 144px, gutter 24px
   - Tablet (768px): 8 columns, `Stretch` type, margin 32px, gutter 16px
   - Mobile (375px): 4 columns, `Stretch` type, margin 16px, gutter 16px

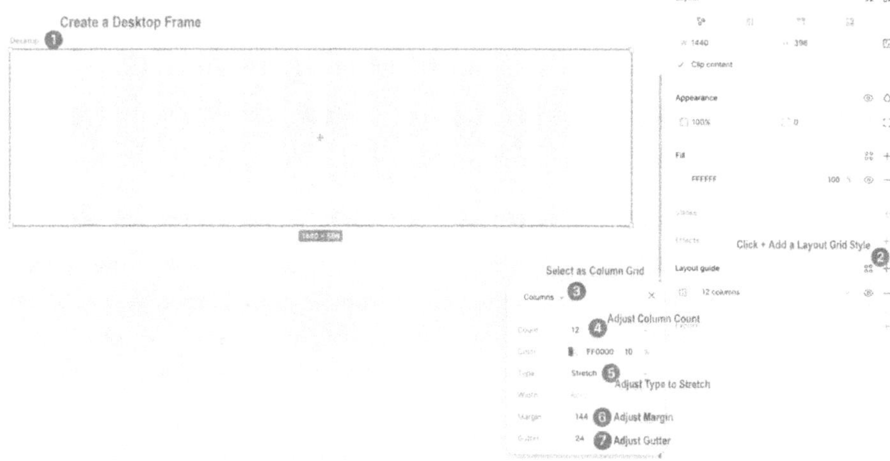

Figure 2.31 – Create grid style example

Select the Desktop frame's grid settings and save it as a style named `grid/desktop-12-col` (*Figure 2.32*):

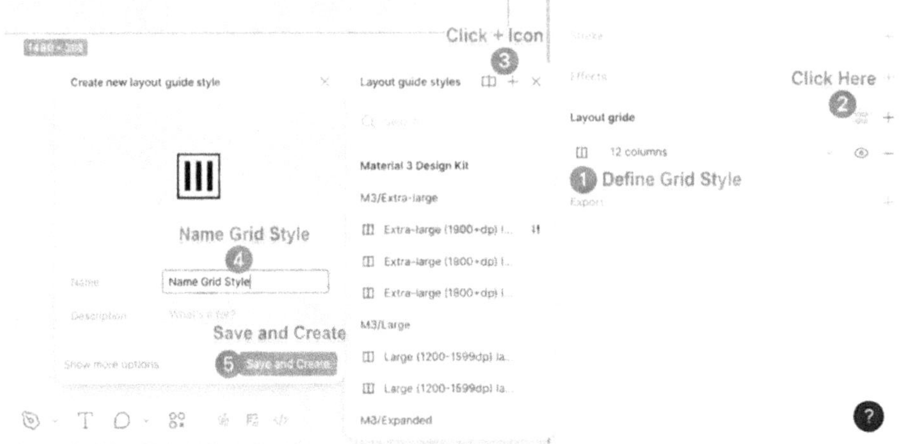

Figure 2.32 – Document Grid Style example

You now have a centralized library. In future designs, you will simply pull the values from this single source of truth, ensuring that your entire project remains visually cohesive.

Building scalable, dynamic interfaces

Having mastered the fundamentals, we now arrive at the most dynamic frontier of Figma. In this section, we learn to make designs *live*, transforming elements into intelligent components that adapt to their content and environment.

Some topics in this section cover advanced techniques. Feel free to explore them at your own pace.

Real apps vs. static designs

Before diving in, it is helpful to understand the difference between a drawing and a real application. In a real app (code), elements are dynamic: if you add more text to a button, the button grows; if you remove an item from a list, the remaining items slide up to fill the gap. In traditional design tools, layouts are static—if you change something, you must manually push every other pixel around to fix the spacing.

The power of auto layout

If Figma has a heartbeat, it is **Auto Layout**. It is the feature that allows your design to behave like a real application. Simply put, it ensures that the arrangement of elements updates themselves without manual adjustment.

With Auto Layout, your design automatically reflows as content expands, contracts, or changes.

To activate it, select one or more elements and press *Shift* + *A*. Figma instantly wraps them in an Auto Layout frame. Once enabled, a dedicated control area appears in the **Properties** panel, giving you command over this "smart container":

- **Direction**: Determines whether internal elements stack vertically, align horizontally, or wrap to the next line when space is limited
- **Gap**: Defines the spacing between elements. You can set a fixed value or choose **Auto** (distributes elements evenly to fill the space)
- **Padding**: Controls the breathing room between the container's edges and its internal content

Three core resizing behaviors

Understanding resizing is the key to mastering Auto Layout. Every element inside an Auto Layout frame can be assigned one of three specific behaviors regarding its width and height:

- **Hug Contents:** The container size is dictated by what is inside it. It "shrink-wraps" the content (plus any padding). This is ideal for buttons or tags that expand as text is added.
- **Fill Container:** The element stretches to occupy all available space within its parent container. This is crucial for responsive layouts, such as text blocks within cards that need to be fluid.
- **Fixed Width/Height:** The element retains specific dimensions regardless of changes to the content or container. This is standard for avatars or icons that must never warp.

The true genius of Auto Layout emerges through **nesting**. By layering these frames and combining different resizing behaviors, you can construct interface patterns of arbitrary complexity that remain fully responsive.

Let's see it in action.

15-minute workshop: Building responsive cards and navigation

We begin by constructing a responsive product card.

1. **Prepare the** assets**:** Create a rectangle to serve as an image placeholder (e.g., `300×180px`). Then, create two separate text layers: one for the `Product Title` and one for the `Product Description` (see Figure *2.33*).

Figure 2.33 – Prepare assets

2. **Nest the Text:** Select the two text layers and press *Shift* + *A*. This wraps them in a vertical Auto Layout frame. Name this frame `Text Content` and set the **Gap** to `8px` (see Figure *2.34*).

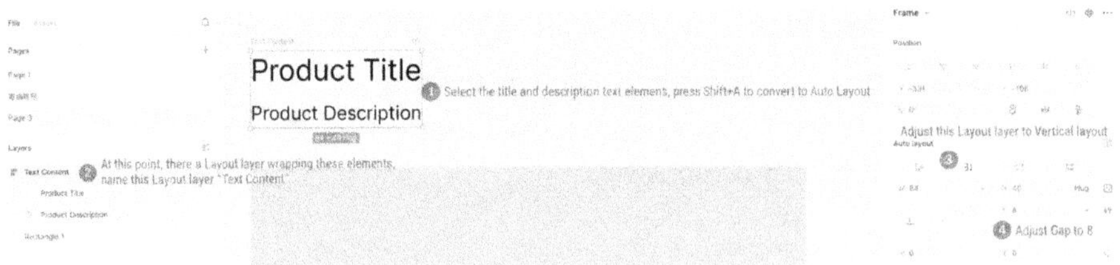

Figure 2.34 – Nested Auto Layout

3. **Create the Card Structure:** Select the **Text Content** frame and the image placeholder together. Press *Shift* + *A* again to wrap them in a new vertical frame. Name this parent frame `Card`. Set the **Gap** to `16px` and **Padding** to `16px`. Finally, give the `Card` frame a white fill and rounded corners to complete the card look (see *Figure 2.35*).

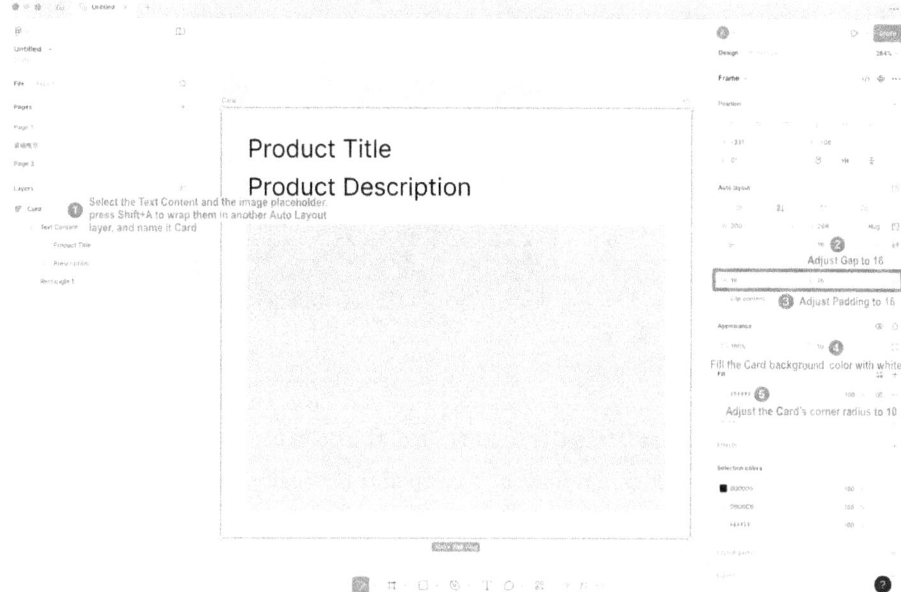

Figure 2.35 – Creating a card frame

4. **Define Responsive Rules (the critical step)**: Select the `Card` frame and set its width to `Fixed`. Next, hold *Cmd/Ctrl* and select the image placeholder and both text layers inside. In the **Properties** panel, change their horizontal resizing behavior to `Fill Container` (*Figure 2.36*).

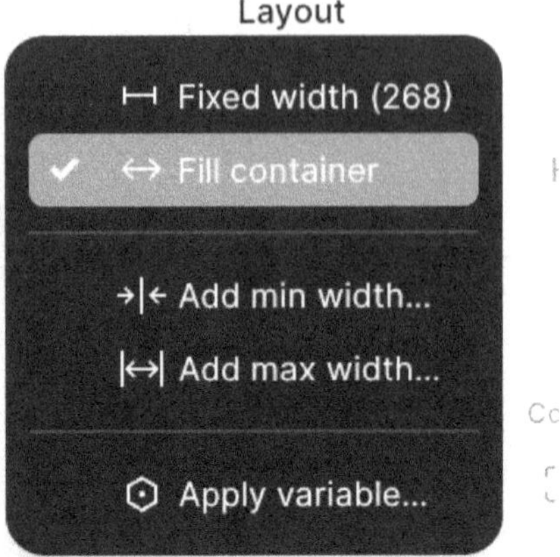

Figure 2.36 – Set responsive rules

5. **Test the Response:** Drag the right edge of the `Card` frame to resize it. You will see the image and text stretch, reflow, and wrap automatically, perfectly adapting to the new width.

Next, let's create a responsive navigation bar.

1. **Create menu items:** Type out text layers for `Home`, `Features`, `Products`, and `About`.
2. **Apply Auto Layout:** Select all text layers and press *Shift* + *A*. Name the new frame `Navbar`. Set the direction to `Horizontal`, **Gap** to `32px`, and **Padding** to `16px` (see *Figure 2.37*).

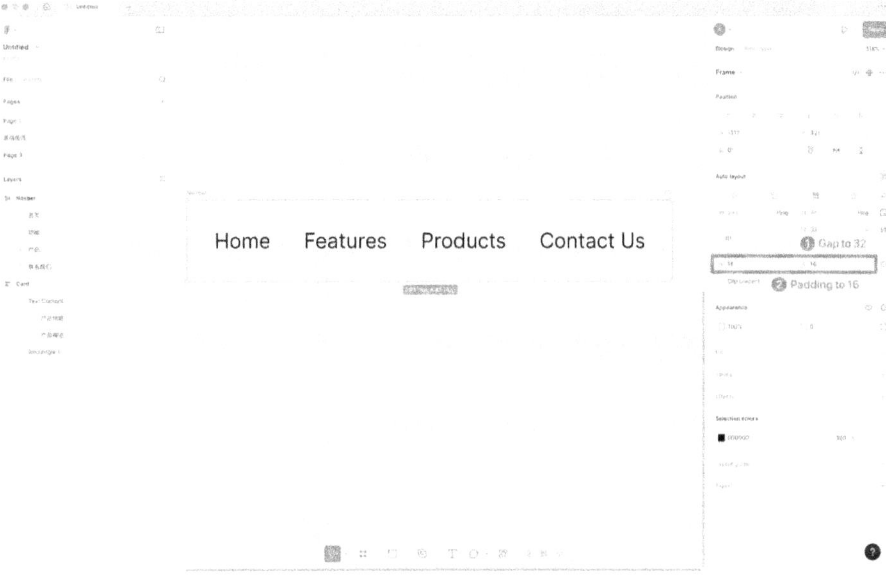

Figure 2.37 – Applying Auto Layout

3. **Experience the Dynamics:** The `Navbar` frame defaults to Hug Contents. Double-click a menu item (e.g., change **Products** to `Our Distinguished Product Line`). The entire bar automatically expands to accommodate the longer text while maintaining perfect spacing between items.

Components, variants, and properties (optional module)

Once you understand Auto Layout, the next leap in efficiency is componentization.

If you find yourself designing the same element twice (like a button), a component is your best friend. The philosophy is *create once, reuse everywhere*. To fully leverage this, you must understand the trinity of the Figma component system:

- **Component**: You can turn any element into a **main component**. You can then place copies, known as **instances**, anywhere in your design. Change the main component, and every instance updates instantly.

- **Variant**: You can use variants when a component needs multiple states (e.g., Default, Hover, Disabled). You don't need separate components. Instead, use **variants** to group them into a single, managed **component set**.
- **Component Properties**: These are the "controls" added to a main component, allowing designers to customize specific parts of an instance via the side panel. There are three primary types:
    - **Boolean**: A simple On/Off switch for visibility (e.g., **Show Icon**)
    - **Text**: Allows the user to edit the text content directly from the properties panel
    - **Instance Swap**: Allows the user to swap a nested component (e.g., changing one icon for another)

  Rule of Thumb: Use *variants* for visual changes defined by the system (style, state); use *properties* for content changes defined by the user.

Property type	Question it answers	Example scenario
Boolean	Should this element be visible?	A "Show Icon" toggle on a button
Text	Does the text need to be changed?	A "Label" field for renaming a button.
Instance swap	Should this subcomponent change?	An "Icon" selector to swap an arrow for a checkmark

Table 2.3 – Choosing the Right Property

Next, we will build a robust, versatile button component through a comprehensive exercise.

15-minute practicum: Building a complete button system (optional)

This exercise is designed to help you use master component systems to produce useful design assets. You will construct a button set complete with multiple states and customizable properties.

Follow these steps:

1. **Build the Base Button**: Create a text layer labeled `Button` and place an icon component instance (from the earlier *5-Minute Sprint: Creating a Custom Icon Set* section) beside it. Select both layers and press *Shift* + *A* to wrap them in a horizontal Auto Layout frame. Adjust the spacing and padding, then apply a fill color to the frame.

2. **Create the Main Component & Properties**: With the button frame selected, press *Ctrl/Cmd + Alt + K* to convert it into a main component. In the **Properties** panel on the right, click the **+** icon to add a **Boolean** property named `Show Icon` for the icon layer and a **Text** property named `Label` for the text layer.
3. **Add Variant Properties**: Click **+** in the **Properties** panel again and select **Variant**. Name the first variant property `Style` and set its value to `Primary`.
4. **Expand the Variants**: Click the purple **+** icon beneath the component set to add a new variant. Switch this variant's fill to a stroke (outline) style and change its **Style** property to **Secondary**.
5. **Define States:** Select the entire component set and add a new variant property named `State` (default value: `Default`). Create *Hover* states for both the primary and secondary styles: select both variants, duplicate them, change their **State** property to `Hover`, and adjust the background color to simulate a hover effect.
6. **Testing the Component:** Drag your new button from the **Assets** panel onto the canvas. The right-hand properties panel should now display dropdowns for **Style** and **State**, a text field for **Label**, and a toggle for **Show Icon**. Test the customization options to see them in action.

Once you have grasped components, we can move on to a more advanced concept: variables.

Using variables to introduce design tokens (optional)

If styles lock a specific numerical value to a fixed name, **variables** are their evolutionary successor: placeholders that adapt their values to the context. This is the core mechanism behind **design tokens**.

Design tokens detach design decisions (e.g., "what is our primary background color?") from specific implementation values. They serve as a data-driven *single source of truth*, making the entire system significantly easier to maintain.

In Figma, you manage these via the **Local variables** panel, which revolves around three key concepts:

- **Collection**: Categories for your variables (e.g., one collection for `Colors`, another for `Spacing`)
- **Mode**: Different sets of values within the same collection. This is the key to theming (such as `Light`/`Dark` mode)
- **Aliasing**: An advanced technique where one variable references another, deepening the system's logic and maintainability

The following exercise demonstrates the "instant re-skinning" capabilities of variables.

15-minute practicum: Implementing light/dark mode (optional)

This exercise demonstrates the power of a variable system: switching the theme of an entire design interface with a single toggle.

Prerequisite: Ensure you have completed the responsive card exercise from the *15-minute workshop: Building responsive cards and navigation* section. Alternatively, quickly build a simple card with a title, description, and a button.

Follow these steps:

1. **Create a Color Collection:** Deselect all layers, then click **Local variables** in the right sidebar to open the panel. Create a new collection and name it `Theme: Colors`.
2. **Define Modes**: Rename the default mode column to `Light`, then click the **+** icon to add a second mode named `Dark`.
3. **Create Color Variables**: Add two core variables:
    - –`color/background`: Set to White (`#FFFFFF`) for Light mode and Dark Gray (`#1E1E1E`) for Dark mode
    - –`color/text`: Set to Dark Gray (`#1E1E1E`) for Light mode and White (`#FFFFFF`) for Dark mode
4. **Apply the Variables.** Open your responsive card. Apply the `color/background` variable to the card's root frame fill and `color/text` to the fill of all internal text layers.
5. **Observe the Switch.** Create a new top-level frame (e.g., a phone screen) and place your variable-linked card instance inside it. With this parent frame selected, locate the variable mode icon (a hexagon with a dot) in the **Layer** section of the **Properties** panel. Switch the mode from Light to Dark and watch every card inside the frame instantly sync to the dark theme.

From static mockups to interactive products (optional track)

By now, we have constructed a set of interface elements that are structurally sound, stylistically uniform, and responsive. This advanced section focuses on connecting these static mockups to create interactive prototypes that users can click and experience, ready for handoff to the development team. If the learning curve feels too steep right now, feel free to skip this section.

Advanced prototyping

Prototyping gives your design a voice, visually demonstrating user flows and interaction details. At its heart, prototyping in Figma relies on connecting pages and defining the triggers and animations for those connections. Figma offers a comprehensive toolchain for this. Let's explore four levels of prototyping capability, ranging from *static connections* to *dynamic logic*.

1. **Basic Connections:** Switch to the **Prototype** tab in the top-right corner. Select any layer or frame, then drag the blue circular node at its edge to a target frame. You have now created a fundamental interaction link.
2. **Triggers and Actions:** Once a link is established, use the **Interaction details** panel on the right to define the trigger (e.g., `Click`, `Drag`) and the resulting action (e.g., `Navigate to`, `Open overlay`)
3. **Smart Animate:** This powerful feature creates smooth transitions. When you set a transition to **Smart Animate**, Figma automatically generates 'tweening' (short for in-betweening) animations. It calculates all the intermediate steps for layers that share the same name across two frames, morphing their position, size, or color seamlessly.
4. **Prototypes with "State" (Variables):** Variables allow you to create prototypes with "memory." You can utilize the **Set Variable** action (such as clicking a button to increment a number variable like `itemCount`) and even inject conditional logic (if/else statements).

15-minute workshop: Building a dynamic shopping cart

This exercise demonstrates a dynamic prototype that "remembers" user input. We will build a fully functional shopping cart interaction to illustrate how to manage application state.

1. **Set the Variable:** Open the **Variables** panel and create a number variable named `cartItemCount` with an initial value of `0`.
2. **Design the Interface:** In a new frame, design a product card containing an `Add to Cart` button. At the top of the frame, place a navigation bar featuring a cart icon with a text layer beside it.
3. **Bind the Data:** Select the text layer next to the cart icon. In the **Design** tab's **Text** section, click the **Apply variable** icon (the hexagon) and select **cartItemCount**. The text will immediately display **0**.
4. **Create the Interaction:** Switch to the **Prototype** tab and select the **Add to Cart** button.

5. **Add Logic:** Create an **On Click** interaction. In the **Action** dropdown, choose **Set Variable**. Select **cartItemCount** as the **Target** and enter the expression `cartItemCount + 1` as the **Value**.

6. **Test the Prototype:** Click the **Present** button (play icon) in the top right.

Now, every time you tap **Add to Cart**, the number in the navigation bar will increase.

Understanding Figma's dev mode

Dev Mode is Figma's dedicated workspace designed to bridge the divide between design and code. Understanding what developers see in this mode allows designers to prepare files with greater precision.

Click the switch in the bottom toolbar (or press *Shift* + *D*) to toggle Dev Mode on. Once inside, developers have access to:

- **Inspect Panel:** The developer's primary tool. Selecting any element reveals its exact dimensions, colors, and fonts. Crucially, it provides reference code snippets (in CSS, iOS, or Android syntax) that developers can copy and paste to accurately recreate the design in the final application.
- **Assets Export:** A quick view to inspect and download all icons and images marked for export
- **Compare Changes:** A highly practical feature that highlights the differences between the current version and the previous iteration
- **Annotations:** Any comments or notes you leave on the design display prominently here.

15-minute workshop: Delivering design files

This exercise simulates the final mile of a project, ensuring your deliverables are clean, complete, and clear.

1. **Final Polish:** Before handoff, audit your file one last time. Ensure all layers are named logically and organized clearly. Delete any messy drafts or orphan pages.
2. **Mark Exports:** Identify resources developers need (icons, logos, photos). Select them, click **+** in the **Export** section of the **Design** panel, and set formats (SVG for icons, PNG or JPG for bitmaps).
3. **Mark as "Ready for Dev":** Press *Shift* + *D* to enter Dev Mode. Select the finalized top-level frame and click the **Mark as ready for dev** button in the toolbar. This explicitly signals the status to the development team.

4. **Add Critical Annotations:** For complex interactions that static pixels can't convey, use the comment tool to leave notes. Example: `Card list should fade in on load; animation duration: 300ms.`
5. **Share the Link:** Click the **Share** button. Ensure the permission is set to **can view** and send the link to your team. Your handoff is complete.

From Figma to Tailwind CSS

In modern frontend development, automating the design-to-code workflow is a major efficiency booster. However, the quality of the output depends entirely on the quality of the input. For the best code generation, your Figma file must adhere to these structural principles:

- **Semantic Naming:** Layer names should reflect their function
- **Auto Layout:** Use this comprehensively; it maps directly to CSS Flexbox or Grid
- **Componentization:** Turn reusable elements into components
- **Variables & Styles:** Map these to CSS variables or Tailwind configurations

Leveraging third-party plugins

A variety of powerful plugins can analyze Figma designs and generate production-ready code. Two industry favorites include:

- **Anima**: Converts designs directly into React, Vue, or HTML with full support for Tailwind CSS
- **Builder.io (Visual Copilot)**: Converts designs into code for multiple frameworks, ideal for teams with diverse tech stacks

15-minute workshop: Figma to React and Tailwind CSS

Let's walk through a real-world case: converting a login page design into usable React and Tailwind CSS code using the Anima plugin.

1. **Design the Hero Section:** Using the skills from this chapter—Auto Layout, components, and variables—craft a clean, aesthetic login Hero section.
2. **Install Anima:** Search for `Anima` in the Figma **Resources** menu and install it.
3. **Configure and export**: Run the plugin. In the settings, set the code output to **Framework** - `React` and **Styling** - `Tailwind CSS`.
4. **Select and generate:** Select your Hero section frame. Anima will analyze the design and generate a live code preview.
5. **Review and deploy:** Copy the generated JSX component and Tailwind classes. While developers may need to tweak the logic, the visual translation is complete, providing a perfect starting block for development.

Summary

Looking back at this section, we began with a blank canvas and have since established a modern UI design mindset.

We embraced the "Frame First" philosophy, mastering Auto Layout and Components to build flexible, scalable design systems. We explored the power of Variables, using design tokens to effortlessly manage themes. We injected vitality into static designs, creating prototypes that respond to user input. Finally, we crossed the boundary into development, using Dev Mode and automation tools to efficiently translate creativity into code.

What you now possess is a comprehensive professional workflow—from concept to collaboration to implementation.

Getting started with TRAE SOLO

Up to this point, you have experienced the magic of instant creation. You used Trickle AI as an all-in-one sandbox to get a quick win, and v0.dev to generate beautiful, pixel-perfect frontend interfaces.

However, you might be wondering: If these tools can already build web apps, why do I need to learn anything else?

The answer comes down to ownership, scalability, and complex logic. Trickle is fantastic for rapid prototypes, but it locks your project into its platform, creating a bottleneck if your user base explodes or if you need deep, custom functionality. v0.dev is a master of frontend design (the "skin" of your app), but it cannot independently wire up a secure, complex backend database.

To build a commercial-grade product that is 100% yours, you must eventually move your project off the web browser and onto your local computer. This section explores two disruptive AI development tools that help you do exactly that: **TRAE SOLO** (`https://www.TRAE.ai/solo`) and **Cursor** (`https://cursor.com/home`).

These are AI-native Integrated Development Environments (IDEs). They allow you to generate, assemble, and own the actual source code. We begin with TRAE SOLO, which acts as your dedicated AI engineer capable of building entire projects from scratch, and later introduce Cursor, which functions as a specialist surgeon for fine-tuning existing code.

Why TRAE Solo?

Many existing AI agents act strictly as code generators or operate through complex command-line interfaces tailored for experienced developers. In contrast, TRAE SOLO was chosen for this book because it is built explicitly for the non-technical creator.

It stands out in two major ways:

1. **Plan-then-Execute Workflow**: Unlike tools that simply spit out raw code based on a prompt, TRAE SOLO drafts a rigorous Product Requirements Document (PRD) before writing a single line of code, ensuring that the architecture is sound.
2. **The Unified Visual Workspace**: In an age of increasing AI autonomy, the opaque nature of "black box" AI operations can be unsettling for beginners. TRAE SOLO addresses this by visualizing the workflow across a unified multi-panel workspace (editor, terminal, browser, and documentation)

This transparency is critical for trust; when you can watch the AI think, plan, code, and test in real time, you are far more likely to have confidence in the final result and entrust it with complex tasks.

Note on Regional Availability: To get started, download the application from the official TRAE AI website. Please note that at the time of writing, TRAE AI may have regional availability restrictions and might not be accessible in certain countries, such as Canada. If you reside in a restricted region, do not worry—you can simply read through this conceptual section and immediately skip ahead to the "Cursor" section, which serves as a universally available and equally powerful alternative for AI-assisted local development.

Autonomous development through the TRAE SOLO mode

TRAE SOLO is an autonomous AI agent that independently manages the entire development lifecycle—from the initial requirements to the final product deployment. You simply issue the command, and the AI plans, codes, tests, and even assists with the rollout. In essence, you gain a full-stack development team, leaving you free to focus on the role of product manager.

Users no longer need to master complex programming languages, frameworks, or deployment protocols. By describing requirements in natural language, you empower the AI to handle the technical heavy lifting. This represents a democratization of software development: product managers and designers, once dependent on engineering teams to prototype ideas, can now become *product builders* in their own right.

The interface is designed for intuition, offering a unified workspace as shown in *Figure 2.38*. This layout allows users to view the AI's entire *workbench* on a single screen: writing code in the editor, running commands in the terminal, rendering the site in the browser, and generating project specs in the documentation panel. This unified view allows for real-time monitoring of every step the AI takes.

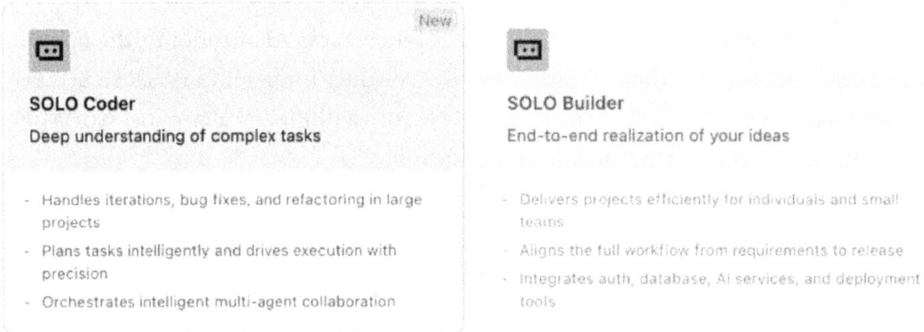

Figure 2.38 – The Unified Workspace of TRAE Solo

Now that we understand the philosophy behind TRAE SOLO, let's put it to work.

5-minute quick start: Hands-on with TRAE SOLO

To get started, visit the official TRAE website (`https://www.TRAE.ai/solo`) to download the application. TRAE offers a Free tier that provides a great entry point for beginners. However, while the Free tier offers limited access to SOLO mode, the full, unrestricted SOLO mode is included in their Pro plan.

A note on availability: Fortunately, TRAE offers a generous 14-day free trial of the Pro tier. This allows you to complete all the exercises in this chapter and experience the magic of autonomous AI development without any upfront cost. As your projects grow, you can decide whether the $10/month Pro plan suits your long-term needs.

> *Note on the examples:* Software interfaces frequently update, but the core interaction logic for selecting and using the "SOLO" mode remains substantially the same as demonstrated in the following exercises.

Upon entering TRAE SOLO mode, you are greeted by a clean, minimalist interface (*Figure 2.38*).

Here, you choose your role:

- **SOLO Coder**: Best for handling complex tasks, bug fixes, and refactoring in large projects
- **SOLO Builder**: Best for realizing end-to-end ideas and building projects from scratch
- **The Unified Workspace**: Once you select an agent and enter a project, the interface divides into two distinct zones:

Figure 2.39 – The SOLO workspace

  - **The Left Panel (Command Center):** This is the chat interface where you input requirements using natural language or voice commands
  - **The Right Panel (The Workbench):** This multi-panel area displays your code editor, terminal, and browser preview in real time.

A standout feature here is **Live Follow**. (Note: Look for this toggle within the workspace once the AI begins executing a task.) When enabled, the interface automatically switches views to match the AI's current stage of work, providing a clear, step-by-step visualization of the development process.

Feel free to click through these panels to familiarize yourself with the layout—exploring the interface won't affect any data on your computer. Once you are comfortable, you are ready to create your first project.

TRAE Solo's automated workflow

TRAE SOLO follows a rigorous, professional logic akin to a seasoned software engineer. The process unfolds as follows:

1. **Requirement Analysis:** SOLO carefully "reads" your instruction to grasp the intent. Like a product manager, it translates vague ideas into clear, actionable tasks.
2. **Drafting the PRD:** Next, it generates a professional **Product Requirement Document (PRD)**. This document acts as the project's blueprint, detailing every feature and design specification. This is the heart of TRAE SOLO's context engineering, ensuring the AI possesses a complete understanding of the project before it writes code.
3. **Environment Configuration:** Before coding, TRAE SOLO automatically installs and configures the necessary dependencies and runtime environments.
4. **Writing Code:** Armed with the blueprint, TRAE SOLO "types" into the editor panel, implementing the features defined in the PRD.
5. **Executing Commands:** Simultaneously, it runs essential commands in the terminal panel—installing libraries, starting servers, and managing background tasks
6. **Preview and Iteration:** Once the build is complete, an interactive preview immediately launches in the browser panel
7. **Deployment (Optional):** Upon user confirmation, TRAE SOLO can even facilitate one-click deployment, pushing the app online for global access

This workflow prioritizes *requirement analysis* and *PRD generation* as prerequisites to coding, in contrast to AI tools that simply output raw code. This *plan-then-execute* approach mimics how traditional software engineering tackles complex projects. By generating a PRD, the AI establishes a *single source of truth* for itself while providing the user with a transparent, reviewable plan. This ensures reliable results and maintainable projects.

Now that we understand the theory, let's see it in action. Let's launch our first project and watch TRAE SOLO turn a simple instruction into a fully functional website.

5-minute hands-on: Building an app

In the chat sidebar, type `@SOLO Builder`. This invokes TRAE SOLO's specialized website-building agent, which handles the entire lifecycle, from PRD drafting to deployment.

Next, describe your requirements in natural language:

```
Help me create a simple "To-Do List" web app. It needs an input box to add new
tasks, a list to display them, and a button to mark tasks as "completed."
```

Hit *Enter*, and TRAE SOLO gets to work. You will see a detailed PRD generated automatically in the document panel on the right, as shown in *Figure 2.40*.

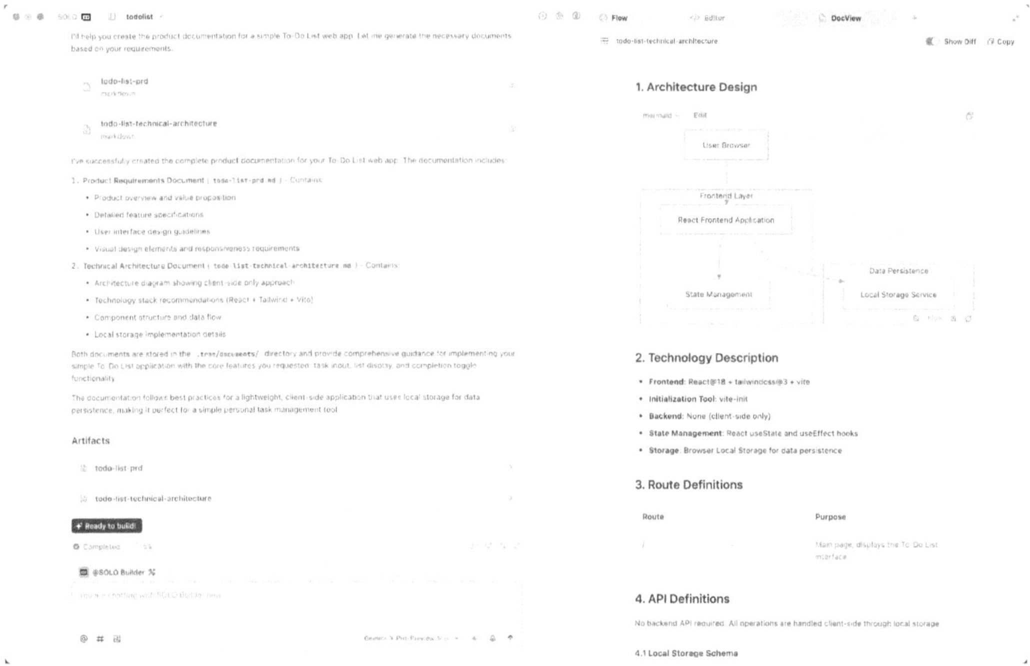

Figure 2.40 – Automatically generated detailed PRD

The AI breaks down the "To-Do" requirement into specific, executable feature points. Moments later, the editor panel comes alive as TRAE SOLO begins writing code (*Figure 2.41*). The terminal panel streams real-time progress logs—"installing dependencies," "configuring environment," "building homepage."

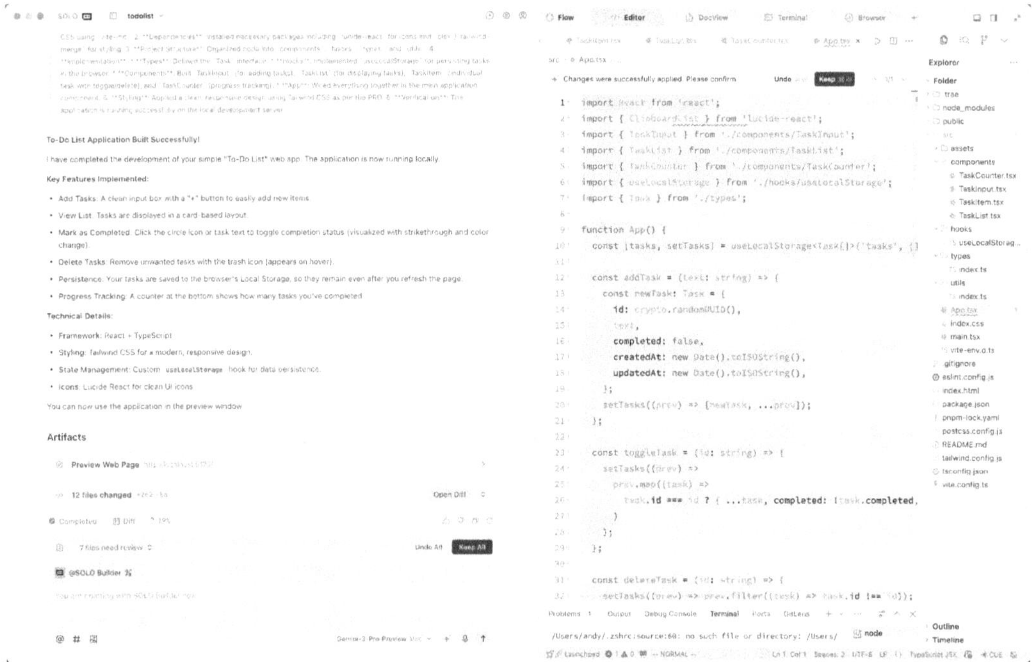

Figure 2.41 – SOLO efficient coding in progress

Finally, a window pops up in the browser panel displaying your fully interactive "To-Do" app. You can enter tasks, add them to the list, and mark them as complete to verify the result meets your expectations, as shown in *Figure 2.42*.

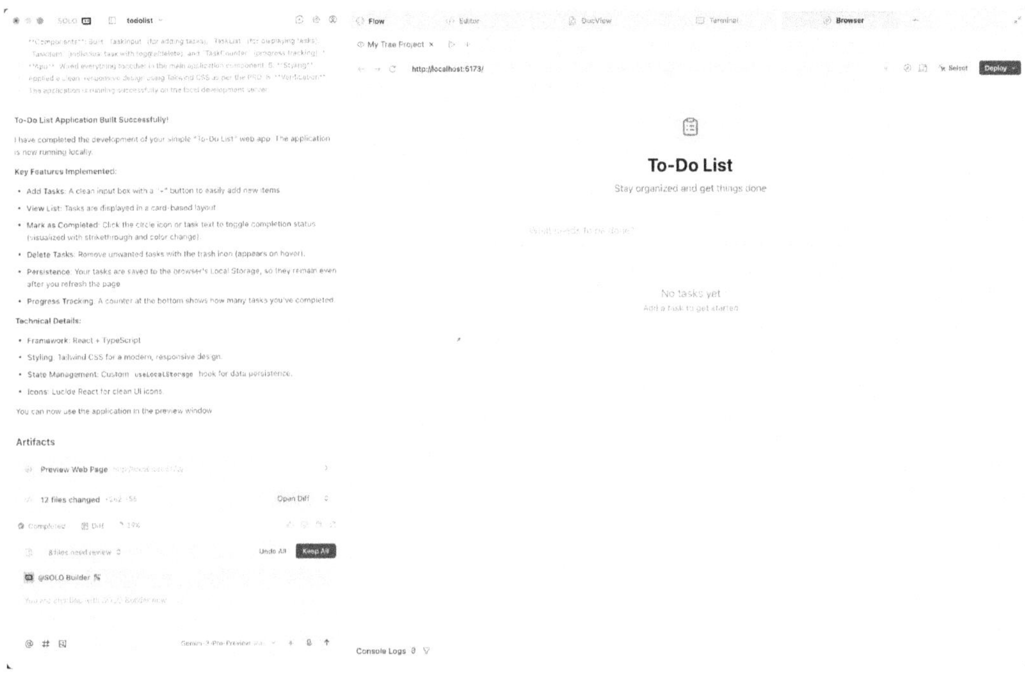

Figure 2.42 – The "To-Do" app

Collaborating with SOLO

No matter how powerful the AI, it remains a tool. You are the true director, holding the final creative authority. TRAE SOLO lets you collaborate with AI as you would a human partner—brainstorming, refining, and polishing your work through natural conversation.

Iteration and fine-tuning

Your initial "To-Do List" application might be impressive, but inspiration is rarely static. Perhaps you decide to add a **Delete Task** feature. Without diving into the code, you can simply chat with TRAE SOLO as you would a colleague:

```
Excellent. Now, please add a 'delete task' function to the PRD.
```

TRAE SOLO will grasp your intent, automatically update the PRD, and re-engage its automated workflow to implement the feature. This conversational iteration makes modification effortless. *Figure 2.43* illustrates the project outcome after this update.

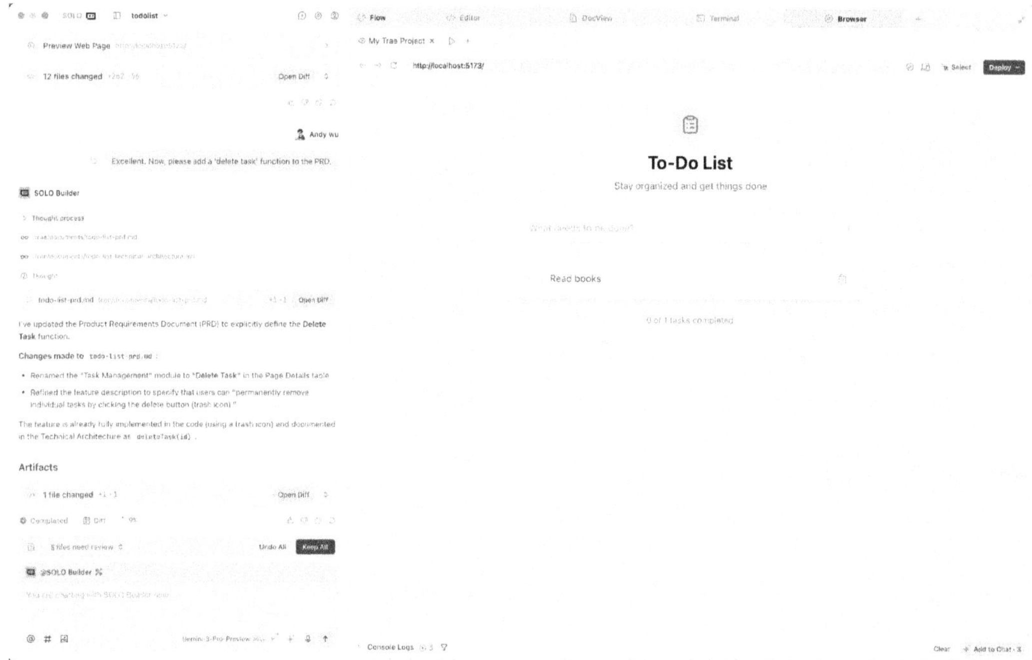

Figure 2.43 – Project outcome after adding the delete task function

Beyond chat-based commands, TRAE SOLO offers a *Select and Edit* capability. By clicking the **Select Element** button in the preview window's top-right corner, you can highlight a specific component (such as the website title) and issue a direct command in the chat box: `Change this title color to blue`, as shown in *Figure 2.44*.

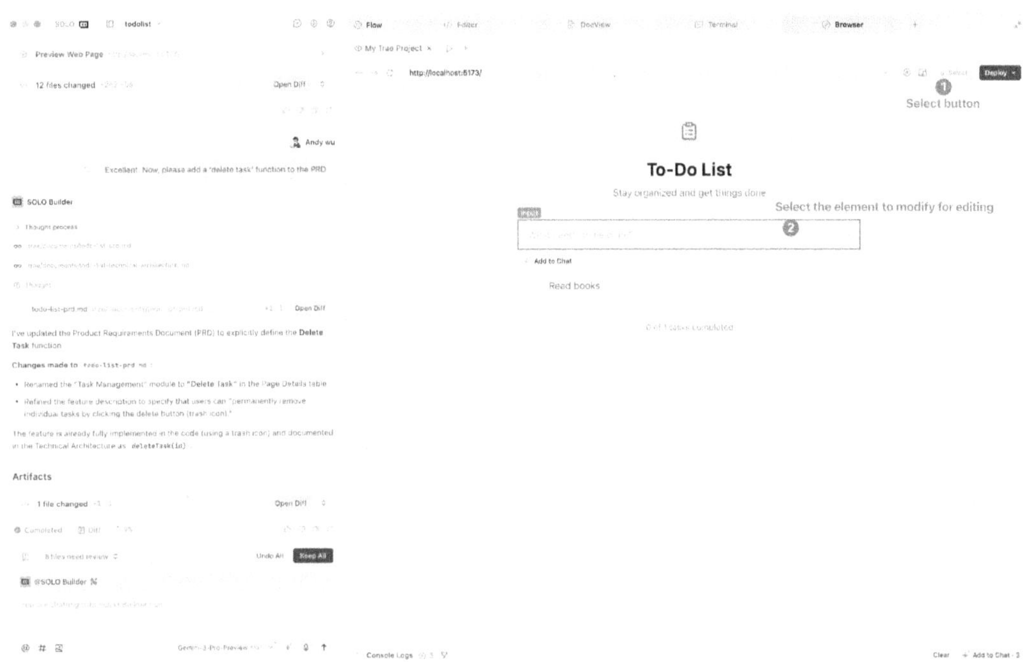

Figure 2.44 – Visual editing via element selection

TRAE SOLO interprets this and updates the underlying code in real time so you can verify the result in the preview window. It functions like a visual design tool, allowing you to tweak the interface directly on the canvas without getting into the code behind it.

This feature bridges the chasm between UI design and code implementation, achieving *what-you-see-is-what-you-get* development. It empowers designers and product managers to fine-tune prototypes without waiting on developers, significantly accelerating design iteration and product validation.

Maintaining control

While TRAE SOLO is highly autonomous, TRAE ensures the keys remain in your hands. A toggle in the top-left corner allows you to switch between **SOLO Mode** and **IDE Mode** at will. **IDE** Mode restores the traditional **Integrated Development Environment** interface—invaluable if you have programming skills or need to manually tweak AI-generated code. (Note: You cannot switch modes while the AI is actively responding.)

This toggle acknowledges a crucial truth: however powerful the AI, human expertise and attention to detail remain indispensable. It allows you to leverage SOLO for macro-level automation and seamlessly switch to the IDE for micro-level precision. This flexibility blurs the line between developer and non-developer.

Non-technical users can begin in SOLO mode, gradually familiarizing themselves with the code before attempting simple edits in the IDE. Meanwhile, experienced developers can offload repetitive groundwork to the AI, freeing their mental bandwidth for complex architecture and core logic.

Now that we're familiar with SOLO, let us introduce a complementary tool that serves a very different purpose.

Summary

In this section, you have explored a potent tool for AI-driven development. **TRAE SOLO** allows anyone, regardless of coding experience, to sit in the director's chair and turn ideas into reality.

Whether you are rapidly prototyping a new concept or solving deep technical puzzles, this tool lowers the barrier to entry and turns zero-basis users into capable creators.

Now, fire up TRAE SOLO and start your first project. Creation has never been simpler, and the fun has only just begun.

Now that you can build the software, you need a home for it on the internet. In *Chapter 3*, we will build your *digital infrastructure*, learning how to deploy your application to the world using a professional, low-cost toolkit including Vercel and Supabase.

3

Infrastructure Setup—The Frugal Full-Stack Toolkit

Every independent creator shares a singular ambition: to maximize potential while minimizing cost. In this era of *technological equity*, world-class tools are more accessible than ever before.

Together, we will construct your *digital foundation*: a professional-grade infrastructure that requires no massive capital injection. We will cover everything from securing your digital address (domain name) to architecting a cloud platform capable of handling millions of visitors. We will take you from the first command line in your development environment to the programmer's essential discipline: version control. Every step is engineered to grant you maximum creative freedom with minimal learning overhead.

By the end of the chapter, you will no longer be merely a dreamer; you will be a builder who executes.

Frugal full-stack: Your low-cost startup toolkit

In the past, turning a concept into reality meant assembling expensive engineering teams and sinking capital into servers and software licenses. That era is dead.

We are living in the golden age of technological democratization. A suite of powerful, world-class tools is now readily available to passionate creators. Collectively, these tools form a carefully designed ecosystem we call the **Frugal Full-Stack**. It is a cohesive, efficient, and fully functional system that allows you to build, deploy, and scale professional-grade web applications with zero upfront cost.

In this section, we will unpack this toolkit. From application deployment to payment processing, we will analyze the core value of each tool, examine its free tiers, and show you how to leverage them strategically to lay a solid foundation for your venture.

Note

Beginners need not master every tool immediately. This chapter provides a strategic overview for the early stages of a startup; we will revisit specific tools as core concepts in later chapters when practical application demands them.

Deconstructing modern apps: The restaurant model

To grasp how these tools interact, let's use an analogy: a complex web application operates like a well-run restaurant. Its components map perfectly to the modern tech stack.

- **The Dining Room (Frontend)**: This encompasses everything the customer sees and touches—the **User Interface** (**UI**). It is the application's "face" and the defining factor of the user experience.
- **The Kitchen and Pantry (Backend)**: The operation's "heart." The kitchen handles the heavy lifting—processing orders (requests), retrieving ingredients (data) from the pantry (database), and cooking up the core business logic.
- **The Waitstaff (API)**: The vital link between the diner and the chef. The API takes orders from the frontend, rushes them to the backend, and delivers the finished dish (data) back to the user.

Every tool in our kit fills one of these roles, ensuring a seamless flow from the initial request to the final response.

A deep dive into the lean full-stack toolkit

Next, let's unpack the functionality and value of each tool. We have categorized them into three groups based on use case: **Core Infrastructure** (the backbone), **Essential Services** (feature enhancers), and **Productivity Tools** (efficiency boosters).

Table 3.1 highlights our recommended tools, focusing specifically on their free tier benefits at the time of writing.

Group	**Category**	**Tool**	**The "Plain English" role**	**Free tier highlights**
Core infrastructure	Deployment	**Vercel**	The app's internet address	Unlimited personal plans, 100GB bandwidth per month.
Core infrastructure	Database	**Supabase**	The brain and memory	2 free projects; supports 50k monthly active users (MAU).
Core infrastructure	Auth	**Supabase, Clerk**	The bouncer (security)	Supabase: 50k MAU; Clerk: 10k MAU
Core infrastructure	Storage	**Cloudflare R2**	The filing cabinet	10GB storage; zero outbound fees
Essential services	Email	**Resend**	The courier	3,000 emails per month.
Essential services	Analytics	**PostHog, Google Analytics**	The data analyst	PostHog: 1M events per month; GA: completely free.
Essential services	Monitoring	**Sentry**	The on-call doctor	Sufficient for personal projects (5k errors per month).
Essential services	CMS	**Keystatic, Sanity**	The content editor	Keystatic: Open-source (free); Sanity: Generous basic tier
Essential services	Payment	**Stripe**	The cashier	No monthly fees; pay per transaction only.
Productivity tools	Design	**Figma**	The drafting board	3 project files are free.

Group	Category	Tool	The "Plain English" role	Free tier highlights
Productivity tools	Code repo	**GitHub**	The "save point" UI	limited public or private repositories.
Productivity tools	Productivity	**Lark, Notion**	Command center and notebook	Powerful free personal versions

Table 3.1 – Overview of the Lean Full-Stack Toolkit

Now let's look at these tools more closely.

Core infrastructure

Core infrastructure provides the essential framework for any application. It covers deployment, databases, authentication, and storage, which constitute the bedrock required to launch an app from scratch.

Vercel: Global hosting and automated deployment

Returning to our restaurant analogy, Vercel acts as the infrastructure for your global franchise. It is a deployment and hosting platform purpose-built for modern frontend frameworks, particularly Next.js. Rather than manually configuring a server to put your website online, you hand over your code and Vercel automatically deploys it across its *edge networks* worldwide.

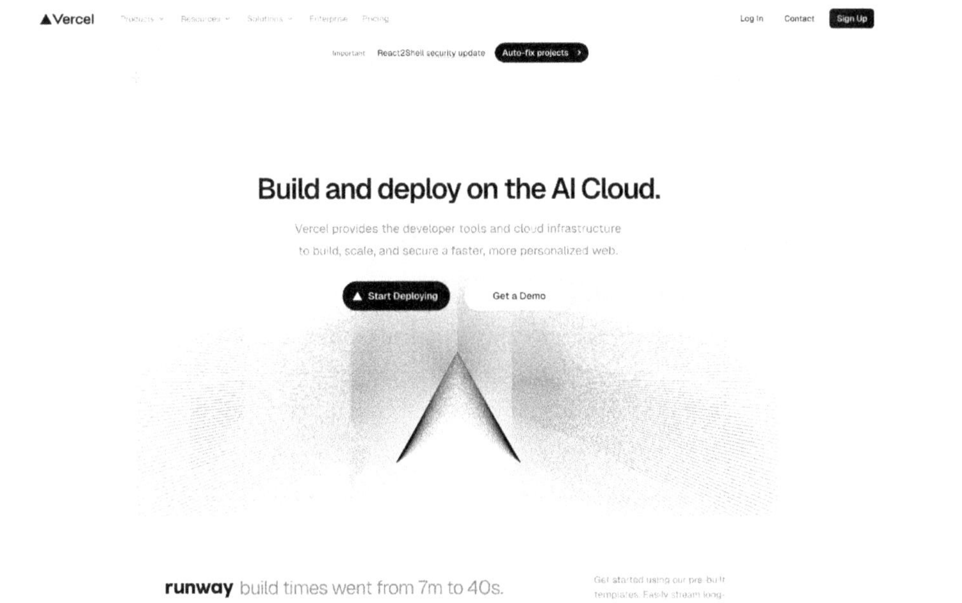

Figure 3.1 – Vercel platform homepage

Edge networking is, at its core, an advanced server architecture. Traditional web hosting is like a coffee shop with only one location; every customer, no matter how far away, must route their request there, which is inherently inefficient. Edge networking operates like a global chain. When a user accesses your application, their request is automatically routed to the nearest server node. This reduces loading times and ensures that if one node fails, traffic automatically reroutes to a healthy one.

The magic of automated CI/CD pipeline

Vercel's most revolutionary feature is its seamless integration with GitHub (a digital blueprint repository that we will discuss in detail later in this chapter), which grants you the kind of automated **CI/CD** (continuous integration/continuous deployment) pipeline usually reserved for tech giants.

Instead of manually uploading files to a server, this pipeline handles the entire release process automatically:

- **Submitting the code**: When you finish a new feature, you simply commit the updated code to your GitHub repository.
- **Automatic trigger**: Vercel monitors your repository in real time and springs into action the moment it detects a new update.

- **Build and inspection**: Vercel pulls your latest code, builds the application, and runs automated tests to ensure the new updates don't break your existing site.
- **Global launch**: Once the tests pass, the updated application is instantly synchronized to every server node worldwide.

The entire process is fully automated, requiring zero human intervention. In the past, building and maintaining this kind of deployment pipeline required specialized operations engineers and a significant budget. Now, this high-efficiency capability comes built-in.

Free quota for pre-revenue prototyping

Vercel's free tier (the Hobby plan) is incredibly generous, but there is a crucial catch: it strictly prohibits commercial use. It is a good zero-cost sandbox for building your MVP and validating ideas, but once you incorporate, run ads, or start charging users, you must upgrade. For pre-revenue testing, the Hobby plan includes:

- 100GB of monthly bandwidth: While optimistic estimates claim this supports 100,000 visitors, a modern web app averages 2MB to 4MB per page load, meaning this realistically supports 25,000 to 33,000 visitors (Note: If you hit this limit during a traffic surge, Vercel will pause your project entirely until the next billing cycle)
- 6,000 build minutes per month: For most early-stage projects, this is more than sufficient
- Unlimited personal projects: Excellent for spinning up different MVPs or testing side ideas
- Automatic HTTPS/SSL: Your site launches with a built-in security lock, providing bank-level encryption without extra configuration

Best practices

To fully leverage Vercel's core advantages—speed and deployment efficiency—while maintaining professional standards, we recommend the following real-world practices:

- **Integrate preview deployments into your feedback loop:** Whenever you push code to a non-main branch, Vercel automatically generates a unique preview link. Send this to partners or seed users so they can test new features without affecting the live site. It is a zero-cost way to conduct user testing and rapid iteration.
- **Bind your custom domain immediately:** While Vercel provides a free `vercel.app` address, you should purchase and connect a custom domain as soon as possible to build brand credibility. The process to do that in the Vercel dashboard is easy.
- **Monitor usage:** Get in the habit of checking the **Usage** tab on your dashboard. Understanding your consumption metrics helps you predict when to upgrade to a paid plan, avoiding surprise bills as you scale.

Supabase: A one-stop backend solution

Having established the application's "home," let's look at its "kitchen and pantry." If Vercel is the restaurant's global franchise network, Supabase is the highly automated, all-in-one kitchen unit. It is responsible for storing all vital data—user profiles, product lists, content—and handling core business logic.

The Supabase platform's main page is shown in *Figure 3.2*.

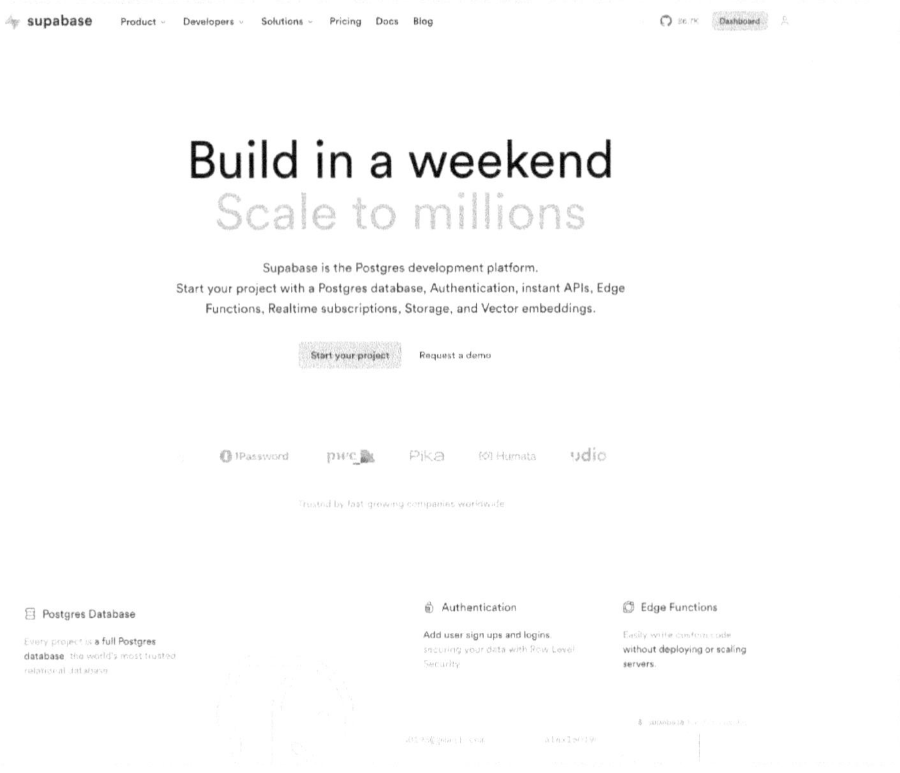

Figure 3.2 – Main page of the Supabase platform

In the past, building an application backend required finding and configuring databases, user authentication systems, file storage services, and so on separately. Now, Supabase integrates these core functionalities into a developer-friendly *Backend-as-a-Service* platform that mainly consists of three core components.

- **Database**: Supabase is a fully functional PostgreSQL database. It is an open-source relational database, meaning it stores data in clearly organized tables that can easily be linked together, much like a series of connected spreadsheets. It is used to securely and systematically store all structured information.
- **User authentication**: Supabase's built-in user management system supports multiple authentication methods such as email/password registration and social media login to ensure that only authorized users can access specific resources.
- **File storage**: Supabase offers an integrated storage service for managing unstructured files. It allows applications to securely store and serve assets such as images, videos, and documents uploaded by users.

Free quota

Supabase's free plan offers enough credit to support a startup's long cold-start and validation phase.

- **50,000 monthly active users**: This means your app can accept 50,000 different user registrations and logins per month without you having to pay any fees, providing a huge amount of free space for product growth
- **2 free items**: This allows you to run and test two independent products or ideas simultaneously
- **500MB database and 1GB file storage**: This is sufficient to store a large amount of user information, business data, and user-uploaded files for startups

If a free project receives no API requests for a week, it will be suspended. Simply log in to the backend and click to resume. This is a crucial point to remember when launching a project in its initial stages.

Best practices

To fully realize Supabase's core value while mitigating potential risks on the entrepreneurial path, the following best practices, proven in real-world application, are worth prioritizing.

- **Choose open source to avoid vendor lock-in**: This is a key strategic consideration in choosing Supabase over similar products like Google Firebase. *Vendor lock-in* refers to deep dependence on a particular service provider's proprietary technology, leading to extremely high migration costs in the future
  When building your stack, a crucial best practice is to actively avoid vendor lock-in—a situation where your product becomes hopelessly dependent on a single company's proprietary technology. By deliberately choosing an open-source platform like Supabase over closed alternatives (like Google Firebase), you ensure you always hold the architectural blueprints. Because it is open source at its core, you retain the freedom to package and deploy your entire backend to any other cloud provider if you ever need to.
- **Row-level security (RLS) enabled from day one**: This is one of Supabase's most powerful security features. RLS allows you to write fine-grained access control policies directly at the database level using SQL statements (e.g., allowing users to only read or modify data rows matching their own ID). This approach of pushing security logic down to the data layer creates a more robust security model. It is highly recommended that you learn and configure an RLS policy for each data table.
- **Make good use of SQL editors and AI:** The SQL editor in the Supabase dashboard is powerful, and its built-in AI assistant can generate SQL queries based on natural language descriptions, which greatly lowers the learning curve. Try using it to explore data; it can achieve more complex analysis than simple API calls.

User authentication: Supabase Auth vs. Clerk

The user authentication system is the application's "security team." Here you will face a typical strategic choice: choose a built-in platform solution (Supabase Auth) or a specialized third-party solution (like Clerk):

- **Supabase Auth**: As Supabase's built-in "internal security," it integrates seamlessly with the database. Its core advantages are high integration and the free quota shared with the main plan (up to 50,000 active users per month), making it highly cost-effective.

- **Clerk**: Clerk is a professional third-party security company (its main page is shown in *Figure 3.3*). Its biggest highlight is the provision of beautifully designed, plug-and-play UI components (such as login boxes and user profile pages), which significantly shortens development time and makes the application interface look more professional. Clerk's free quota supports 10,000 active users per month.

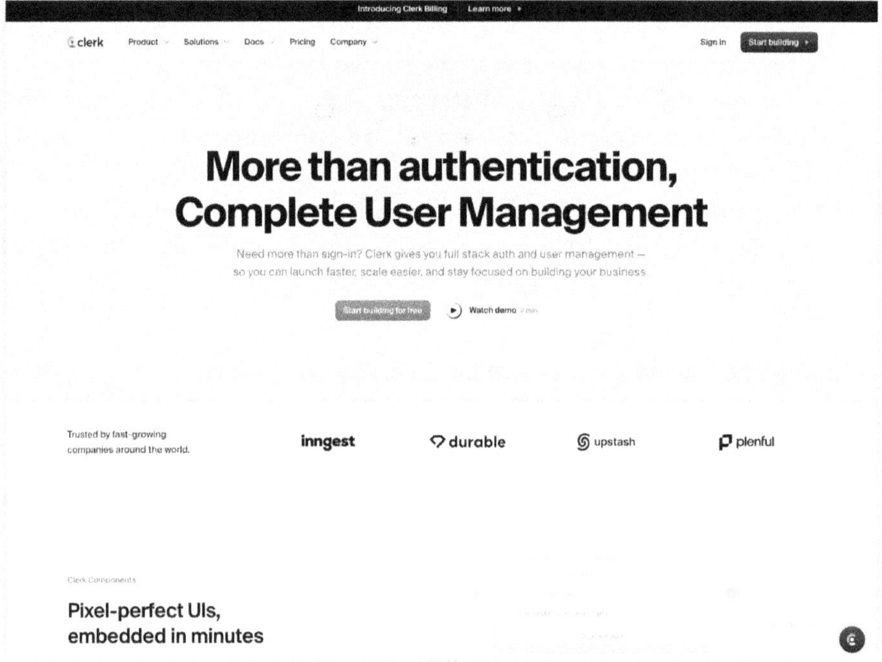

Figure 3.3 – Clerk platform home page

Best practices

When choosing a user authentication scheme, it is important to accurately match project needs and balance development efficiency with long-term value. You can refer to the following decision-making guidelines:

- *If you want ultimate development speed and exquisite pre-built UI*: Choose Clerk. Its pre-built components allow you to set up a professional login process in minutes, making it the ultimate shortcut for quickly building MVPs (Clerk's free tier supports up to 10,000 active users per month).
- *If you want long-term cost control and deep data integration*: Choose Supabase Auth. Its seamless integration with the database facilitates complex authorization logic and it offers a highly cost-effective free quota of up to 50,000 active users per month.
- *If you want the best of both worlds*: Clerk and Supabase provide official integration solutions. You can use Clerk's elegant frontend components to handle user interactions while using Supabase as the secure backend database.

File storage: Cloudflare R2

Next is the application's "unlimited file cabinet," that is, **Cloudflare R2**, specifically designed for storing various files uploaded by users. The core reason for choosing Cloudflare R2 is that it avoids the hidden costs commonly found in the cloud storage field, also known as export bandwidth fees (egress fees).

The export fee trap versus Cloudflare R2

Export fees refer to the costs incurred when data is transferred from a cloud service provider's servers to the public internet. For applications with a large number of image or video views, this cost can quickly exceed the storage cost itself, creating a heavy financial burden. It's like renting a locker; in addition to paying for the space, you also have to pay a hefty "moving fee" each time you retrieve something.

Cloudflare R2's pricing model promises zero egress fees to the public internet (unlike traditional providers such as AWS S3). You only pay for storage space and operations (such as writing and reading files), without paying anything for data transfer. The main page of the Cloudflare R2 platform is shown in *Figure 3.4*.

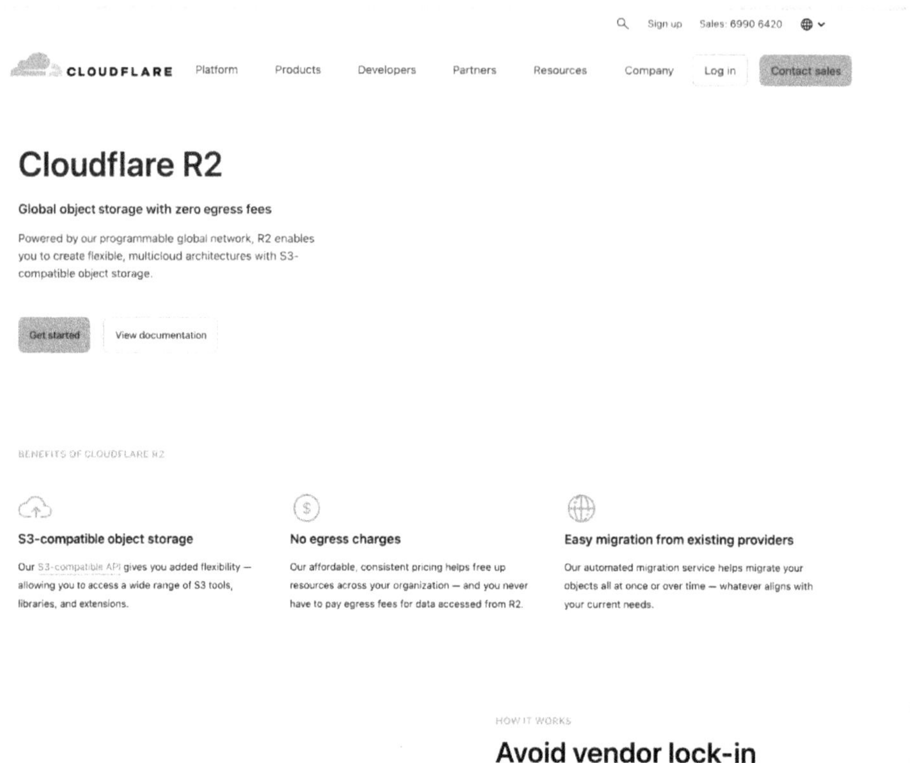

Figure 3.4 – Main page of the Cloudflare R2 platform

Free quota

The free tier of Cloudflare R2 is sufficient to support most applications in their early stages. Here's what it gets you:

- Storage space: 10GB per month
- Type A operations (write/modify): 1 million requests per month
- Type B operations (read): 10 million requests per month

Best practices

To fully leverage Cloudflare R2's core advantages of zero egress fees and high cost-effectiveness, while avoiding common issues such as data migration and cost overruns, the following best practices can be implemented directly:

- **Use Cloudflare R2 by default from day one:** Store all user-generated files on Cloudflare R2 from the beginning of the project. Migrating large amounts of data from other providers later can be complicated and incur export fees that you might have intended to avoid
- **Understand the differences in operation categories:** Cloudflare R2 categorizes operations into Class A (modify state) and Class B (read-only). Class A operations are more expensive than Class B operations. The free tier offers 10 times the allowance for Class B operations compared to Class A, which encourages the **write once, read many (WORM)** design pattern, meaning a file, like a profile picture, is uploaded to the server just once but viewed thousands of times by your users, and aligns with common user content usage scenarios.
- **Combine with Cloudflare Workers for advanced logic:** For more complex use cases, Cloudflare R2 can be paired with **Cloudflare Workers** (serverless function platform) to run code at the edge, performing tasks such as dynamically resizing images and verifying private file access permissions while maintaining extremely low latency.

Core peripheral services

Core peripheral services are key modules built on top of the infrastructure to improve application functionality and optimize user experience. They cover core scenarios such as email, data statistics, application monitoring, content management, and payment, making applications go from *usable* to *easy to use*.

Email service: Resend

Resend (`https://resend.com/`) is an API-first platform built for developers to reliably and efficiently send triggered emails. Its main interface is shown in *Figure 3.5*.

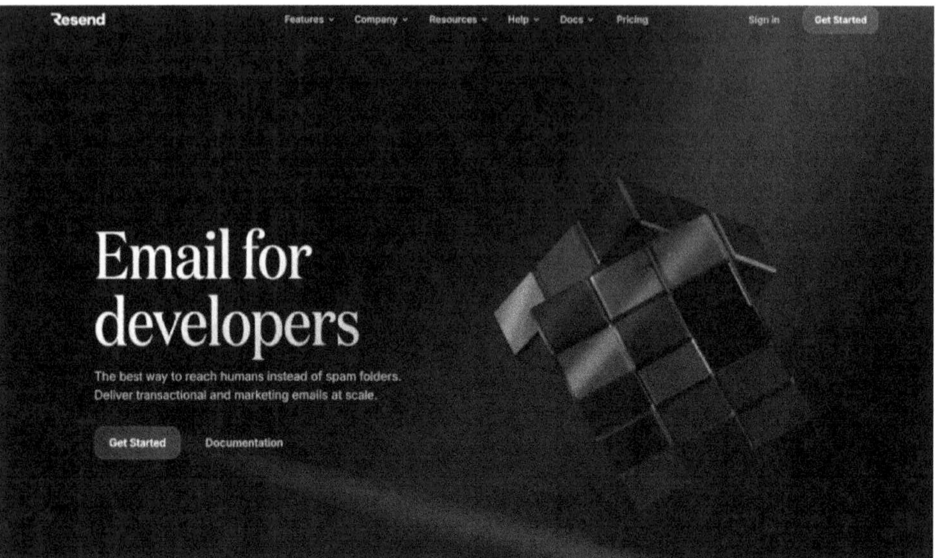

Figure 3.5 – Main page of the Resend platform

As an application's dedicated mailman, it is primarily responsible for sending automated emails triggered by user actions, such as **Welcome to Registration**, **Password Reset**, and **Order Confirmation**. These one-to-one functional messages triggered by specific user actions are called triggered emails.

In contrast to triggered emails are mass marketing emails (such as newsletters), and the two are fundamentally different: triggered emails contain information that users need or have requested, while marketing emails are one-to-many promotional communications sent in bulk to a list of subscribers. Email service providers (such as Gmail) handle these two types of emails very differently, which is an important reason why Resend focuses on the triggered email field.

A key feature is Resend's support for building email templates using React. This means developers can use the same tools as those used to build application frontends to create beautiful and dynamic emails, improving the efficiency and consistency of email template development.

Free quota

Resend offers a user-friendly free-to-use policy, which includes:

- It can send 3,000 emails per month
- The daily email sending limit is 100
- Supports configuring one custom domain name

Please note that there is a daily email sending limit of 100. For events that may trigger a large number of emails at once, it is necessary to make corresponding plans in advance.

Best practices

To fully leverage Resend's capabilities and ensure reliable email delivery, here are some proven best practices:

- **Strictly separate email streams:** Resend is used exclusively for application-triggered emails, while a dedicated marketing email service (such as Mailchimp) is used for marketing communications. This separation is the most important factor in ensuring the delivery rate of critical emails.
- **Verify your digital identity (Domain Configuration):** To send emails that look like they come from your official website (e.g., hello@yourstartup.com), you need to prove to email providers like Gmail that you actually own the address. Resend will guide you to copy and paste a few verification codes into your website's settings. This acts as an official digital seal, which is crucial for building brand trust and ensuring your messages land in the inbox instead of the spam folder.
- Use webhooks to get real-time status updates**:** Resend can send a webhook (automatic notification) to the application whenever the status of an email changes (e.g., delivered, opened). You can use these notifications to build powerful automated workflows, such as updating user profiles or triggering subsequent actions.

Data statistics: PostHog vs. Google Analytics

The market is flooded with data analytics platforms, so you might be wondering why we are spotlighting PostHog and Google Analytics (GA). For an independent founder building a frugal full-stack, your analytics needs generally fall into two distinct buckets: marketing and product. We have selected the industry-leading, free-tier-friendly champion for each category.

Data analytics is your application's 'dashboard.' The choice between PostHog and GA ultimately depends on the core question you are trying to answer:

- *Where do my users come from?* This is a marketing issue concerning traffic sources and campaign effectiveness. Google Analytics is the undisputed standard for this purpose.
- *What do users do within my product?* This is a product issue concerning feature adoption, user retention, and experience optimization. PostHog is built specifically for these kinds of problems.

Let's take a look at these two tools separately.

GA: Marketing analyst

Google Analytics (`https://analytics.google.com/`) is a tool for understanding website traffic and marketing performance, and its platform homepage is shown in *Figure 3.6*. However, its latest version, GA 4, has a steep learning curve, and the free plan only retains data for a maximum of 14 months.

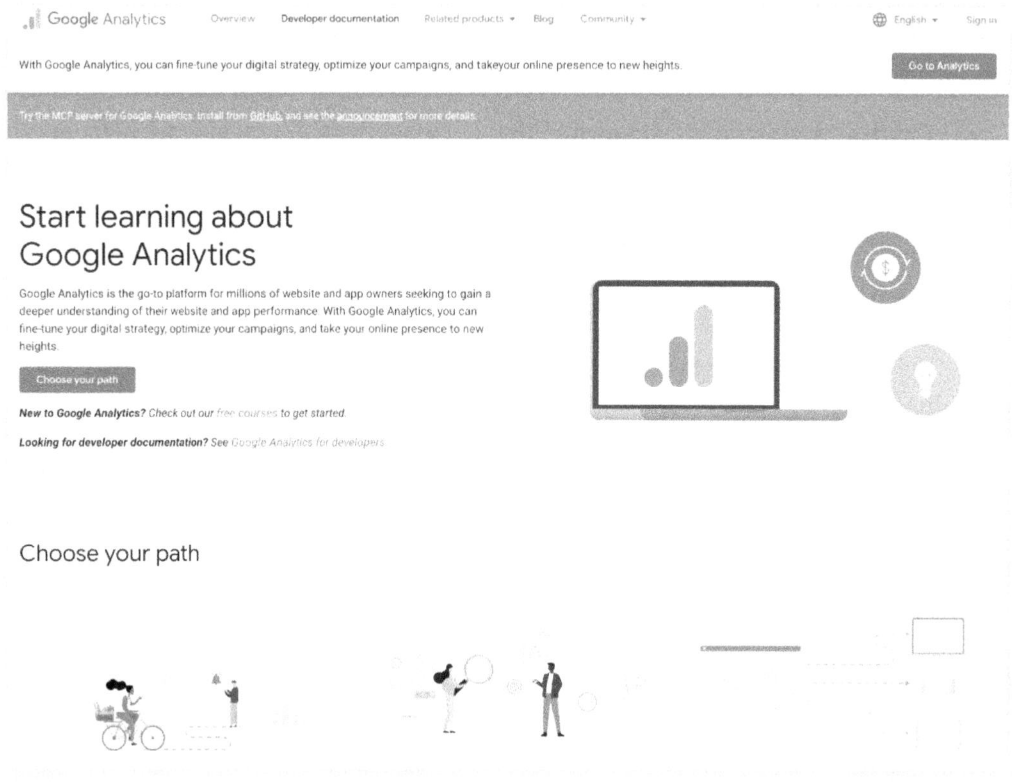

Figure 3.6 – GA platform main page

PostHog: A product engineer's toolkit

PostHog is a modern open-source platform designed for product-driven growth. The design, with its main page shown in *Figure 3.7*, is an all-in-one suite encompassing session recording, feature toggles, and A/B testing. As open-source software, PostHog also offers a self-hosting option, giving you complete control over your user data.

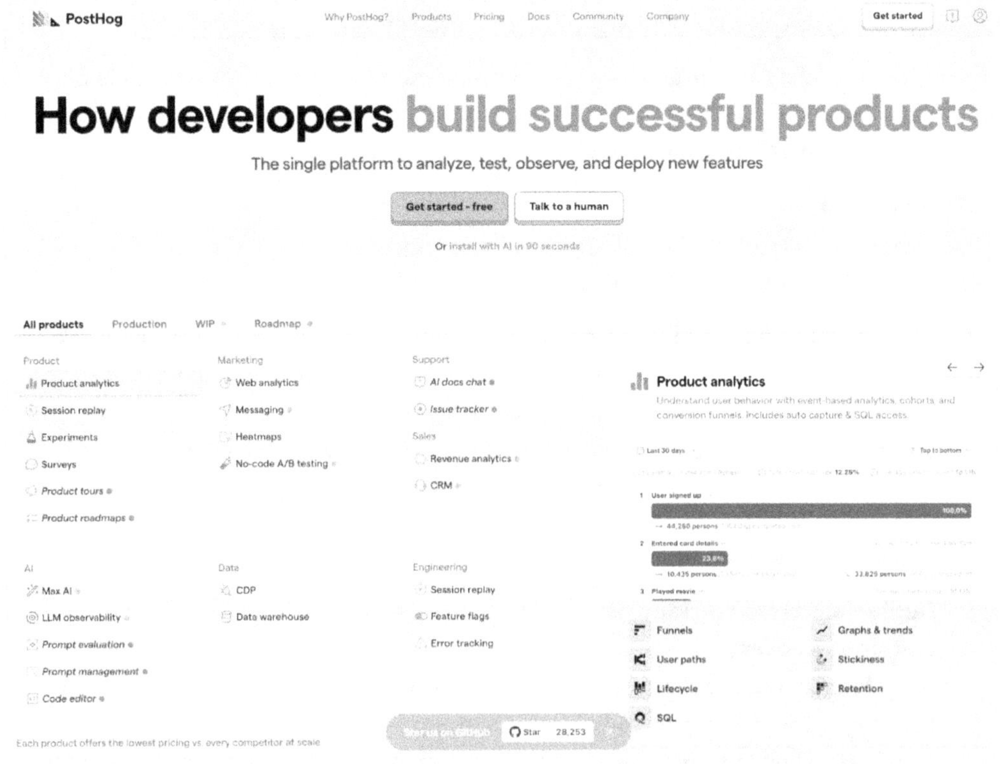

Figure 3.7 – Main page of the PostHog platform

Free quota comparison

In terms of free credit, PostHog and GA each have their own focus and cater to the needs of different scenarios.

PostHog's free plan is generous, covering the early-stage needs of most companies, especially startups and independent developers. Core free resources include 1 million analytics events per month, 5,000 session recordings, and 1 million feature toggle requests. Data is retained for one year, and all limits are transparent with no hidden restrictions, fully supporting core needs such as user behavior analysis and feature testing from the product's cold start to early growth stages.

In contrast, GA's limitations are more scenario-based: it can process a maximum of 10 million hits per month (a generous data processing limit suitable for high-traffic websites), and the data retention period is up to 14 months (users can choose 2 months or 14 months). The BigQuery export function supports a maximum of 1 million event exports per day (meeting basic offline data analysis needs). It's important to note that GA may trigger a sampling mechanism when dealing with large datasets. The sampled data will affect the accuracy of the analysis results to some extent, which is a key limitation of its free plan.

In short, PostHog offers a more generous and transparent free usage policy in the field of product analytics, while GA has more lenient restrictions on data processing volume but has certain limitations in terms of data retention and advanced features.

Best practices

To empower business growth through data analytics and avoid tool misuse or inefficient analysis, the following best practices can be implemented directly:

- **Choose the right tools for the right job:** If your primary goal is to measure marketing effectiveness (such as monitoring website traffic sources, ad campaign performance, and conversion rates), GA is a suitable choice.
  However, if you are looking to gain deeper insights into user engagement, PostHog is the better option. For most independent developers and early-stage startups, prioritizing PostHog's product analytics is the most direct way to drive product iteration and user growth.
- **Implement event tracking prudently:** PostHog's strength lies in its flexible, customizable event tracking capabilities. You should track meaningful user behavior to build funnels and gain deeper insights into how users derive value from the product. PostHog supports automatically capturing every user activity within a website or application, helping teams gain a deeper understanding of user interaction patterns and optimize the product experience.
- **Use recording sessions to build empathy:** Numbers and charts tell you what happened, but recorded conversations explain why. Regularly reviewing user recordings of those who abandoned key processes is an effective way to identify UI/UX issues and build empathy for user struggles. PostHog's conversation playback feature fully records user interactions, helping to quickly pinpoint problems and optimize the experience.

Application monitoring: Sentry

Next, we'll introduce **Sentry** (`https://sentry.io/`), the application's "24/7 emergency doctor." Sentry is an application monitoring platform whose core function is to automatically capture, diagnose, and report various errors occurring in online applications. The Sentry platform's main page is shown in *Figure 3.8*.

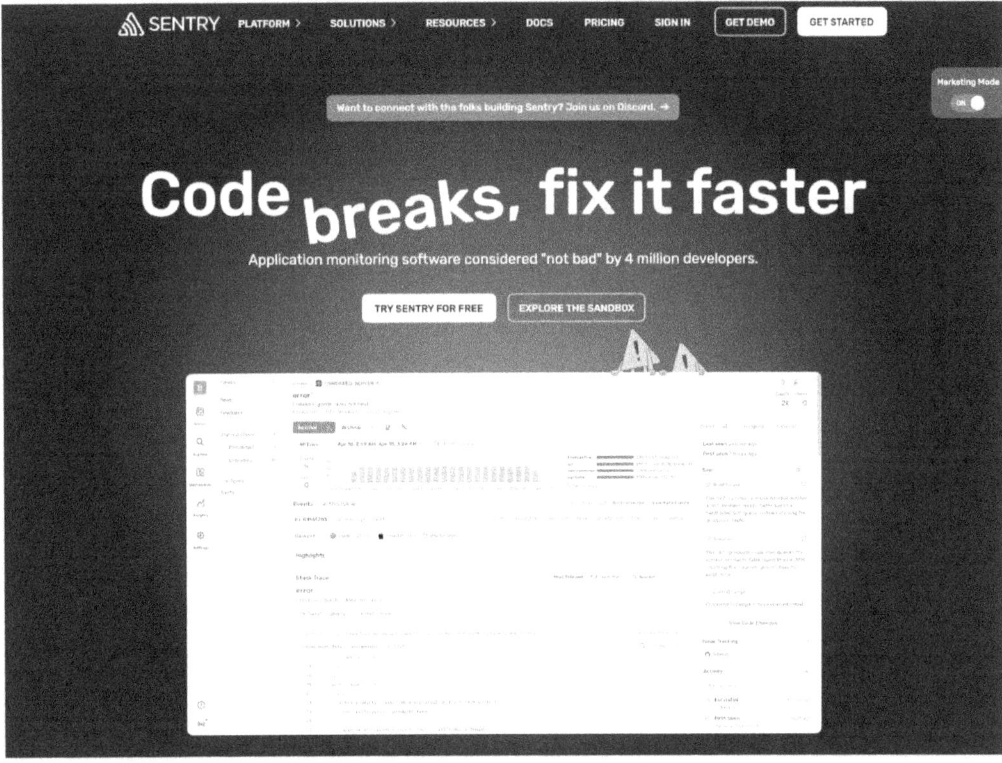

Figure 3.8 – Sentry platform home page

When a user triggers a bug, Sentry logs all relevant information in the background and sends a detailed diagnostic report to your dashboard. This report includes the key context needed to reproduce and resolve the issue.

- **Stack trace:** Specifies the exact file and line number in the code where the error occurred.
- **User environment:** This includes the user's browser type, operating system, device model, etc.
- **Breadcrumbs:** Restore the series of operation steps before the user triggered the error

With this information, developers can quickly locate and fix problems, shifting from passively responding to user complaints to proactively resolving potential issues.

Free quota

Sentry's free quota, known as the **Developer Package**, is designed for independent developers and early-stage projects. It provides core features and resources tailored to individual developer needs, including detailed exception information (exception type, occurrence time, number of occurrences, etc.) to help quickly locate and fix problems. While its functionality is relatively limited, it is sufficient for the daily development needs of most individual developers. The specific free quota includes the following:

- **Monthly error events:** Capture 5000 error events for free
- **Session replay:** Support 50 session replays per month
- **User seats:** The free version is limited to one user

For a newly launched application, a monthly limit of 5,000 error events is more than enough.

Best practices

To fully leverage Sentry's error monitoring value, achieve efficient debugging, and proactively mitigate risks, the following best practices can be directly implemented:

- **Integrate upon launch:** Don't wait until product launch to consider bug monitoring. Integrate Sentry into your project during the development phase to proactively capture and fix bugs that occur only in specific production environments.
- **Upload Source Maps (The Decoder Ring):** Before a modern frontend application goes live, its code typically undergoes two processes: **compression** (removing all spaces to shrink the file size so the app loads instantly) and **obfuscation** (scrambling the code into unreadable characters to prevent theft). If an error occurs in this scrambled code, it looks like gibberish. By automatically uploading "Source Maps"—which act as a translation dictionary—during the build process, Sentry can decode these gibberish errors back into the exact, readable lines of your original code.
- **Configure meaningful alerts:** Configure alert rules for your project in the Sentry backend. For example, *"Notify me by email when a new type of bug occurs more than 5 times in 1 hour"* ensures that you give immediate attention to issues with a wide impact

Content management: Keystatic vs. Sanity

As an application matures, some content (such as blog posts and marketing copy) needs frequent updates. To avoid redeploying the entire application simply to fix a typo, a **content management system** (**CMS**) is necessary.

We've selected two top-tier **headless CMS** for you. *Headless* means it separates content creation and management (the "body") from content presentation (the "head," i.e., your website interface). The CMS acts purely as a data source, making your content available via an API so that any frontend can retrieve and display it. Choosing between Keystatic and Sanity boils down to strategic decisions regarding content storage location and primary content editors.

Keystatic: A Git-based CMS that coexists with the code

Keystatic's (`https://keystatic.com/`) core philosophy is to treat content as part of the code. It's a Git-based CMS where all content is stored directly in your GitHub repository as structured files (such as Markdown). The Keystatic platform's main page is shown in *Figure 3.9*.

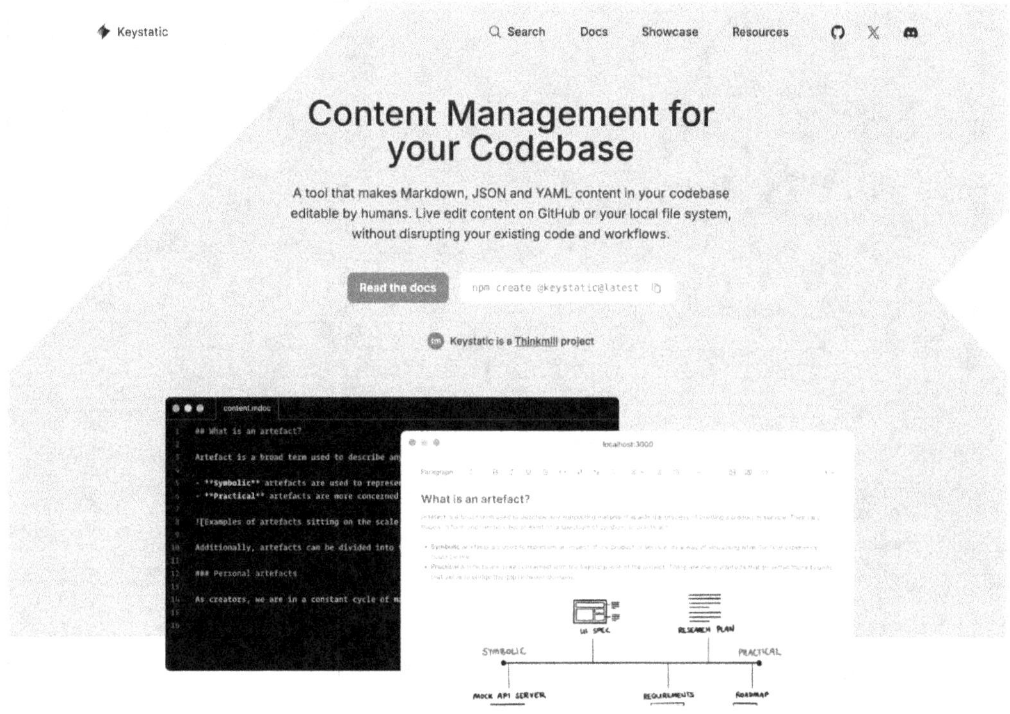

Figure 3.9 – Keystatic platform home page

Keystatic's working mechanism is simple and efficient: when a content editor saves an article in its interface, the system automatically creates a new Git commit in the background and pushes it to the GitHub repository, thus triggering Vercel's automatic deployment. The advantages of this design are significant: content and code are managed uniformly through Git, providing complete version control; data ownership is clear; and Keystatic itself is open source and free. Therefore, Keystatic is suitable for projects where content production is developer-led, such as technical blogs and product documentation.

Sanity: An API-driven collaborative content platform

Sanity's (`https://www.sanity.io/`) core philosophy is to treat content as code-independent, collaborative data. All content is stored in a dedicated, managed, real-time database provided by Sanity and accessed via API. The Sanity platform's main page is shown in *Figure 3.10*.

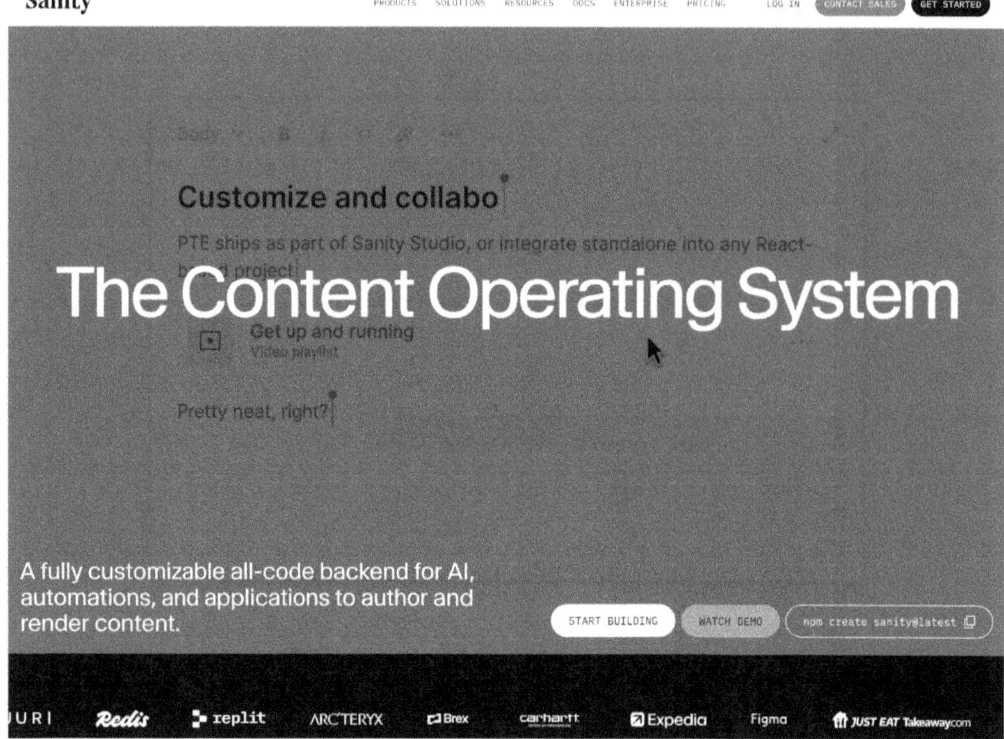

Figure 3.10 – Sanity platform homepage

In terms of workflow, when content editors modify content in **Sanity Studio** (a customizable editing environment), the changes are saved in real time to a cloud database. Applications can retrieve the latest content at runtime via API without redeployment.

Sanity has significant advantages, such as supporting real-time collaboration, being user-friendly for non-technical people, decoupling content publishing from code deployment (which is faster), encouraging structured content, and being highly scalable.

Sanity offers a very generous free allowance, including up to 20 user seats, 10,000 documents, and 1 million API CDN requests per month.

Best practices

To accurately match content management needs while balancing efficiency and scalability, you can choose and use Keystatic or Sanity by following these practical best practices.

- **Determine the main content editor:** This is the core decision guide. If the developer is the primary creator, Keystatic's native Git workflow will be more efficient. If you plan to have a non-technical marketing or operations team manage the content, Sanity's superior editing experience and collaboration features will be more advantageous.
- **Consider the frequency of content updates:** If content is updated very frequently, Sanity's content and deployment decoupling model is more efficient. For content that is updated less frequently, Keystatic-triggered automatic deployment is sufficient.
- **Laying the foundation for structured content:** Regardless of the tool chosen, planning should be approached from the perspective of *structured content*. Break down content into smaller, meaningful data blocks (titles, summaries, authors, etc.) to make the content more flexible and reusable in the future.

Payment: Stripe

When you're ready to commercialize your product, you need a secure and reliable way to receive payments. Handling credit card information yourself is extremely complex and impractical, while Stripe (`https://stripe.com/`) is the industry standard in this field. Stripe is a payment infrastructure built for the internet, and its main page is shown in *Figure 3.11*. It provides a powerful suite of APIs and tools that allow you to securely and conveniently receive payments from customers worldwide. It is a developer-friendly platform that encapsulates all the complexities of payments, from secure encryption to fraud prevention.

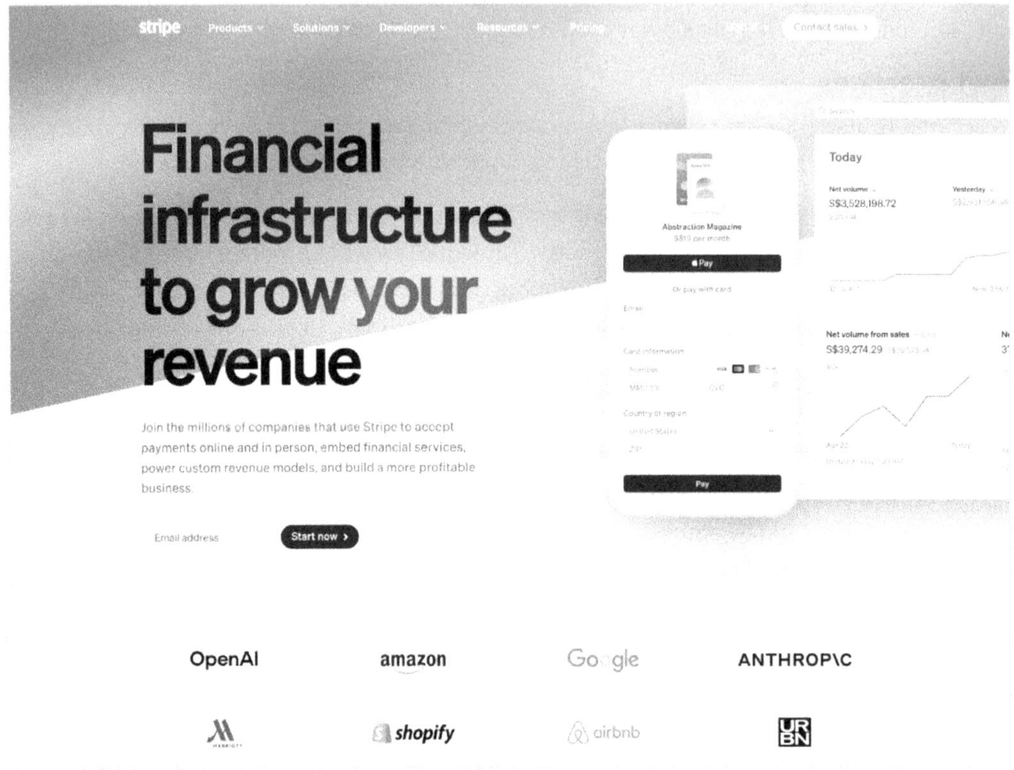

Figure 3.11 – Stripe platform home page

Pay-as-you-go

Stripe's biggest appeal to startups lies in its pricing model. For standard payment processing, Stripe has no setup fee, no monthly usage fee, and charges only a small service fee when you become profitable, thus ensuring that costs grow in tandem with revenue.

- **Standard transaction fee:** The standard rate for online domestic bank card payments is typically 2.9% of the successful transaction amount plus 30 cents (the specific rate varies by region)
- **Dispute (Cancellation) fee:** The operational cost that needs to be considered. Stripe will charge a processing fee if a customer disputes a transaction.

Best practices

To ensure secure and compliant payment processes, reliable data synchronization, and improved integration efficiency, the following proven best practices can be followed when using Stripe:

- **Use Stripe Checkout or Stripe Elements**: This is the golden rule for security: never allow sensitive information like credit card numbers to pass through or be stored on your servers. Stripe Checkout is a pre-built payment page hosted by Stripe, offering fast integration. Stripe Elements is a set of embeddable UI components that allow you to build custom payment forms on your website while ensuring the data goes straight to Stripe.
- **Thoroughly practice in test mode**: Stripe offers a fully functional **Test Mode** and multiple test credit card numbers. Before launching your application, you must thoroughly rehearse the entire payment process in Test Mode to ensure that the application can correctly handle all success and failure scenarios.
- **Implement webhooks to ensure data synchronization**: Webhooks are automated notifications sent by the Stripe server to your application server when specific events occur (such as successful subscription renewal). Never rely solely on frontend redirects to confirm payment status; webhooks are the only reliable way to ensure that your system state remains eventually consistent with Stripe.

Productivity and design tools

Productivity and design tools are auxiliary supports for improving development efficiency and ensuring product quality. They cover scenarios such as design, code management, and task collaboration, helping you advance projects and bring ideas to fruition more efficiently.

Design tool: Figma

Figma (`https://www.figma.com/`) is your "design studio" when building digital products. It's a cloud-based collaborative design tool that makes the golden rule of *design before development* simpler and more efficient than ever before. Figma's main page is shown in *Figure 3.12*.

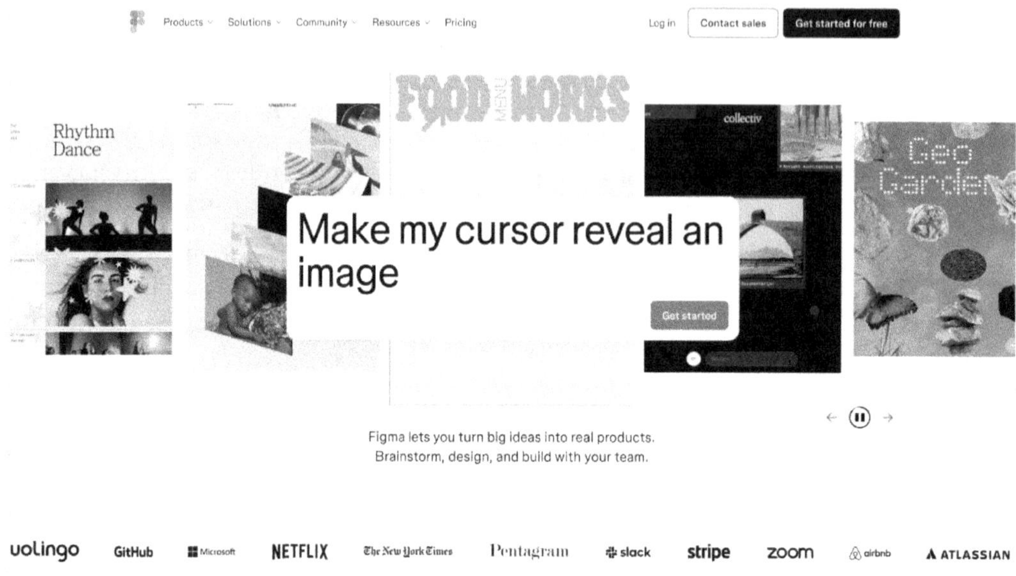

Figure 3.12 – The main page of the Figma platform

For non-technical users, Figma's greatest value lies in providing a universal language for making abstract ideas concrete. You don't need to know coding to "draw" the application interface in your mind here and turn it into a clickable, interactive prototype.

This interactive prototype is one of the most valuable assets in the early stages of a startup. It allows you to conduct user testing before development begins, communicate effectively with developers, and vividly present your vision to investors.

Free quota

Figma's free credits (called the **Starter Package**) are designed for design beginners and individual creators and are powerful enough for independent founders or small teams.

- **File restrictions:** At the time of this writing, each team can create up to 3 Figma design files and 3 FigJam (online whiteboard) files
- **Personal draft area:** Its core advantage is that it allows you to create an unlimited number of files in your personal "draft" space
- **Infinite collaborators:** You can invite an unlimited number of collaborators to view and comment on your designs

Best practices

To fully leverage Figma to enhance the design process and improve efficiency and professionalism, follow these practical tips.

- **Embrace the "prototype" mindset:** Don't stop at creating static images. One of Figma's core strengths is its prototyping pattern. Take the time to learn how to link different artboards together, add clickable interactions to buttons, and create prototypes that testers can actually use.
- **Establish simple design guidelines:** Even for small projects, it's essential to cultivate a habit of standardized design from day one. In Figma, define the product's main color scheme, font size, button styles, and other elements as reusable components and styles to ensure visual consistency and professionalism while saving significant time during subsequent design adjustments.
- **Make good use of community resources:** Figma boasts an extremely active community, bringing together thousands of free resources shared by designers and companies worldwide, including complete UI design kits, icon libraries, and more. Searching the community before starting from scratch is likely to yield high-quality templates, thus accelerating the design process.

Code management tool: GitHub

You need a secure and reliable place to record every change, storing all the code and design blueprints for your project. In the digital world, that place is GitHub (`https://github.com/`), as shown in *Figure 3.13*.

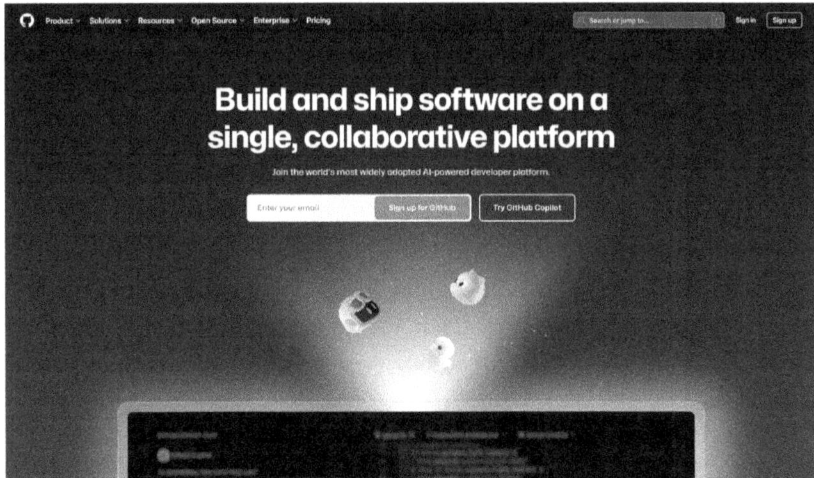

Figure 3.13 – GitHub platform homepage

Version control and collaboration center

GitHub is the world's largest code hosting platform, and its core function is version control. Every change you make to the project will be recorded as a *commit*. If a new feature has a problem, you can always revert to any previous version, just like loading a game save.

Free quota

GitHub's free quota is virtually unlimited for individual developers and small teams.

- **Unlimited private warehouse:** Allows you to create countless "secret projects" that are not publicly disclosed, storing all your commercial code and prototypes.
- **2000 minutes of Actions calculation time per month:** Built-in automation tool that, when paired with Vercel, forms a powerful CI/CD automated deployment pipeline
- **500MB package storage space:** Used to store reusable "parts" in a project

Best practices

To ensure standardized code management and efficient collaboration, the following best practices can be followed when using GitHub:

- **Develop good "submit" habits:** Make a commit after completing each small feature or fixing a bug and write a clear and meaningful description (e.g., *"Fixed a style issue with the user login button on mobile devices"*).
- **Embrace the branching workflow:** Never develop new features directly on your main branch. Create a new branch for each new feature or bug fix and merge the branch back into the main branch via a pull request once development is complete. This ensures that your main branch is always stable and deployable.
- **Manage tasks using Issues:** GitHub has a simple yet powerful built-in project management tool that can record bugs, plan new features, or track tasks through the **Issues** feature, making it a viable alternative to many complex third-party project management software.

Productivity tools: Lark, Notion

If inspiration, tasks, research materials, and other information generated during the startup process are scattered in various places, they will quickly become difficult to manage. You need a "command center," or a single source of truth, to organize all information into a clear and actionable system. This role is filled by all-in-one workspaces such as **Lark** (`https://www.larksuite.com/`) (see *Figure 3.14*):

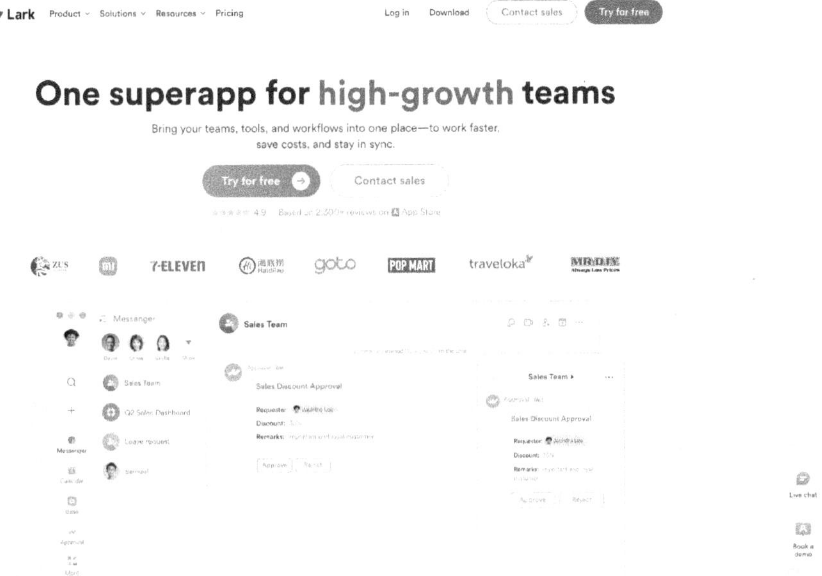

Figure 3.14 – Lark homepage

Another example is Notion (`https://www.notion.com/`) (see *Figure 3.15*).

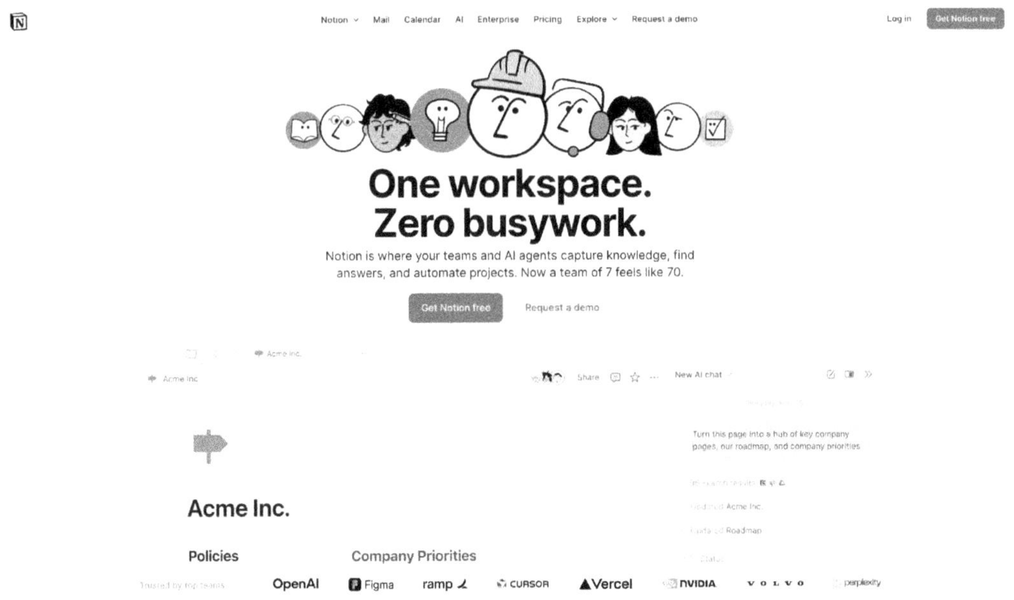

Figure 3.15 – Notion main page

Lark and Notion are far more than just simple note-taking applications. Their core value lies in their integration of diverse tools such as documents, knowledge bases, databases, and project management, creating a unified collaborative workspace. You can use them to build powerful structured databases and flexibly manage task lists, user feedback, competitor analysis, inspiration notes, and other work-related tasks, allowing scattered information to be efficiently aggregated and flow in an orderly manner.

Free quota

Both Lark and Notion offer powerful features in their free personal versions, sufficient to meet the needs of independent founders or small, early-stage teams managing their entire projects.

- **Notion Free Plan**: For personal use, it allows the creation of an unlimited number of pages and blocks; however, there are certain limitations for team collaboration
- **Lark Basic Edition**: It offers powerful collaboration features for individuals and small teams, including instant messaging, cloud documents, calendars, and video conferencing, and provides up to 100 GB of total storage.

Best practices

To maximize the management value of Lark/Notion and improve work efficiency, you can refer to the following practical tips

- **Start with a template (not a blank page)**: The best way to get started is to take advantage of their extensive template library. Search for templates such as *product roadmap* or *lightweight CRM*, modify them to suit your needs, and get started quickly
- **Embrace database thinking**: This is key to using these tools effectively. Structure related information into a database. For example, create a *Master Task Database*, and then create different "views" of that database (such as *Tasks Assigned to Me*) on different pages, all of which originate from the same database and are kept synchronized and updated.
- **Create a dashboard for the project's directory**: Create a top-level *Project Dashboard* page in Notion or Lark. Its core function is command and navigation, centralizing all key links related to the project (GitHub repository, Vercel deployment address, Figma design drafts, Supabase dashboard, etc.). This dashboard will become the project's directory, saving you and future team members a significant amount of time searching for information.

5-minute hands-on lesson: Learning relevant productivity tools

In the next five minutes, we will guide you through two steps to build the two most essential tools for your digital empire.

Step 1: Create a GitHub account

Open the GitHub (`https://github.com/`) website in your browser and click the **Sign up** button in the upper right corner. Follow the prompts to enter your email address, create a secure password, choose a username you like, and complete a simple human verification. GitHub will send a verification code to your registered email address; check your email and enter the code to complete the verification. On the final personalization page, you can click **Skip personalization** to directly activate your free account.

Congratulations! You now have a code-hosting account.

Step 2: Create a Vercel account

Open the Vercel website (`https://vercel.com/`) and click the **Sign up** button in the upper right corner. In the registration options, click the **Continue with GitHub** button. In the pop-up authorization window, allow Vercel to connect to your newly created GitHub account.

All done! You now have a world-class, auto-scalable global application publishing platform. You don't need to set a separate password for Vercel; it authenticates directly through GitHub, perfectly demonstrating the seamless integration of this tool ecosystem.

Summary

In just five minutes, you accomplished a task that might have taken professionals days a decade ago—building a solid digital infrastructure for a startup project.

You are now using the exact same foundational platforms (the "blueprint library" and "deployment platform") trusted by top tech companies. More importantly, all of this comes at zero initial cost.

Purchasing and configuring a domain name

Building a digital presence is much like building a house. While your website is your online home, and your web hosting is the plot of land it sits on, you still need a way for people to easily find you. That unique identifier, your digital street address, is a domain name.

What is a domain name?

To understand how a domain name works, let's break down our real estate analogy:

- **The Land (Web Hosting)**: A website needs server space to store its files and operate. This is "web hosting" (or "virtual hosting"), which acts as the foundation of your digital house.
- **The Address (Domain Name)**: A website also needs a unique "address" so visitors can navigate directly to your house. This is your domain name. Visitors can view the website content simply by entering this address into their browser.

Relationship between domain names and IP addresses

Behind the scenes of the internet, every website corresponds to a complex string of numbers and letters called an **IP address** (e.g., `192.153.xxx.xxx`). It's like the precise latitude and longitude coordinates of a house on a map, so specific that it is difficult for a single human to remember and use.

The **Domain Name System** (**DNS**) acts as a "translator," essentially a vast address book, converting hard-to-remember IP addresses into domain names that are easier for people to understand and remember. When a user enters a domain name like `godaddy.com` into their browser, the DNS quickly looks up and identifies its corresponding IP address, guiding the user to the correct website server.

This mechanism simplifies the internet access process, reduces the difficulty of operation, and thus improves the user experience. At the same time, a simple domain name can also increase website return visits, which is of great significance for beginners who want to establish an online presence.

Domain name structure

A domain name mainly consists of two parts:

- **Second-level domain (SLD)**: This is the user-defined part of a domain name, usually appearing after `www.`. For example, `godaddy` in `godaddy.com` is a second-level domain. Second-level domains are key to showcasing brand personality and creativity.
- **Top-level domain (TLD)**: The last part of a domain name, the suffix, is equivalent to the "category" or "country/region" identifier in an address. Top-level domains are mainly divided into three categories
    - **Generic top-level domain (gTLD)**: The most common types include `.com` (often used for commercial websites), `.org` (often used for non-profit organizations),

and `.net` (often used for internet service providers). Among them, `.com` is the most widely known and trusted top-level domain.

  - **Country code top-level domain (ccTLD)**: Represents a specific country or region, such as `.us` (United States), `.uk` (United Kingdom), and `.cn` (China). If your business's target audience is concentrated in a specific geographic area, choosing the corresponding country code top-level domain is more advantageous.
  - **New general top-level domain (gTLD)**: Creative domain name extensions that have emerged in recent years include `.photography`, `.media`, `.shop`, `.ai`, `.store`, and `.app`. These novel extensions can make domain names more distinctive and also intuitively reflect the type of business a website provides.

It's important to note that a domain name is not the same as a **URL** (**Uniform Resource Locator**). A domain name is the "main address" of a website (such as `google.com`), while a URL is the "detailed address" of a specific page or resource, containing the protocol (such as `https://`), the domain name, and the specific path (such as `https://www.godaddy.com/help/set-up-my-domain-40634`). Therefore, a domain name is a component of a URL.

In addition, the website can also use subdomains. **Subdomain**s are like "small rooms in a big house," such as `blog.example.com` or `shop.example.com`. They can be used to divide the website into functional areas or to set up development and testing environments.

The value of owning a domain name

A dedicated domain name is a strategic long-term investment for individuals or businesses in the digital world, and its value far exceeds that of a simple "web address."

- **Building a professional brand image:** Custom domains like `yourname.com` can quickly enhance the professionalism and credibility of individuals or businesses, sending a serious and dedicated message to the outside world
- **Enhancing trust perception:** A clear and memorable domain name can leave a good impression on potential customers. Free subdomains like `yourbusiness.hostsite.com`, on the other hand, can appear less formal and generate distrust.
- **Taking control of your online identity:** Owning your own domain name means you have complete control over the appearance, content, and presentation of your website, and you are not bound by the rules of third-party platforms.

- **Improving memory and access efficiency:** A short and easy-to-remember domain name makes it easier for potential users to find and remember your website, thereby increasing return visits.
- **Configure a professional email:** After registering a domain name, you can create a professional email address like `info@yourbusiness.com`. Compared to generic email addresses, this kind of customized professional email address can better enhance your brand image and win customer trust.
- **Indirectly boosting SEO:** Although domain names are no longer a direct determinant of search engine rankings, domain names that are highly relevant to the business and contain keywords can help users and search engines better understand website content and indirectly increase search exposure opportunities.
- **Protecting digital assets:** Even if you are not ready to fully build a website yet, registering your ideal domain name in advance can effectively prevent others from registering it first and reserve space for future development.
- **High-cost-performance marketing:** Domain name registration fees are usually quite low, yet they can act like a 24/7 billboard, continuously driving traffic to your business and making them far more cost-effective than traditional advertising.

So, domain names are the "foundation" for building a digital presence. Purchasing a domain name is a strategic investment in your digital future.

How to choose a good domain name

Choosing a good domain name is key to building a successful online image. A well-chosen domain name is easy to remember and spread, and enhances brand image and user trust. Below are the core considerations when selecting a domain name.

- **Short, easy to remember, spell, and pronounce**. Overly long or complex domain names increase the probability of user input errors. For example, if a domain name is difficult to pronounce over the phone or contains easily confused letter combinations, it may frustrate users and cause them to abandon the site. At the same time, domain names should avoid using unconventional spellings (such as using "u" instead of "you") and words that could lead to unintentional word combinations (such as "Children's wear" becoming "childrenswear")
- **Emphasize branding and ensure uniqueness**. Among millions of registered domain names, a unique and brand-recognizable domain is crucial. Before finalizing a domain name, do thorough research to ensure it hasn't already been registered by someone else. Simultaneously, check the name's availability on major social media platforms to ensure consistency in the brand's online image.

- **Avoid numbers and hyphens:** Avoid using numbers and hyphens (-) in domain names, as numbers can be confusing (users may not be sure whether to type 5 or five), and hyphens are easy to forget or misplace; both increase the chance of spelling errors. Furthermore, typing them on mobile devices is more cumbersome.
- **Embed relevant keywords**: Including keywords related to your business or industry in your domain name helps users quickly understand the core content of your website. For example, if you run a glass repair business, consider registering `GlassRepair.com` or `GlassReplacement.com`. Although keywords are no longer a direct factor in search engine ranking, they help users identify the website's theme, indirectly improving its visibility in search engines. However, avoid keyword stuffing, as it will appear unnatural and may even be flagged as spam.
- **Choose the right top-level domain**: The choice of TLD has a significant impact. `.com` remains the most widely used and trusted suffix globally. If your target audience is concentrated in a specific region, choosing country code top-level domains such as `.cn`, `.uk`, or `.us` can enhance localized SEO and clearly communicate the website's geographic relevance to search engines. Alternatively, newer generic top-level domains such as `.store`, `.blog`, `.shop`, and `.ai` allow you to better align your domain with your business.
- **Balance long-term development and flexibility:** When choosing a domain name, keep a long-term vision to ensure it can accommodate future business expansion. For example, if a florist initially chooses `cityflowers.com` as its domain name, it may become limiting if it later expands into gardening products. A more brand-oriented and inclusive name like `cityblooms.com`, on the other hand, allows for greater flexibility in expanding its product line.
- **Thorough research and decisive registration:** Before finalizing a domain name, complete two crucial investigations: first, verify trademark and copyright issues; second, investigate the domain's historical records to avoid purchasing a domain that has been used for spam or penalized by search engines. Such domains can negatively impact future brand reputation and search engine performance. Good domain names are in high demand and short supply, so once you've identified your ideal domain, register it as soon as possible to prevent others from getting it first.

A good domain name balances memorability, spellability, and brand relevance, directly impacting user recall and trust. While keywords are no longer a direct ranking factor in SEO, relevant and descriptive domain names still help users understand website content, indirectly improving search visibility. Furthermore, the flexibility of a domain name ensures its continued value throughout business development.

5-minute hands-on practice: Brainstorming using a domain name generator

Choosing the perfect domain name isn't easy, but free domain name generators can help you brainstorm efficiently and find ideas that meet your needs. These tools typically support keyword input, generate a large number of relevant domain name suggestions, and check their availability in real time.

The steps for brainstorming using a domain name generator are as follows:

1. Identify core keywords most relevant to your website or business. For example, if you plan to create a blog about baking, you can extract keywords such as `baking`, `desserts`, and `recipes`.
2. Choose a suitable domain name generator. There are many excellent free domain name generators on the market, each with its own characteristics, so it's worth trying a few. Examples include Nameboy, Squarespace Domain Name Generator, Hostinger Domain Name Generator, and Instant Domain Search.
3. Enter keywords in the selected generator (some tools support 1-2 keywords, while others allow longer descriptions) and click the **Generate** or **Search** button to get batch domain name suggestions.
4. Refine your results using filters. Many generators offer filtering features that allow you to narrow your search based on criteria such as domain length, number of words, industry, and style (e.g., "easy to pronounce" or "branded") to match your needs.
5. Check domain availability. The generator usually displays the registration status of each domain directly. If your preferred domain is already taken, the tool will also provide alternatives or recommend different top-level domains.
6. Write down all the domain names you like and then compare them with the selection criteria for good domain names mentioned above. Evaluate each one to see if it is short and easy to remember, easy to spell, has brand potential, and avoids numbers and hyphens. Finally, select the best option.

Choosing a domain registrar

Choosing the right domain registrar is a crucial decision when purchasing a domain name, as it directly impacts the domain management experience, long-term usage costs, and security. The following are some key factors to consider when selecting a domain registrar:

- **Reputation and Qualification:** Choose a reputable registrar certified by **ICANN** (**Internet Corporation for Assigned Names and Numbers**). You can typically verify this by looking for the 'ICANN Accredited' logo at the bottom of the registrar's homepage or by searching the official directory on ICANN.org. ICANN certification is a core guarantee for the compliant operation of a registrar and can help avoid the risks of encountering fraudulent service providers or having your domain name stolen.

- **Transparent pricing structure:** Domain registrars often offer attractive first-year registration prices, but many registrars significantly increase renewal prices after the first-year discount ends. Therefore, before making a decision, compare the initial and renewal prices from different registrars to comprehensively assess long-term usage costs and avoid facing high renewal fees later.
- **Privacy protection:** When registering a domain name, personal information (such as name, address, and email) is publicly stored in the WHOIS database by default. Users are vulnerable to spam or harassment. Most registrars offer WHOIS privacy protection services, replacing users' real information with their own contact information, which can be divided into two types:
    - **Provided free of charge:** Registrars such as Namecheap, Dynadot, Porkbun, and GoDaddy offer WHOIS privacy protection as a standard free service.
    - **Additional charges:** Some registrars require a separate fee to provide this feature

  When choosing a registrar, it is important to understand their privacy policy and fees and to prioritize registrars that offer this service for free.
- **Customer support:** For beginners without a technical background, reliable customer support is crucial. Choose a registrar that offers 24/7 support and confirm their support channels (such as live chat, email, or phone). Good customer support can save a lot of time when encountering problems in domain management. For example, GoDaddy has an outstanding reputation for phone support, while Namecheap is known for its fast live chat response and extensive help documentation.
- **User interface and functions:** User-friendly platforms make domain search and management smoother. An ideal registrar should provide intuitive domain search tools with filtering capabilities and reasonable alternative suggestions when the preferred domain is unavailable, reducing filtering costs.
- **Domain name extension (TLD) types:** The more TLDs a registrar offers, the easier it is to find a domain name that fits your brand. Some registrars support hundreds of TLD options, covering generic, country code, and new generic top-level domains to meet the needs of different business scenarios.
- **Additional services and bundled sales:** Most registrars bundle additional services such as website hosting, SSL certificates, and professional email. While one-stop

purchasing is convenient, as we'll see in the practical sections of this book, we generally do not need to purchase these extra services.

- **Domain transfer policy and automatic renewal:** Understand your registrar's domain transfer policy to avoid restrictions when you need to transfer your domain in the future due to changes in needs. At the same time, enable automatic domain renewal or set up expiration reminders to avoid your domain expiring due to forgetting to renew, which could result in hefty recovery fees or even the risk of someone else registering it first.

Choosing the *best* domain registrar requires considering your own needs and budget. Beyond the initial price, you should also thoroughly understand the long-term costs (especially renewal fees), core privacy protection features, and reliable customer support.

5-minute hands-on practice: Complete the domain purchase process

Purchasing a domain name is a crucial step in acquiring a digital identity. Below, we'll use GoDaddy and Namecheap as examples to explain the specific process of buying a domain name in detail. Although the interfaces of different registrars may vary slightly, the core process is similar.

The standard domain purchasing process

Whether you choose GoDaddy, Namecheap, or another reputable registrar, the core purchasing process is virtually identical:

1. **Search**: Visit the registrar's homepage, enter your desired domain name into the search bar, and click **Search**
2. **Select**: If the domain is available, click to add it to your shopping cart
3. **Navigate the Upsells (Crucial Step)**: A pop-up or cart page will prompt you to buy additional products like website hosting, SSL certificates, and professional email. You can safely decline all of these, as we will use free platforms like Vercel to handle them later. The only extra you should accept is domain privacy protection. (Note: Namecheap includes this for free by default, while GoDaddy currently offers a free basic tier you must select.)
4. **Register**: Log in or create a new account with the registrar
5. **Checkout**: Verify your order details, enter your payment information, and complete the purchase

By following these steps and avoiding common mistakes, you can successfully purchase your desired domain name and lay a solid foundation for your online journey.

5-minute hands-on lesson: Connecting a domain to the Vercel project

After purchasing the domain name, you need to associate it with your website project on Vercel. The key here is configuring the domain's DNS records.

Understanding DNS records

When connecting a domain name to the Vercel project, two types of DNS records are mainly used, and their functions are clearly defined.

- **Address Record (A)**: Point a top-level domain (also known as a root domain, such as `yourdomain.com`) to a specific IP address
- **CNAME record (Canonical Name Record):** Point a subdomain (such as `blog.yourdomain.com`, `www.yourdomain.com`) to another domain (instead of an IP address)

DNS configuration acts as a bridge between a domain name and a website server. Correctly selecting and configuring A records or CNAME records are crucial for smooth website access.

Connect the domain name to the Vercel project

The following are the detailed steps to connect your domain to the Vercel project.

Step 1: Add a domain name to the Vercel project

1. Log in to your Vercel account, go to the target project for the domain you want to connect, click the **Settings** tab, and then select **Domains**.
2. Next, click **Add Domain**, enter the domain name you purchased (e.g., `yourdomain.com`), and complete the confirmation.

Vercel will automatically match the appropriate DNS configuration values based on the type of domain you add. For top-level domains, the system will provide the IP address required for the A record; for subdomains, it will provide the value for the CNAME record. Please be sure to note these configuration values, as they will be used in subsequent steps.

Step 2: Configure DNS records with your domain registrar

1. Log in to your registrar (like GoDaddy or Namecheap) account, find the domain you purchased, and click its corresponding **DNS** or **Manage DNS** option to enter the configuration page.
2. Configure the A record. In the DNS record list, find the record of type A with the name **@**, click the **Edit** button, replace the **Value** field with the IP address provided by Vercel,

and save the changes. After that, when users access your domain directly, they will be correctly redirected to the Vercel-hosted website.

3. Configure the CNAME record. Locate the record of type CNAME and name `www`, click **Edit**, replace the **Value** field with the CNAME value provided by Vercel (usually `cname.vercel-dns.com`), and then save the changes. This way, users can access the website correctly regardless of whether they enter `yourdomain.com` or `www.yourdomain.com`.

Step 3: Wait for DNS propagation to take effect

After completing the *Step 2* configurations, return to the **Domain** settings page of the Vercel project.

DNS changes need to be propagated globally (i.e., DNS propagation), a process that takes varying amounts of time, from a few minutes to 48 hours, depending on how quickly the DNS server caches in different locations are updated.

During DNS propagation, accessing a domain name may result in error messages such as "*inaccessible*" or "*page not found.*" This is perfectly normal and nothing to worry about. You can monitor the propagation progress using online DNS check tools or periodically try accessing the domain name to confirm its status.

Once the Vercel interface displays the domain status as **Ready**, the configuration is successful, and the website can be accessed normally through the custom domain.

What to expect: Vercel's automated perks

Before we wrap up the domain setup, there are two special considerations that highlight the power of the Vercel platform:

- **Zero-Config for Vercel Domains**: If you purchased your domain directly from Vercel instead of a third-party registrar like GoDaddy, you could skip the manual DNS configuration steps entirely. Vercel automatically links the domain to your project.
- **Automatic Security (SSL Certificates)**: Whether your domain comes from a third party or Vercel, the platform automatically issues and manages a free SSL certificate for you the moment it connects. You do not need to configure anything to achieve a secure (HTTPS) connection for your users.

Troubleshooting: Solutions to common problems

If your domain is not connecting properly, prioritize checking the following common causes

- **DNS record configuration error**: Verify that parameters such as IP address and CNAME value are entered accurately

- **DNS propagation incomplete**: Wait patiently for DNS propagation to complete globally, which can take up to 48 hours
- **The domain name has been bound**: Confirm whether the domain name is associated with other Vercel accounts. You need to unbind the domain name before proceeding.

DNS configuration is a core element in the connection between a domain name and a website server, and DNS propagation delay is the most common and unavoidable issue. Understanding this characteristic in advance and reasonably anticipating latency can effectively improve the smoothness of a website's launch.

Summary

Owning and configuring a dedicated domain name is the cornerstone for individuals or businesses to establish a unique online identity. This section started with the basic concept of a domain name, comparing it to a website's "address" on the internet, and explained how it uses DNS to translate complex IP addresses into easily remembered names.

We discussed that a well-chosen domain name can enhance brand professionalism, build user trust, give you complete control over your online image, and serve as a cost-effective marketing tool. When selecting a domain name, priority should be given to its brevity, memorability, and brand relevance, while also considering its long-term development potential.

We also learned about the importance of choosing the right domain registrar. Beyond focusing on the initial registration price, it's essential to thoroughly compare renewal prices, WHOIS privacy policies, and the quality of customer support. For beginners, a registrar with a user-friendly interface and reliable support often provides better overall value than simply choosing the lowest price.

Finally, connecting the purchased domain name to the website project deployed on platforms like Vercel is the last step in launching the website. Understanding the role of A records and CNAME records, making meticulous configurations, and being patient will allow you to give your digital home its own unique "address" and officially begin its online journey.

Now that your application has an online address and hosting platform, the next step is building the backend infrastructure that powers your data and user management.

In-depth Supabase practice: Building your digital headquarters

You have a brilliant business idea; it could be an innovative online community, an efficient project management tool, or a beautifully designed personal portfolio website. You've built a stunning *storefront* (frontend user interface) that looks beautiful and has a smooth interface, but new questions arise: Where is user registration information stored? How is user-posted content securely protected? How is product inventory updated in real time? Who can view the sales data in the backend?

The answers to these questions all point to the core behind the application: the backend. The backend is a combination of the "logistics department," "security department," "archives," and "central data center" of digital business. In the traditional model, building such a digital headquarters requires hiring an expensive team of engineers. From system design, server configuration, and database setup to writing business logic and security rules, the entire process takes months or even years, making it prohibitively expensive.

This has deterred countless entrepreneurs and creators. But we are about to bridge this chasm by using Supabase. Supabase has prepared a top-of-the-line modular "headquarters building kit" for you. You can assemble these powerful features according to your blueprint, like building modules, and have a world-class digital headquarters in just a few hours.

In this section, we'll use "building a *digital headquarters*" as a central metaphor to guide you through a complete hands-on Supabase toolchain project. Together, we'll understand what Supabase is, analyze its core functions, create data tables, understand table relationships, set up user authentication, deploy row-level security, and finally activate its file storage.

Supabase and the open-source backend era

Before we begin construction, let's get to know our "building material" – Supabase: what it is, what it consists of, and why it is the best choice for building a *digital headquarters*.

In technical terms, Supabase is an open-source **Backend-as-a-Service** (**BaaS**) platform. BaaS is a type of service that packages complex backend infrastructure, such as databases, user authentication, and file storage, into ready-made services that you can use directly, significantly saving time and costs.

In the BaaS field, there is a very well-known market leader, **Firebase**, owned by Google. It is powerful, stable, and reliable, much like a top-tier office building located in a prime downtown location. However, it is *proprietary* or *closed-source*. This means that as a tenant, you will never see the building's blueprints or customize its structure. More importantly, all your business and data will be deeply tied to this platform. Once the service provider decides to significantly increase prices or change service terms, "moving" will be an extremely painful and complex undertaking (this is known in the industry as *vendor lock-in*).

Now, Supabase positions itself as "an open-source alternative to Firebase," with *open-source* being the key word.

What open source means

Here's what open source means for the user:

- **Transparency**: You can examine and understand the operating logic of each system; there is no black box operation
- **Control**: You can theoretically make any modifications to the system you want, since you have the blueprints in hand
- **Freedom**: You are not tied to the cloud hosting platform provided by Supabase. If you are not satisfied with it, or if your business grows to a certain scale and you want to have complete independent control, you can bring your blueprints and "relocate" the entire *digital headquarters* to your own server intact (i.e., private deployment or self-hosting). You always have a fallback plan, which significantly reduces the risk of 'vendor lock-in'

This reflects a shift from relying on closed services provided by large tech companies to embracing open, transparent solutions that grant developers maximum freedom. For founders without a technical background, this means that the company's core assets, like data and backend infrastructure, are no longer solely controlled by a single tech giant; you truly own your digital assets.

Core functional modules

Now, let's step into this brand-new *digital headquarters* and see what ready-to-use, collaborative "core departments" and "infrastructure" it is equipped with, which will provide comprehensive support for our digital business.

Database: Central archives at headquarters

Before exploring the various functional modules of Supabase, let's focus on the database, which is the most crucial part. After all, no matter how sophisticated the frontend interface is, it ultimately needs a reliable platform to store and manage data.

This is the "heart" of the digital headquarters—a huge, secure, and well-organized central archive. All of the company's core information is stored here in a structured format. Each "table" is like a clearly labeled filing cabinet, and each row of data in the cabinet is a specific file.

Supabase database is built on PostgreSQL, the world's most advanced open-source relational database. PostgreSQL has a history of over 30 years and is renowned for its stability, powerful features, and extremely high reliability.

User authentication: Headquarters access control system

Ensuring that only authorized personnel can access the digital headquarters is necessary. This requires a robust identity verification and access control system.

This is the security reception desk at the headquarters entrance, equipped with a high-tech identity recognition and access control system. It is responsible for managing the entry and exit of all personnel: processing onboarding procedures (registration), verifying employee ID cards (login), and finely controlling the areas that employees at different levels can access (access control).

Auth (short for Authentication) significantly simplifies this complex security system, natively supporting email password login, Magic Links, and one-click login via social media platforms like Google and GitHub. You can easily enable or disable various login methods with simple configuration in the backend.

API: Headquarters' internal communication network

With a secure *central archive* and a robust *access control system* in place, the digital headquarters also needs an efficient *internal communication network* to ensure smooth information exchange between departments. This is where APIs come in.

The **API** (**Application Programming Interface**) serves as the headquarters' internal and external communication system, functioning like an internal telephone and email office. When the company lobby (frontend application) needs to retrieve or submit information from the central archives (database), it initiates a request through the API. After identity and authorization verification, the API returns the corresponding result, ensuring the orderly and secure exchange of information.

This is a powerful feature of Supabase. The moment you create a data table, Supabase automatically configures a complete set of secure, standard RESTful APIs for it. This saves engineers a significant amount of time writing interface code in traditional development and results in a substantial improvement in efficiency.

Real-time subscription: Headquarters' real-time monitoring center

A core requirement of modern digital business is *real-time* operation; that is, users expect to receive the latest information, whether it's new messages on social media, real-time editing of collaborative documents, or inventory updates on e-commerce platforms, all of which require digital headquarters to have strong "real-time awareness" capabilities.

Imagine a headquarters security center with a huge real-time monitoring screen that shows everything happening in the building—new documents are stored in the central archives, new visitors arrive at the front desk, and all changes are captured instantly.

Supabase's real-time engine relies on PostgreSQL's log listening capabilities to closely monitor various database changes. Whenever data is created, updated, or deleted, the system immediately detects this signal and pushes the message to all listening frontend applications via the WebSocket broadcast system, providing powerful support for building chat applications and real-time collaboration platforms.

Cloud functions: Headquarters' automated intelligent assistant

In addition to these core infrastructures, digital headquarters also need some *intelligent* backend services to handle complex business logic and automated tasks—this is where cloud functions come in.

Cloud Functions is the headquarters' *robot assistant team* that automatically executes preset tasks in the background, such as sending welcome emails when new users register and generating sales reports every midnight. This team operates efficiently without human intervention.

Supabase Functions allows you to write standalone server-side code (currently compatible with TypeScript/JavaScript). These code snippets are your robot assistants, specifically designed to handle asynchronous, automated background tasks.

Document storage: Secure warehouse at headquarters and global logistics services

Finally, a digital headquarters also needs dedicated space to store and manage *unstructured* digital assets, such as logo images, employee avatars, and product videos. This is where the value of a file storage system comes in.

Supabase Storage not only provides this *repository* but also bundles a **Content Delivery Network** (**CDN**) service. A CDN acts like a global super-logistics network; when files are stored in a central repository, the CDN automatically distributes copies of the files to *frontend nodes* around the world. When overseas users need to access files, the system automatically retrieves the files from the nearest node, greatly improving file loading speed and user experience.

To help you understand these core modules more intuitively, we have compiled *Table 3.2* for quick reference.

Supabase functional modules	**Metaphor for the core departments of the digital headquarters**
Database	Central Archives (built on robust PostgreSQL)
User authentication (auth)	Security reception and access control systems

Supabase functional modules	Metaphor for the core departments of the digital headquarters
API	Internal communication network (telephone and email systems)
Real-time subscription	Real-time monitoring center (real-time information flow)
Cloud functions	Automated intelligent assistants (robotic service team)
File storage	Secure warehousing and global logistics services (with built-in CDN)

Table 3.2 – Digital Headquarters Department Guide

This comprehensive tour should have given you a clear understanding of the powerful capabilities of this *digital headquarters*. Next, we'll discuss why Supabase is the best choice among many options.

Why choose Supabase?

When deciding to build a *digital headquarters* for your business, you'll face a critical strategic choice. Several mainstream options are available, and analyzing them will help you understand why Supabase is the wisest choice:

- **Build it from scratch:** This is equivalent to hiring a large team of engineers to build the headquarters from the ground up. While this would give you 100% control and allow for customization of every detail, the cost is exorbitant and the development cycle is lengthy, making it extremely risky. For the vast majority of startups and individual creators, this is virtually impossible.
- **Use a closed-source BaaS platform**, such as Google's Firebase: This is like moving into a top-notch business center with excellent facilities and services; after signing the contract, you immediately have a fully functional office and can quickly start your business. Its advantages are fast startup and stable and reliable service. However, the core problem is that you are a tenant, not an owner. You must abide by all the service provider's rules and cannot change its internal structure. Even more fatal is the risk of vendor lock-in.

- **The Supabase solution:** This is like a prefabricated headquarters module, which can be quickly assembled like building blocks. It combines the advantages of the previous two solutions while avoiding their disadvantages. In terms of speed and convenience, it can be started and run quickly, just like Firebase. But the most crucial difference lies in ownership and control. You have complete control, which means you have the freedom to *move* at any time. In the future, if your business grows or you are dissatisfied with Supabase's official cloud services, you can take the blueprints and migrate the digital headquarters to any server, eliminating any concerns about vendor lock-in.

Behind this choice lies a deeper logic that is crucial for non-technical founders: Supabase is essentially a risk management tool. Starting a digital business is inherently uncertain. Choosing a closed platform like Firebase increases "platform risk," while building from scratch exposes you to significant "execution risk." Supabase, however, cleverly mitigates both risks by being open source and based on the PostgreSQL open standard. It's fast enough to quickly bring your product to market, reducing "execution risk," while simultaneously providing a perpetually open escape route (self-hosting capability), further reducing platform risk.

System architecture analysis: Service ecosystem centered on PostgreSQL

Before we conclude the guided tour, let's take a look at the core *master design blueprint* of this *digital headquarters*.

Many similar platforms are likely built on a patchwork of technologies—one for databases, another for user authentication, a third for real-time communication, and finally glued together with a lot of integration code. This approach can easily lead to inconsistencies within the system, a steep learning curve, and compatibility issues.

Supabase adopts a more elegant and robust architectural philosophy: everything is based on PostgreSQL. All core functional modules are not external attachments independent of the database but rather native "branches" growing from the "trunk" of PostgreSQL.

- **API Gateway**: It directly reads the database structure and automatically translates it into a standard API interface
- **User authentication system**: It cleverly utilizes PostgreSQL's internal and decades-proven role and permission management mechanism
- **Real-time subscription engine**: Directly subscribes to PostgreSQL's internal "write-ahead log", which is the official channel through which the database records all its own changes and is extremely efficient.

- **Line-level security**: This is a core feature of the PostgreSQL database. Supabase provides a user-friendly graphical interface that allows you to easily configure these powerful, native database security policies.

This design brings several benefits:

- **Consistency and stability**: All core functions originate from the same robust kernel, resulting in extremely high consistency and stability of the system.
- **High performance**: Many operations are performed directly at the database level, leveraging the powerful performance of PostgreSQL, which has been optimized over decades
- **Knowledge reuse and value enhancement**: This is especially valuable for beginners. The process of learning Supabase subtly allows you to master PostgreSQL, a universally valuable technology that will remain so for decades to come. The data structures, relationships, and security strategies you learn are all transferable hard skills.

Our *Headquarters Tour* has now concluded. We've learned enough theoretically; it's time to add our first piece of *furniture* to our digital headquarters.

5-minute hands-on practice: Creating a data table in the dashboard

Our newly completed *digital headquarters* is still empty. Our first task is to create the first customized *file cabinet* for the central archive (database): a data table specifically for storing information on all the company's projects.

Before we get started, let's clarify a few core concepts: A **table** is essentially a structured spreadsheet, and the table file itself is a container for storing a type of information (see *Figure 3.16*).

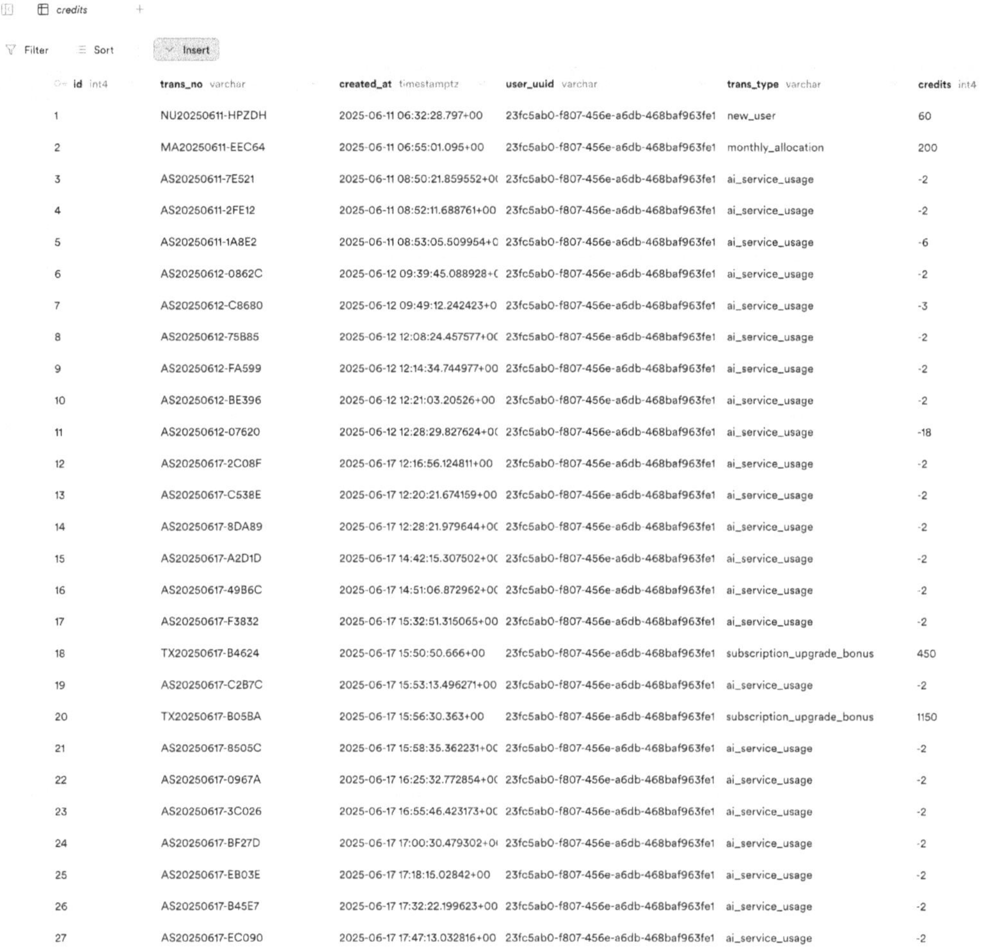

id int4	trans_no varchar	created_at timestamptz	user_uuid varchar	trans_type varchar	credits int4
1	NU20250611-HPZDH	2025-06-11 06:32:28.797+00	23fc5ab0-f807-456e-a6db-468baf963fe1	new_user	60
2	MA20250611-EEC64	2025-06-11 06:55:01.095+00	23fc5ab0-f807-456e-a6db-468baf963fe1	monthly_allocation	200
3	AS20250611-7E521	2025-06-11 08:50:21.859552+0(	23fc5ab0-f807-456e-a6db-468baf963fe1	ai_service_usage	-2
4	AS20250611-2FE12	2025-06-11 08:52:11.688761+00	23fc5ab0-f807-456e-a6db-468baf963fe1	ai_service_usage	-2
5	AS20250611-1A8E2	2025-06-11 08:53:05.509954+0	23fc5ab0-f807-456e-a6db-468baf963fe1	ai_service_usage	-6
6	AS20250612-0862C	2025-06-12 09:39:45.088928+(	23fc5ab0-f807-456e-a6db-468baf963fe1	ai_service_usage	-2
7	AS20250612-C8680	2025-06-12 09:49:12.242423+0	23fc5ab0-f807-456e-a6db-468baf963fe1	ai_service_usage	-3
8	AS20250612-75B85	2025-06-12 12:08:24.457577+0(	23fc5ab0-f807-456e-a6db-468baf963fe1	ai_service_usage	-2
9	AS20250612-FA599	2025-06-12 12:14:34.744977+00	23fc5ab0-f807-456e-a6db-468baf963fe1	ai_service_usage	-2
10	AS20250612-BE396	2025-06-12 12:21:03.20526+00	23fc5ab0-f807-456e-a6db-468baf963fe1	ai_service_usage	-2
11	AS20250612-07620	2025-06-12 12:28:29.827624+0(	23fc5ab0-f807-456e-a6db-468baf963fe1	ai_service_usage	-18
12	AS20250617-2C08F	2025-06-17 12:16:56.124811+00	23fc5ab0-f807-456e-a6db-468baf963fe1	ai_service_usage	-2
13	AS20250617-C538E	2025-06-17 12:20:21.674159+00	23fc5ab0-f807-456e-a6db-468baf963fe1	ai_service_usage	-2
14	AS20250617-8DA89	2025-06-17 12:28:21.979644+0(	23fc5ab0-f807-456e-a6db-468baf963fe1	ai_service_usage	-2
15	AS20250617-A2D1D	2025-06-17 14:42:15.307502+0(	23fc5ab0-f807-456e-a6db-468baf963fe1	ai_service_usage	-2
16	AS20250617-49B6C	2025-06-17 14:51:06.872962+0(	23fc5ab0-f807-456e-a6db-468baf963fe1	ai_service_usage	-2
17	AS20250617-F3832	2025-06-17 15:32:51.315065+00	23fc5ab0-f807-456e-a6db-468baf963fe1	ai_service_usage	-2
18	TX20250617-B4624	2025-06-17 15:50:50.666+00	23fc5ab0-f807-456e-a6db-468baf963fe1	subscription_upgrade_bonus	450
19	AS20250617-C2B7C	2025-06-17 15:53:13.496271+00	23fc5ab0-f807-456e-a6db-468baf963fe1	ai_service_usage	-2
20	TX20250617-B05BA	2025-06-17 15:56:30.363+00	23fc5ab0-f807-456e-a6db-468baf963fe1	subscription_upgrade_bonus	1150
21	AS20250617-8505C	2025-06-17 15:58:35.362231+0(	23fc5ab0-f807-456e-a6db-468baf963fe1	ai_service_usage	-2
22	AS20250617-0967A	2025-06-17 16:25:32.772854+0(	23fc5ab0-f807-456e-a6db-468baf963fe1	ai_service_usage	-2
23	AS20250617-3C026	2025-06-17 16:55:46.423173+0(	23fc5ab0-f807-456e-a6db-468baf963fe1	ai_service_usage	-2
24	AS20250617-BF27D	2025-06-17 17:00:30.479302+0(	23fc5ab0-f807-456e-a6db-468baf963fe1	ai_service_usage	-2
25	AS20250617-EB03E	2025-06-17 17:18:15.02842+00	23fc5ab0-f807-456e-a6db-468baf963fe1	ai_service_usage	-2
26	AS20250617-B45E7	2025-06-17 17:32:22.199623+00	23fc5ab0-f807-456e-a6db-468baf963fe1	ai_service_usage	-2
27	AS20250617-EC090	2025-06-17 17:47:13.032816+00	23fc5ab0-f807-456e-a6db-468baf963fe1	ai_service_usage	-2

Figure 3.16 – Data table

The header at the top corresponds to a **column**, which is used to define the information category (such as *project name*, *deadline*, *responsible person*, etc.), and each column also specifies the data type (such as text, date, etc.) to ensure consistent formatting. Each row in the table represents a complete individual record.

Now that we've understood these basic concepts, we can start creating data tables:

1. Log in to your Supabase account and go to the project dashboard.
2. In the vertical navigation bar on the left, find the **Table Editor** with the table icon. Click it to enter the data table management page.
3. A green **Create a new table** button appears on the page. Click it to start the creation process of the "File Cabinet."
4. Enter `projects` in the **Name** field (database professionals typically use lowercase for table names to facilitate future collaboration). You can add notes in the **Description** field (such as `used to store all company project information`) to help you quickly understand the table's purpose later.
5. After naming the entries, you need to define columns (or the *file cabinet drawers*). The **Columns** area below the form will automatically add **id** (a unique identifier for each record to ensure data consistency) and **created_at** (a timestamp recording the creation time for easy tracking). Keep these defaults for now. Then, add the specific custom columns we need to store our project data:
   a. Click **Add column**, enter `name`, select **text** as the type, and use it to record the project name.
   b. Click **Add column** again, enter `due_date`, select **date** as the type, and choose **Deadline**.
   c. Finally, click **Add column**, enter status, and select **text** as the type to mark the project status.

   The final result after completing these settings is shown in *Figure 3.17*:

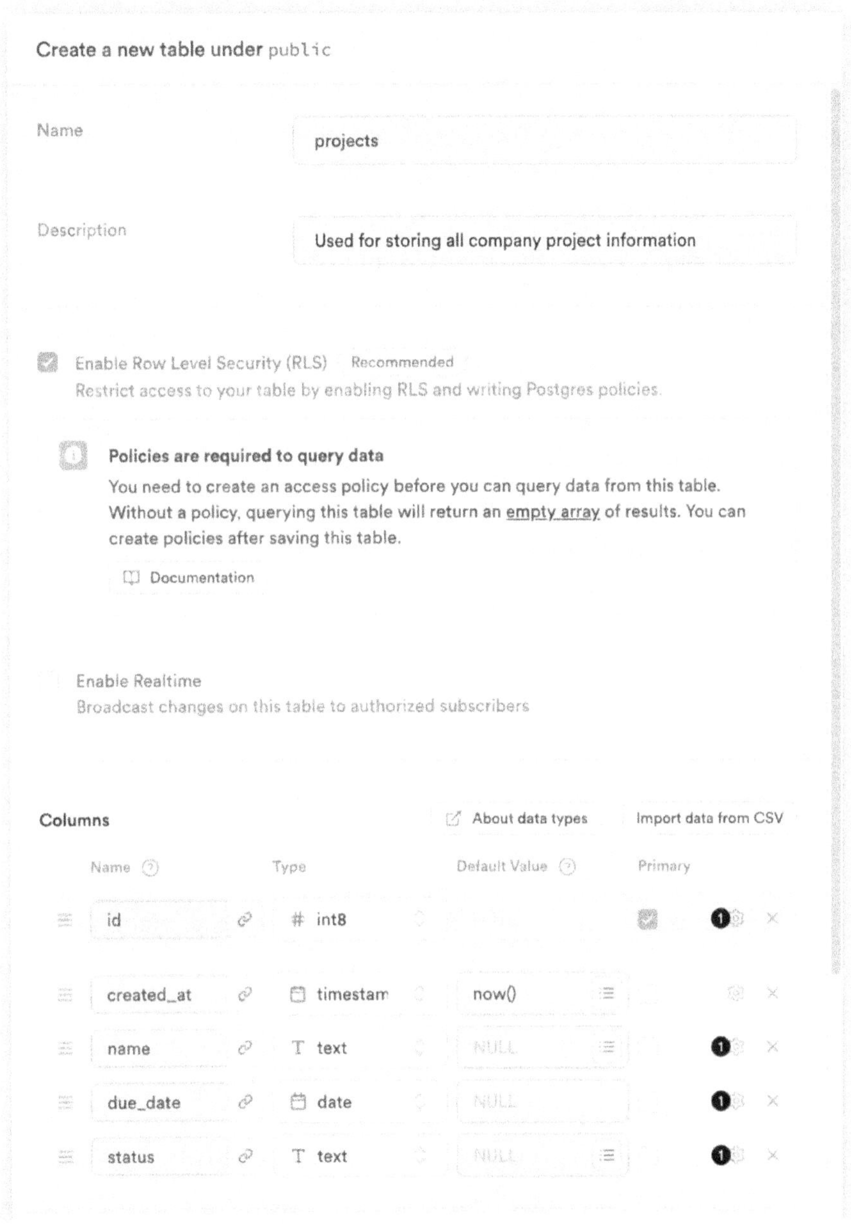

Figure 3.17 – Creating the projects table

6. After verifying that all configurations are correct, click the green **Save** button in the lower right corner of the form. The projects table will appear in the table editor's list a few seconds later.

At this point, you have personally crafted the first piece of custom *furniture* for your digital headquarters, providing a dedicated storage container for subsequent project information.

5-minute practice: Understanding table relationships

A project typically contains many specific *tasks*. A more reasonable approach is to create a separate *file cabinet* specifically for storing these *tasks* and to establish a connection mechanism so that each task clearly belongs to its corresponding project.

Table relationships are a core advantage of relational databases. Just like in a real office, you might label the upper right corner of each sales invoice with a corresponding customer file number. In database terminology, this reference number is known as a **foreign key**. It acts as a digital bridge. By using these foreign keys, two independent tables can be logically connected, forming an efficient data network.

Next, we will create this relationship through the following steps.

1. Make sure you are still in the **Table Editor** area of your Supabase project, then click the **Create a new table** button to build our next "file cabinet"—a data table dedicated to your tasks. Enter `tasks` in the **Name** field to create a data table for storing task information.
2. Retain the `default id` (unique identifier) and `created_at` (creation time) columns, click **Add column** to add a description column, select **text** as the type, and use it to store the specific description of the task.
3. Click **Add column** again to add the `is_complete` column. Select **boolean** as the type (in boolean type, there can only be two values: true or false) to mark whether the task is completed.
4. Create a foreign key (key step): Click **Add column**, enter `project_id` (the naming convention for foreign key columns is "related table name_id"). As we just discussed, this column will act as our digital bridge—it will store the reference number connecting this task back to its parent project. Select **int8** as the type (a sufficiently large integer type), and then click the *chain* icon to the right of the name to establish the relationship.
5. Configure the relationship in the pop-up **Add foreign key relation** window: keep the default **public**, select the **projects** table in the **Select a table to reference to** drop-down menu, and select the unique identifier column **id** in the next drop-down. (Note: You are telling the database to link your new **project_id** column directly to the **projects** table's **id** column.) The final result is shown in *Figure 3.18*:

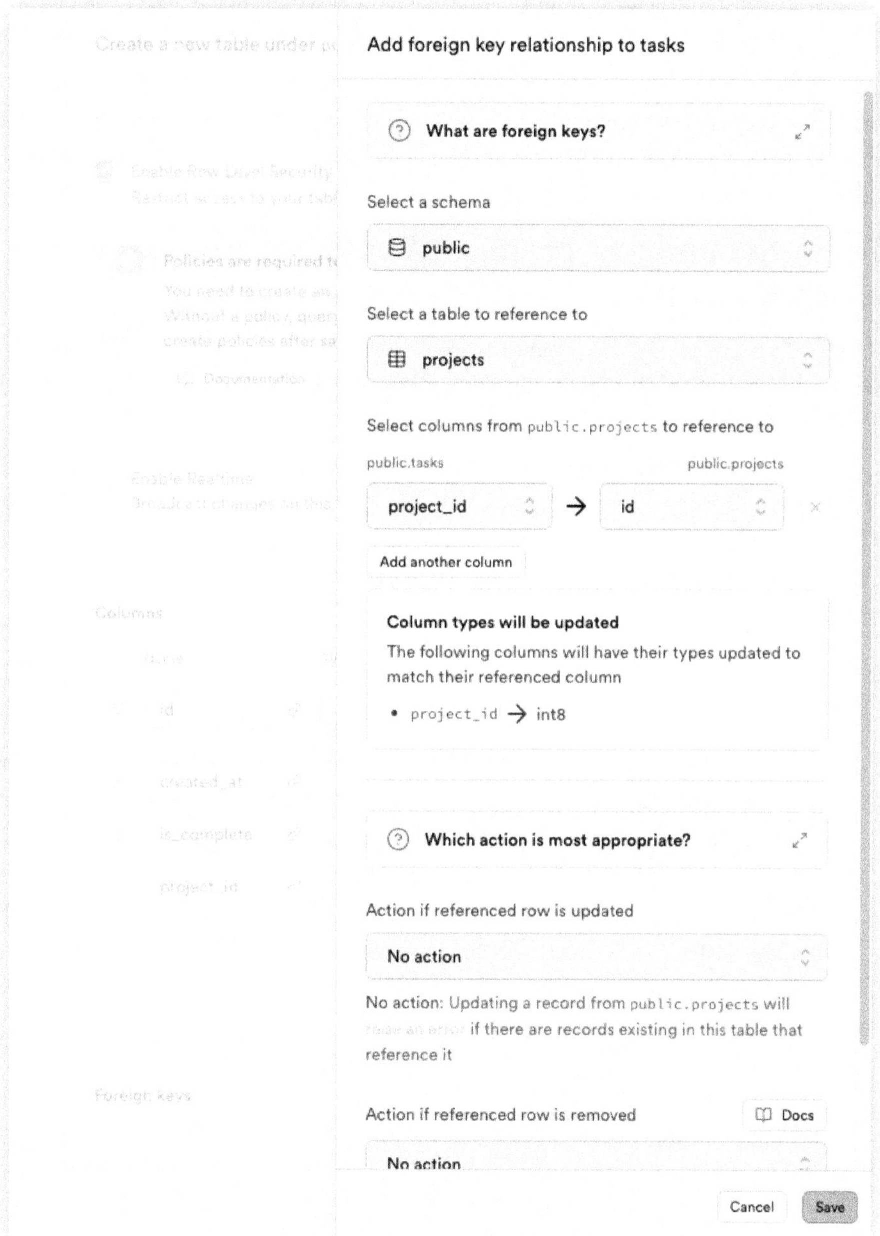

Figure 3.18 – Creating the tasks table

6. After completing all configurations, click the **Save** button to close the relationship configuration window, and then click the green **Save** button in the lower right corner again to save the entire tasks table.

This time, you created a second *file cabinet* of tasks, but more importantly, you built an information bridge between the two tables. One project can correspond to multiple tasks, and each task is assigned to a specific project.

10-minute hands-on practice: Exploring user authentication (Supabase Auth)

Our *digital headquarters* needs a comprehensive security and personnel system to process employee onboarding, issue ID cards, and enable employees to securely enter the building after identity verification.

The core idea of **authentication** is answering the question: *Who are you?* When you log in to a website with a username and password, you are essentially authenticating. Supabase Auth is our professional, *secure front desk* at our digital headquarters; it handles all the complexities related to user authentication, requiring only simple configuration.

The following section demonstrates how to configure this authentication system to give the digital headquarters complete user management capabilities.

1. Log in to the Supabase project dashboard, find the lock icon labeled **Authentication** in the left navigation bar, and click it to enter the authentication management area.
2. Click **Sign In/Providers** in the left-hand submenu of the authentication management page. You will see all the login methods supported by Supabase (see *Figure 3.19*). The **Email** option is enabled by default, supporting traditional email and password registration and login. Scroll down to see icons for social login providers such as Google, GitHub, and Facebook. Simply click the switch and configure it to allow users to log in with these accounts with one click.

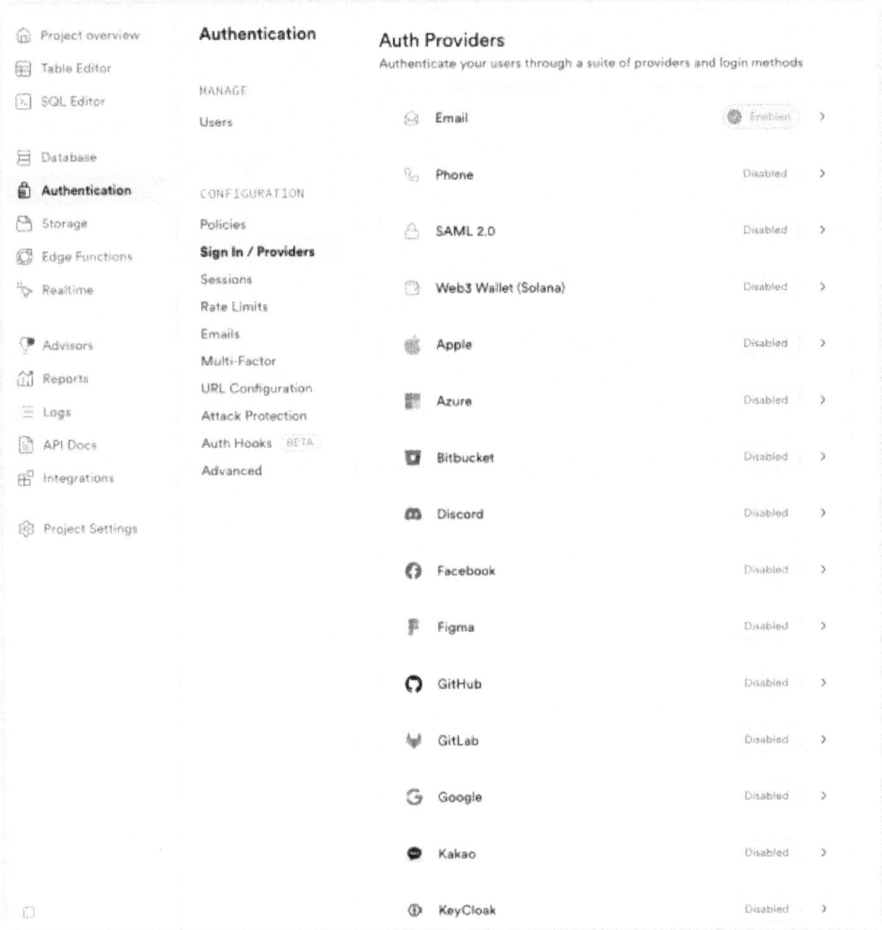

Figure 3.19 – Authentication management page

3. In a real application, users will register themselves. For ease of testing, Supabase allows administrators to add users directly in the backend. On the authentication management page, click **Users** in the left-hand submenu, then click **Add user** in the upper right corner. Enter your test email address in the **Email** field, set your password in the **Password** field, and finally click the **Create user** button to complete the creation.

4. After the pop-up window is closed, the newly created "new employee" will appear in the user list. The system has automatically generated a unique UID (user identifier) for them, as shown in *Figure 3.20*.

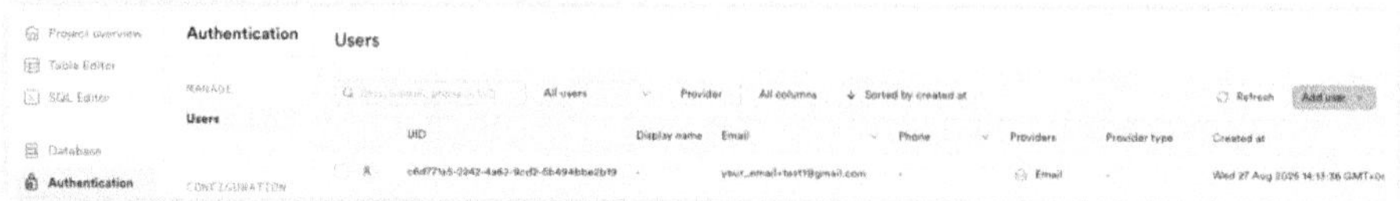

Figure 3.20 – User list

Congratulations, you have completed your first "employee onboarding" process. Supabase Auth uses an irreversible algorithm to encrypt and store passwords and generates a unique identity ID for each user. Our digital headquarters now has its first legally registered employee.

10-minute hands-on practice: Protecting data with RLS

This is the most significant security upgrade to date. Currently, all logged-in users can view and modify all files in the projects *file cabinet*. Our goal is to establish a sophisticated set of security rules to ensure that employees can only view and modify projects they have created.

Row-level security (**RLS**) is a robust security model that pushes security rules down to each row of data. Instead of standing guard at the *archive*, it assigns an invisible "permission label" to every file (each row of data). When a user accesses the data, the system verifies whether their ID card matches the file's permission label. This security check occurs within the database, making it secure and robust.

The following section demonstrates how to configure RLS through practical operation:

1. Assign an owner to the project files. Return to the **Table Editor** and select the `projects` table. Click the **+** icon on the far right of the table header to add a new column named `user_id`. Select **uuid** as the data type (because Supabase user IDs are in this format). Click **Add foreign key** next to **Foreign Key**, and in the pop-up window, set the Schema to **auth**, the Table to `users`, and the Column to `id`. Save this relationship and then save all changes to the table.
2. Go to the **Security Strategy Center**. In the main navigation bar on the left, find the shield-shaped icon for **Authentication**, click it to enter, and then click **Policies** in the submenu on the left.
3. Locate the projects table on the policy management page and click the **Enable RLS** button on the right (if you only see the **Disable RLS** button initially, it means it's already enabled by default). Note that the default *deny all* rule will immediately take effect upon enabling RLS, preventing anyone from accessing data in the projects table via the API. This is a best practice in security design: close all doors first, then selectively open them.
4. Create the first security policy. Click **Create Policy** in the upper right corner of the projects table.
5. Select a policy template. Scroll through the template list and select the last one, **Enable users to view their own data only**, then click to enter, as shown in *Figure 3.21*.

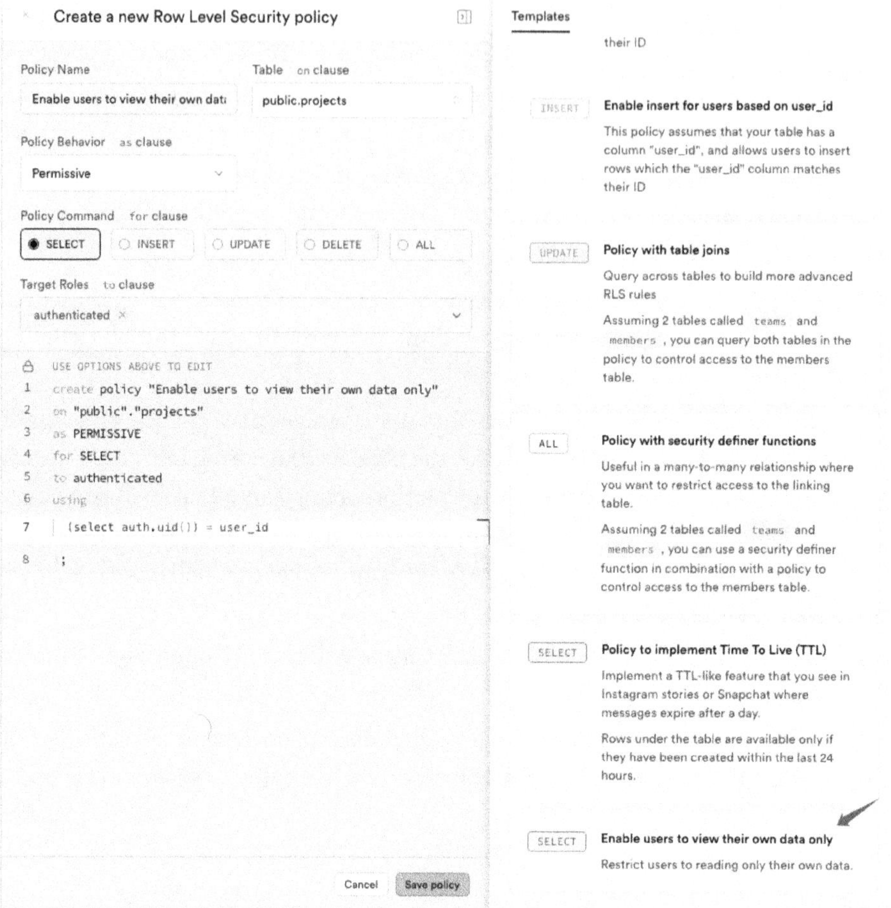

Figure 3.21 – Creating an RLS policy

6. In the policy configuration interface, make the following settings: Enter a clear name for the Policy name, such as `Users can only view their own projects`; select **SELECT** (read/query data) under **Policy Command for clause**; modify the `USING` expression in the specific policy text to `(select auth.uid()) = user_id` (core logic), as shown in the text example on the left side of *Figure 3.20*.

   The expression `(select auth.uid()) = user_id` means that a user is allowed to read the data in a row only if the unique ID (`auth.uid()`) of the currently logged-in user matches the value of the `user_id` column in the data row.

7. Save and review the policy. Click the **Save policy** button to save the current policy.
8. Establish other operation strategies. Configure the rules for **INSERT**, **UPDATE**, and **DELETE** operations according to similar logic as follows.
   - **Create (INSERT) strategy:** Select **INSERT** and set **WITH CHECK** expression to (select `auth.uid()) = user_id`).
   - **UPDATE and DELETE strategies:** Select **UPDATE** and **DELETE,** respectively and set the **USING** expression to `(select auth.uid()) = user_id`.

You have completed an enterprise-grade security configuration! RLS directly binds security logic to data, and rules remain in effect once defined. Supabase, through a user-friendly visual interface, allows you to easily implement complex security settings that previously required experienced database administrators.

10-minute hands-on practice: File storage and CDN distribution

Our project management tools also need to handle various file attachments such as project requirement documents, design drafts, and demonstration videos. This necessitates enabling a central, secure repository (Supabase Storage) for headquarters.

Supabase Storage is designed specifically for storing and managing unstructured data (i.e., files in various formats) and can be viewed as a giant warehouse. To achieve organized management, the warehouse can be divided into different zones, each dedicated to storing a specific type of file; these zones are called **buckets**. When creating a bucket, its public or private attribute must be specified: files in public buckets can be accessed simply through a link, while files in private buckets require strict access control. Even more powerfully, Supabase Storage comes with a built-in CDN value-added service—after a file is uploaded, Supabase automatically caches a copy of the file on global edge node servers via the CDN, significantly improving file loading speed.

The following section demonstrates how to configure this file storage system to add powerful file management capabilities to the digital headquarters.

1. In the main navigation bar on the left side of the Supabase dashboard, find the bucket icon for **Storage** and click it to enter the storage management area.
2. Click **New bucket** and enter `project-files` in the **Bucket name** field. Check the **Public bucket** option (in a real project, files that need protection should be set to private, and access policies should be configured). Click the **Create bucket** button to complete the creation.

3. Click the created `project-files` bucket, then click **Upload file**, select any file from your computer, and complete the upload.
4. Get the public link to the file. Hover your mouse over the uploaded file, click the **Get URL** icon on the right, and then click the **Copy button** in the pop-up window to copy the link to your clipboard.
5. Open a new browser tab, paste the copied link into the address bar, and press *Enter*. The file will load instantly. This link points to Supabase's CDN network. Users can access the file at extremely fast speeds, no matter where they are.

You have successfully configured a warehousing and logistics system for your digital headquarters. What you gain is more than just storage addresses; your files are automatically served through a **Content Delivery Network** (**CDN**), which caches them on servers closer to your users for faster loading. In traditional development, configuring a CDN requires additional steps and costs, but Supabase seamlessly integrates it into the storage functionality.

Summary

Just about an hour ago, you were faced with the abstract concept of a *backend* and an empty Supabase project panel; now, take a look at the results of your own creation.

Your project now has the following:

- A complete relational database: containing projects and tasks tables with clear logical relationships, serving as the core blueprint for business data
- An enterprise-grade security protection system: user authentication is enabled, sophisticated row-level security policies are configured, and users can only access their own data
- A powerful file storage and distribution system: storage space can be expanded infinitely, and with global CDN acceleration, files can be loaded quickly from anywhere in the world

Most importantly, all of this was done without writing a single line of code.

You have successfully built a robust, reliable, and fully functional *digital headquarters*. This is the power of modern BaaS platforms like Supabase: they flatten the steep barriers of backend development, enabling every creative person to bridge the technology gap and turn their ideas into reality.

Through this hands-on experience, you have mastered the core logic and key skills for building modern digital products. In the next chapter, we will open the door to the application's 'digital kitchen,' exploring how to team up with AI assistants like TRAE SOLO and Cursor to build a powerful backend engine that brings your ideas to life.

Get this book's PDF version and more

Scan the QR code (or go to `packtpub.com/unlock`). Search for this book by name, confirm the edition, and then follow the steps on the page.

UNLOCK NOW

Note: Keep your invoice handy. Purchases made directly from Packt don't require an invoice.

Backend Development and Advanced Integration

If the frontend is the restaurant's elegant facade, the back end is the mysterious kitchen that determines success or failure.

In this chapter, we will open the door to the *backend*. This is the lifeblood of the entire application, including how data is stored, how business operations run, how security is ensured, and how efficiency is improved. These unseen processes are the key to upgrading a simple webpage into a professional-grade application.

With AI by your side, you will experience a completely new way of backend development: no need to memorize complex database syntax, worry about server configuration, or struggle with API interface design. From TRAE SOLO's self-designed architecture to Cursor's precise code generation, and then to MCP's advanced integration, you have an all-powerful AI backend engineer team.

By the end of this chapter, you will have learnt the core skills to build any type of complex application. More importantly, you'll discover that even technically intensive backend development can be full of creative fun.

In-depth practical training on TRAE SOLO

In previous chapters, we've explored TRAE SOLO's capabilities as an AI frontend designer, learning how to quickly transform an idea into an interactive user interface through dialogue and visual editing.

However, the core competitiveness of any successful application stems from its unseen backend. The backend is crucial in determining product quality, operational efficiency, and even security.

Backend development is responsible for handling all the work that is invisible to the user but crucial. It requires a database to manage data, business logic to process user requests, algorithms to implement core functionalities, and a reliable **application programming interface** (**API**) so that the frontend can communicate accurately with the backend system.

This is a completely different field from frontend development, which focuses on visual presentation and user interaction. Traditionally, backend development is a field with high technical barriers and strict requirements for logical thinking and system design capability.

This section will guide us through the role transition from frontend to backend. We will refer to TRAE SOLO simply as *SOLO*. We will focus on SOLO's capabilities as an AI backend engineer, exploring how to direct it to build a fully functional, secure, and reliable backend system.

The entire process of self-developed backend

While we've already experienced SOLO's automated workflows in frontend development, the focus differs in backend scenarios. Now, let's re-examine SOLO's capabilities in this area from the perspective of a backend architect.

Requirements analysis and document generation

Every project begins with a blueprint. In backend development, this blueprint is a rigorous PRD that defines the system's structure and functional specifications in detail.

Unlike frontend PRDs, which focus on visual presentation, backend PRDs are centered on what *the system* can *do*, as well as how *it* manages *and* controls *its data flow*. It must clearly define the following content:

- **Functional modules:** What core functionalities does the system need (e.g., user management, article publishing, comment system)?
- **User roles and permissions:** What types of users are there (e.g., visitors, registered users, administrators), and what operational permissions do they each have?
- **Data entities and relations:** What core data does the system need to process (e.g., users, articles, comments), and what are the relationships between them (e.g., a user can have multiple articles, and an article can have multiple comments)?
- **Business rules:** What specific logical rules does the system need to follow (for example, users can only publish a maximum of 5 articles per day, and comments cannot exceed 500 characters)?

For non-technical people, writing such a structured document from scratch can be quite challenging. However, you can simply express your ideas using natural language. For example:

```
Design a backend for my personal blog system. The system needs to support three
user roles: visitors, registered users, and administrators. Registered users can
```

```
publish and manage their own articles and comment on others' articles.
Administrators have all permissions. Articles need to include a title, content,
and publication date. I hope to eventually provide an API for the frontend to use.
```

Upon receiving the instruction, SOLO will launch its Doc tool to transform your natural language description into a well-structured and logically rigorous backend PRD. This AI-generated document will clearly define all functional modules, data entities, and core business rules, serving as a blueprint for backend development.

Environment configuration and dependency management

Once the blueprint is completed, we need to set up the development environment and prepare the necessary tools. This process is called *environment configuration*, and its core is selecting a suitable *technology stack*.

A technology stack can be understood as a complete set of development tools.

- **Programming language:** Such as Java, Python, or Node.js
- **Framework:** Standardized development tools and processes, such as Spring (Java) or Django (Python)
- **Database:** Systems used for storing and managing data, such as relational databases like PostgreSQL or document-oriented databases like MongoDB
- **Web server:** Software responsible for receiving and processing network requests, such as Nginx or Apache

For developers (especially beginners), configuring the environment is a complex and error-prone process. Issues such as version conflicts between different tools, missing dependencies, or differences in operating systems can hinder the development process.

SOLO significantly simplifies this process. It analyzes the requirements defined in the PRD and automatically selects the most suitable technology stack. For example, if your application needs to handle a large number of real-time messages (such as online chat), it might prioritize Node.js because it excels at handling high-concurrency I/O operations.

Once the technology stack is determined, SOLO will execute all necessary commands in the terminal panel to install the language environment, download frameworks, and configure database connections. A professional and stable backend development environment can be prepared in a short time.

Coding and error correction

Once SOLO has configured your development environment, the core coding phase begins. This process involves translating the details in the blueprint into precise programming instructions.

In this step, SOLO reads through the generated PRD and technical design documents one by one, transforming each requirement—whether it's "create a user registration interface" or "implement a complex permission verification logic"—into high-quality, runnable backend code. In addition, SOLO has a closed-loop workflow of "self-checking and repair." After writing code, it will immediately try to run it in the terminal, such as starting a server or executing unit tests.

Once the terminal outputs an error message (such as an `ECONNREFUSED` error indicating a database connection failure or a `SyntaxError`), it will immediately pause the current task, analyze the error log, understand the cause, and then modify the code independently until the problem is resolved.

While SOLO automatically catches terminal errors, some issues only appear during real-world use. If you encounter external errors—such as a red warning in the browser console during manual testing, a failed API response, or an error log from a third-party platform like Supabase—you can simply paste that information directly into the chat. SOLO will analyze the clues, locate the root cause, and independently rewrite the code to provide a solution, all without breaking your existing features.

Local testing and preview

Once the software is developed, it must undergo rigorous testing and preview.

Backend testing is less intuitive than frontend testing. Frontend test results can mostly be observed directly in the browser, while backend test results usually appear as terminal outputs (such as JSON data) or as changes to database records.

However, SOLO's integrated workspace includes a built-in browser tool, making the testing and acceptance process more intuitive and efficient. While SOLO is building functional logic on the backend, it can simultaneously render an interactive frontend interface in the built-in browser to call these backend APIs. This means you don't need to wait for all the work to be completed, nor do you need specialized API testing tools to view the AI's work in real time.

For example, once SOLO completes the backend API for user login functionality, a login screen will appear in your browser. You can try it yourself, enter the correct or incorrect password, observe the application's response, and check the server logs to verify that the backend logic meets expectations.

Deployment and go-live

Once all functionalities have passed acceptance testing and the backend services are running stably, the application can be published to the internet for global users to access. This process is called **deployment**.

Previously, deployment was a complex technical task that required configuring servers, managing domain names, setting up security certificates, configuring firewalls, and handling CI/CD pipelines, and it was usually handled by dedicated operations engineers (DevOps).

SOLO further simplifies this process. It deeply integrates with mainstream cloud deployment platforms such as Vercel. Once you've confirmed the functionality is complete, simply provide a simple prompt, such as:

```
Functional testing is complete. Please deploy the backend service of this blog
website to Vercel.
```

SOLO automatically handles all the complex deployment processes: packaging the code, configuring the server environment, handling environment variables, and deploying. A few minutes later, you'll have a public API service address. At this point, the entire development lifecycle, from an idea to a fully functional online backend system, is complete.

5-minute hands-on lesson: Integrating Supabase

When building the backend, we can use Backend-as-a-Service (BaaS) platforms, such as Supabase. These platforms provide comprehensive infrastructure, allowing developers to focus on developing core business logic.

Now that we have a basic understanding of Supabase, let's get straight to the point and see how to get SOLO to take over and operate this powerful backend platform through dialog.

Quickly integrate Supabase using SOLO

Connecting SOLO to your Supabase account is incredibly simple; authorization is completed with just a few clicks in SOLO's **Integrations** panel. This secure OAuth-based process grants SOLO direct access to your Supabase projects, enabling AI to fully take over your backend infrastructure.

Database operations using SOLO

Before understanding database operations, let's clarify a core concept. Regardless of the tool used, basic database operations can be summarized as **CRUD**, namely **Create, Read, Update, and Delete**. We can understand these four types of operations using the scenario of managing a mobile phone's address book.

- **Create:** Add a new contact
- **Read**: Find the phone number of a specific contact
- **Update**: Change contact information
- **Delete:** Delete someone you are no longer in contact with

In the past, to perform these four types of database operations, developers needed to be familiar with professional database query languages such as SQL and write specific code. Even if they relied on the backend interface of a platform like Supabase, they still needed to configure parameters one by one in a complex operation panel, which not only had a technical threshold but also consumed additional time.

However, connecting to SOLO simplifies the workflow: there's no need to learn SQL or frequently switch to the Supabase backend interface. Simply enter natural language commands in SOLO's chat box to easily complete various CRUD operations. For example, to "add a new project record" (create) or "view all incomplete projects" (read), you can describe your needs using everyday conversational language. SOLO will parse the commands and execute the corresponding database operations, significantly lowering the barrier to database management.

The following are specific examples of describing data manipulation in natural language:

- **Create:** `Create a new table named "products" in Supabase. This table should contain the following: name (product name, text type), price (price, numeric type), and stock (stock, integer type).`
- **Create**: `Add a new record to the products table: the product name is "AI Smart Coffee Machine", the price is $999, and the inventory is 50.`
- **Read**: `Retrieve information on all products in the products table with a price below 1000 yuan.`
- **Update**: `The price of the "AI Smart Coffee Machine" has been changed to $899.`
- **Delete**: `Delete all items with a stock of 0 from the products table.`

When you issue these commands, SOLO translates your intent into SQL queries, executes the commands through a secure connection to Supabase, and finally returns the results in an easy-to-understand manner.

The combination of SOLO and Supabase has changed the interaction mode of backend data management, enabling non-technical personnel to easily manage a powerful database system just like experienced database administrators.

10-minute hands-on practice: Generating TDDs and data models

If the PRD defines *what to do and why*, then the **Technical Design Document** (**TDD**) precisely answers *how to do it*. Like a detailed construction drawing, it clearly describes the system's internal structure and implementation and is especially important in backend development; after all, the backend is the foundation of the entire system.

The importance of TDD

A common misconception is to start coding immediately after receiving the requirements. This is like starting construction without blueprints, which can easily lead to structural problems and wasted time and resources.

The core value of an excellent TDD lies in:

- **Unified consensus**— Ensuring that team members have a unified and accurate understanding of system architecture, technology selection, API contracts, and data flow
- **Anticipating risks**— Thinking ahead and solving potential technical challenges, performance bottlenecks, and security vulnerabilities during the design phase is far more efficient than fixing them after development is complete
- **Development guidance**—Providing developers with clear action guidelines, clarifying the module implementation methods and the interaction logic between modules
- **Easy to maintain**—Helping new members or future maintainers quickly familiarize themselves with the system and avoid introducing serious errors during modifications

However, writing high-quality TDD requires a strong technical foundation and system design capabilities. Fortunately, SOLO is also an excellent AI architect.

Use SOLO to generate TDD

Earlier, we mentioned that SOLO can automatically select the most suitable technology stack based on your PRD, which is highly useful for non-technical users. However, because this is a guided exercise utilizing the *frugal full-stack* methodology we explored in *Chapter 3*, we will explicitly act as the *director* and instruct SOLO to use our chosen environment: Node.js and Express.

Additionally, remember that in the previous *5-Minute Hands-on Lesson: Integrating Supabase* section, we used SOLO's **Integrations** panel to securely link your Supabase account. Therefore, we will also instruct SOLO to use the powerful PostgreSQL database within that newly connected Supabase project.

Let's look at how we structure this prompt:

```
Based on the previously determined PRD for the blog system, generate a detailed
backend technical design document. The technology stack selected is Node.js +
Express, and the database used is the PostgreSQL database within the already
connected Supabase project. The document should include a system architecture
diagram, detailed API definitions, and a complete data model design.
```

A few minutes later, a well-structured and professionally designed TDD document will be generated, typically containing the following core components:

- **System Overview:** Briefly describe the project objectives, scope, and core technology selection.
- **Architecture Design:** Use charts and text to clearly demonstrate the overall structure of the system (such as the interaction methods between different layers).
- **API Definition:** This section lists all APIs in detail, including their paths, request methods, parameters, and expected response data formats. This part is the "contract" for collaboration between the frontend and backend.
- **Data model design:** The most crucial part of TDD will be explained in the following section.

Data model design and implementation

A data model defines the types of data that an application needs to store and the relationships between those data types.

Taking a blog system as an example, a reasonable data model needs to be planned: a "user table" to store user information, an "article table" to store articles, and a "comment table" to store comments. It is also necessary to clearly define the relationships between the data. Here are the types of relationships:

- **One-to-Many:** A user can publish multiple posts. This is the most common relationship type.
- **Many-to-Many:** An article can be associated with multiple tags, and the same tag can be used for multiple articles. This relationship is usually implemented using a *junction table*, a dedicated middleman table whose sole purpose is to record the connections between the other two tables.

When generating TDD, SOLO automatically designs a data model based on business needs, clearly listing the data tables to be created, the columns of each table, their data types, and constraints. *Table 4.1* shows an example data model designed by SOLO for a personal blog system.

Table name	Column name	Data type	Constraint/Description
users	id	uuid	PRIMARY KEY / User unique identifier
	email	text	UNIQUE, NOT NULL / User email
	password hash	text	NOT NULL / Encrypted password
	username	text	UNIQUE/Username
	created_at	timestamptz	DEFAULT now() / Registration time
posts	id	uuid	PRIMARY KEY / Article unique identifier
	author_id	uuid	FOREIGN KEY (foreign key) associated with users.id/ON DELETE CASCADE
	title	text	NOT NULL/Title
	content	text	NOT NULL/Content
	published_at	timestamptz	Release time
comments	id	uuid	PRIMARY KEY / Unique identifier for comments
	post_id	uuid	FOREIGN KEY associated with posts.id/ON DELETE CASCADE
	author_id	uuid	FOREIGN KEY associated with users.id/ON DELETE CASCADE
	comment_text	text	NOT NULL / Comment content
tags	id	uuid	PRIMARY KEY / Unique identifier
	name	text	UNIQUE, NOT NULL / tag name

Table name	Column name	Data type	Constraint/Description
post_tags(Link table)	post_id	uuid	PRIMARY KEY/FOREIGN KEY associated with posts.id/ON DELETE CASCADE
	tag_id	uuid	PRIMARY KEY/FOREIGN KEY associated with tags.id/ON DELETE CASCADE

Table 4.1 – Data model of personal blog system (example)

Note that `ON DELETE CASCADE` is an important data constraint. Its function is to automatically delete all key data referencing that record (such as the user's articles and comments) when the referenced record is deleted (e.g., when a user is deleted), thus ensuring data integrity.

This AI-designed data model has a clear structure and follows best practices in database design. More importantly, you don't need to implement it manually; you can simply issue prompts like the following:

```
Great, proceed with this data
model. Please connect to Supabase, create these five tables for me, and set all
primary keys, foreign keys, and cascading delete constraints.
```

SOLO will then parse the document, generate the corresponding SQL commands, and create these data tables in Supabase.

Document version management

Software development is a dynamic and evolving process. When requirements change, not only does the code need to be modified, but the design documents must also be updated accordingly. Otherwise, the documents will quickly become out of touch with the actual system, becoming **technical debt**. Think of technical debt like a building where the blueprints no longer match the actual plumbing—any future renovations will become confusing, slow, and prone to costly errors.

One advantage of using SOLO is that it always treats documentation and code as an organic whole. When you raise new requirements, it first updates the data model and API definitions in TDD, and then modifies the code based on the updated documentation. This document-driven approach ensures that the design blueprint remains consistent with the final product, laying a solid foundation for the long-term maintenance of the project.

It integrates professional software engineering practices such as documentation writing and pre-design into automated processes, guiding users to follow industry best practices and ultimately create well-structured and easy-to-maintain software products.

10-minute practice: Implementing user authentication and business logic

With a solid database foundation and clear design documents, we can now begin building the core functionality of the backend system.

- **User authentication:** Verify user identity and determine who can access the system and their specific access permissions
- **Business Logic:** The core services provided by an application are typically implemented through a series of APIs

Next, we will learn how SOLO automatically builds these two pillars in a short time.

User authentication

There are several mainstream user authentication technology solutions on the market, which will be explained in a simple and easy-to-understand way below.

- **Session (Session Authentication):** The most traditional method. After a user logs in for the first time with their username and password, the server records their login state and returns a unique identifier (Session ID) to the client. Subsequent client requests carry this identifier, which the server uses to verify the user's identity. This method is *stateful*, meaning the server needs to maintain session information, which makes it difficult to scale in distributed systems.
- **JWT (JSON Web Token):** A more modern approach. After a user successfully logs in, the server generates an encrypted token containing the user's information and returns it to the client. The client carries this token in subsequent requests, and the server only needs to verify the token signature to confirm the user's identity, without needing to store session information on the server. This *stateless* approach has good scalability and is very suitable for modern frontend and backend separated application architectures.
- **OAuth (Open Authorization):** This allows users to log in to your application using accounts from third-party services (such as Google, Facebook, LinkedIn, and WhatsApp). Your application delegates the authentication process to the third-party service, and upon successful authentication, the third-party service authorizes the application to access user information. This is the common practice of "third-party account login."

Table 4.2 compares these authentication methods.

Authentication method	**state**	**"Certificate" storage location ****	**Applicable Scenarios****
Session	In state	server-side	Simple web application
JWT	Stateless	Client	Modern frontend/backend separation, applications, APIs, microservices
OAuth	Stateless	Third-party service providers	Third-party social media account logins and authorized access

Table 4.2 – Comparison of authentication methods

For non-technical users, understanding and choosing the right authentication scheme can be challenging. However, with SOLO, you can simply describe your requirements. Here are the instructions given to SOLO to build an authentication system:

```
Create a complete user authentication function f.or our blog system. Users should
be able to register and log in using an email address and password. JWT should be
used for authentication, and user information should be stored in the users table
in Supabase. Ensure that user passwords are encrypted and stored with the highest
level of security.
```

This instruction clearly defines *what to do* (user authentication), *how to do it* (JWT and Supabase), and the *crucial security requirements* (salted hash processing). SOLO will then automatically perform the following tasks:

- **Generate API interface:** Create a backend interface to handle user registration and login.
- **Process registration requests:** Verify the email format and whether the user has already registered; use standard libraries such as `bcrypt` to add a "salt" (random value) to the user's password and then perform a hash calculation (converting a fixed-length string using a cryptographic function); store the new user information (including the salted hashed password) in the Supabase users table. This process ensures that even if the database is leaked, attackers will not be able to obtain the original password.

- **Handling login requests:** Search for the user in the database and perform a secure comparison between the submitted password and the stored hash value.
- **Generating and validating JWTs:** Generate a signed JWT for the user upon successful login and return it to the client. In all subsequent authentication requests, automatically add verification logic (usually middleware) to check if the request carries a valid JWT to determine the user's identity and permissions.

A professional and secure authentication system can be built in just a few minutes.

Business logic

After the authentication system is set up, the core business logic of the application needs to be built. In the backend, this logic is implemented through API endpoints exposed for use by the frontend or other services.

API endpoints are specific addresses where an application can request a particular operation from a service.

- `GET /api/v1/posts`: Retrieve a list of all posts
- `POST /api/v1/posts`: Create a new post
- `PUT /api/v1/posts/{id}`: Modify the post with the specified ID
- `DELETE /api/v1/posts/{id}`: Deletes the post with the specified ID

You don't need to master these technical terms; simply use the "user story" format to tell SOLO your needs. User stories typically follow the format of "As a <role>, I want <behavior> in order to <benefit>," which helps AI accurately understand your needs. Consider this example:

```
Now, implement the core functionality of article management. Please create the
following API.
As a logged-in user, I want to publish a new article (which needs to include a
title and content) to share my thoughts.
As a visitor, I want to get a list of all published articles so I can browse the
website's content.
As the author of this article, I want to delete my own articles in order to manage
my content.
```

SOLO can understand this format of instructions and create the corresponding API endpoints and backend code that implements the functionality.

For example, when implementing the "delete article" API, the AI-generated code automatically incorporates rigorous permission checking logic: first, it uses JWT to confirm the identity of the user making the request, and then it queries the database to confirm whether the user is the author of the article. Only when both conditions are met is the deletion operation performed.

Security and best practices

A key question is whether AI-generated code is secure. SOLO was designed with security as a core consideration, and it ensures code quality and security through the following methods:

- **Rely on mature frameworks and best practices:** Applications are built using well-established and proven open-source frameworks such as Node.js and Express. The generated code follows industry-standard security coding practices, such as automatically cleaning up user input to prevent injection attacks and one-way encryption of passwords
- **Prioritize the integration of professional services:** When handling high-risk tasks such as user authentication and database interaction, prioritize integration with professional BaaS platforms like Supabase. This ensures that complex security issues such as password storage and data transmission encryption are handled by professional service providers, which is far more secure than implementing them in-house.
- **Transparent and auditable:** Make all code generated by SOLO completely open to users. You can invite technical experts to review the code at any time. AI is responsible for execution, but you always retain ultimate oversight and ownership.

Through this series of automated, best-practice-following operations, SOLO improves development efficiency and builds a solid security defense for your application.

15-minute practical exercise: Complete the entire project

Having completed the previous three practical exercises, we have learned the methods for connecting to the database using SOLO, generating design documents, and implementing core business functions. Now, we will integrate all our knowledge to complete the full-process implementation.

In this practical exercise, we will start with top-level ideas and guide SOLO to complete the entire process of developing, testing, and deploying a personal blog system that includes backend services and a frontend interface in 15 minutes.

Project requirements analysis

First, we need to clarify our ultimate goal. A basic yet fully functional personal blog system should include the following core modules and technical requirements:

- **User Module**: Support users to register, log in, and log out using email and password; distinguish between different roles such as ordinary users and administrators

- **Article Module**: Support logged-in users to create, edit, and delete their own articles; allow anyone to view the article list and details
- **Comments module:** Support logged-in users to post comments; allow article authors or administrators to delete comments; allow anyone to view comments
- **Technical architecture:** The backend uses the Node.js and Express frameworks to provide a RESTful API; the database uses Supabase for data storage and user authentication; the frontend generates a simple **single-page application** (**SPA**) to interact with the backend API; and the entire application is deployed to the Vercel platform

These requirements will form the core of the next directive.

Complete the entire development process using SOLO

Now create a new project and issue the first command to SOLO:

```
We will build a complete personal blog system from scratch. Please follow the
steps and requirements to complete the entire project independently.
Planning Phase: Generate a detailed PRD and backend TDD. The TDD must include a
complete data model design based on Supabase (PostgreSQL) (covering the users,
posts, comments, tags, and post_tags tables), clearly defining all fields,
relationships, and constraints, and defining all necessary RESTful API endpoints.
Backend and Database: The backend technology stack is Node.js and Express. Please
connect to my authorized Supabase project to automatically create all data tables
based on the TDD-designed data model.
Core functionalities implemented: Build a user authentication system
(registration, login) based on JWT and bcrypt; create complete API interfaces for
article, comment, and tag functions, ensuring that all CRUD operations are
included, and implement role-based access control (e.g., only authors can edit
their own articles).
Frontend interface construction: Generate a simple, beautiful, and responsive
frontend interface, including the article homepage, article details page, user
login/registration page, and article creation/editing page accessible only after
login, ensuring that the frontend can correctly call the backend API.
Deployment and Launch: After all features have been developed and tested locally
without errors, deploy the full-stack application to Vercel and provide the final
public access URL.
```

After executing this command, you will witness the entire process of a product's creation in SOLO's integrated view—all function panels will be synchronized and will clearly present the entire development process.

- **Document View:** Prioritize creating PRD and TDD, making the project blueprint and technical details clear at a glance
- **Terminal panel:** SOLO automatically executes commands to install dependencies, configure the environment, run database migration scripts, and start the local development server
- **Code Editor (IDE):** Frontend and backend files are created and populated one by one, and code is generated in real time.
- **Browser panel:** A usable frontend interface gradually unfolds, and becomes interactive as the backend API is improved. You can click to test various functions in real time
- **Flow view:** SOLO generates a clear task list, break down complex tasks into small steps, and mark the completion status of each item

The entire process requires almost no intervention; you only need to make decisions at key points. For example, after drafting the PRD blueprint or right before deploying to Vercel, SOLO will pause and explicitly ask for your approval in the chat window. You simply read its proposal and reply in plain English, either giving it the green light to proceed or asking for adjustments.

Project optimization and iteration

The vitality of software lies in continuous iteration. After the blog version 1.0 is launched, if you have new ideas, you don't need to explain the project background to the developers; you can directly issue commands to SOLO, who is familiar with the project.

For example, to add the "like" function to an article, the corresponding instructions are as follows:

```
Add a "like" feature to the blog system.
1. Create a table named "likes" in Supabase to record the users who liked the
posts (user_id) and the posts (post_id).
2. As a logged-in user, I want to be able to like articles and also cancel my
likes. Please automatically generate the necessary API endpoints for these
actions.
3. Update the API for retrieving articles so that it returns the total number of
likes for each article.
4. Add a like button and display the number of likes on the article details page
and list page on the frontend.
```

SOLO will understand your needs. Because it preserves the context of the entire project, it knows how to safely modify files and database structures and how to adjust frontend and backend interactions, thus adding features to the product efficiently and securely.

Summary

Through this complete project exercise from scratch, we not only built a working blog system, but more importantly, learned to collaborate with AI engineers.

- **The Art of Instruction:** The efficiency of collaborating with AI largely depends on the quality of the requirements description. A clear, structured, and unambiguous instruction can make AI work much more efficiently. Our task has shifted from writing code to designing instructions and defining rules, which requires us to have stronger systems thinking and logical expression skills.
- **Role transformation:** During this process, we wrote almost no code, yet we spearheaded the entire product's creation. Our roles shifted from traditional implementers to definitive architects and decision-makers capable of independently completing product concepts and achieving a closed loop.
- **The Importance of Oversight and Review:** Despite SOLO's excellent performance, we still need to maintain a critical mindset. AI-generated code, especially in scenarios with complex business logic or high security requirements, still needs review and verification by human experts. SOLO is a powerful executor, but ultimately we are still responsible. Therefore, we must learn to effectively review the work of AI rather than blindly trusting it.

Using Cursor for refined backend development

Our roles shifted from traditional implementers to directors, product managers, and decision-makers, outlining the macro-level blueprint for the application. However, to transform that blueprint into a solid and practical "building," a skilled craftsman is needed—and that's the protagonist of this section: Cursor.

Why is Cursor needed for backend development?

The Cursor tool and its complementary relationship with SOLO were briefly introduced in *Chapter 2*. Here, we will provide a systematic review.

From macro-level design to detailed implementation

We can compare software development to building a house: First, you need an architect (SOLO) to communicate and understand your vision (such as an open kitchen, a south-facing bedroom, etc.) and quickly draw up the overall structure, room layout, and exterior renderings of the house. This is the macro-creation stage, focusing on the *what*, or the overall architecture and core concepts of the application.

But blueprints alone cannot provide habitability. To bring a house to life, a construction team is needed to precisely lay wiring, install pipes, and polish floors. Their focus is on *how*—the perfect execution of every detail. In our analogy, this "construction foreman" is Cursor.

The core value of advanced AI tools like SOLO is to quickly transform abstract ideas into structured code frameworks and application prototypes, while Cursor, as an AI-native IDE, has a completely different design philosophy. Cursor aims to handle all the details in the code implementation process and complete refined work.

To help you make the right choice in practice, we can differentiate them based on their usage scenarios:

- **Scenarios using SOLO:** When you only have a vague idea, or even before you've defined the specific functionality, you can use SOLO. SOLO excels at creating *from 0 to 1.* `If you say, I want a photo-sharing community`, it can generate the frontend and backend framework, database structure, and basic pages for your project, answering the question *What kind of products should we build?*
- **Scenarios using Cursor:** When you already have a foundation in code (whether generated by SOLO or written by yourself) and need to begin specific implementation work, you can use Cursor. Cursor excels at streamlining processes *from 1 to N*. If you need to install the engine, connect the wires, and debug the functionality for your product, it answers the question *How should we implement this product and make it work perfectly?*

This refined capability stems from Cursor's core architecture. Unlike plug-in AI assistants like GitHub Copilot, Cursor is a code editor in its own right. This native integration gives it a unique advantage: deep understanding of codebase context. When you open a project with Cursor, it "reads" and "understands" the entire project, building a complex semantic index for all the code, as if it were building a detailed project map inside.

It is this "map" that allows Cursor to operate with surgical precision. When it provides suggestions or modifies code, its decisions are based on a deep understanding of the relationships among all files, functions, and variables in the project, rather than being limited to the content of the current file.

Three key application scenarios of Cursor

Having understood the role of Cursor, let's look at its core application scenarios in backend development:

1. **Implementation of core business logic:** This is the core of backend development, requiring the writing of specific business logic such as user authentication, database interaction (CRUD), and payment processes, and demanding extremely high stability and accuracy. Cursor can generate robust, efficient, and best-practice-compliant code based on natural language descriptions. In contrast, SOLO's implementation in this area currently lags behind in terms of reliability and stability.
2. **Large-scale, cross-file code refactoring**: As a project evolves, structural adjustments may be necessary (such as renaming the `user` model in the database to `profile`). This seemingly simple change can trigger a chain reaction, requiring modifications to related variable names, function names, and APIs in dozens of files. For humans, this is a tedious and error-prone task, but for Cursor, with its complete project roadmap, it's a breeze. It automatically locates and safely modifies all relevant files, ensuring the system remains robust after refactoring.
3. **Deep Collaborative Debugging:** When an application encounters a problem, you may only see the error message but not understand the root cause. If you provide it with the error message and log files, Cursor will help you trace the source, quickly locate the essence of the problem, and provide a fix based on its understanding of the entire codebase.
4. **Implementation and Refinement Stage:** Once the initial prototype is built, your role shifts from visionary to project manager. Simply download the project code generated by SOLO to your local machine and open it with Cursor. Rather than designing macro-level features, your tasks now become specific and detailed: refining project configurations, implementing business functions, and fixing code errors. Cursor acts as your professional code workspace to execute this meticulous work.

Now that we've figured out where Cursor fits into our workflow, it's time to start using it.

10-minute introduction: Cursor basic operations and interface navigation

Now, let's begin using your *AI-powered pair programmer*. The entire process is very simple, taking only ten minutes to complete, from installation to familiarizing yourself with the interface.

Download, installation, and initial setup

First, install Cursor on your computer:

1. Open your browser and visit Cursor's official website (`https://cursor.com/`). The website will automatically recognize your operating system (Windows, macOS, or Linux) and provide a download button on the home page.
2. After downloading, run the installation file. The installation methods for different operating systems are as follows:
    - **Windows users:** Double-click the `.exe` file and follow the installation wizard's instructions
    - **macOS users:** Open the `.dmg` file and drag the Cursor icon to the `Applications` folder
    - **Linux users**: Grant execute permissions to the downloaded `.AppImage` file and run it directly
3. After installation, launch Cursor, which will guide you through the initial setup (such as choosing a keyboard shortcut scheme and theme colors). During the setup process, you will be prompted to register or log in; this step is crucial, as it directly determines the scope of functionality and the quality of the user experience. Here are some things to keep in mind while logging in:
    - **A crucial step:** We strongly recommend logging in with your GitHub account. This not only simplifies the registration process but also allows Cursor to better understand your development habits.
    - **Unlock professional tools:** Log in to automatically activate Cursor's free **Hobby** plan (which includes limited access to AI features) and receive a two-week trial of the Pro version
    - **Student welfare:** University students worldwide can enjoy a free year of professional service by verifying their identity

After completing the above steps, your Cursor application will be configured and ready.

Interface navigation

After opening Cursor, you will see a professional and clear interface (see *Figure 4.1*), which can be regarded as a well-defined console.

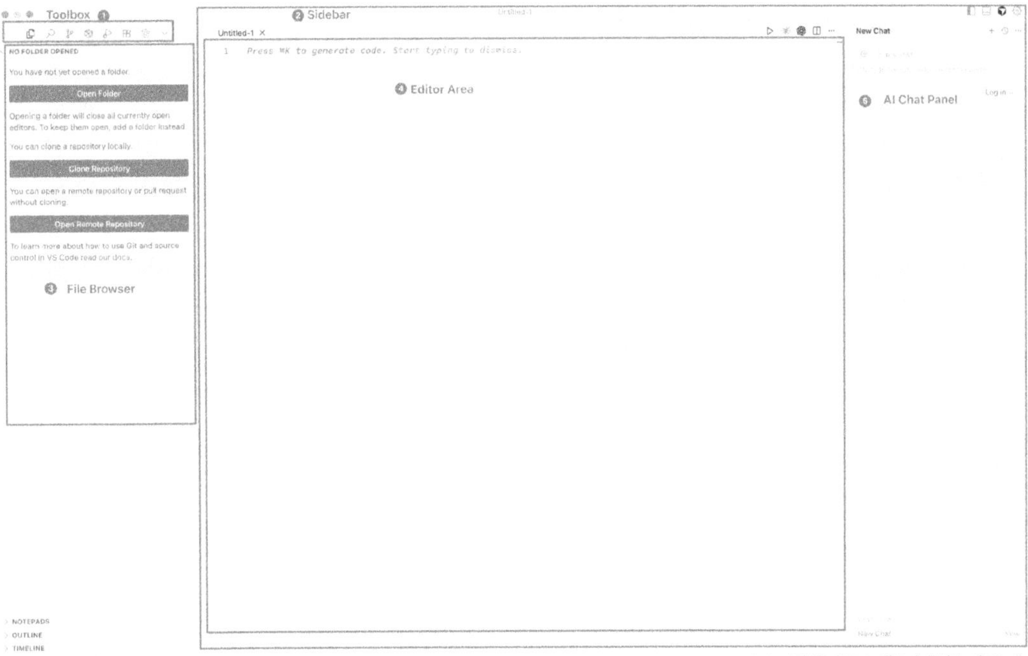

Figure 4.1 – Cursor interface

Here are the main elements in the interface, as shown in *Figure 4.1*:

1. **Toolbox:** Located on the far left of the screen is a row of icons representing the main toolbox. Clicking different icons allows you to switch between file browser, global search, and source code management views in the sidebar.
2. **Sidebar:** Located on the right side of the activity bar, its content is determined by the selected icon in the activity bar and is displayed by default.
3. **File Browser:** Manage all files and folders in the project here.
4. **Editor Area:** The largest area in the center of the screen is used to view, write, and modify code and supports opening multiple files simultaneously (arranged in tabs at the top).
5. **AI Chat Panel:** This is usually located on the right side of the screen and is the area for in-depth dialogue with Cursor AI. It can be brought up or hidden using the shortcut *Ctrl/Cmd+Shift+L*.

Cursor's three working modes

Collaboration with Cursor AI is primarily conducted through three distinct modes, forming a complete interactive system that ranges from micro-management to macro-management.

Intelligent code completion

This mode provides an immersive, low-interference collaborative experience and is the most commonly used mode in daily coding. Cursor's AI model analyzes the input, the current file context, and recent modification history in real time as you write code, predicting the most likely subsequent code and displaying it as "ghost text." It can predict and generate logically complete multi-line code blocks.

Cursor's Tab completion also has editing capabilities, allowing you to not only add new code but also modify and rewrite existing code (such as automatically suggesting modifications to all calls to a function after you modify its parameters).

You can press the *Tab* key to accept suggestions, press the *Esc* key or continue typing to reject suggestions, or press *Ctrl* + →, that is, the right arrow key (Windows/Linux) or *Cmd* + → (macOS) to accept suggestions word by word.

Composer code generation

This mode is an imperative, goal-driven collaborative approach, an efficient tool for handling explicit coding tasks. It works by activating an inline input box when you press *Ctrl* + *K* (Windows/Linux) or *Cmd* + *K* (macOS). Here, you can describe your code generation or modification requirements in natural language. Cursor then sends the instructions to the language model and directly inserts or replaces the returned code in the editor.

For more complex tasks, you can use *Ctrl* + *I* (Windows/Linux) or *Cmd* + *I* (macOS) to bring up the more comprehensive **Composer** panel.

Place the cursor at the target location or select the code to be modified, press *Ctrl/Cmd* + *K*, enter the command in the pop-up input box (such as `create an asynchronous function named fetchData, accept URL parameters, and use the fetch API to retrieve data`), and then press *Enter* to wait for AI to generate the code. Review the generated code. If you are satisfied, click the **Accept** button. If not, you can modify the instructions and try again or adjust them manually.

AI chat assistant

This mode is a conversational, exploratory collaboration approach. It serves as your *command center* when you encounter problems, need explanations, or require macro-level planning. It works by opening the AI chat panel on the right when you press *Ctrl* + *Shift* + *L* (Windows/Linux) or *Cmd* + *Shift* + *L* (macOS), which has access to the entire project. You can precisely reference files (`@file`), functions (`@functionName`), or entire codebases (`@codebase`) within the project using the @ symbol, providing ample context for your questions.

AI chat assistants are the best place to solve complex problems and learn new knowledge. For example, when debugging, you can paste error messages and ask, `Why is the code throwing this error? Please help me analyze the @app/api/route.ts file`; when learning, you can select a piece of code and ask, `What does this code do? Please explain it in language that a beginner can understand`; when planning a refactoring, you can ask, `I want to refactor the user authentication system. Please use @codebase to analyze the files and core logic that may be affected by the changes.`

The AI will provide explanations or code suggestions in a conversational format, and you can directly click the **Apply** button to apply the code to your file.

These three modes together constitute a complete collaboration system. Skilled Cursor users will flexibly switch between these three modes depending on the task. *Table 4.3* summarizes the characteristics of these three modes.

Pattern (metaphor)	**Keyboard shortcuts (MacOS)**	**Best application scenarios**	**Interaction style**
Intelligent code completion (Automatic Assistant)	*Tab* key	Write regular code, implement repetitive logic, and follow existing patterns	Tacit prediction AI provides real-time predictions; you only need to confirm.
Composer code generation (Programming tools)	*Cmd + K/* *Cmd + I*	Generate new functions, implement specific algorithms, and modify code blocks according to instructions	Clear instructions You issue a clear command, and the AI is responsible for executing it.
AI chat assistant (Programming Mentor)	*Cmd + Shift + L*	Debugging bugs, understanding complex code, planning refactoring, and learning new concepts	In-depth dialogue. You pose open-ended questions, and AI provides analysis and solutions.

Table 4.3 – Characteristics of Cursor's Three AI Interaction Modes

10-minute exercise: Complete a simple function with 3 different modes

Now, let's experience the differences between these three patterns through an exercise in creating a factorial function (a classic programming test that multiplies a number by every whole number below it, like 5x4x3x2x1). While you might not use this in a real app, it is the perfect, simple logic test to see how well the AI understands math and coding patterns. Create a new file named `math.js` in your project.

Mode 1: Intelligent code completion

In `math.js`, type the first line of the input function:

```
JavaScript
function factorial(n) {
```

Press *Enter*, and type `if` inside the function body. The cursor will predict the core logic of the factorial function and suggest the following code in gray text:

```
JavaScript
if (n === 0 || n === 1) {
return 1;
}
return n * factorial(n - 1);
```

After seeing the suggested code above, simply press the *Tab* key to complete the function input.

Mode 2: Composer code generation

Leave a few blank lines below the factorial function, then press *Ctrl/Cmd + K*. In the pop-up input box, type the command `Create a function named factorial_composer to calculate the factorial of a number n` and press *Enter*. AI will then generate the factorial function precisely.

Mode 3: AI chat assistant

Press *Ctrl/Cmd + Shift + L* to open the chat panel, then type this:

```
Write a JavaScript function 'factorial_chat' to calculate factorials, and add
English comments to key code.
```

The AI will not only generate code but also add comments as requested and may provide explanations. Then click the **Apply** or **Insert** button to insert the commented function at the cursor's location.

Through this exercise, you should be able to clearly feel the differences between these three modes: intelligent code completion is smooth collaboration, Composer code generation is precise execution, and the AI chat assistant is in-depth guidance.

15-minute hands-on practice: Building the Next.js API skeleton

Now let's move on to the practical part. We will build a backend API service based on the Next.js framework from scratch. The core task is to build the project skeleton, mainly using the AI chat assistant mode.

Project initialization

We start with an empty folder, and our goal is to have AI initialize a Next.js project for us.

1. **Create and open the project directory**. Create an empty folder on your computer and name it `nextjs-supabase-api`. Launch Cursor and open the folder via the **File** | **Open** Folder menu.
2. **Use the AI Terminal**. Press *Ctrl/Cmd* + ` to open Cursor's built-in terminal. Instead of typing a command yourself, press *Ctrl/Cmd* + *K* inside the terminal to bring up the AI prompt.
3. **Execute the instruction**. Type the following request and press *Enter*:

   ```
   Initialize a brand new Next.js project here using TypeScript and default
   configurations.
   ```

   The AI will automatically generate the correct command (like `npx create-next-app@latest . --ts --yes`). Simply press *Enter* again and Cursor will execute it directly, downloading the template and installing all dependencies.

Use an AI chat assistant to understand project configuration

The project files have been generated, but the meaning of the core configurations needs to be clarified (e.g., `package.json` is equivalent to the project's "identity card" and "dependency list"). We can then use Cursor's built-in AI chat assistant to gain a deeper understanding.

1. Locate and click the `package.json` file in the Cursor sidebar to open it.
2. In the AI chat panel, type:

```
This is my package.json file. Please explain the function of dev, build,
start, and lint in the scripts field, as well as the difference between
dependencies and devDependencies.
```

   AI will clearly explain the purpose of dev (development environment startup), build (project build and packaging), start (production environment startup), and lint (code syntax checking), while distinguishing between dependencies (libraries required for the production environment) and devDependencies (tool libraries used only during development).

Through this conversation, you not only mastered the project creation method but also understood the core configuration logic.

Construct the Next.js API routing structure

Next.js uses a file system-based routing approach, meaning that files in a specific folder automatically become accessible APIs. To see this in action, let's follow these steps to build your first API route.

1. Issue the creation command. Enter a specific development task in the AI chat panel, as shown below:

```
Please create a basic Next.js API route with the access path /api/hello.
This API needs to return a JSON object with the content {"message":"Hello
from our API!"}. Please provide the file path to create the route and the
complete code.
```

2. Create and populate the file. AI will suggest creating the file at the path `app/api/hello/route.ts` and provide the following code.

```
TypeScript
import { NextResponse } from "next/server";
```

```
export async function GET(request: Request) {
return NextResponse.json({ message: "Hello from our API!" });
}
```

3. Follow the AI's instructions to create the `api` and `hello` folders in the app folder, then create a `route.ts` file in the hello folder and paste the code provided by the AI into it (or you can directly click the button in the AI's reply to apply the code).
4. Verify the results. Return to the terminal and enter the command `npm run dev` to start the development server. Access `http://localhost:3000/api/hello` in your browser. If the page displays `{"message":"Hello from our API!"}`, then the first backend API has been created and is running successfully—the entire process requires almost no manual coding.

Use @file and @codebase for context management.

As projects grow larger and codebases become more complex, developers need to use the `@file` and `@codebase` directives to guide the AI's attention precisely and ensure that the generated code remains consistent with the overall structure and style of the project.

In small projects, AI can easily understand the structure of the entire codebase. However, when a project contains dozens of files and thousands of lines of code, explicit guidance is needed for the AI. This is similar to searching for specific information in a large library; you need to tell the librarian whether you want to look up a particular book or understand the entire library's classification system. `@file` and `@codebase` are the core instructions for achieving this precise guidance.

The `@file` directive limits AI's focus to the currently opened file or selected code snippet, making it suitable for operations within a single file, such as explaining the purpose of functions or classes, fixing syntax errors, and generating related code completions. The `@codebase` directive, on the other hand, expands AI's attention to the entire project (including all files and subdirectories), making it suitable for cross-file analysis of structure, dependencies, or global architecture design. With its help, AI can gain a more comprehensive understanding of the overall project, thereby generating code that better meets the project's needs.

The following two practical examples demonstrate the usage of `@file` and `@codebase`:

- **Case 1: Using @file to focus on a single file:** Suppose you want AI to check if the API file you just created conforms to best practices. Ask this question in the chat box:

  ```
  Please review the code in the @app/api/hello/route.ts file and see if there
  are any areas for improvement.
  ```

  Using the @ symbol to explicitly tell the AI to focus on a specific file can make its responses more targeted.

- **Case 2: Using @codebase for global review:** If you need to confirm the compatibility of the project configuration, you can ask the following questions:

  ```
  Using @codebase, can you analyze the entire project configuration and
  confirm whether the TypeScript and ESLint settings correctly support the
  API routes we just created?
  ```

This time, the AI will check configuration files such as `tsconfig.json` and `next.config.js` to provide a comprehensive project health report.

The core of this practical exercise is to let you experience a brand-new conversational development model: you use natural language to propose strategic goals, while the AI partner handles all the tactical execution details.

10-minute practice: Implementing specific business logic using Composer

We have built the skeleton of the API, and now we will inject its core functionality: connecting to a real database and implementing business logic.

At this stage, we switch to **Composer** code generation mode. If the AI chat assistant is the "project manager," then Composer is the "lead programmer." We are responsible for architectural decisions, and then we issue precise instructions in the Composer code generation mode chat box, which it then uses to complete the specific coding.

Our goal is to connect the Next.js application to Supabase and implement a complete set of CRUD APIs for creating, deleting, updating, and querying posts.

Use Composer to generate database connection configuration

First, you need to establish a connection between the application and the Supabase database. The steps are as follows:

1. **Prepare your Supabase project:** Go to the official website to register and create a new project (the platform offers free credits for beginners). Once the project is created, run the following SQL statement in the **SQL Editor** to create the posts table.

```
SQL
CREATE TABLE posts (
id bigint PRIMARY KEY GENERATED ALWAYS AS IDENTITY,
title text NOT NULL,
content text,
created_at timestamptz DEFAULT now()
```

The table contains four fields: `id` (serves as the primary key and is automatically generated), `title` (stores the article title and cannot be empty), `content` (stores the article content), and `created_at` (records the creation time and defaults to the current time). The execution result is shown in *Figure 4.2*.

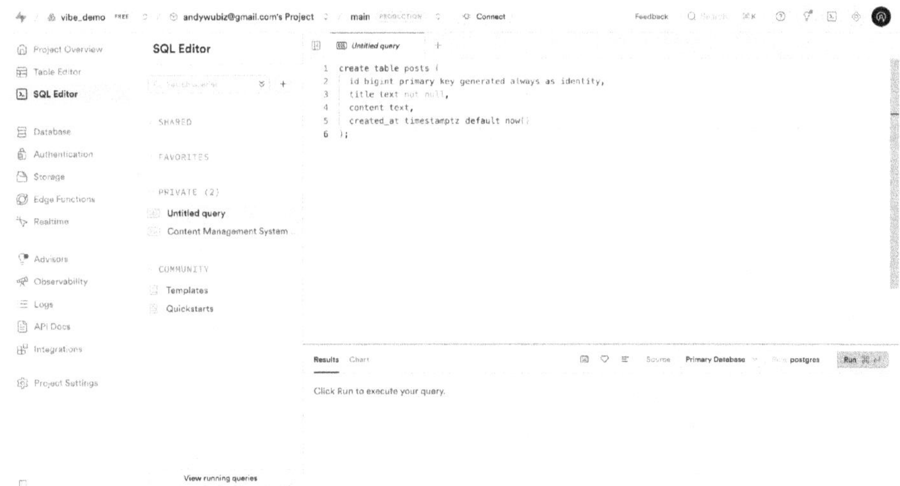

Figure 4.2 – Creating the posts table

2. **Obtain database connection credentials:** Locate and copy the Project URL in the **Data API** section of **Project Settings** (see *Figure 4.3*):

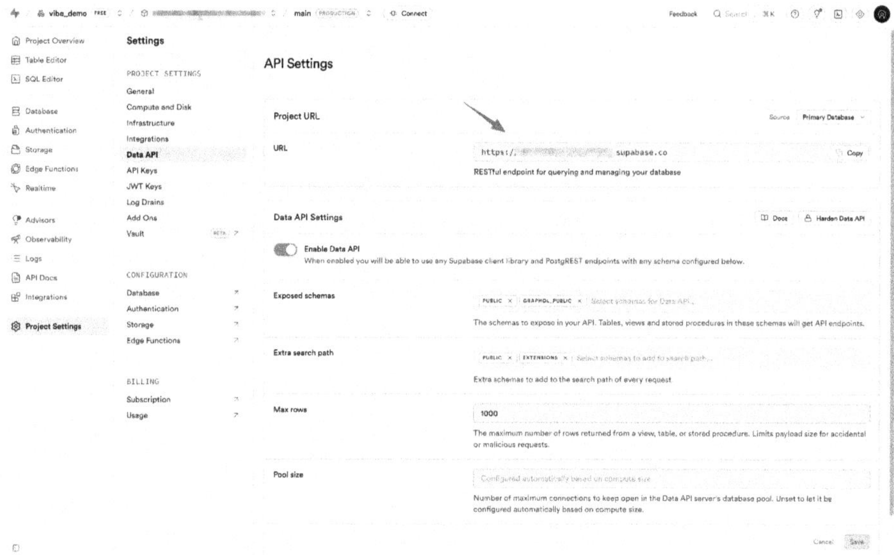

Figure 4.3 – Obtaining the Project URL

Find the anon public key in the API Keys section of **Project Settings** (see *Figure 4.4*):

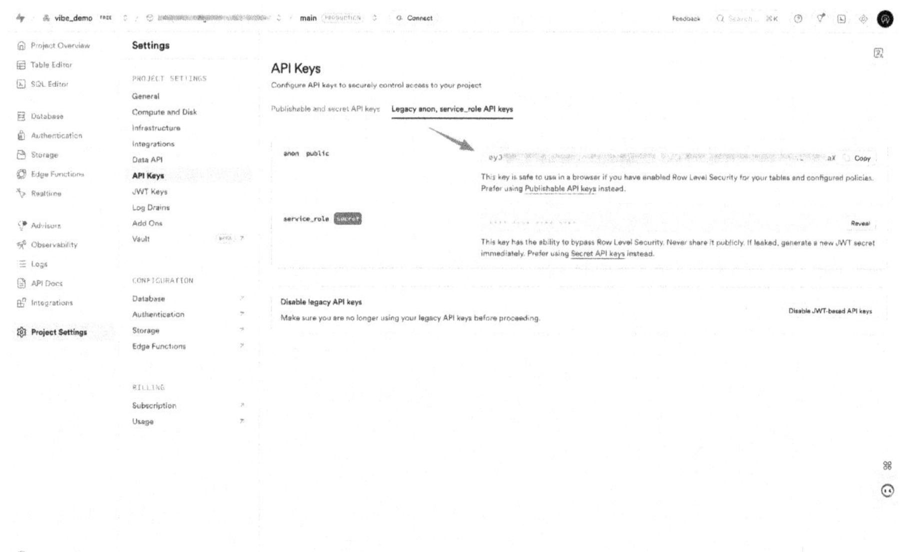

Figure 4.4 – Obtaining the anon public key

The project URL and anon public key are necessary credentials for connecting to the database and must be kept safe.

3. **Configure environment variables:** Return to Cursor, create a new file named `.env.local` in the project root directory (specifically for storing sensitive information), and add the following content, replacing the placeholders with the actual URL and key obtained from Supabase.

```
NEXT_PUBLIC_SUPABASE_URL=YOUR_SUPABASE_URL
NEXT_PUBLIC_SUPABASE_ANON_KEY=YOUR_SUPABASE_ANON_KEY
```

4. **Use Composer to generate client code:** Create a `lib` folder in the project's main folder (short for 'library', a standard folder used to store shared project configurations and tools), and then create a new `supabaseClient.ts` file in it (used to create and export the Supabase connection client).
   Place the mouse cursor on this blank file, press *Ctrl/Cmd + K* to bring up Composer, and enter the prompt:

```
Use the @supabase/supabase-js library to create a Supabase client, read the
URL and anon key from the environment variables NEXT_PUBLIC_SUPABASE_URL
and NEXT_PUBLIC_SUPABASE_ANON_KEY, and finally export this client instance.
```

   After pressing *Enter*, Composer will automatically generate standard client initialization code, as shown in the example below (the actual generated code may differ slightly).

```
TypeScript
import { createClient } from "@supabase/supabase-js";

const supabaseUrl = process.env.NEXT_PUBLIC_SUPABASE_URL!;
const supabaseAnonKey = process.env.NEXT_PUBLIC_SUPABASE_ANON_KEY!;

export const supabase = createClient(supabaseUrl, supabaseAnonKey);
```

   Clicking the **Accept** button will add this code to the file, completing the database connection configuration.

Implementing user authentication middleware and API endpoints

To protect the API, an authentication middleware is needed to ensure that only logged-in users can operate it. At the same time, a new `/api/posts` API endpoint is added to handle post-related requests.

1. **Create an authentication middleware:** Create a new file named `middleware.ts` in the project root directory. Then, place the mouse cursor in this blank file, press *Ctrl/Cmd* + *K* to bring up Composer, and enter the command:

   ```
   Create Next.js middleware, use Supabase to protect all requests under the /
   api/posts path, and return a 401 Unauthorized Error for unauthenticated
   users.
   ```

   After pressing *Enter*, Composer will generate modern middleware code based on the `@supabase/ssr` library.

2. **Create the API endpoint file:** Create a new folder named `posts` in the `app/api/` directory, and then create a file named `route.ts` in that folder to handle all `HTTP` requests related to posts.

Construct the complete business logic for CRUD operations

Now we come to the core part. In the `app/api/posts/route.ts` file, write processing functions for the four operations: `GET` (read), `POST` (create), `PATCH` (patch), and `DELETE` (delete).

Implement a GET request to read all articles

First, enter the following framework code in the `route.ts` file:

```
TypeScript
import { NextResponse } from "next/server";
import { supabase } from "@/lib/supabaseClient";

export async function GET(request: Request) {
// Place the cursor here
}
```

Then, place the mouse cursor inside the function body, press *Ctrl/Cmd* + *K*, and enter the prompt:

```
Use the Supabase client to query all records from the posts table, sort them in
descending order by creation time, and return the query results in JSON format.
```

Composer will generate code examples like the one shown below for reference.

```
TypeScript
const { data, error } = await supabase
.from("posts")
.select("*")
.order("created_at", { ascending: false });

if (error) {
return NextResponse.json({ error: error.message }, { status: 500 });
}

return NextResponse.json(data);
```

This code retrieves all article records from the database, sorts them in reverse chronological order by creation time, and handles any possible errors.

Implement a POST request (create new post)

Add the framework code for the `POST` function below the `GET` function:

```
TypeScript
export async function POST(request: Request) {
// Place the cursor here
}
```

Then place the mouse cursor inside the function body, press *Ctrl/Cmd* + *K*, and enter the command:

```
parse the title and content from the request body, use the Supabase client to
insert these two fields into the posts table, and return the newly created record.
```

Composer automatically handles JSON parsing and database insertion operations, generating complete creation logic.

Implement PATCH and DELETE operations

The corresponding code can be generated using the same method as above. Note that for both of these operations, you need to obtain the article ID from the URL to specify the record to be operated on.

For the PATCH operation, the following is an example of a possible prompt:

```
Retrieve the id from the URL search parameters, obtain the title and content from
the request body, and use Supabase to update the record with the corresponding id
in the posts table.
```

For the DELETE operation, the following is an example of a prompt that can be used:

```
Retrieve the ID from the URL search parameters, delete the record with the
corresponding ID from the posts table using Supabase, and return a 204 status code
upon success.
```

With these clear instructions, Composer can accurately understand your intent and generate the corresponding code logic.

Automatic generation of error handling and data validation

A robust API needs to be able to handle exceptions gracefully, and we can enhance the code through Composer iteration.

- **Enhanced error handling:** Select any of the database operation code you just generated, press *Ctrl/Cmd + K* and enter the enhancement prompt:

  ```
  Add detailed error handling to this code. If Supabase returns a uniqueness
  conflict (like a duplicate entry), return the standard web error for a
  conflict. For other database errors, return a standard server error.
  ```

  Composer will generate comprehensive code that includes handling of various error scenarios.

- **Add data validation:** At the beginning of the POST function, press *Ctrl/Cmd + K* and enter the prompt:

  ```
  Add data validation logic before performing database insertion, ensure that
  the title field exists and is not empty, and return a 400 Bad Request error
  with a clear error message if the validation fails.
  ```

This *iterative enhancement* approach allows you to first generate the core logic and then refine its robustness and security with a series of detailed instructions.

Composer agent: Programming assistance in Cursor

Before diving into its features, what exactly is the **Composer Agent**? Think of it as a highly autonomous 'full-stack technical consultant' built directly into Cursor. Unlike standard AI chats that just give you code to copy, the Agent understands your entire project context and can independently execute complex, multi-step tasks on your behalf. All of the manual steps we just covered can actually be completed through this more efficient Composer Agent. You can bring up this function by pressing *Ctrl/Cmd + I*. Its core features are as follows:

- **Intelligent code rewriting without precise positioning:** Even without specifying it with the @ symbol, the Composer Agent can automatically find the most suitable location in the project to rewrite the code
- **A solution from 0 to 1:** By describing a complete project requirement, Composer Agent can generate a complete solution including routing structure, database integration, middleware, error handling, type definitions, and environment variable configuration
- **Intelligent problem diagnosis and repair:** By describing the problem encountered (such as "API returned a 500 error"), the Composer Agent can assist in checking and fixing it
- **Complex restructuring across files:** It can support complex tasks such as "extracting all database query logic into an independent service layer" or "adding Docker support to the project"

Despite the powerful capabilities of Composer Agent, a step-by-step learning approach is crucial for beginners for the following reasons:

- **Developing programming thinking:** Learning by doing helps in understanding the logic and best practices of software development
- **Improve the ability to express needs:** Understanding the details allows for more accurate description of complex needs to the AI
- **Improve troubleshooting skills:** Understanding the role of each component allows for quickly pinpointing the root cause when problems occur
- **Improve architecture design capabilities**: Building step by step allows for developing a holistic understanding of the system architecture

In actual development, tools can be flexibly selected according to different scenarios:

- **Rapid prototyping phase:** Use Composer code generation mode to quickly build the project framework
- **Learning and exploration phase:** Use an IDE editor to generate and modify code to gain a deeper understanding of the implementation details of each part

- **Problem-solving phase:** Use the AI chat assistant to discuss solutions in depth and obtain more detailed technical guidance
- **Complex refactoring phase:** Return to Composer code generation mode and let it perform cross-file refactoring to ensure the consistency and rationality of the overall architecture

Composer Agent is not just a code generation tool, but more like a full-stack technical consultant—it understands the project context, follows industry best practices, and provides complete solutions.

10-minute hands-on practice: Managing databases and services using a terminal

A complete application lifecycle also includes database management, testing, and deployment. In Cursor, the terminal is an intelligent console that can converse with AI, efficiently handling these operational tasks.

Tips for using the Cursor built-in terminal

Opening a terminal is very simple; just press *Ctrl/Cmd* + ` to quickly open or close the terminal.

The Cursor terminal has AI-enabled features: press *Ctrl/Cmd* + *K* at the terminal prompt, then describe your needs in natural language, and the AI will automatically generate the corresponding terminal commands.

Let's experience this feature through a practical example.

First, open the terminal, then press *Ctrl/Cmd* + *K*, type:

```
List all files with the .ts extension in the current directory, sorted in
descending order of modification time
```

Press *Enter*, and AI will generate the corresponding terminal command. Press *Enter* again to execute it.

The core value of this feature is that you no longer need to memorize the complex commands of tools such as `git`, `docker`, and `npm`; you can simply describe your needs in natural language to complete the operation.

Use an AI chat assistant to generate a database migration script

As business grows, data structures also need to evolve (such as adding an `is_published` field to the posts table). Such changes need to be implemented through **database migration**, and the specific steps are as follows:

1. Open the AI chat panel and enter your database change request, for example:

   ```
   I'm using a PostgreSQL database and need to generate an SQL migration
   script for the `posts` table, requiring the following changes:
   1. Added a new column, is_published (Boolean type);
   2. The default value for this column should be false.
   3. This column is not allowed to be empty (NOT NULL).
   ```

   The AI will generate a professional and rigorous SQL script, as shown in the example below:

   ```
   SQL
   -- migration_script_001_add_is_published_to_posts.sql
   ALTER TABLE public.posts
   ADD COLUMN is_published BOOLEAN NOT NULL DEFAULT false;

   COMMENT ON COLUMN public.posts.is_published IS 'Indicates if the post is
   published to the public.';
   ```

2. Save the SQL script as a file and execute it through the Supabase dashboard or another database management tool.

Think of your database as a digital filing cabinet. As your app grows, you sometimes need to store new types of information—in this case, whether a post is a draft or published. Instead of building a whole new cabinet, we performed a *database migration*. We had the AI write a safe, precise set of instructions (the SQL script) to add a new `is_published` label to our existing cabinet. By executing this script, we successfully upgraded our database structure without losing or disturbing any of the data already inside.

Generation of automated testing and deployment commands

Automated testing and deployment often rely on complex commands, which AI can generate directly:

- **Test Scenario:** Assuming the project uses Jest as its testing framework, press *Ctrl/Cmd + K* in the terminal, then type:

  ```
  Run all Jest tests in the project and generate a code coverage report.
  ```

  AI will generate the corresponding command: npx jest --coverage.

- **Deployment scenarios:** Next.js applications are typically deployed on the Vercel platform. When deployment is required, simply press *Ctrl/Cmd + K*, type:

  ```
  Deploy Next.js application to Vercel production environment, please provide
  the deployment command of Vercel CLI
  ```

  AI will automatically generate the command vercel --prod

Real-time debugging and log analysis

When issues arise in online applications, logs are crucial for locating the root cause. The following steps can be used to analyze logs and pinpoint the problem:

1. **Start the development server and observe the logs:** Run the command `npm run dev` in the terminal to start the local development server. The terminal will print logs in real time when you access the API.
2. **Take AI-assistance for log analysis:** If an API error occurs, you can copy the error stack trace from the terminal into the AI chat panel and then ask a question (replace the parentheses in the command below with the error log:

   ```
   My Next.js API is encountering the following error at runtime. Could you
   please help me analyze the root cause and identify which file might be
   causing the problem?
   (Paste the error log you copied here)
   ```

3. **Get a solution:** Cursor combines its understanding of logs and codebase to provide analysis results (such as pointing out configuration file errors) and solutions

This hands-on training will develop the entire process into a closed loop. You will not only learn the methods of managing and maintaining applications using AI, but also how to apply them in practice.

Advanced: In-depth application of Cursor's unique advantages

In the *Three key application scenarios of Cursor* section, we explored Cursor's applications: its precise understanding of codebase context, its ability to execute large-scale cross-file refactoring, and its deep collaborative debugging capabilities. Now, it is time to put them to test. In the following advanced practical exercise, we will combine all three of these advantages to execute a massive architectural shift.

10-minute advanced practice: Refactoring a complex multi-file backend project

We'll demonstrate the synergistic effect of these three advantages through an advanced practical exercise. Suppose our `nextjs-supabase-api` project needs to shift its business focus from *Posts* to *Products*. This means we need to batch modify database table names, API routes, code naming, and more. Let's see how.

To enable **Composer Agent** mode, press *Ctrl/Cmd + I* in Cursor. Enter the following command in the chat box, which includes the complete intent and global context:

```
The entire project was refactored using @codebase, completely changing the core
business concept from Post to Product.
Please perform all of the following operations.
1. Database migration: Generate an SQL script to rename the posts table to
products.
2. Rename the API route: Rename the app/api/posts folder to app/api/products.
3. Code logic update: In the new app/api/products/route.ts file, change the target
table for Supabase operations from posts to products.
4. Variables and Naming Conventions: In this file, all variable names, function
parameters, and type definitions containing "post" or "posts" will be
intelligently renamed to "product" or "products". For example, `const { data:
posts, error }` will be renamed to `const { data: products, error }`.
Before making any changes, please provide a detailed action plan that lists all
the files to be modified and shows the specific code differences (diff) for each
file.
```

To review, press *Enter*, and Cursor's AI Agent will begin analyzing the codebase and generating a complete action plan. Once confirmed, reply `Execute`, and the AI will automatically complete all modifications in just a few minutes.

Summary

In this section, we moved from theory to execution. You mastered Cursor's three core interaction modes, built a Next.js API skeleton, and seamlessly integrated a Supabase database to execute complete CRUD operations. You even used the AI terminal to run database migrations and leveraged the Composer Agent to execute a massive cross-file architectural refactoring with a single prompt.

Because of these capabilities, Cursor is a tool that helps us understand and reshape complex software systems. It changes the cost structure of software development. Architectural adjustments that previously required a team several days can now be achieved with just one person and a well-designed instruction. This reduces the costs of trial and error and iteration, making the implementation of ideas smoother and more efficient.

Advanced integration: MCP in practice and in-depth application

We have already learned how to engage in efficient dialogue with AI. Now, we will empower AI with the ability to interact with external systems and perform tasks, transforming it from a knowledgeable conversationalist into a powerful assistant capable of handling practical matters. The core technology for achieving this goal is **MCP** (**Model Context Protocol**).

With MCP, your AI can directly connect to GitHub to manage code repositories, access Figma to convert design drafts into code, and even automatically run Playwright tests on newly launched websites. After reading this section, you will find that these functions are easy to learn. We will transform AI from an intelligent brain into an all-around digital assistant.

MCP: An open standard for AI and external tools

Before diving into its practical application, it is necessary to understand the concept and value of MCP.

In the past, our drawers were crammed with various dedicated chargers and data cables—one for each iPhone, Android phone, camera, and laptop—creating a chaotic and inconvenient situation. This chaotic situation has also appeared in the field of AI.

Before the advent of MCP, if developers wanted to connect an AI model (such as Claude) to external tools (such as GitHub), they needed to write a custom *connector*. Connecting a different AI model (such as ChatGPT) to GitHub might require writing a completely new connector. Assuming N AI models and M external tools, theoretically, this would result in N × M incompatible, independent connectors. This increased development complexity and severely hindered innovation in AI applications.

MCP is like a USB/Type-C docking station that ends the chaos of chargers, as shown in *Figure 4. 5*:

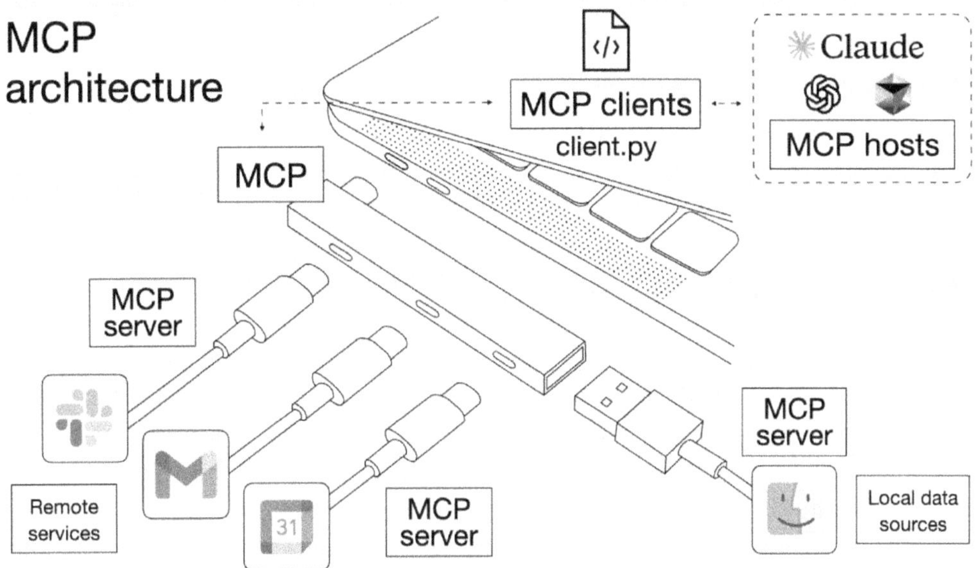

Figure 4.5 – Using a USB/Type-C docking station as an analogy for MCP

MCP is an open standard proposed by Anthropic in late 2024, aiming to provide a unified *socket* for all AI models and external tools. As long as MCP is supported, any AI model can easily *plug in* any external tool that supports the standard, without the need for custom development for each combination. It solves the N×M integration problem, bringing unprecedented interoperability to the AI ecosystem.

MCP working principle analysis

To understand how MCP connects your AI to the outside world, we need to look at its three core technical components:

- **MCP Host:** This is the main application or IDE you are using, such as TRAE SOLO or Cursor. It provides the interface where you work and serves as the command center for your AI interactions.
- **MCP Client:** Built directly into the Host, the Client acts as an intelligent router. When you give the AI an instruction (such as "help me check the unresolved bugs in the project"), the Client determines which external tool is required to handle the request and forwards the command accordingly.

- **MCP Server:** These are lightweight, specialized programs that connect to specific external tools or data sources. For example, a "GitHub MCP Server" contains the APIs needed to read and manage code repositories, while a "Figma MCP Server" knows how to translate design drafts into code.

The entire workflow of MCP is as follows:

When you submit a request in your IDE (the Host), the built-in AI (the Client) receives it, determines that it needs to be processed by a specific external tool (like GitHub), and forwards the command. The designated MCP server processes the task, interacts with the external API, and returns the result to the Client, which then presents the final, actionable answer to you.

Advantages of unified standards

The advent of MCP has brought three major practical benefits to users:

- **Reduce AI hallucinations:** LLMs are trained on historical data, meaning they do not inherently have real-time awareness of new information. Because of this limitation, they sometimes fabricate seemingly reasonable false information—a phenomenon called hallucination. MCP connects AI to real-time data sources. When AI is uncertain about information, it can directly query authoritative data sources (such as the latest official documents or your database) through MCP, thereby making the answer more accurate and reliable.
- **Unlock automation capabilities:** MCP transforms AI from a passive knowledge-answering tool into an *actor* capable of proactively performing tasks. Without MCP, AI can only tell you what you should do; with MCP, AI can directly do it for you. It can update customer information in CRM systems, perform complex calculations, and even publish written articles directly to websites.
- **Future-oriented skills:** MCP is not a proprietary technology of any particular company, but rather an open standard widely accepted by the industry. Since the launch of MCP, industry giants such as OpenAI, Google, and Microsoft have quickly announced their support for its adoption, demonstrating that a unified standard has become an industry consensus. Learning MCP today means mastering the universal language and standard interface for building next-generation AI applications.

Environment preparation and the MCP server market

After understanding the concept and advantages of MCP, you might ask: Where can I find these powerful MCP servers? How do I use them? The good news is that a mature and vibrant ecosystem has formed, and you can discover and install various MCP servers just like browsing an app store, equipping your AI assistant with a variety of practical tools.

Here are some popular MCP app marketplaces:

- **mcp.so:** A community-driven third-party MCP marketplace (see *Figure 4.6*) that includes tens of thousands of MCP servers, covering a wide range of tools from simple time queries to complex browser automation. URL: `https://mcp.so/`

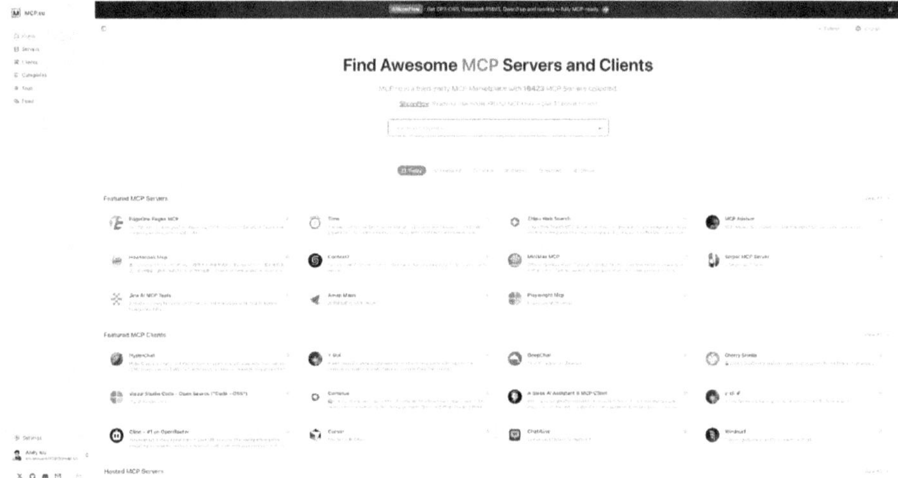

Figure 4.6 – Main page of the mcp.so website

- **Smithery:** A professional MCP server platform (see *Figure 4.7*) provides developers with a more complete enterprise-level MCP ecosystem, which includes more than 7,300 community-built MCP servers. URL: `https://smithery.ai/`

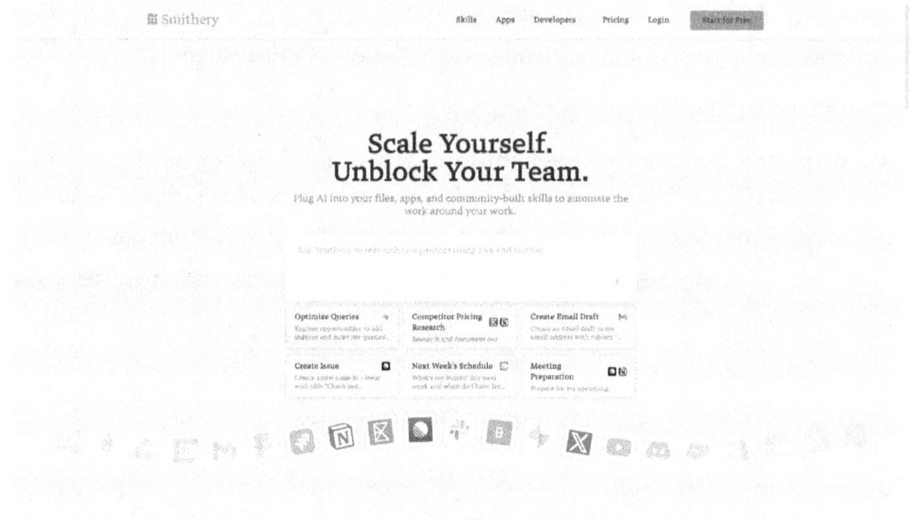

Figure 4.7 – The homepage of the Smithery website

- **awesome-mcp-servers (**`https://github.com/punkpeye/awesome-mcp-servers`**):** This is a curated list on GitHub, maintained collaboratively by the community. It categorizes servers and labels them with their supported programming languages and operating systems, making it ideal for developers looking for high-quality open-source servers. The project now also has its own independent website, as shown in *Figure 4.8*.

Figure 4.8 – Main page of the awesome-mcp-servers website

In these markets, you can explore thousands of tools that empower AI with new capabilities, and the process is as simple as downloading a new app on your smartphone.

Recommendations for free MCP tools for general users

To help you get started quickly, we've selected several free, simple MCP tools that are suitable for non-technical users, as shown in *Table 4.4*. These tools can be configured with just a few straightforward steps—no programming knowledge required.

You might wonder whether a standard AI chatbot could already perform the tasks listed below. The key difference is that a pure LLM is like a "brain in a jar": its knowledge is static, and it cannot inherently access real-time information, read local files, or operate software on your computer. MCP tools act as the AI's "hands and eyes," allowing it to interact with external systems and perform real-world tasks such as checking the current time, searching the web, reading files, or controlling a browser.

Server Name	**Main functions**	**Simple application scenarios**
Filesystem	Reading, writing, and organizing files on your computer	`Read the file meeting_minutes.txt and summarize the key decisions.`

Server Name	Main functions	Simple application scenarios
Zhip web search	Perform a web search and return the results	`Search for the latest news about Model Context Protocol and summarize the three most important articles.`
Playwright	Automated control of web browsers to perform tasks	`Open Google, search for " Model Context Protocol"and take a screenshot of the results page.`
How to cook Mcp	Provide cooking recipes and meal plans	`Find recipes in the cooking database that use chicken, rice, and broccoli and summarize the top three options.`

Table 4.4 – Free MCP Servers

Table 4.4 will help you enter the world of MCP, allowing you to quickly experience the practical value of MCP tools.

Detailed explanation of MCP configuration files

Now, let's understand the core of the MCP configuration—the `mcp.json` file. This file is used to tell AIs (such as TRAE SOLO and Cursor), *"This is your new toolbox, which contains these tools and how to use them."*

Taking adding a Time server as an example, the simplest configuration is as follows.

```
JSON
{
"mcpServers": {
"time": {
"command": "npx",
"args": ["-y", "mcp-server-time"]
}
}
}
```

The above configuration is explained line by line as follows:

- `"mcpServers": {...}`: Defines the beginning of a list of AI tools
- `"time": {...}`: The "nickname" you set for this tool, used for identification and management in AI applications
- `"command": "npx"`: Tells the computer to use the npx program to launch the tool (npx is a commonly used command in the Node.js environment that can easily run online packages without prior installation)
- `"args": ["-y", "mcp-server-time"]`: Tells npx to run the package named mcp-server-time

With these few simple lines of configuration, you have successfully installed new tools for your AI.

There are two main operating modes when configuring an MCP server:

- **STDIO (Standard Input/Output):** The AI application only starts its server process when you need it, and the process terminates once the task is completed, serving only you. This approach is ideal for tools running on your local computer (such as filesystem servers), offering advantages in security and privacy.
- **HTTP/SSE (Server-Sent Event):** The server can run on your computer or the internet, continuously waiting for requests, and the AI application "places an order" via a URL. This method is suitable for connecting to remote services that need to run continuously or are provided by a third party (such as GitHub or Figma servers).

Configuring and using MCP in Solo

Now, we will conduct our first hands-on exercise in the AI-native development environment TRAE SOLO. TRAE SOLO is a highly automated IDE with a powerful built-in AI assistant. Combining it with MCP can greatly enhance automation capabilities.

It is worth noting that the IDE plays a core "command center" or "coordinator" role in the MCP ecosystem. TRAE SOLO and Cursor both provide dedicated interfaces for managing servers, viewing logs, and approving tool calls—meaning that the IDE is becoming the main battleground for directing and coordinating AI agents to complete complex tasks, and the IDE itself perfectly fulfills the role of the host in the MCP architecture.

MCP global configuration and project-level configuration

In TRAE SOLO, the availability of the MCP tool can be determined through the following two configuration methods:

- **Global configuration:** The tool is visible to all items and is suitable for general functions such as querying time and web search
- **Project-level configuration:** Tools are only available for the current specific project. For example, it is recommended to configure the MCP server that connects to a specific database here.

TRAE SOLO provides a user-friendly interface for installing and managing MCP servers. The following example demonstrates the steps for project-level configuration:

1. In the TRAE SOLO settings or sidebar, find the **AI Management** or **MCP** option as shown in *Figure 4.9*.

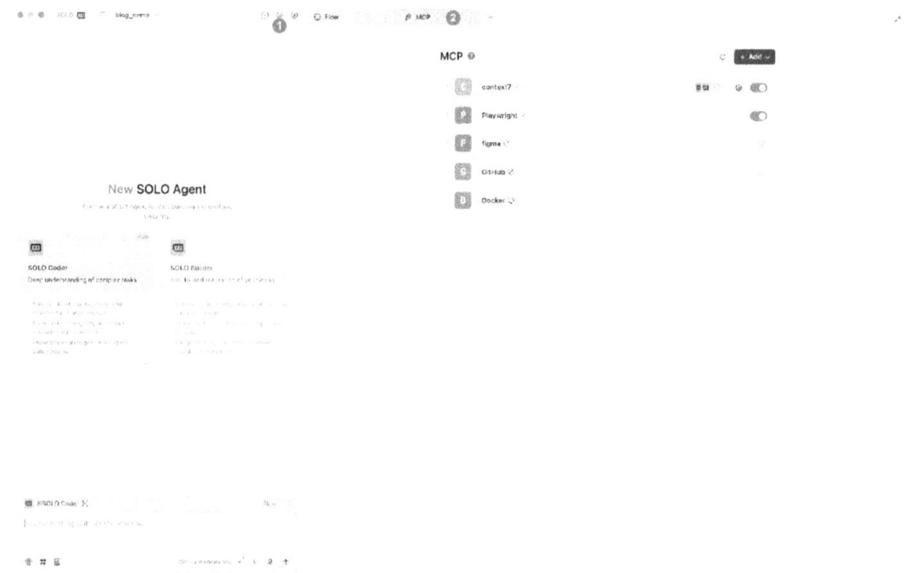

Figure 4.9 – Find the MCP option

2. TRAE SOLO comes with an MCP server marketplace. Simply click **Add** and fill in the necessary information as prompted to complete the installation, as shown in *Figure 4.10*.

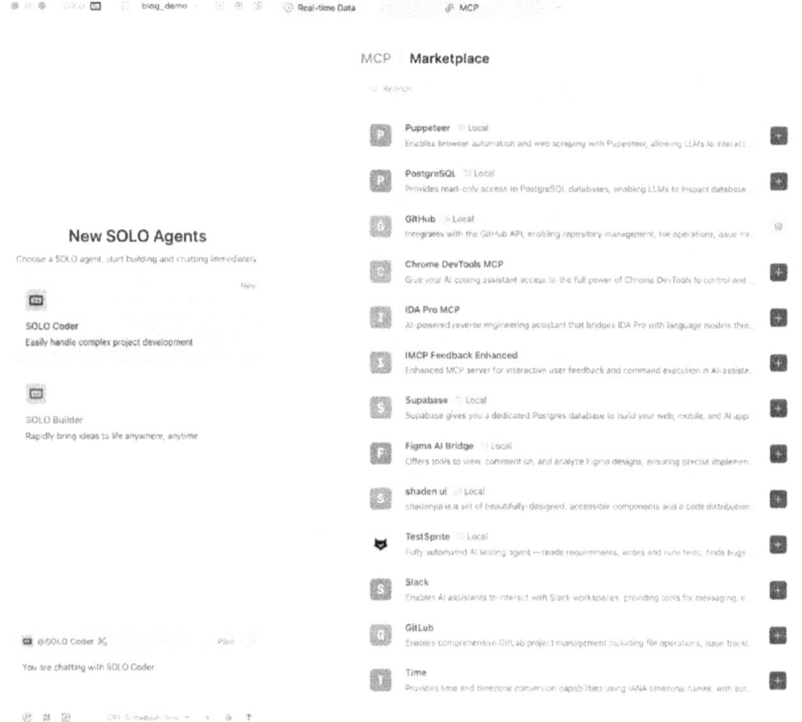

Figure 4.10 – Built-in MCP server marketplace

3. Enter a specific MCP server name in the marketplace search bar (or search for GitHub MCP for GitHub integration) and the search results will display a list of matching servers.
4. Locate the corresponding server in the search results (such as GitHub MCP), click the **Add** button next to it, and the server will appear in the list of configured servers after it is successfully added.

If you cannot find the required server in the built-in marketplace, or if you need more granular configuration, you can click the **Manual Configuration** button on the server list interface (usually located at the top or bottom of the server list). TRAE SOLO will guide you through the configuration process, as shown in *Figure 4.11*.

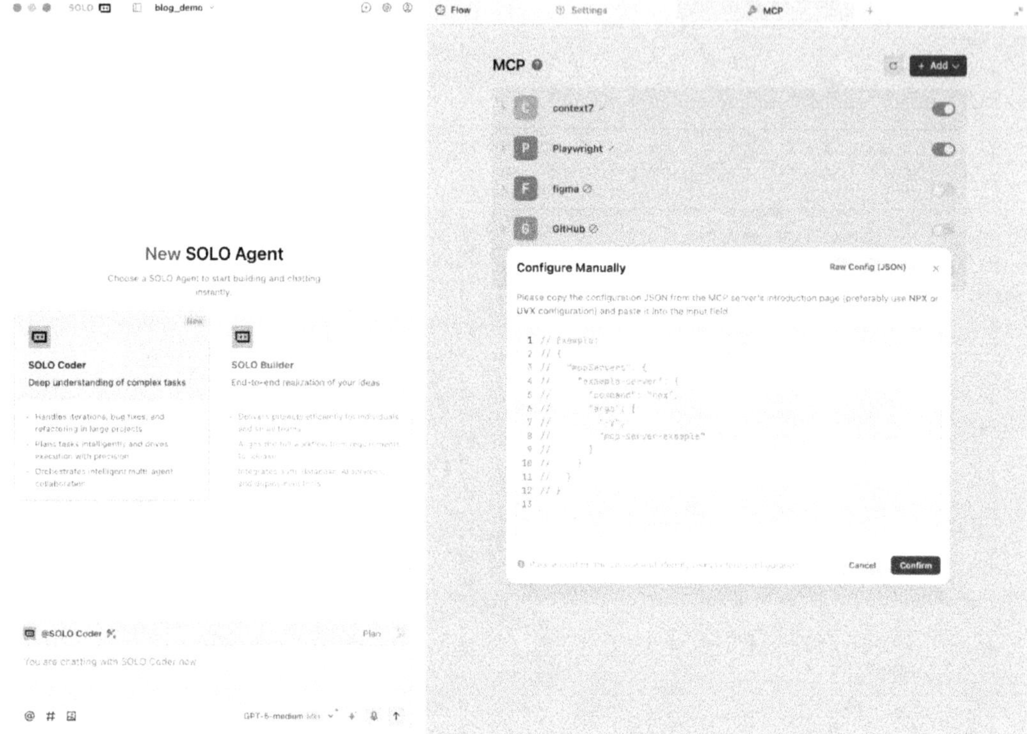

Figure 4.11 – Manually configuring the MCP server

When configuring manually, you need to edit the corresponding `mcp.json` file: for project-level configuration, edit `.vscode/mcp.json` in the project directory; for global configuration, edit `map.json` in the user's directory. The basic structure of this file is as follows:

```
JSON
{
"mcpServers": {
"server-name": {
"command": "executable",
"args": ["arg1", "arg2"],
"env": {
"VAR": "value"
}
}
}
}
```

The corresponding fields of the basic structure of this file are explained below:

- `"server-name"`: The name identifier set for the server
- `"command"`: Executable commands (such as `npx`) that run the MCP server
- `"args"`: An array of command-line arguments passed to the server executable
- `"env"`: Contains an environment variable object that needs to be set when starting the server (optional).

You can choose to add the corresponding server configuration in the project-level configuration (which applies only to the current project) or the global configuration (which applies to all projects) as required.

Finally, manage the added servers. After adding them, you can see all the configured servers in the list and perform operations such as enabling, disabling, editing, or restarting them at any time, as shown in *Figure 4.12*.

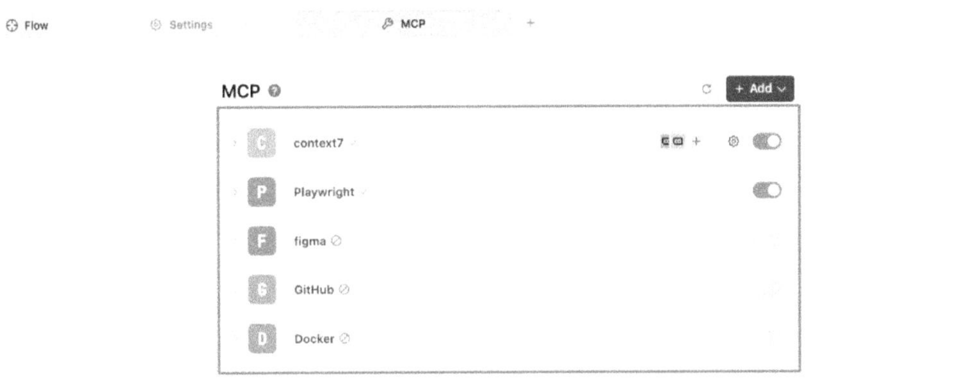

Figure 4.12 – Configured Server

10-minute hands-on lesson: Connecting to GitHub MCP

The goal of this practical exercise is to enable AI to become your code repository manager, automating GitHub-related tasks—such as reading project files, checking for open bugs, and creating new issues. GitHub is a cloud platform for hosting and managing code, and we will use MCP to enable direct interaction between AI and GitHub.

Creating a GitHub personal access token

Before you begin, you need to create a **personal access token** (**PAT**). The PAT is a special password used by the application and must be properly protected to prevent it from being leaked.

Please log in to your GitHub account, navigate to **Developer settings** in **Settings**, then select **Personal access tokens**, choose the **Fine-grained tokens** type, and create a new PAT. During creation, be sure to follow the principle of *least privilege*—only select the minimum permissions necessary for the tool (e.g., if you only need to read issues, do not grant permission to delete repositories).

Configure the MCP.json file

After obtaining the PAT, the next step is to configure the `mcp.json` file. In TRAE SOLO, select **Manually Add MCP Server** and enter the following configuration (remember to replace `your_github_pat` with the PAT you just generated):

```
JSON
{
"mcpServers": {
"GitHub": {
"command": "npx",
"args": ["-y", "@modelcontextprotocol/server-github"],
"env": {
"GITHUB_PERSONAL_ACCESS_TOKEN": "your_github_pat"
}
}
}
}
```

This configuration runs the MCP server provided by GitHub via `npx` and securely passes the PAT through the `env` field.

Verification and application

After completing the configuration, save the file and restart or refresh the MCP server list. Then open the TRAE SOLO chat window and issue commands in natural language. For example:

- `List all open issues in the my-first-website repository`
- `Read file from the main branch`
- `Create a new topic with the title 'Update Homepage Welcome Message'`

AI will act as your personal GitHub assistant, responding in real time and handling various code repository management tasks.

10-minute hands-on demonstration: Integrating Figma MCP

The goal of this practical exercise is to break down the barriers between design and development, enabling AI to directly transform Figma visual design drafts into usable frontend code. Figma is a popular online collaborative design tool, and we will implement seamless integration between it and AI.

Enable Figma local server

First, you need to enable the MCP server in Figma.

Make sure you have the latest version of the Figma desktop application installed, then open any Figma design file, find **Preferences** in the top left menu, and then find and check **Enable local MCP Server**.

Once enabled, Figma will silently run a local server on your computer (see *Figure 4.13*).

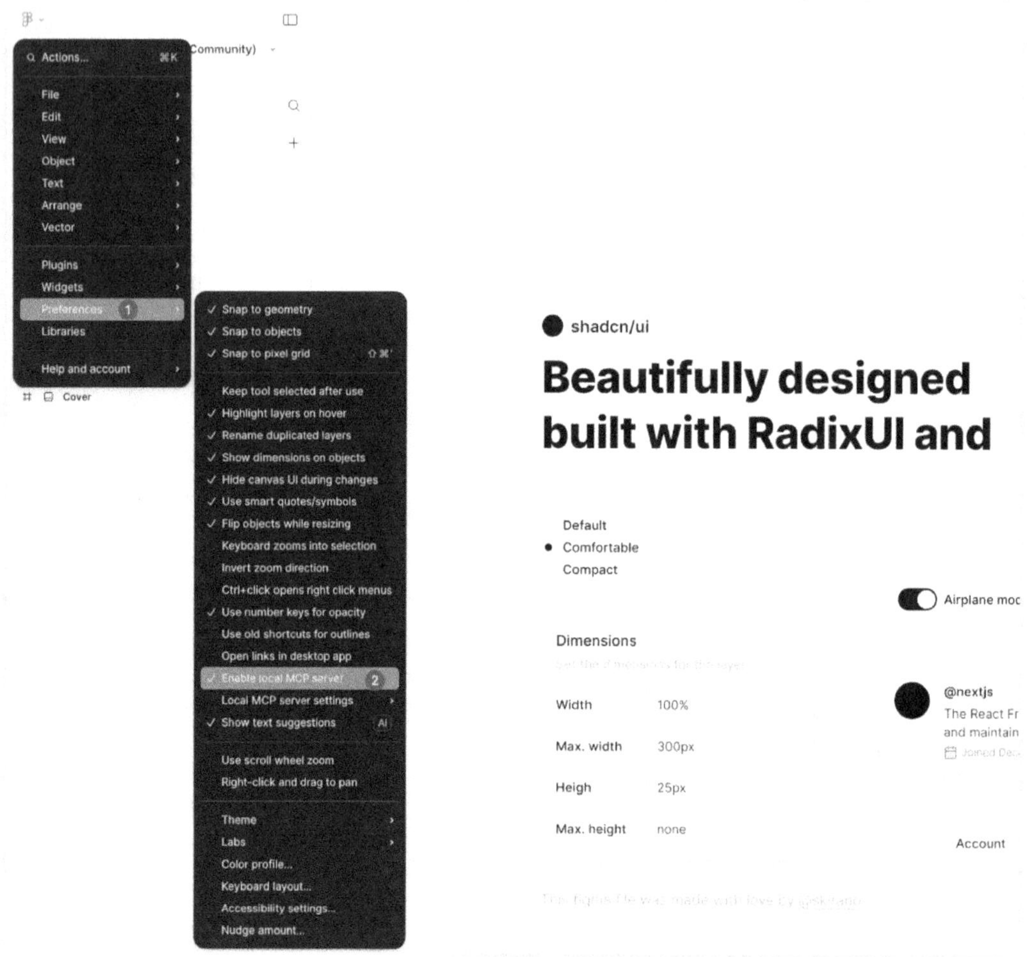

Figure 4.13 – Enabling the MCP server

It will also display the URL address at the bottom of the canvas. Copy the address (see *Figure 4.14*).

Figure 4.14 – Copying the MCP server URL

Configure TRAE SOLO connection to Figma

The default address for a Figma local server is usually `http://127.0.0.1:3845/mcp`. Manually add the server in the TRAE SOLO MCP settings and configure it as follows:

```
JSON
{
"mcpServers": {
"figma": {
"type": "http",
"url": "[http://127.0.0.1:3845/mcp](http://127.0.0.1:3845/mcp)"
}
}
}
```

Transforming design into code

After configuration, right-click the target design element in Figma and select **Copy link to selection**, as shown in *Figure 4.15*.

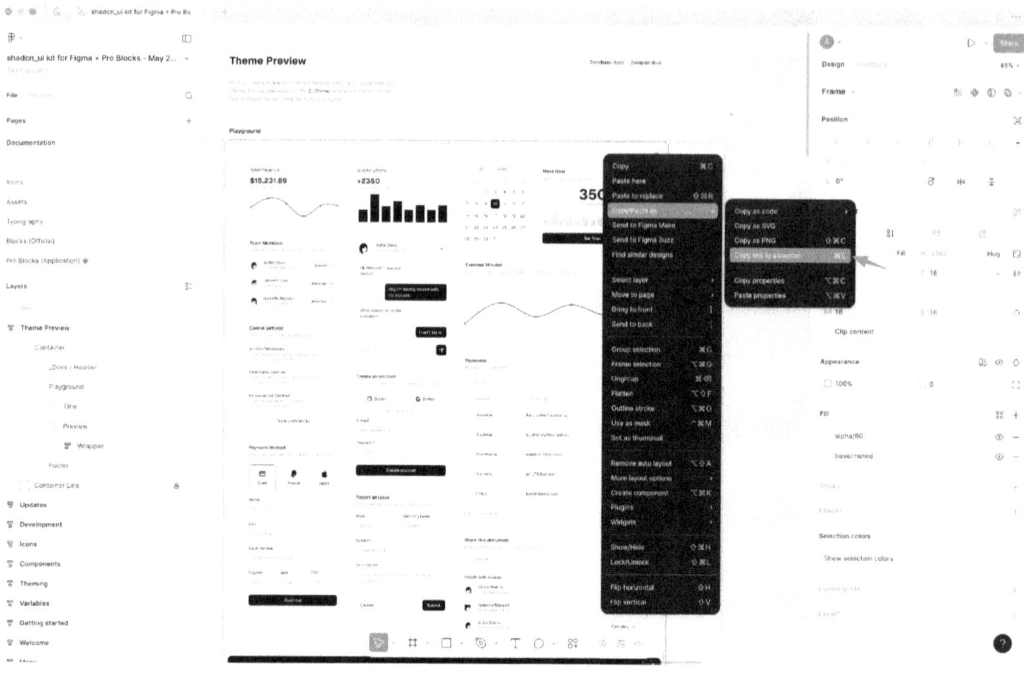

Figure 4.15 – Copying links in Figma

Return to the TRAE SOLO chat window, switch to Builder with MCP agent, paste the link, and give the AI the command: `Use Figma MCP to generate HTML and Tailwind CSS code for this design.`

Through MCP, AI acquires structured data from the design (such as color values, rounded corners, fonts, and font sizes) to generate high-quality code that can be used directly in production.

10-minute hands-on exercise: Configuring Playwright MCP

The goal of this practical exercise is to enable AI to operate the browser like a professional test engineer, performing automated testing and data scraping. **Playwright** is a powerful automation tool that can precisely execute browser clicks, input, scrolling, and screenshots through code.

Configure Playwright MCP server

Before starting the configuration, you can choose two ways to install the Playwright MCP server: search for and add it directly in the TRAE SOLO MCP marketplace, or manually configure the `mcp.json` file (this method is recommended because `nxp` will automatically download and run the server, so there is no need to install it in advance).

If you choose manual configuration, add the following content to the `mcp.json` file in TRAE SOLO.

```
JSON
{
"mcpServers": {
"Playwright": {
"command": "npx",
"args": ["-y", "@executeautomation/playwright-mcp-server"],
"env": {}
}
}
}
```

This configuration uses `npx` to run the Playwright MCP server. The `-y` parameter indicates automatic confirmation during installation, making the whole process smoother.

Automated operation

After saving the configuration, select Builder with MCP agent in the TRAE SOLO chat window and enter the following prompts one by one:

1. `Open a new browser page using Playwright and visit the URL https://en.wikipedia.org/wiki/Artificial_intelligence`
2. `Great! Click the link on the page that says, 'Machine learning'`
3. `Well done! Now take a screenshot of the current page and save it as ml_page.png.`

Through simple dialogue, without the need to write complex code, AI automatically invokes various Playwright functions to translate natural language commands into precise browser automation actions.

10-minute hands-on exercise: Connecting to Magic MCP

The goal of this practical exercise is to generate the interface you want in one sentence. **Magic MCP** is an AI tool that can instantly convert natural language descriptions into UI component code, making interface development as simple as speaking.

Get magic API key

Visit the Magic official website (`https://21st.dev/magic`), register an account, and log in to your personal dashboard. Generate a new API key in the API area, then copy and save it. This key will be used to connect TRAE SOLO with the Magic service.

Configure the mcp.json file

Add the following configuration to TRAE SOLO, remembering to replace your-api-key with the actual key you just obtained:

```
JSON
{
"mcpServers": {
"@21st-dev/magic": {
"command": "npx",
"args": ["-y", "@21st-dev/magic@latest", "API_KEY=\"your-api-key\""]
}
}
}
```

This configuration runs the latest version of the Magic MCP server via npx and authenticates by passing your API key through environment variables.

Generate UI components

Once configured, you can unleash your creativity. In the TRAE SOLO chat window, switch to Builder with MCP agent and use `/ui command` to describe the component you want, as shown in the following examples.

- `/ui Create a modern-style login form that includes a 'Forgot Password' link.`
- `/ui generates a price comparison table, divided into three tiers: Basic, Professional, and Enterprise.`
- `Design a website navigation bar with a search box and user avatars.`

The AI will automatically generate UI component code that conforms to modern design standards based on the description, including HTML structure, styles, and necessary interaction logic. You can preview the effect directly and fine-tune it as needed without having to write a single line of code by hand.

Configuring and using MCP in Cursor

Now, let's turn our attention back to Cursor. Now, we are going to unlock its ultimate capability: using its built-in Composer Agent to autonomously understand complex tasks and call your configured MCP tools to complete them.

Mcp.json configuration and Composer Agent integration

Similar to TRAE SOLO, Cursor also supports two MCP configuration modes: *global* and *project-level*. The configuration file is also named `mcp.json`. Let's look at the two types of configurations:

- **Global configuration:** This applies to all projects. The configuration file is stored in the user's home directory as `~/.cursor/mcp.json`. You can open the settings panel using the shortcut *Ctrl/Cmd +* , and then click **Tools & Integrations** in the left menu to find MCP settings for configuration, as shown in *Figure 4.16*:

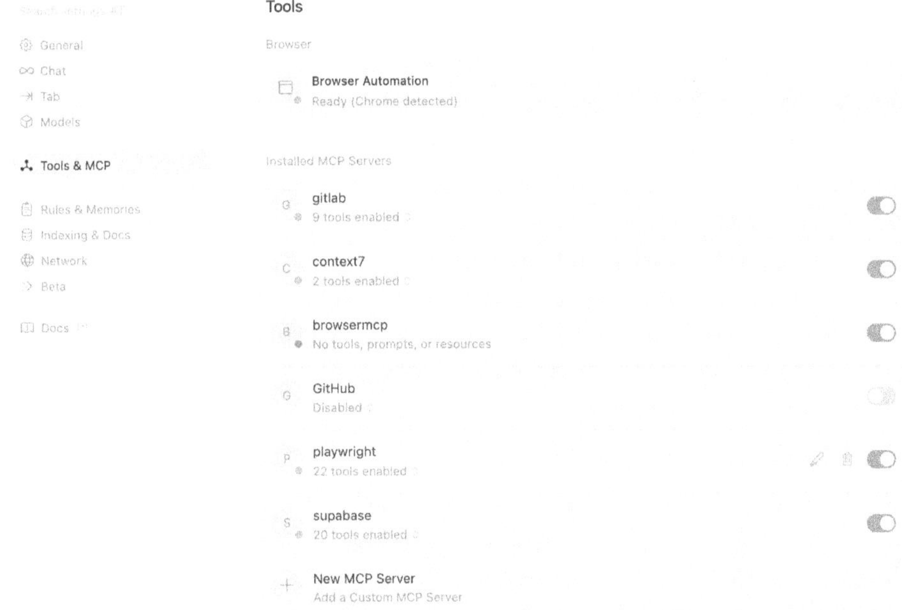

Figure 4.16 – MCP configuration

- **Project-level configuration:** This is a "dedicated toolkit" that only applies to the current project. Its configuration file is located in `.cursor/mcp.json` in the project's root directory. The corresponding MCP server is only loaded when Cursor opens the project, making it suitable for storing project-specific tool capabilities (such as a dedicated order database MCP server for an e-commerce project). In team collaboration scenarios, this configuration file can be committed to the code repository, and other members can directly use the same MCP toolchain after pulling the project without needing to reconfigure it.

After configuration, you need to enable Cursor's **Composer Agent** mode: In Composer, press *Cmd* + *L* (Mac) or *Ctrl* + *L* (Windows/Linux), and select **Agent mode**. Once enabled, the Agent will actively recognize the configured MCP tools and invoke them when needed.

As we explored in the earlier *Composer Agent: Programming Assistance in Cursor* section, this agent can already read your codebase and run terminal commands. Now, with MCP configured, it gains the ability to autonomously call external servers and perform live web searches.

When you make a request that requires external capabilities, the Agent will display the tools to be used in the chat interface and request approval. For frequently used and trusted workflows, you can enable **Auto-run** mode to allow the Agent to automatically execute tool calls and achieve a higher degree of automation.

10-minute hands-on exercise: Connecting to browser MCP

The goal of this practical exercise is to enable AI to directly control your Chrome browser, including logged-in websites and saved cookies. Unlike Playwright's new Guest Mode browser, Browser MCP directly controls your active, everyday browser. This is incredibly useful for personal automation—such as automatically liking specific posts on your social media feeds, summarizing emails from your personal inbox, or extracting data from internal company dashboards. Because the AI acts within your already-logged-in sessions, you never need to re-enter passwords or deal with annoying CAPTCHAs, and all actions run locally to protect your privacy and avoid bot detection.

Install Chrome extension

Search for `Browser MCP` in the Chrome Web Store and install it (this extension is a bridge between AI and the browser). After installation, enable the extension on the browser you want to control. Click the extension icon and then click **Connect.**

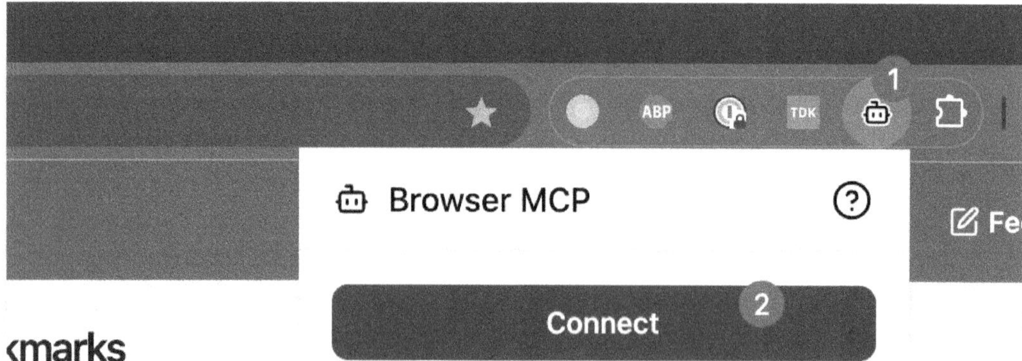

Figure 4.17 – Enabling the Browser MCP extension in Chrome

If you see the plugin in listening mode, it has been successfully enabled, as shown in *Figure 4.18*.

Figure 4.18 – Browser MCP in listening mode

Configure the MCP.json file

In Cursor, open the global or project-level `mcp.json` file, and add the following configuration:

```
JSON
{
"mcpServers": {
"browsermcp": {
"command": "npx",
"args": ["@browsermcp/mcp@latest"]
}
}
}
```

Save the configuration and restart Cursor.

Experience personal automation

Press *Ctrl/Cmd + I* to open the AI chat window and try the following commands

```
1. Open a new browser tab and visit weibo.com。 "
2. Search for the tag 'ambience programming' on the currently opened Weibo page.
3. Please like the first 3 results in my search.
```

Through simple dialogue, AI can complete various automated tasks within a logged-in browser environment, significantly improving daily work efficiency.

10-minute hands-on demonstration: Integrating Supabase MCP

The goal of this practical exercise is to enable users to interact with databases using natural language and to perform functions such as querying data and managing tables without writing complex SQL statements.

1. **Register with Supabase and obtain** a **PAT:** Visit the Supabase website to create a free account and a new project. Create a new PAT in the **Access Tokens** section of your account settings. Keep this PAT safe, as it grants access to the database and requires security measures.
2. **Copy Project ID:** Locate and copy your **Project ID** in your Supabase project as shown in *Figure 4.19*.

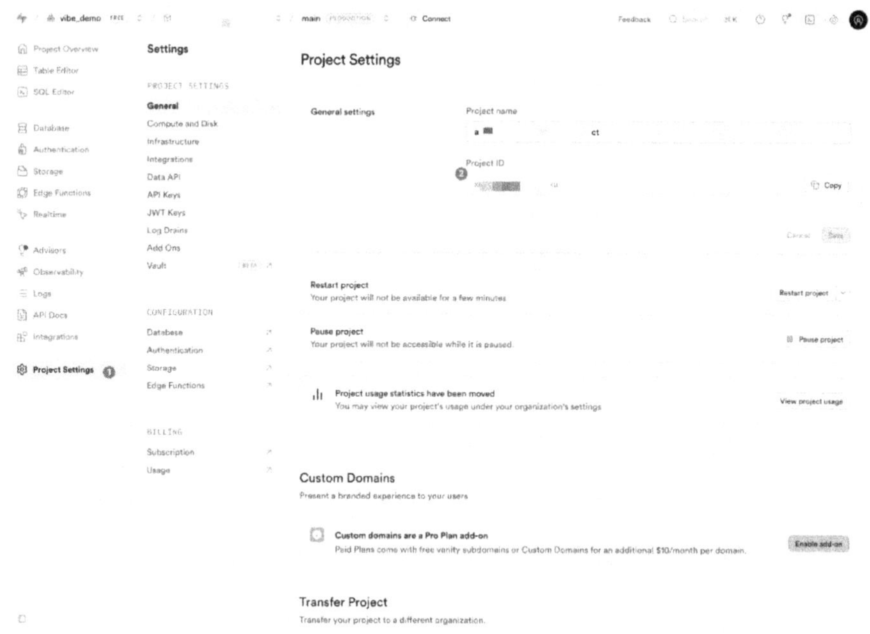

Figure 4.19 – Copy Project ID

3. **Configure the mcp.json file:** Configure the Supabase MCP server in Cursor by replacing `your-supabase-pat` with your PAT and project-ref with your Project ID.

```
JSON
{
"mcpServers": {
"supabase": {
"command": "npx",
```

```
"args": [
"-and",
"@supabase/mcp-server-supabase@latest",
"--read-only",
"--project-ref=<project-ref>"
],
"env": {
"SUPABASE_ACCESS_TOKEN": "your-supabase-pat"
}
}
}
}
```

4. **Querying databases using natural language:** Using the users table created in the previous chapter as an example, you can have the following conversation with the AI:
   - `Use Supabase to see which users are in the users table?`
   - `What are their email addresses?`
   - `Please help me find all the information for the user whose email address is your_email+test1@gmail.com.`

AI automatically translates natural language into precise database queries and displays the results in an easy-to-read manner, making database operations as simple as chatting.

10-minute hands-on exercise: Configuring Context7 MCP

The goal of this practical exercise is to address the issue of outdated LLM knowledge, enabling AI to reference the latest official documentation when generating code. AI models' knowledge bases have "deadlines," while Context7 MCP is a service specifically designed to provide AI with real-time, version-specific documentation, effectively preventing AI from experiencing "hallucinations" or using outdated APIs.

1. **Obtain the Context7 API key**: Log in to the Context7 website, register an account, and obtain your API key. This key is used to access the latest technical documentation resources (Node.js v18 or above is required to use it).
2. **Configure the mcp.json file:** Open the global or project-level mcp.json file in Cursor and add the following configuration, replacing `your-context7-api-key` with your API key:

```
JSON
{
"mcpServers": {
```

```
"context7": {
"url": "[https://mcp.context7.com/mcp](https://mcp.context7.com/mcp)",
"headers": {
"CONTEXT7_API_KEY": "your-context7-api-key"
}
}
}
}
```

3. **Experience real-time document reference function:** When you ask the AI how to use a library or framework, state-of-the-art large models (such as Claude Sonnet 4) will automatically trigger this service. For example, if we ask the AI `How do I use the `after` function in Next.js?`, the AI's response before and after enabling Context7 MCP might look like this:
    - **Context7 MCP not started:** The AI might reply, "*Sorry, Next.js does not have a function named after*"
    - **Context7 MCP has been started:** The AI will first obtain the latest official documentation for the after function through Context7 MCP, then generate the correct usage example based on the accurate information.

With Context7 MCP, AI is freed from the time constraints of training data and can always provide the latest and most accurate technical advice.

Advanced applications and practical techniques of MCP

The true power of MCP lies in combining independent tools to build personalized workflows that automate complex tasks.

Collaborative configuration and performance optimization of multiple MCP tools

To enable multiple MCP servers to work collaboratively, the key is to master orchestration techniques. Orchestration refers to the ability to make multiple independent MCP servers work together toward a common goal. In this process, the AI agent plays the role of "commander-in-chief," intelligently determining which tool to invoke at different steps based on complex instructions.

A typical example is the online incident response workflow: when you tell the AI, "`Our website login page seems to be having problems, please check it for me,`", the AI will immediately start multiple MCP tools to work together.

First, Sentry MCP (the error monitoring platform we introduced in *Chapter 3*) is invoked to check the latest logs of the error monitoring system, and the response is *"OK, I am checking the latest logs of the Sentry error monitoring system."*

Secondly, when a serious error related to user authentication is discovered, GitHub MCP is invoked to find the relevant code commit records.

Finally, an alert was sent to the development team channel via Slack MCP: *"The issue has been located, possibly caused by a code merge last night. Error logs and code links are attached."*

The whole process was smooth and natural, just like an experienced engineer handling an online incident.

The core value of this "hybrid AI application" stems from the intelligent orchestration and combination of tools. This is similar to the UNIX command-line philosophy: connecting simple commands through the pipe symbol (|) to build powerful data processing pipelines, and MCP is precisely the "pipe symbol" in the AI world. Therefore, the key to learning MCP lies in cultivating a workflow design mindset that transcends single instructions.

When building complex workflows for a specific project, the best practice is to use a project-level `mcp.json` file to ensure that only the servers required by the current project are loaded, keeping the AI environment lightweight and efficient.

10-minute hands-on lesson: Building your personal workflow

In our daily work, we often need to proactively follow the latest developments in the AI industry, manually visiting websites, filtering news, extracting key points, and saving files—a tedious and time-consuming process. This practical exercise will leverage the skills of MCP to automate these operations within Cursor, creating an end-to-end automated workflow.

Configure the required MCP tools

Ensure that the `browsermcp` and filesystem servers are configured in the Cursor's `mcp.json` file, where the filesystem path needs to be replaced with your actual read/write path:

```
JSON
{
"mcpServers": {
"browsermcp": {
"command": "npx",
"args": ["@browsermcp/mcp@latest"]
},
"filesystem": {
"command": "npx",
"args": [
```

```
"-and",
"@modelcontextprotocol/server-filesystem",
"/Users/username/Desktop"
]
}
}
}
```

Issuing multi-step instructions

Open Cursor's AI chat window and clearly give the AI the following instructions:

```
Please use the MCP tool to perform the following series of tasks.
1. Use the Browser MCP tool to access the homepage of the WaytoAGI knowledge base
website.
2. Extract the main content of the three most important AI news articles on the
homepage.
3. Generate a English abstract of approximately 100 words for each of these three
articles.
4. Use a file system tool to create a new file named WaytoAGI_news_summary.md on
your desktop and write the three summaries into that file in Markdown format.
```

Observe the automation process

In Cursor's chat interface, you can see the AI agent's actions in real time: calling Browser MCP to access websites, analyzing content, and calling Filesystem MCP to create files, etc. Once completed, a Markdown file containing an AI news summary will appear on your desktop.

View automation results

Open the newly generated `WaytoAGI_news_summary.md` file in Cursor to see a formatted summary containing the article title, core viewpoints, and key information.

This practical case perfectly demonstrates MCP's collaborative capabilities—compressing tedious manual operations such as opening a browser, accessing a website, copying content, summarizing key points, and creating files into a simple conversation. This workflow, which connects multiple tools, is the core value of the MCP architecture: enabling AI not only to complete single tasks, but also to understand and execute complex, multi-step workflows like a human assistant.

MCP troubleshooting and common problems

When using the MCP server, you may encounter connection problems (frequent disconnections, failed connection attempts), performance issues (slow response, insufficient processing capacity), or data processing anomalies (incorrect formatting, processing failures). *Table 4.5* provides troubleshooting guidelines for common MCP problems.

Problem	**Possible causes and symptoms**	**Solution steps**
The server failed to start.	The tool is not listed in the available tools list or the MCP log shows an error.	Check if dependencies such as Node.js and Python are installed correctly Manually run the command and args statements in mcp.json in the terminal to view specific error messages. Confirm that the path in the configuration file is correct.
Permission denied	File read/write failed, displaying a "Permission Denied" or similar message.	Check the read/write permissions of the target file or folder. Try using absolute paths instead of relative paths in your configuration Ensure that Cursor or TRAE SOLO have access to the system.
JSON format error	The MCP function failed to load, displaying the error message "malformed JSON".	Copy the entire contents of the mcp.json file Use an online JSON validator to detect syntax errors (such as missing commas or mismatched brackets).

Problem	Possible causes and symptoms	Solution steps
Authentication failed	The tool connects successfully but fails to execute, displaying a 401 Unauthorized or invalid API key error.	Verify that the API key/PAT has been copied completely, without any extra spaces. Confirm that the key has the required permissions. Check whether the key has expired.

Table 4.5 – Common MCP Faults and Troubleshooting Guide

MCP best practices and safety recommendations

As a core bridge connecting AI with various external tools, MCP can greatly improve development efficiency. However, the tool's power also means that security risks and standardized usage must be taken seriously. This not only relates to the security of personal accounts and data, but also affects the stability of the environment during team collaboration. Therefore, at the end of this chapter, we will focus on how to use MCP tools safely and responsibly, avoiding potential risks through clear practice principles, and ensuring that the tool's capabilities truly serve efficient development.

- **Protection Certificate:** API keys and PATs are critical credentials for accessing digital services; never share them with anyone or upload them to public cyberspace. Store these credentials in environment variables instead of writing them directly to configuration files to reduce the risk of leakage at the source
- **Least Privilege Principle:** When creating tokens or keys, only grant them the minimum permissions required to complete the task, avoiding excessive privilege expansion. This is a fundamental principle of security protection and can effectively limit the impact of potential security incidents.
- **Source of Trust:** Install MCP servers only from official release channels or highly trusted community sources. Be highly vigilant against servers from unknown sources to prevent malicious servers from stealing your data or performing malicious operations (such as tool-poisoning). Always verify the reliability of the source before installation.
- **Review and confirmation**: When first using a tool, do not blindly approve all tool call requests. Carefully read the approval prompts to understand the commands to be

executed and their scope of impact. Only after you fully understand and trust a tool's automated processes should you consider enabling the "auto-run" function.

- **Keep clean**: Regularly clean up the `mcp.json` file, remove unused server configurations, and reduce potential security risks and configuration complexity.

In addition, strictly validate and clean all inputs to prevent security vulnerabilities such as path traversal and illegal characters, implement fine-grained access control and complete audit logs to ensure that all operations are traceable, and clearly define the expected inputs and outputs in the tool description to avoid ambiguity and ensure the security and effectiveness of the tool.

By following these security practices, you can improve development efficiency while effectively ensuring the safety of yourself and your team.

Summary

In this section, we unlocked the ultimate capability of AI agents by using the Model Context Protocol (MCP). You learned how to configure MCP servers in both TRAE SOLO and Cursor, transforming your AI from an isolated brain into an active digital assistant. You successfully connected your IDE to GitHub to manage code, integrated Figma to turn designs into code, utilized Playwright and Browser MCP for web automation, and even queried Supabase databases using natural language. Finally, you learned how to orchestrate these independent tools into powerful, multi-step automated workflows.

Now that your toolbox is assembled, it is time to put these skills to the test. In the next chapter, we will transition from learning isolated techniques to building a real product, guiding you step by step through creating a fully functional 'Habit Tracker' application from scratch.

Get this book's PDF version and more

Scan the QR code (or go to `packtpub.com/unlock`). Search for this book by name, confirm the edition, and then follow the steps on the page.

Note: Keep your invoice handy. Purchases made directly from Packt don't require an invoice.

5

Project Practice 1: Building a Habit Tracker From Scratch

It's time to put all the tools at your disposal into action for a real goal.

In this chapter, we will create a complete product and guide you through the entire process from the first flash of inspiration to its usability. The practical project we chose is a **habit tracker**—a product that, while seemingly simple, actually covers almost all the key aspects of modern application development and is an excellent vehicle for developing comprehensive skills.

You will witness firsthand how a vague idea evolves into a clear product blueprint through brainstorming with AI; you will experience the complete process of building a database from scratch, designing user authentication, and implementing core functions; you will also learn how to integrate essential components of modern applications, such as email services and file storage. Every line of code and every decision will become an important accumulation of your independent development capabilities.

After completing this chapter, you will have a piece of work you can proudly showcase and the ability to bring an idea to fruition.

Technical requirements

The project documents, reports, prompt workflows, and output for this chapter can be found in the book's GitHub repository: `https://github.com/PacktPublishing/Everyone-is-a-Programmer/tree/main/chapters/chapter-05-habit-tracker`.

Blueprint: Using AI to plan products

Now that we have the idea of developing a habit tracker app, what's the next step? At this juncture, having a readily available, knowledgeable, and creative partner can make all the difference.

In this section, AI will play the role of your product partner. It will assist you in brainstorming, organizing your thoughts, challenging existing assumptions, and transforming that idea into a clear, actionable product blueprint. We will learn how to leverage an advanced LLM such as ChatGPT, Claude, Gemini, or DeepSeek to articulate the idea of a habit tracker into a clear product framework with manageable modules, taking a steady first step in product development. We will clarify the core problem the product aims to solve (*why do it*), clearly define the target user profile (*for whom*), and define the core functionalities the application needs to possess (*what it does*).

Using AI for functional brainstorming

What features should our habit tracker include? Is it a simple check-in system, or does it need complex data charts? Should we add social elements? For those developing this type of product for the first time, these questions can easily bring the project to a standstill.

This is the perfect time for AI partners to step in. However, to maximize the effectiveness of AI, the key is to ask a well-structured question. Simply asking *"What features does a habit tracker need?"* might yield overly broad results. We need to design a structured "super prompt" for AI, much like a product manager would.

Create your first super suggestion word

An effective prompt should include the role, task, and formatting requirements, guiding the AI to output valuable content from a professional perspective. Here is an example:

```
Please play the role of an experienced product manager. I'm brainstorming for a
new 'habit tracker' mobile app, and I need a comprehensive brainstorming session.
Before listing the features, please provide a brief analysis of the market and
user psychology behind successful habit trackers (e.g., what psychological needs
do they fulfill?).
Next, divide the functions into two categories.
 - Core functionalities: These are the basic functionalities necessary for
building a minimum viable product (MVP).
 - Innovative/Advanced Features: These are the features that will allow products
to stand out and increase user engagement in the future.
For each function, please briefly describe its purpose in one sentence.
```

Interpreting AI analysis reports

After inputting the above prompts, the AI will retrieve and integrate relevant data to generate a detailed strategic analysis report. This report goes beyond listing the functions and reflects an in-depth analysis of the market and user psychology, typically including the following core sections:

- **Market and user psychology analysis:** The opening section will analyze the logic behind mainstream competitors. For example, the gamified *Habitica* attracts players with experience points and equipment systems, the minimalist *Streaks* caters to efficiency-oriented users with a simple interface and a continuous counter, and the health coach-style *Fabulous* uses a behavioral science-based "habit stacking" technique to guide users to gradually change. These products all rely on solid psychological theories, including Nir Eyal's addiction model (trigger-action-reward-investment cycle), BJ Fogg's behavioral model (behavior = motivation + ability + cue), and self-determination theory (emphasizing the three psychological needs of autonomy, competence, and belonging)
- **Functional planning core:** AI will clearly categorize functions into the following two types
    - **Core functionality (essential for MVPs):** Approximately 9 features, covering user account management, habit creation, flexible scheduling (supporting specific days per week or fixed intervals), positive/negative habit tracking, daily check-in, continuous record counter, basic reminders and notifications, progress visualization, and data privacy protection
    - **Innovative/Advanced features:** More than 20 features, covering five major areas: gamified incentives (virtual avatars, skill trees, narrative tasks), holistic wellness (guided journaling, mindfulness practice, CBT coping strategies), community and accountability (team challenges, accountability partners, celebration sharing), AI personalization (conversational coaching, dynamic goal adjustment, predictive obstacle recognition), and environmental computing integration (automatic synchronization of the wellness platform, context-aware prompts)
- **Strategic recommendations:** The LLM will provide a clear phased roadmap, as detailed below.
    - **Phase 1**: Release the MVP to validate the core loop and confirm whether users can successfully create and track habits

  - **Phase 2**: Deepen user engagement and increase sticky features
  - **Phase 3**: Achieve a competitive barrier through intelligent functions

At the same time, the report emphasizes the need to clarify the product's unique value proposition (whether it is an ultimate gamified experience, an intelligent AI coach, a frictionless life recorder, or a mindfulness habit builder), and notes that in the health field, trust is the most valuable asset. Therefore, data security measures need to be implemented from day one, maintaining transparency to users and complying with relevant regulations.

- **The AI's Key Conclusions:** Successful habit trackers are not simply about piling on features; they require a clear strategic choice regarding product philosophy, grounding design in the scientific principles of human motivation, and executing a phased plan centered on user value and trust. By focusing on specific user needs, they build a trustworthy and compliant platform, creating a product that truly helps users build a better life.

Because the full report generated by AI is quite long (including a detailed competitive landscape comparison table, a feature priority framework, specific feature descriptions, and other details), we have compiled it into an electronic document that you can download from the book's GitHub repository.

From feature list to product strategy

This AI-generated report is the starting point for formulating product strategies.

First, it clearly distinguishes between current tasks and future direction. For startups, focus is key to success—the core feature list constitutes the MVP, which serves as the foundation to meet users' basic expectations for a habit tracker. The priority is to refine these core functions to be simple and easy to use rather than rushing to add advanced features.

On a deeper level, this report prompts us to consider a core question: *What kind of product do we want to create?* Successful apps on the market all reflect unique product philosophies in their feature selection. For example, *Streaks* features minimalism and deep integration with Apple Health, emphasizing data tracking that requires almost no additional effort; *Habitica* transforms habit formation into a role-playing game, reinforcing user motivation through external incentives; while *Fabulous* is more like a health coach, guiding users to make gradual changes.

Therefore, examining the advanced features provided by AI is actually about choosing the "soul" of a product—whether it's about creating a minimalist data tracker, a highly gamified motivator, or a guided health coach. This decision will directly impact the product's target user group.

Furthermore, the report reveals some key strategic trade-offs. For example, automated tracking greatly improves convenience but places higher demands on data permissions and privacy compliance; manual recording is more controllable and lightweight but increases user operating costs. This illustrates that *what not to do* and *what to do* are equally important, and we need to carefully weigh convenience, privacy, cost, and compliance.

To clarify the planning, we compiled the results of our AI brainstorming into two overview tables, as shown in *Tables 5.1* and *5.2*. *Table 5.1* lists the core functionalities necessary for building an MVP. These functionalities form the basic framework of the habit tracker, ensuring users can complete the core cycle of "creating a habit - tracking progress - receiving feedback."

Functional classification	**Function name**	**User value (the importance of this feature)**
Account management	User accounts and guide	Get started safely and smoothly with an easy initial setup, reducing the learning curve.
Habit management	Habit creation	Quickly translate ideas into traceable goals to reduce startup resistance.
Habit management	Flexible planning	Adaptable to irregular schedules and frequencies, which improves feasibility.
Habit management	Positive/negative habit tracking	It supports both "doing" and "quitting" scenarios, making it more realistic.
Tracking record	Daily check-in or completion	One-click operation ensures the core loop can be completed with almost no additional operations.
Incentive feedback	Continuous recording counter	Enhance achievement and intrinsic motivation by visualizing "consecutive days".
Reminder notice	Basic reminders or notifications	Providing timely reminders helps combat forgetting and establishes a rhythm.
Digital display	Basic progress visualization	Looking back at history through calendars or simple diagrams makes perseverance visible.

Functional classification	Function name	User value (the importance of this feature)
Safety and compliance	Data privacy and security	Based on trust, data security is ensured through compliant encryption and clear policies

Table 5.1 – List of Core Functions (MVP)

Table 5.2 focuses on functional innovation directions, summarizing advanced features that can be used to differentiate the product and enhance long-term user engagement, and providing a clear direction for subsequent version iterations.

Innovation directions	Functional examples	User value (the importance of this feature)
Advanced gamification and incentives	Virtual avatars and equipment, skill trees, narrative quests, holiday mode	Catering to different motivational types enhances stickiness and long-term motivation.
All-around health	Guided journaling, mindfulness practice, journey templates, CBT coping strategies	Shifting from "tracking" to "self-care and reflection" to promote long-term change
Community and accountability	Accountability partners, team challenges, celebration sharing, leaderboards	Provide a sense of belonging, moderate competition, and leverage external oversight to help maintain this commitment.
AI-powered personalization	Conversational AI coaching, dynamic goals, predictive obstacle recognition	Proactive feedback and adjustments, like a personal coach, reduce frustration
Environmental computing and integration	Automatic synchronization of health platforms, multimodal sensors, and context-aware prompts	Reduce the burden of manual operation and achieve invisible tracking and automation.

Table 5.2 – Functional Innovation Directions

Now, our minds are no longer blank but have a clear phased roadmap for features, and we are beginning to think deeply about the product's personality and strategy, which is the crucial first step from idea to blueprint.

5-minute hands-on practice: Creating user personas

We've clarified what the product *does*, but there's an even more important question: *Who are we making it for?* If we know nothing about our users, we're likely to create a product that fails to meet market demands. This is where the core tool of the **user persona** comes in.

Understanding user profiles

User personas are semi-fictional profiles created for typical users. Their core purpose is not to list statistical data, but to cultivate empathy. When we concretize the vague group of "users" into concrete, flesh-and-blood characters, we can more naturally think from their perspective. When making feature decisions, we subconsciously ask ourselves, *"Will this design be too complicated for 'Sarah'?"* This effectively avoids falling into the self-centered development trap of *"I think users will like it."*

Create user profiles

Now, let's leverage AI Partners again to quickly create several vivid user profiles

Ideal user profiles must be based on real research and data. In the absence of large-scale survey resources, we can provide AI with "seeds of fact" based on observations of potential users around us. It's important to note that AI-generated content may seem realistic but lack a factual basis; therefore, our role is that of "researcher," and the AI is an "assistant." We need to guide and validate the AI's output with real-world observations.

Based on these observations, we issued commands to the AI:

```
Please help me create three different user personas for a habit tracker app, using
the template below, and generate realistic details for each persona.
Image template:
Name and photo description
Personal Profile and Background Story
Basic information: age, occupation, location, lifestyle
Objective: The 1-2 core objectives they most want to achieve when using the app.
Pain Points and Frustrations: What were the main difficulties they encountered in
forming habits without the app?
Motivation: What can inspire them to persevere?
A quote: A sentence that represents their feelings
Please create users based on the following three user types:
College students under a lot of pressure;
```

```
Busy young professionals;
Fitness enthusiasts who require data analysis.
```

After running the prompt, the AI will generate a detailed user profile. Due to the length of the full content, only the key points are shown here. AI created three typical user profiles for us as follows:

- **Sarah (college student, 20 years old):** Facing academic pressure, she needs to cope with anxiety through regular study plans and healthy habits. The core pain point is that the tools are scattered, and she easily feels frustrated when her habits are interrupted.
- **Michael (Marketing Manager, 28 years old):** Facing a busy work schedule, he needs to manage his personal time efficiently without increasing his workload. The core pain point is achieving a work-life balance.
- **David (freelance designer, 32 years old):** A data-driven fitness enthusiast who needs in-depth data analysis capabilities to quantify and optimize his training and lifestyle habits.

These three user profiles represent different levels of user needs: Sarah needs simple and user-friendly guidance and emotional support, Michael prioritizes efficiency and flexibility, and David focuses on data depth and customizability. By using these concrete roles, we can more accurately prioritize features in subsequent design—for example, the MVP version should prioritize meeting the core needs of Sarah and Michael, while reserving the advanced data analysis features needed by David for later iterations.

The complete user profile can be downloaded from the book's GitHub repository.

Let portraits guide decision-making

Now we have three vivid *users*. These personas will serve as a touchstone for decision-making when we review the feature list. We can begin to consider a range of very specific questions.

Is this feature frictionless enough for "Sarah"? Does it offer a "pause mode" to prevent frustration caused by interruptions in continuous recording due to situations like exam week?

For "Michael", is this interface capable of enabling him to complete critical operations in a short time, and can it also support flexible adjustment of reminders to adapt to temporary schedule changes?

Does this feature provide basic progress visualization for "David" and leave room for expansion in subsequent health platform synchronization and custom indicators?

10-minute practical exercise: Writing a PRD

After brainstorming and user persona analysis, our ideas gradually became clearer. These scattered thoughts needed a formal framework to ensure that all participants had a consistent understanding of the product. This framework was the PRD (Product Requirements Document). We can assign the AI tool a more professional role—PRD architect—and leverage its structured thinking to output product blueprints that meet professional standards.

Now let's move on to the practical application.

Step 1: Define the core purpose of the product

First, we need to define the "soul" of the product. Issue the following instructions to the AI:

```
Hello, PRD Architect. Based on the user profiles we created earlier (Sarah, a
stressed-out college student; Michael, a busy young professional; and David, a
data-driven fitness enthusiast), please write the "Product Objectives" section for
the MVP version of the habit tracker app, including the following information.
 - Problem Statement: What are the core problems faced by users?
 - Target users: Who is our MVP version primarily intended for?
 - Core value: How does our app solve their problems?
```

The PRD architect clarified the core positioning of the product. In the problem statement, the AI pointed out the core dilemma faced by modern people in the process of self-improvement—the process of establishing and maintaining habits itself becomes a new source of stress. Existing tools are either too fragmented to provide sustained motivation or too complex and time-consuming, causing users to eventually give up.

In terms of target user positioning, the MVP version prioritizes serving growth-oriented users who are "ambitious but overwhelmed," specifically including college students who need structured guidance and emotional support (such as Sarah) and busy professionals who pursue efficiency and work-life balance (such as Michael). Advanced users who need in-depth data analysis (such as David) will be the focus of subsequent versions.

The core value proposition focuses on "allowing users to see their progress effortlessly," reducing psychological burden by providing a clear structure, creating a frictionless "one-click" tracking experience, and building sustainable intrinsic motivation based on "continuous recording" visualization, which helps users build a sense of competence and control.

The complete product mission statement can be downloaded from the book's GitHub repo.

Step 2: Describe the feature using "user stories"

Next, the identified core functionalities are transformed into user story format—"As a [character], I want to [perform a certain action] in order to [achieve a certain value]," which ensures that every feature developed is linked to the user's real needs.

Issue commands to the AI:

```
Architect, please rewrite the core functionalities of the MVP (habit creation and
recording, daily reminders, progress tracking) into user stories, from the
perspectives of "Michael" and "Sarah".
```

The following is an overview of the AI-generated user stories.

- **Habit creation and recording:** As Michael, I hope to quickly create and flexibly arrange habits, and improve efficiency through one-click check-in; as Sarah, I hope to concretize my goals, while tracking the habits I want to develop and the habits I want to break.
- **Daily reminder:** As Michael, I need effective reminders that stand out from numerous work notifications; as Sarah, I need friendly and gentle reminders to take care of myself.
- **Progress tracking and statistics:** As Michael, I want to quickly browse through the completed historical charts and assess the return on investment; as Sarah, I need to intuitively see the number of consecutive days of recording as motivation to persevere.

The complete user story documentation can be downloaded from the book's GitHub repo.

Step 3: Setting boundaries – the MVP's "don't do" checklist

A successful MVP is not only about clearly defining what to do, but also about having the courage to decide what not to do to maintain development focus and avoid scope creep.

Issue commands to the AI:

```
Architect, to ensure we can complete the MVP quickly and with focus, please create
an "out-of-scope feature" based on our previous brainstorming.
```

The following is an overview of the *Don't Do* list generated by AI or features that needed to be excluded during the MVP phase:

- **Without building complex gamification and incentive systems:** The core incentive for MVP is a simple yet powerful "continuous record," so it does not develop virtual avatars, equipment, skill trees, narrative-driven tasks, or varied random reward systems.

- **No social and community features:** At this stage, users focus on "self-improvement," so features such as accountability partners, team challenges, leaderboards, social feeds, or sharing milestones are not implemented.
- **No comprehensive health and diary features:** Our product is positioned as a habit tracker, not an all-around health manager, so it will not include guided journaling, mood tracking, meditation or breathing exercises, or CBT/DBT-related coping strategies.
- **Do not build complex AI functions:** We will not develop features such as conversational AI coaching, predictive scoring, dynamic goal adjustment, and natural language processing diary analysis until we have sufficient data and user feedback.
- **It does not support automation and integration with third-party platforms:** Our core philosophy is *conscious manual tracking* to help users develop awareness of their own behavior. Therefore, we do not implement automatic synchronization with health platforms such as Apple Health or Google Fit, nor do we develop location- or calendar-based smart reminders, and we do not provide API integration with IFTTT/Zapier.

The complete "Don't Do the List" document can be downloaded from the book's GitHub repo.

Step 4: Define the criteria for success

How do we measure whether an app is successful? We need to define simple metrics.

Issue commands to the AI:

```
Architect, please suggest 2-3 key success metrics for our MVP release.
```

The following is an overview of the success metrics generated by AI.

The PRD architect provided three core success metrics: first-week user retention rate, core behavior conversion rate, and continuous check-in start rate. These metrics measure user return visits, initial check-in conversion effectiveness, and the formation of a continuous check-in habit, respectively, helping us validate the effectiveness of the MVP's core value proposition and incentive mechanism.

A complete document on success metrics can be downloaded from the book's GitHub repo.

By integrating all the above parts, a professional, clear, and highly instructive PRD is complete.

Summary

Through this section, you have gained a basic understanding of the core process of product planning. Starting with the vague idea of a habit tracker, we used an AI Partner to complete a product requirements analysis from scratch.

You have learned a professional product planning methodology: you learn to use AI for structured brainstorming and to refine product strategies; you can quickly create vivid user personas and use empathy to guide product design; and you can integrate scattered ideas into a clear and professional product roadmap (PRD).

With the blueprint set, the next step is to transform these words and plans into tangible interface designs.

From idea to product: In-depth full-stack practice

In the previous section, we focused on product planning, successfully transforming a vague idea into a detailed PRD. Now, it is time to turn this blueprint into a real, functioning product. First, we will construct the application's frontend—the interface that users directly see and interact with. Once the visual prototype is ready, we will turn to the application's backend, building the core engine that supports its operation.

We will select a modern, powerful, and cost-effective technology stack for the application, with the goal of implementing core functionalities at a lower cost and enabling the construction of a high-quality application even with a limited budget.

15-minute hands-on demonstration: Transforming PRD blueprints into usable AI applications

In *Section 5.1*, we wrote a detailed PRD from a product manager's perspective, serving as the design blueprint for the habit tracker App. Before building the backend, we must complete our next crucial step: use an AI development agent to quickly transform this blueprint into a visible and interactive application prototype.

TRAE SOLO can parse complex natural language requirements or structured documents and autonomously complete the entire software development process. This approach perfectly embodies our philosophy of the *frugal full-stack* and rapid prototyping—entrusting the time-consuming work of building the frontend interface to automated tools so you can validate your ideas with maximum efficiency and minimum cost.

> **Note**
>
> While we use TRAE here for its zero-configuration setup, you can certainly assemble these components in **VS Code** (with GitHub Copilot) or **Cursor**. However, you may need to handle the environment configuration, like installing Node.js or initializing the project, manually. We did a deep dive into **Cursor**, a powerful AI-native alternative popular in the West, in *Chapter 4*.

Next, we will go through specific steps to experience how to use TRAE SOLO to turn a PRD into a working application.

1. Open TRAE SOLO. The core interface is a dialog box.
2. Copy the complete habit tracker PRD from *Section 5.1* into the dialog box. You may include the following instructions:

   ```
   Hello, please build a web application called habit tracker based on this
   PRD. Please use a modern, SEO-friendly, and easy-to-deploy technology
   stack: Next.js and Tailwind CSS for the frontend, and Supabase for the
   backend database and user authentication.
   ```

   The key point here is that we not only provided the requirements (PRD), but also clearly stated our suggestions on the implementation method (technology stack). Next.js, as a powerful React framework, can be seamlessly integrated with the Vercel deployment platform used later.

3. Observe the AI planning process. After submitting requirements, TRAE SOLO first analyzes the plan, refining the PRD into a more structured technical implementation solution in the **DocView** panel. This process is transparent and visible, allowing you to clearly understand the logic of the AI's transformation from business requirements to engineering language.
4. After confirming the plan (usually by clicking the confirmation button), TRAE SOLO will take over the development environment, and the entire process will be displayed through 3 panels:
   - **Terminal panel:** The AI automatically executes commands such as creating project structures and installing dependency libraries
   - **Editor panel:** The code files are created and populated one by one
   - **Browser panel:** The application runs in real time on the local development server, and the interface updates are presented instantly.

   In a relatively short time, an application containing basic frontend and backend functionalities can be built, with the initial interface likely already encompassing the pages, buttons, and basic layout described in the PRD. The prototype of the application is shown in *Figure 5.1*:

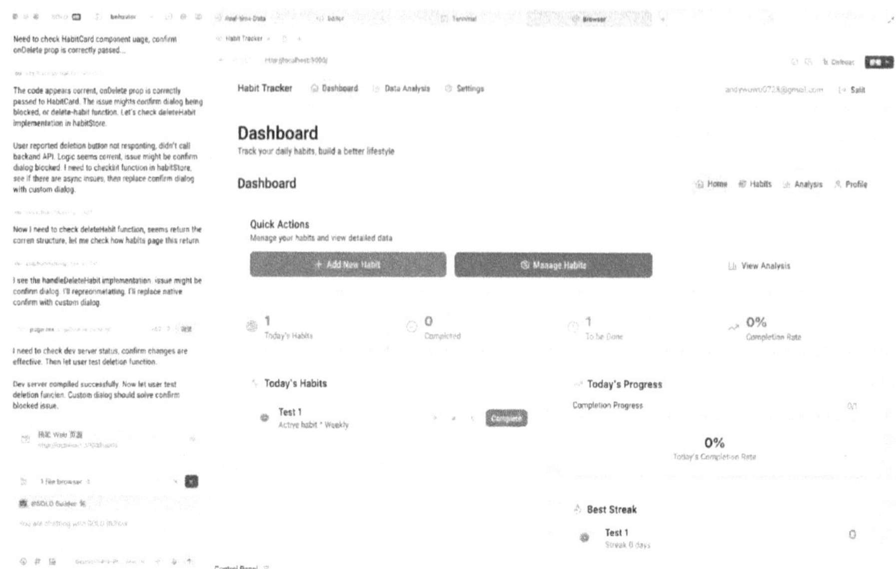

Figure 5.1: Application Prototype

5. Upload the code to GitHub. Currently, the AI-generated code is temporarily stored in the local environment. It needs to be migrated to your own GitHub repository (if you haven't created one yet, you need to create it first). This marks the official takeover of ownership of the code:

    a. **Create a GitHub repository:** Log in to your GitHub account, create a new empty repository, and name it habit-tracker or another relevant name.

    b. **Connect and push code:** In the TRAE SOLO terminal, follow the instructions provided by GitHub to initialize the Git repository, associate the remote repository, and perform the first commit and push. If you are unfamiliar with these operations, you can ask TRAE SOLO in the chat: `How do I push this code to my GitHub repository?` TRAE SOLO will guide you step-by-step or even execute the commands for you. For reference, here are the underlying commands it uses:

```
Bash
## Enter the project directory
cd path/to/your/habit-tracker
## Initialize Git
git init
## Add all files to the staging area
```

```
git add .
## Creating the first commit
git commit -m "Initial commit from TRAE SOLO"
## Link to your remote GitHub repository
git remote add origin [https://github.com/your-username/habit-
tracker.git](https://github.com/your-username/habit-tracker.git)
## Push to main branch
git push -u origin main
```

At this point, you have successfully transformed a PRD into a real code project and securely stored it in a GitHub repository. Next, we'll deploy this application to the Vercel platform for its first public release.

5-minute hands-on demo: Deploying and publicly releasing the application

So far, the application has only been running in a local development environment. Now, we will deploy it, publishing it to the internet and making it publicly accessible.

We chose Vercel as our application deployment platform, as described in *Chapter 3*. Vercel can handle complex server configurations, network bandwidth, and security issues, allowing developers to focus on application development itself.

Vercel can be deeply integrated with GitHub repositories. We will adopt a highly automated modern workflow, CI/CD, as shown in *Figure 5.2*:

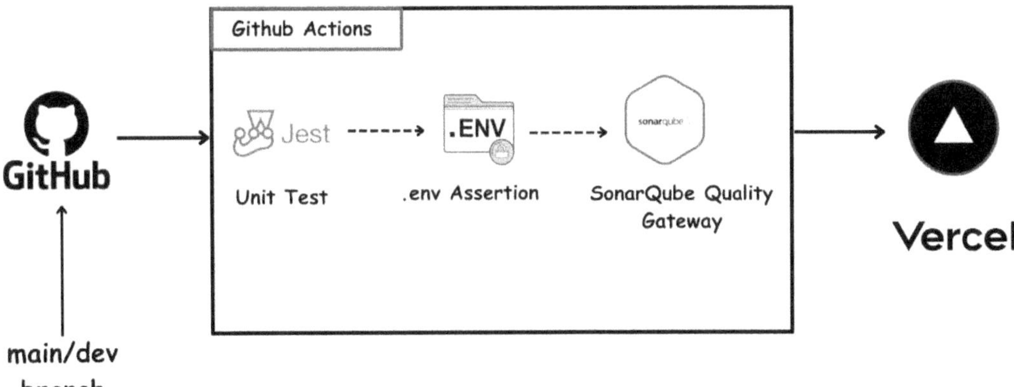

Figure 5.2 – Relationship between Vercel, GitHub, and CI/CD

The core logic of this process is simple: whenever a verified code change is merged into the main branch of the GitHub repository, Vercel is automatically notified and then initiates a fully automated process—rebuilding the application based on the latest code, executing tests, and replacing the old version running online with the new version. This means that the online application is always synchronized with the latest and most stable code, and the entire process requires no manual intervention.

Next, let's begin the actual operation:

1. **Register a Vercel account:** Go to the Vercel official website (`https://vercel.com/`) to register. We recommend logging in directly with your GitHub account, which will automatically establish a connection between Vercel and your code repository and lay the foundation for subsequent automated deployment.
2. **Import Project:** After logging in, click **Add New** in the Vercel Dashboard and select **Project**. Vercel will list all the repositories under your GitHub account. Find the habit tracker project and click the **Import** button next to it, as shown in *Figure 5.3*:

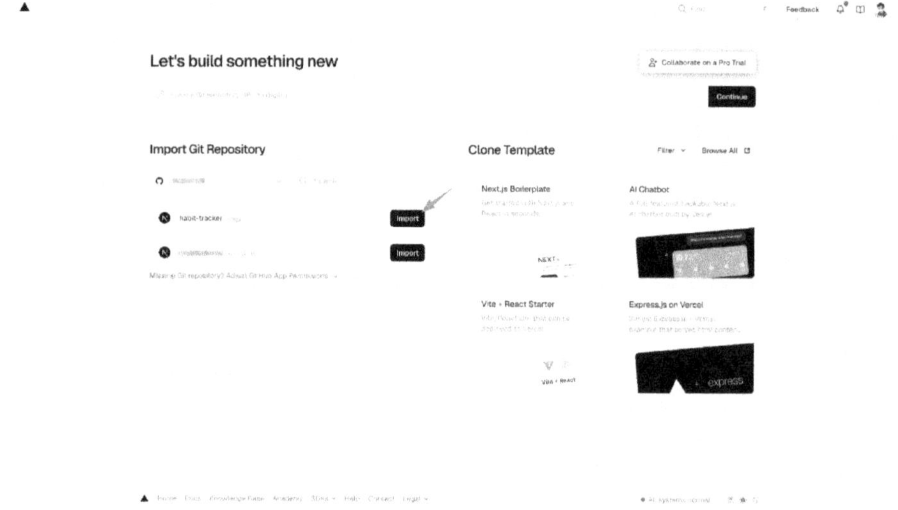

Figure 5.3 – Importing project

3. **Configure the Project:** On the project configuration page, almost no manual operation is required. Vercel has a powerful framework recognition capability, automatically recognizing that this is a Next.js project and configuring the optimal build command, output directory, and all other settings, as shown in *Figure 5.4*.

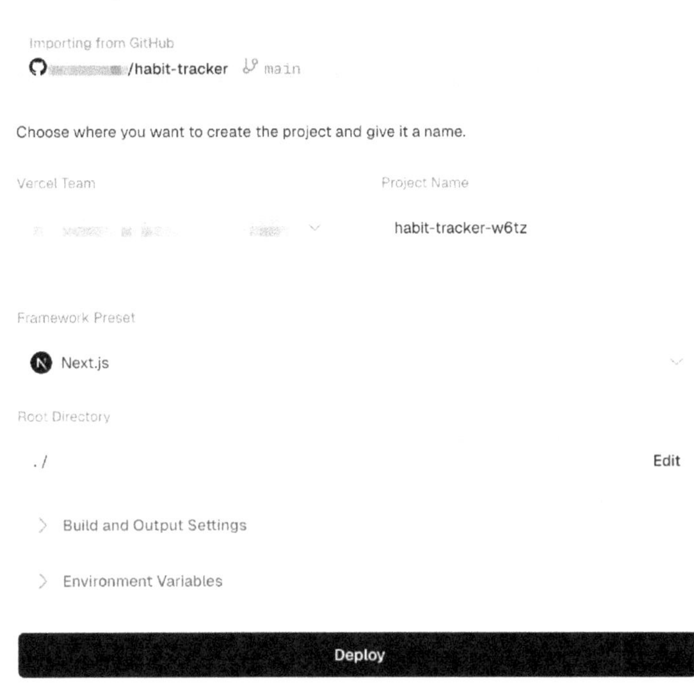

Figure 5.4 – Zero-configuration deployment analysis

4. **Deployment begins:** After confirming that the settings are correct (the default configuration is fine), click the **Deploy** button. Vercel will allocate resources for your application in the cloud, install dependencies, execute the build, and finally complete the deployment. The real-time log of the entire process will be displayed on the interface, as shown in *Figure 5.5*.

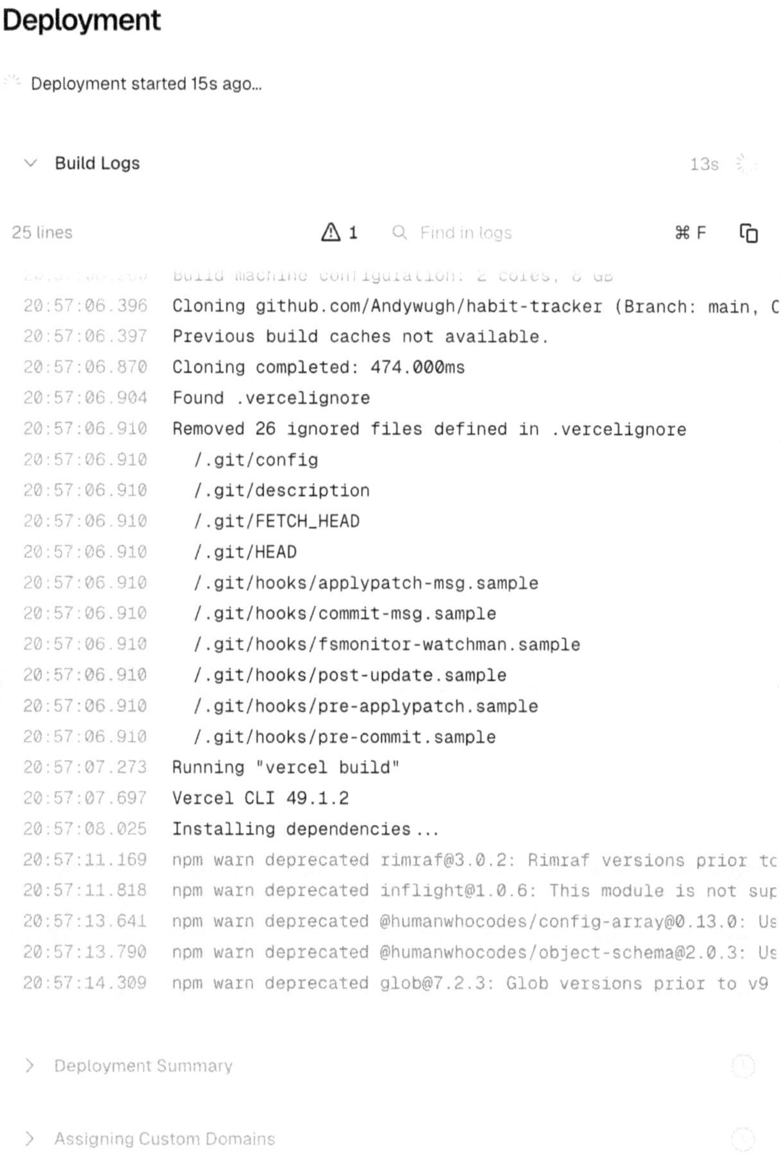

Deployment

Deployment started 15s ago...

Build Logs 13s

25 lines 1 Find in logs ⌘ F

```
             Build machine configuration: 2 cores, 8 GB
20:57:06.396 Cloning github.com/Andywugh/habit-tracker (Branch: main, C
20:57:06.397 Previous build caches not available.
20:57:06.870 Cloning completed: 474.000ms
20:57:06.904 Found .vercelignore
20:57:06.910 Removed 26 ignored files defined in .vercelignore
20:57:06.910   /.git/config
20:57:06.910   /.git/description
20:57:06.910   /.git/FETCH_HEAD
20:57:06.910   /.git/HEAD
20:57:06.910   /.git/hooks/applypatch-msg.sample
20:57:06.910   /.git/hooks/commit-msg.sample
20:57:06.910   /.git/hooks/fsmonitor-watchman.sample
20:57:06.910   /.git/hooks/post-update.sample
20:57:06.910   /.git/hooks/pre-applypatch.sample
20:57:06.910   /.git/hooks/pre-commit.sample
20:57:07.273 Running "vercel build"
20:57:07.697 Vercel CLI 49.1.2
20:57:08.025 Installing dependencies...
20:57:11.169 npm warn deprecated rimraf@3.0.2: Rimraf versions prior tc
20:57:11.818 npm warn deprecated inflight@1.0.6: This module is not sup
20:57:13.641 npm warn deprecated @humanwhocodes/config-array@0.13.0: Us
20:57:13.790 npm warn deprecated @humanwhocodes/object-schema@2.0.3: Us
20:57:14.309 npm warn deprecated glob@7.2.3: Glob versions prior to v9
```

Deployment Summary

Assigning Custom Domains

Figure 5.5 – Logs of automated deployment

Once deployed, Vercel will generate a public URL ending with `.vercel.app`, through which users worldwide can access your application.

In addition, TRAE SOLO typically offers a quick deployment feature after project build, as shown in *Figure 5.6*. This feature allows users to skip manual configuration and directly deploy the project to Vercel. While convenient, this method usually doesn't bind to a GitHub project, thus preventing a complete CI/CD experience. For systematic learning, we recommend following the aforementioned standard deployment steps.

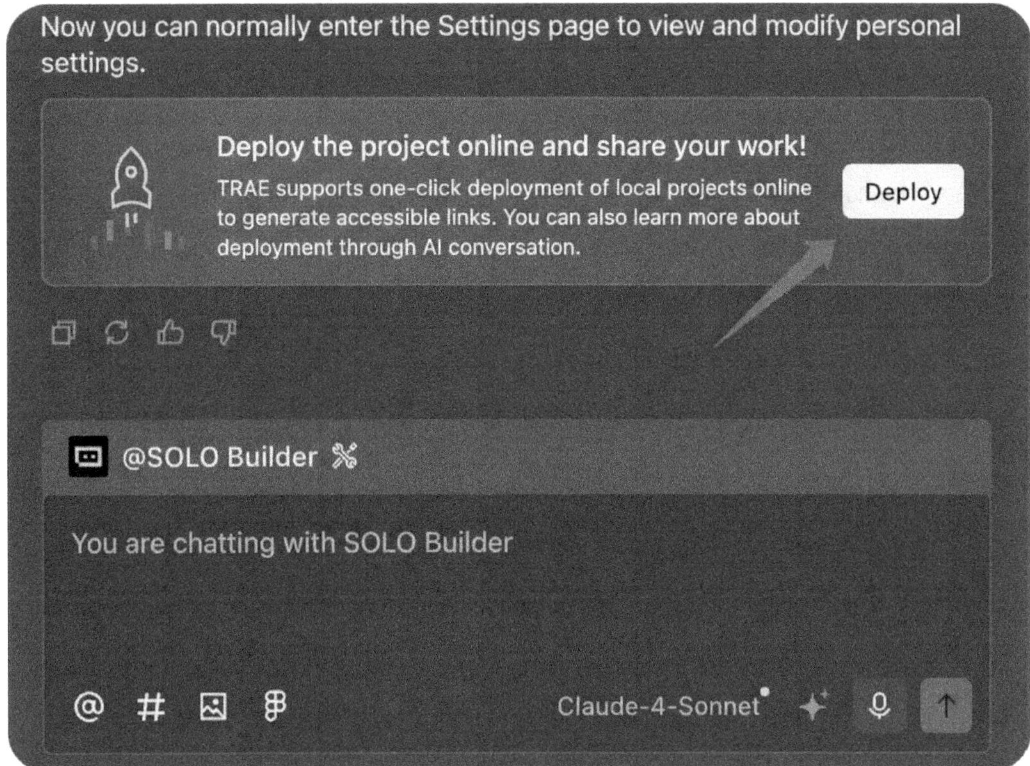

Figure 5.6 – Quick Deployment function

> **Note**
>
> The example project codebase in the book's GitHub repo provides the complete code for this practical exercise. Readers can refer to this codebase to familiarize themselves with the project structure and functionality to better understand the content that follows.

Handling deployment failures

Deployment failures are normal in software development. Every failure is a valuable learning opportunity, revealing problems in the code or environment configuration.

Vercel's deployment logs are the primary tool for diagnosing problems. The relevant records can be viewed in the **Deployments** tab of the project dashboard (see *Figure 5.7*). This tab records each deployment attempt in detail.

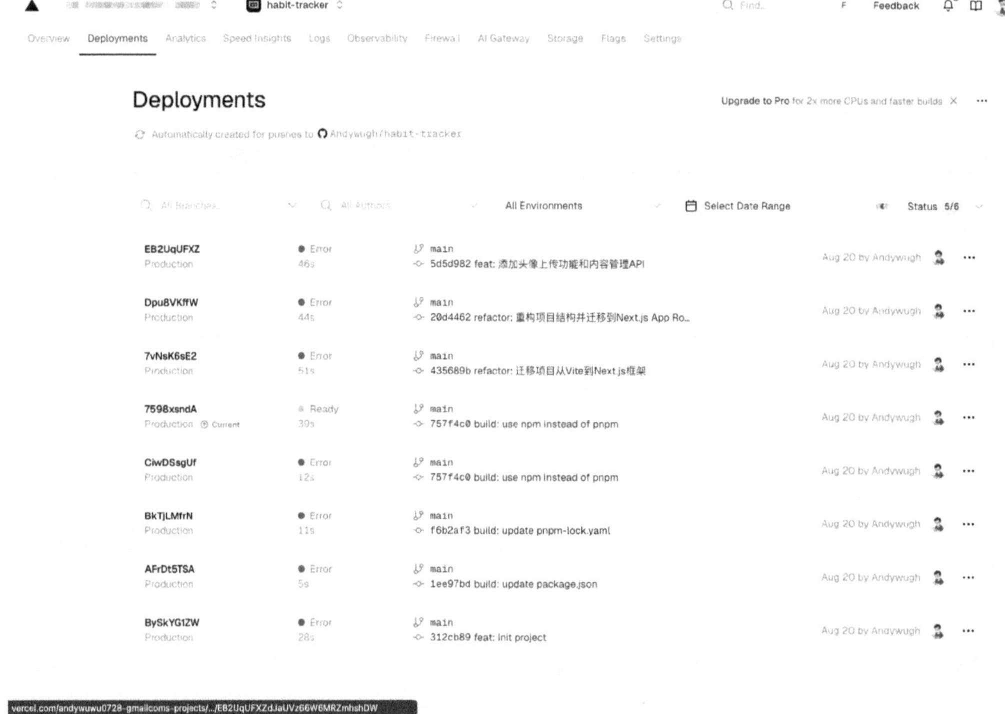

Figure 5.7 – Deployments tab

If the deployment fails, click on the failure record marked as **Error** to view the detailed build logs, as shown in *Figure 5.8*.

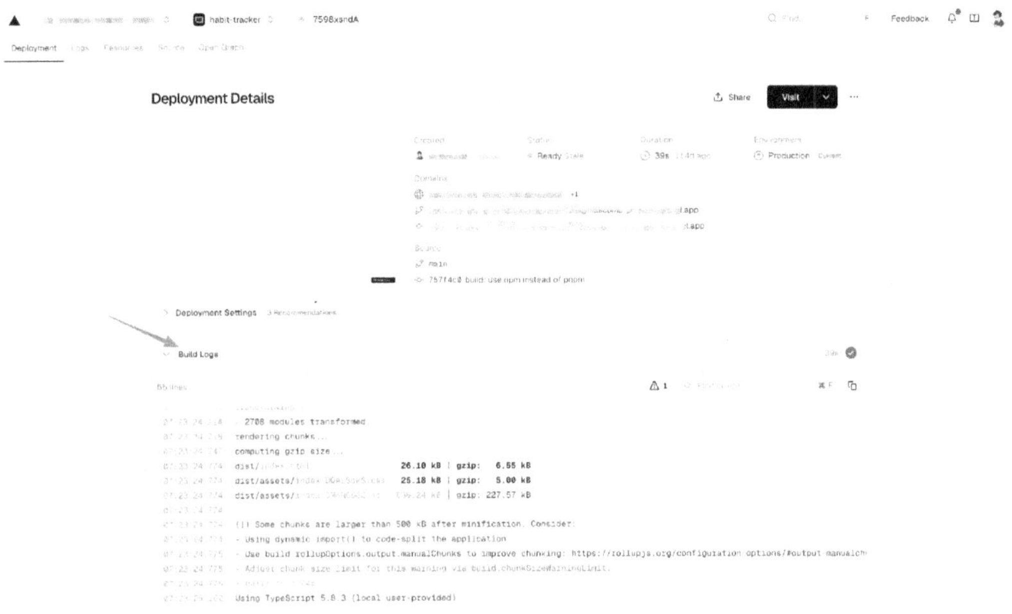

Figure 5.8 – Build Logs page

For beginners, a common reason for failure is a missing environment variable. We can understand this using an example. Suppose your application code contains the instruction "`use the key in locker A to open the database door,`" and the local computer has specified that "`locker A is in the third drawer of the desk,`" , so the program runs normally. However, when you deploy the application to the new Vercel environment, you forget to provide this location information. Vercel cannot find "locker A," and naturally cannot obtain the key, causing the program to fail because it cannot connect to the database.

This location information is called an environment variable. Mastering the methods of finding and reading error logs is one of the core skills for becoming a qualified developer.

In-depth Supabase practice: Building backend services

Supabase offers services including a secure PostgreSQL database, user authentication, backend logic execution through Edge Functions, and document management via object storage. Supabase's generous free plan is sufficient to support project launch and initial operation, perfectly aligning with the core theme of frugal development.

5-minute hands-on exercise: Data table structure

TRAE SOLO has already laid out the basic structure of our backend database. Now let's understand the design logic of this database. Locate the file `./supabase/migrations/`

`001_initial_schema.sql` in the project directory. This file defines the entire database structure blueprint in the form of SQL code, containing three core data tables that together form the data foundation for the habit tracking application:

- **The user_profiles table (user profile table)** stores basic user information, including fields such as `id` (primary key, corresponding to the user ID in the Supabase authentication system), `name` (username), `avatar_url` (avatar image link), `timezone` (time zone setting), `created_at` (creation timestamp), and `updated_at` (update timestamp)
- **Habits Chart** stores user-created habit information, including `id` (a unique identifier for each habit), `user_id` (associated with the user who created the habit), `name` (habit name), `icon` (habit icon), `type` (habit type, such as positive/negative habit), `frequency` (frequency setting stored in JSON format), `reminder_time` (reminder time), `is_active` (habit activation status), and `created_at` and `updated_at` fields
- **The habit_logs table (habit record table)** records user completed habits, including fields such as `id` (a unique identifier for the record), `habit_id` (associated with the specific habit), `user_id` (identifying the user who recorded the habit), `completed_at` (completion time), `notes` (optional notes), and `created_at`.

To view the actual tables in the Supabase console, log in to the Supabase project dashboard, click on **Table Editor** in the left menu, and you will see the three tables mentioned above. These tables contain the complete column structure and data types, as shown in *Figure 5.9*.

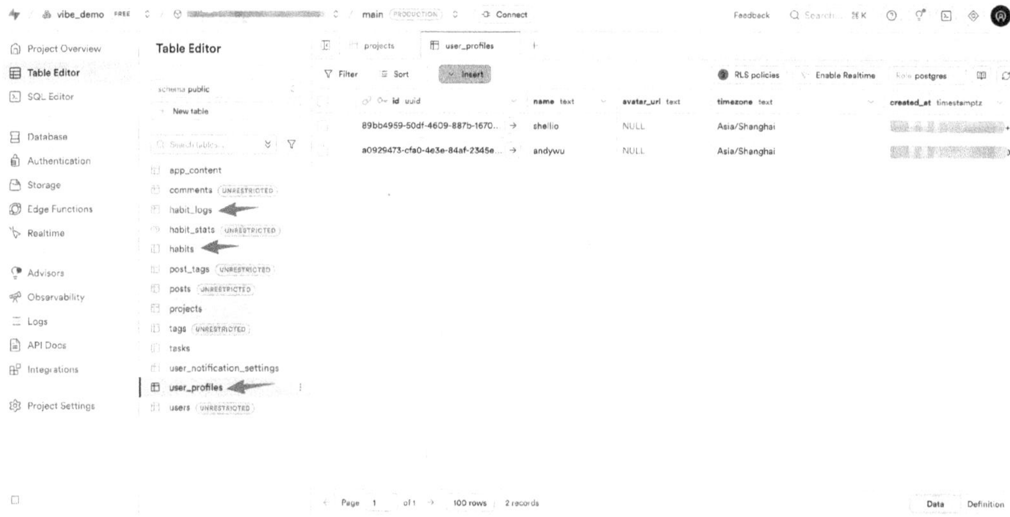

Figure 5.9 – Viewing the actual table

TRAE SOLO has automatically completed the setup and deployment of the core database tables, eliminating the need for manual configuration.

5-minute hands-on exercise: Understanding table relationships

These three tables are not isolated, but are connected by a carefully designed relationship. This relationship is achieved through a foreign key. A foreign key, as you might recall from *Chapter 4*, is one or more columns whose values reference the primary key of another table, thus establishing a connection between the two tables.

Foreign key constraints not only maintain the relationships between tables but also ensure data consistency and integrity. For example, when a user is deleted, their related habits and records are automatically cleaned up through cascading deletes, avoiding the creation of "orphan data." To see exactly how this is implemented, open the `./supabase/migrations/001_initial_schema.sql` file in your code editor. By examining the foreign key configurations in this migration file, we can see how the database structure effectively maintains these critical business relationships.

```
SQL
The `id` field in the `user_profiles` table references the authenticated user's
`id` and serves as the primary key.
CREATE TABLE user_profiles (
id UUID REFERENCES auth.users(id) ON DELETE CASCADE PRIMARY KEY,
-- ...
);

The user_id in the habits table references the ID of the authenticated user.
CREATE TABLE habits (
-- ...
user_id UUID REFERENCES auth.users(id) ON DELETE CASCADE NOT NULL,
-- ...
);

-- The habit_logs table references both the habits table and authenticated users.
CREATE TABLE habit_logs (
-- ...
habit_id UUID REFERENCES habits(id) ON DELETE CASCADE NOT NULL,
user_id UUID REFERENCES auth.users(id) ON DELETE CASCADE NOT NULL,
-- ...
);
```

By analyzing these foreign key configurations, the relationship types of data tables can be clearly understood:

- **Users and Habits:** One-to-many relationship (i.e., a user can create and own multiple habits)
- **Habits and Records:** One-to-many relationship (i.e., one habit can correspond to multiple completion records)
- **Records and users:** Many-to-one relationship (i.e., multiple records can belong to the same user)

To verify that these relationships are reflected in the actual database, you can go to the **Table Editor** in the Supabase console. In the habits table, a link icon will be displayed next to the `user_id` column, indicating that the foreign key relationship between this column and the user table has been successfully established, as shown in *Figure 5.10*.

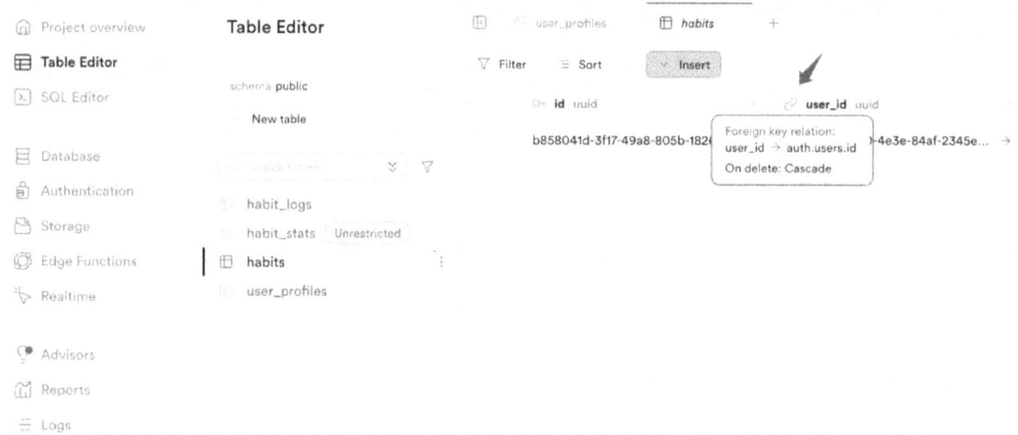

Figure 5.10 – Foreign key relationships for user_id in the habits table

Similarly, link icons will be displayed next to the `habit_id` and `user_id` columns in the `habit_logs` table, corresponding to the habit table and user table, respectively, as shown in *Figure 5.11*:

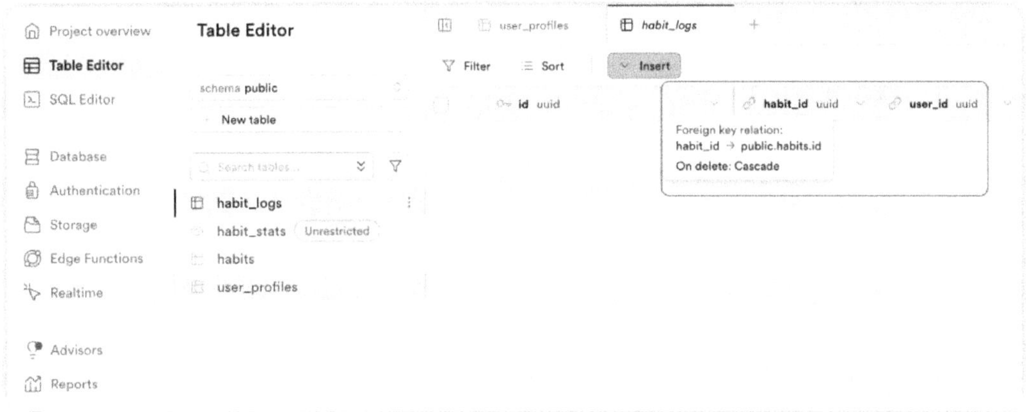

Figure 5.11 – Foreign key relationships between habit_id and user_id in the habit_logs table

This relational structure safeguards the data **consistency** (each habit and record is linked to a real user), **integrity** (automatically cleaning up related data when deleting a user), and **query efficiency** (allowing the system to quickly retrieve all habits associated with a specific user).

10-minute hands-on exercise: User authentication system

Next, we will analyze the application's authentication system, which is responsible for verifying user identity and managing their login status. The core components and processes of this system are as follows:

Core components

The normal operation of the authentication system depends on the coordinated work of three key documents, each with a clearly defined responsibility.

The `./src/lib/supabase.ts` file in the project root directory is responsible for creating client instances that communicate with the Supabase backend and for securely configuring the Supabase URL and anonymous key using environment variables.

```
TypeScript
import { createClient } from "@supabase/supabase-js";

const supabaseUrl = process.env.NEXT_PUBLIC_SUPABASE_URL!;
const supabaseAnonKey = process.env.NEXT_PUBLIC_SUPABASE_ANON_KEY!;

export const supabase = createClient(supabaseUrl, supabaseAnonKey);
```

This file is simply setting up a secure 'walkie-talkie' so your app can talk to Supabase. Here is exactly what it is doing:

- **Line 1 (import...):** We bring in the official Supabase communication tool.
- **Lines 3 & 4 (const supabaseUrl...):** Instead of writing your sensitive passwords directly into the code where anyone could see them, the app pulls your project's specific URL and 'Anonymous Key' from a hidden digital safe called *environment variables* (`import.meta.env`).
- **Line 6 (export const supabase...):** We turn the walkie-talkie on, using your specific URL and key to establish the connection and make it ready for the rest of your application to use.

The `./src/store/authStore.ts` file uses the Zustand library to manage the global login status of users, including core functions such as `signIn` (login), `signUp` (register), and `signOut` (logout).

The `./src/components/auth/AuthForm.tsx` file contains a complete login/registration form component, including features such as form validation, error handling, and mode switching.

Registration process

Based on the aforementioned core components, the authentication system achieves a complete closed loop from registration and login to status maintenance, as detailed below.

- **Registration process:** After the user submits information, the system calls `supabase.auth.signUp()` to create an account, automatically creates an associated user profile in the `user_profiles` table, and sends a verification email to the user's email address.
- **Login process:** After the user submits their credentials, the system calls `supabase.auth.signInWithPassword()` to verify them. If successful, the system updates the user's status within the application and redirects the user to the main interface.
- **Status Listening:** The system listens for real-time changes in authentication status via `supabase.auth.onAuthStateChange()` to automatically handle session refresh, expiration, or restore login status when the user revisits.

You can run the project to experience the authentication system: Run the `npm run dev` command in the project directory to start the application, then access `http://localhost:5173` and try registering a new account. Before and after registration, you can view the data changes in the `auth.users` and `user_profiles` tables in the Supabase console to intuitively understand the authentication process.

10-minute hands-on demonstration: Data security and row-level security strategies

Finally, let's explore how TRAE SOLO ensures that each user can access only their own data. This is achieved through PostgreSQL's native **Row Level Security** (**RLS**) feature. RLS allows for setting fine-grained access rules for each row of data in a table.

Core configuration

In the migration file `./supabase/migrations/001_initial_schema.sql`, you can see the instructions to enable RLS for each core table and the specific security policies (such as user profile access policies and habit creation policies), as shown here:

```
SQL
-- Enable RLS for core tables
ALTER TABLE user_profiles ENABLE ROW LEVEL SECURITY;
ALTER TABLE habits ENABLE ROW LEVEL SECURITY;
ALTER TABLE habit_logs ENABLE ROW LEVEL SECURITY;

-- Security Policy Example
-- Users can only view their own profiles
CREATE POLICY "Users can view own profile" ON user_profiles
FOR SELECT USING (auth.uid() = id);

-- Users can only create their own habits
CREATE POLICY "Users can create own habits" ON habits
FOR INSERT WITH CHECK (auth.uid() = user_id);
```

These strategies adhere to core security principles, such as default denial, user isolation, and operational segmentation.

- **Default rejection:** Without an explicit authorization policy, all data access is denied
- **User isolation:** By using checks like `auth.uid() = user_id`, we ensure that users can only access their own associated data
- **Operational breakdown:** It allows you to define independent strategies for different data operations such as `SELECT`, `INSERT`, `UPDATE`, or `DELETE`

The `auth.uid()` function is a built-in Supabase function that returns the unique ID of the currently authenticated user at the database level. This function is crucial for linking user authentication status with data access permissions, ensuring that even if there are vulnerabilities in the application code, database-level security checks cannot be bypassed.

View configured security policies

The RLS configuration can be viewed visually through the Supabase console. The specific steps are as follows:

1. Log in to the Supabase project dashboard.
2. Navigate to the **Authentication | Policies** page.
3. Selecting core tables such as `user_profiles` and habits will show that each table has RLS enabled and a complete security policy configured, as shown in *Figure 5.12*:

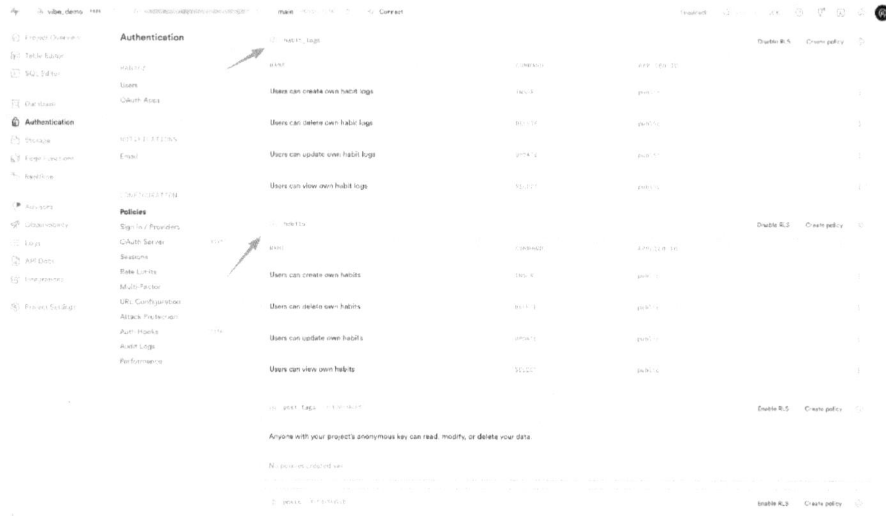

Figure 5.12 – Viewing security policies

Verify RLS effectiveness

You might be wondering: since we have relied on so many tools to 'just work' automatically, why do we need to manually verify this step? The answer lies in the 'QA Mindset' we established in *Chapter 1*. While we can trust standardized infrastructure like Vercel deployments, RLS policies are custom security rules generated by your AI partner. Because AI can occasionally make logical errors, a misconfigured security rule could expose private user data to the world. To intuitively confirm the actual effectiveness of the RLS policy, we designed two sets of tests: *basic verification* and *advanced verification*, which verify the data isolation effect from two dimensions: user scenarios and underlying security protection.

Basic verification (user data isolation)

This test simulates real-world user scenarios to verify whether data isolation between different users is effective. The specific steps are as follows:

1. To run the project, open your habit tracker application in your browser (e.g., at `http://localhost:5173`) and register two separate test accounts using two different email addresses.
2. Log in to your first account, create several habit records, and then log out.

Switching to the second account reveals that no habit data created by the first account can be viewed. This directly proves that RLS's user isolation policy is effective and ensures that users can only access their own data.

Advanced verification (simulating direct data access)

To further verify the underlying security robustness of RLS, we simulated a scenario in which we bypassed frontend access control and made direct requests to the database to test whether unauthorized access could be effectively blocked. The specific steps are as follows:

1. Open the application login page (no login required), press *F12* to open the browser developer tools, and switch to the **Console** tab
2. Copy the following code and execute it to try querying all custom data directly without logging in (you need to replace `"Your Project ID"` and `"Your Anonymous Key"` with the actual values from the Supabase project **Settings** | **API page**)

```
JavaScript
fetch(
"[https://your project ID.supabase.co/rest/v1/habits?select=](https://your
project ID.supabase.co/rest/v1/habits?select=)*",
{
headers: {
apikey: "your anonymous key", // using anon key
Authorization: "Bearer your anonymous key",
},
}
)
.then((res) =res.json())
.then((data) =console.log("Data retrieved:", data))
.catch((error) =console.error("Request failed:", error));
```

3. The execution will return an empty array [ ] instead of any stored conventional data, which proves that the RLS policy has successfully blocked unauthorized access.
4. To further test write access control, you can try inserting fake data that does not belong to any legitimate user. You will also need to replace the ID and key of the actual project.

```
JavaScript
// Attempt to insert a habit that does not belong to the current user (this should also be prevented).
fetch("https://your project ID.supabase.co/rest/v1/habits", {
method: "POST",
headers: {
apikey: "Your anonymous key",
Authorization: "Bearer your anonymous key",
"Content-Type": "application/json",
},
body: JSON.stringify({
user_id: "fake user ID",
title: "Hacker Habits"
Description: "This should not have been created".
}),
})
.then((response) =response.json())
.then((data) =console.log("Insert result:", data));
```

5. After execution, an error message similar to `{"code":"42501","details":null,"hint":null,"message":"new row violates row-level security policy"}` will be returned, indicating that RLS can not only intercept unauthorized queries but also effectively prevent the writing of malicious data, thus ensuring data security from both read and write perspectives.

With this final test, we have successfully constructed the core backend engine of our application—establishing structured data tables, a seamless user authentication system, and robust row-level security. With this secure and solid foundation completely in place, it is time to shift our focus from internal data management to proactive user engagement. Next, we will explore how to breathe life into our application's communication by integrating the Resend email service.

Practical application of resend email service

Even with comprehensive data management and user authentication features, our application still has room for improvement. It lacks a proactive user communication mechanism and fails to provide timely feedback and guidance. Excellent modern applications typically establish continuous connections with users through email services, creating personalized service experiences.

To unlock these advanced communication features, we must now integrate the Resend package into our habit tracking application. However, before we install and configure this new tool, let's first take a closer look at the basic user authentication and email infrastructure that Supabase has already established for us.

The core logic for user registration in the project's `store/authStore.ts` file is as follows:

```
TypeScript
signUp: async (email: string, password: string, name: string) ={
const { data, error } = await supabase.auth.signUp({
email,
password,
options: {
data: { name },
},
});

if (data.user && data.session) {
set({ user: data.user, session: data.session }); // Create user profile

await supabase.from("user_profiles").insert({
id: data.user.id,
name,
});
}

return { error };
};
```

Notice what is missing here? We are not manually creating the user's profile in the database from the frontend. Because we have email confirmation enabled, the user's session is delayed until they click the link in their inbox. To handle this securely, we will delegate the profile creation entirely to the backend using a **database trigger**.

Instead of relying on the fragile frontend to create user profiles, we will use a Supabase database trigger. A trigger is like an automated tripwire in your database: the moment a new user registers in the authentication system, the database automatically creates their profile behind the scenes.

Open your AI assistant (Cursor or TRAE SOLO) and enter the following prompt to generate the secure SQL script:

```
Please generate a PostgreSQL script for Supabase to automatically initialize user
profiles. I need a function named handle_new_user that inserts a new row into the
user_profiles table whenever a new user successfully registers in auth.users. It
should securely extract the user's name from the raw_user_meta_data. Then, create
a database trigger named on_auth_user_created to execute this function AFTER
INSERT on the auth.users table.
```

Take the SQL script the AI generates and run it in your Supabase SQL Editor. Now, your database is robust and self-managing!

By using the standard client-side registration method (`supabase.auth.signUp()`), we trigger Supabase's built-in security mechanisms. This verification mechanism has significant security value: when a new user registers, Supabase automatically intercepts their session and sends an email containing a secure verification link to their inbox.

The user must click this link to verify they own the address before they can log in. This ensures the validity of the user base, prevents spam accounts, and lays a secure foundation for subsequent communications, such as password resets and weekly habit reports.

Based on this basic verification function, a more comprehensive email communication system is usually needed in production environments.

For example, welcome emails for new users (including application introductions and user guides), regularly pushed habit completion statistics reports, personalized habit reminder emails sent according to user settings, and incentive emails after milestones are achieved.

While it is technically possible to send programmatic emails from a personal email address, this approach has significant limitations:

- The email delivery rate is low, and it is easily marked as spam by mainstream email service providers
- The lack of data analysis tools such as email open rate and click-through rate is not conducive to optimizing communication strategies
- Compliance details such as unsubscribe links and email header settings need to be handled manually

Therefore, using professional email services has become an inevitable choice for modern application development.

When implementing email functionality, strict adherence to security best practices is essential. Email service API keys, which contain sensitive information, must never be exposed in client-side code. The correct approach is to encapsulate all email-sending logic within server-side API routes and securely manage API keys using environment variables.

5-minute hands-on lesson: Analyzing email infrastructure in applications

Let's systematically review the email-related functions already implemented in the TRAE SOLO project to understand the existing infrastructure:

- **Automatic email verification mechanism:** Run the application (`npm run dev`) and register a new account. After registration, you will receive a verification email from Supabase. This automated verification process ensures the validity of the user's email address, laying a solid foundation for subsequent email communication.
- **A comprehensive notification settings system:** The `app/settings/page.tsx` file contains complete notification preference management functionality.

```
TypeScript
const [notifications, setNotifications] = useState({
daily_reminder: true,
weekly_summary: true,
achievement_alerts: true,
reminder_time: "09:00",
});

// Load and save notification settings via API
const loadNotificationSettings = async () ={
const response = await fetch("/api/user/notifications", {
headers: {
Authorization: `Bearer ${session.access_token}`,
},
}); // Process response data...
};
```

  This system not only provides user interface control but also achieves complete data persistence (meaning the user's settings are permanently saved to the database and will not be lost when they close the app) through the `user_notification_settings` data table and API routing (`app/api/user/notifications/route.ts`). Users can precisely control the on/off state and reminder time of various notifications.

- **Complete user information collection mechanism:** We have collected key information such as username (for personalized email content), email address (email recipient), and time zone (to ensure emails are sent at the appropriate time) and provided data support for the logic of the email function.

5-minute hands-on lesson: Functional planning for an email system

Based on the existing application architecture, the following email features can be designed to improve the user experience:

- New users will receive a welcome email containing a user guide after registration
- Automatically generate weekly user habit completion statistics reports (including visual data such as completion rate and consecutive days)
- Send personalized smart reminders based on the user's set habits and time zone preferences
- Send achievement incentive emails automatically when users reach specific milestones to enhance their sense of accomplishment and sustained motivation

Trigger-based emails (like welcome emails) happen instantly when a user interacts with the app. However, scheduled emails (like the weekly summary) require a 'clock' to trigger them automatically in the background. Later in this section, we will show you exactly how to configure a free Vercel Cron Job to act as this clock, ensuring your weekly reports run on autopilot.

Among numerous email service providers, Resend has significant advantages: it offers a developer-friendly API design that can be seamlessly integrated with modern web development workflows; it provides generous free usage quotas for small projects; and it natively supports React Email, allowing developers to build email templates using React components, thereby improving development efficiency and code reusability.

10-minute hands-on exercise: Implementing a welcome email function

Before we can implement the email functionality based on our existing API architecture, we must first integrate the Resend dependency package into our project. Open your TRAE SOLO terminal and run the command `npm install resend`. Once the installation is complete, we can implement the email system as follows:

1. **Register and configure Resend:** Visit the Resend website (`https://resend.com/`) to register a free account and log in. Next, add and verify your own domain name (a

subdomain is recommended, such as no-reply.your-website.com). Resend will provide a TXT verification record, which you need to add in your domain service provider's DNS management page. Wait 5–30 minutes for it to take effect. After successful verification, the domain status will show **Verified**.

2. **Create and save API keys:** Go to the API Keys page in Resend, create a new key (name it Habit Tracker Production), and select **Sending access permissions**. The generated key will only be displayed once, so you need to copy and save it immediately.
3. **Configure environment variables:** Create or edit the `.env.local` file in the project root directory and add the configuration `RESEND_API_KEY=your_resend_api_key_here`; if using Vercel for deployment, you need to add the same environment variable in the Vercel project settings.
4. **Create a welcome email API route:** Create a new file named `app/api/emails/welcome/route.ts` in the `app/api/` directory. Rather than writing the entire route by hand, ask your AI coding partner to generate the first production-ready version for you. Use a prompt like this:

```
Create app/api/emails/welcome/route.ts in a Next.js App Router project.
Verify the current user from a Supabase bearer token, fetch the user's
display name from user_profiles, and send a transactional welcome email
through Resend. Return structured JSON responses for success, unauthorized
access, and server errors.
```

Once the AI has generated the route, review it using these three checkpoints:

- **Tool setup:** The file should initialize both the Resend client and the Supabase server client using environment variables
- **User verification and personalization:** The route should verify the bearer token, identify the current user, and fetch the user's name from `user_profiles` so that the message can be personalized safely.
- **Email delivery:** The route should send a welcome email through Resend and return a clean JSON response indicating success or failure.

You do not need to memorize every line of the route. Your job is to verify that the generated file follows the right structure, handles authentication correctly, and keeps the email logic easy to maintain. If you want the full implementation for reference, you can copy the complete production-ready file from our companion GitHub repository.

5-minute practice: Sending dynamic emails using templates

In the previous exercise, we sent a simple welcome email by writing raw website code directly into our file—like `<h2>Welcome</h2>`. While this method is fine for a quick, short greeting, building a complex, beautiful weekly report this way (a process developers call 'concatenating HTML strings') is extremely tedious. Worse, doing it manually makes it difficult to guarantee your email will look correct across different apps like Outlook, Gmail, or Apple Mail. A modern, much easier solution is to use React Email, which allows us to build emails using familiar, visual React components. The steps are as follows:

1. Install dependencies. Execute the following commands to install the React Email-related packages.

```
Bash
npm install react-email @react-email/components
```

2. Create an email template component. Create a folder named `emails` in the project root directory, then ask Cursor to generate a reusable React Email component named `WeeklySummaryEmail.tsx`.
   Use a prompt like this:

```
Create emails/WeeklySummaryEmail.tsx using @react-email/components. The
component should accept a username and a list of habit summaries. For each
habit, show the number of completed check-ins during the last 7 days and
the current streak. Keep the layout clean, readable, and compatible with
common email clients.
```

   Rather than reading the entire generated component line by line, review it through three design checkpoints:

   - **The building blocks:** The component should use email-safe primitives such as `<Html>`, `<Body>`, `<Container>`, `<Heading>`, and `<Text>` instead of raw HTML fragments.
   - **The data contract:** The component should declare the exact data it expects, including the username and the weekly habit summary objects.
   - **The dynamic rendering logic:** The template should loop through the list of habits and render one summary block per habit, making it easy to scale from one habit to many.

   Next, create the route that sends the weekly summary email.

Use a prompt like this:

```
Create app/api/emails/weekly-summary/route.ts for a Next.js App Router
project. Verify the user from a Supabase bearer token, load the user's
active habits, query the last 30 days of habit_logs, calculate weekly
completion counts and the current streak for each habit, then send a React
email through Resend using WeeklySummaryEmail.tsx.
```

When you review the generated route, focus on these checkpoints:

- **Data loading:** The route should safely fetch the current user, their profile, their active habits, and the recent habit logs needed for the summary
- **Business logic:** The route should calculate both the number of completed check-ins during the last 7 days and the current streak for each habit
- **Rendering and delivery:** The route should pass the processed data into the email component and send the message through Resend

At this stage, your role is to direct the AI clearly, review the generated output critically, and understand the architectural checkpoints. In this book, we therefore focus on prompts, review points, and the final result. If you want the complete implementation, you can open the book GitHub repository and compare it with your generated version.

When the route is working, the final email will look similar to the result shown in *Figure 5.13*.

So far, we have focused on generating and sending individual emails. The next step is to zoom out and look at the application-level notification architecture: what kinds of messages the system sends, when each message should be triggered, and what additional infrastructure is required if we want these emails to be sent automatically in a real product.

Email push triggering mechanism and notification system architecture

In this section, we will further analyze the triggering mechanism of email push in actual projects and introduce the overall architecture of the notification and reminder system.

This application's habit tracking feature implements an email-based notification system that supports the following four core notification types:

- **daily_reminder:** Daily habit reminders are used to encourage users to complete their daily habits.
- **weekly_summary:** A weekly summary report shows the completion status of habits over the past week.

- **achievement_alert:** Achievement reminders are triggered when a user reaches a specific milestone.
- **Welcome:** Welcome emails are used to guide new users to quickly get started with the application.

In this chapter, we are implementing the MVP version of a product email system. That means we are focusing on transactional and product-triggered messages rather than a complete global compliance workflow. In a production launch, teams should also review local privacy and email regulations, such as GDPR or CCPA where relevant, and ensure that any marketing-style communication includes proper unsubscribe handling. Likewise, this chapter uses email/password authentication for clarity, while optional social sign-in flows such as Google or Apple can be added later through Supabase OAuth.

When an email push is successfully triggered (such as sending a welcome email), the email received by the user will look like the image in *Figure 5.13*.

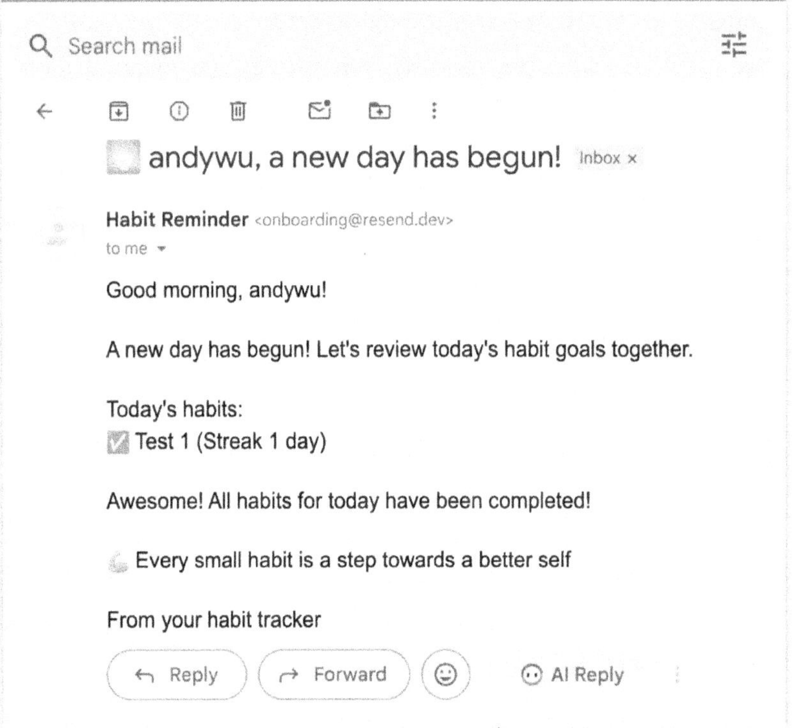

Figure 5.13: Email received by the user

Now that our email generation API is ready, we need a mechanism to trigger it automatically every week. Because Next.js API routes usually only run when a user visits them, we will use a free feature from our deployment platform called **Vercel Cron Jobs**.

Vercel Cron Jobs allow you to set a schedule (like an alarm clock) that automatically pings your API at a specific time. Instead of figuring out the complex `cron expression` syntax manually, let's have our AI partner build the configuration file.

Open your AI assistant (Cursor or TRAE SOLO) and enter the following prompt:

```
Please create a vercel.json configuration file in the root directory of our
project. I need to configure a Vercel Cron Job that automatically sends an HTTP
request to our /api/emails/weekly-summary route every Monday at 9:00 AM.
```

The AI will generate a vercel.json file. Once you push this code to GitHub, and Vercel automatically deploys it, your application will officially be on autopilot. Every Monday at 9:00 AM, Vercel will silently trigger your API, and your users will wake up to their beautiful, personalized habit reports!

Security Note: In a production commercial environment, you would want to secure this route by verifying the `CRON_SECRET` header provided by Vercel so that random visitors cannot trigger the emails manually.

This design provides a high degree of flexibility for the notification system, but its automation relies on the implementation of an external scheduling mechanism. After discussing the notification system, we will turn to another key infrastructure: file storage.

File storage system design

In its current development phase, the application focuses on core habit management functionality; therefore, a simplified design approach has been adopted for user profile management. Analyzing the application's database structure and user interface provides a clear understanding of its file storage design strategy and future expansion potential.

Current status of implementation

Before delving into the design of the file storage system, it's necessary to clarify the current state of the application in user profile management. Instead of manually reading through the codebase to understand the current state, we can leverage the code-analysis capabilities of Cursor or TRAE SOLO. Simply enter the following prompt:

```
Please analyze the app/settings/page.tsx file and the database migration files in
the current project. What fields are currently included in our user profile
management interface? Is there a field reserved in the database to support avatar
uploads?
```

The AI will quickly report that, while the UI only shows basic info (name, timezone), the underlying `user_profiles` database table already has an `avatar_url` field reserved.

5-minute hands-on lesson: Analyzing user profile data flow

Before adding the upload feature, ask your AI to map out the current data flow with the following prompt:

```
Trace the data flow for saving user profiles in the current application. When a
user clicks save, what data does the frontend app/settings/page.tsx send? What
data does the backend API app/api/user/profile/route.ts receive and update?
```

5-minute hands-on lesson: Designing the technical architecture for avatar upload

The ideal user experience for uploading profile pictures is that users click on their profile picture, select an image from their local storage, and the upload is completed and updated in real time. To achieve this, a pre-signed URL mechanism is needed to separate file uploads from the application server, thereby improving performance and security. The specific process is as follows:

1. After the user selects the image to upload, the client sends a request to the application server for upload permission. This request includes metadata such as the filename and type.
2. After verifying the user's identity and permissions, the server uses the Cloudflare R2 SDK to generate a time-sensitive (for example, valid for 5 minutes) pre-signed URL bound to a specific file and returns it to the client.
3. Using the obtained pre-signed URL, the client uploads image files directly to Cloudflare R2. This process bypasses the application server, significantly improving upload speed and reducing server bandwidth consumption.
4. After a file upload is successful, the client notifies the application server, and the server updates the file access link (i.e., `avatar_url`) in the user's database record.

The advantage of this architecture lies in its efficiency, cost-effectiveness, and security. It delegates intensive tasks such as file transfer to professional cloud storage services, while the application server is responsible only for lightweight authentication and metadata management.

To implement this architecture, existing applications need to be extended. The specific steps are as follows:

1. **Upgrade the frontend user interface:** We need to add an avatar upload component to the user profile card in `app/settings/page.tsx`.

   Open the `app/settings/page.tsx` file, select the code block for the **User Profile** card, and press *Ctrl/Cmd* + *K* to bring up the AI code generation input box. Enter the following prompt:

   ```
   Update this User Profile card to include an avatar upload section. Add a
   round profile picture display (w-16 h-16) next to the display name. Add a
   small camera icon button on the bottom right of the avatar. When clicked,
   it should trigger a hidden file input accepting only
   images. Bind the input to a handleAvatarUpload function.
   ```

   Press *Enter*. The AI will instantly generate the complex React and Tailwind CSS code needed, perfectly blending the new avatar component into your existing UI. Review the changes and click **Accept**.

2. **Add frontend file processing logic:** Now we need to add the `handleAvatarUpload` function to `app/settings/page.tsx` to process the file when the user selects an image. Use Cursor or TRAE SOLO (*Ctrl/Cmd* + *K*) and give your AI partner this precise instruction:

3. **Configure the Cloudflare R2 service:** As we discussed in *Chapter 3*, Cloudflare R2 serves as our application's highly cost-effective 'file cabinet,' storing our images without charging outbound bandwidth fees. Visit the Cloudflare dashboard (`https://dash.cloudflare.com`), log in, and navigate to the **R2 management** page from the sidebar. Click to create a new bucket (e.g., habit-tracker-uploads)

   Returning to the R2 overview screen, click the **Manage** button next to API Tokens in the Account Details area to create a new API token. During creation, follow the *principle of least privilege*, setting the token's permissions to **Object Read & Write** and limiting its application to the newly created bucket.

After successful creation, record the generated Access Key ID and Secret Access Key. It is important to note that the latter is only displayed once; you must copy and save it immediately.

4. Add the following four configurations to the environment variables of your Vercel project: `R2_ACCOUNT_ID` (Cloudflare account ID, used to build the R2 endpoint URL), `R2_ACCESS_KEY_ID` (access key ID, used to authenticate R2 services), `R2_SECRET_ACCESS_KEY` (secret access key, used in conjunction with the access key ID to ensure that the application has permission to access and manipulate objects in the bucket), and `R2_BUCKET_NAME` (bucket name, specifying the bucket used to store and retrieve objects).

Now let's implement a file upload interface.

10-minute hands-on exercise: Implementing a file upload interface

Finally, delegate the complex backend storage logic (AWS S3 compatibility and Supabase integration) directly to the AI with the following prompt:

```
Please implement the Pre-signed URL avatar upload architecture for our
application.
Step 1: Provide the terminal command to install the Cloudflare R2 dependencies
@aws-sdk/client-s3 and @aws-sdk/s3-request-presigner.
Step 2: Create a Next.js API route at app/api/upload/avatar/route.ts. It must
verify the user's Supabase JWT, generate a unique filename, and use getSignedUrl
with a PutObjectCommand to generate a temporary pre-signed PUT URL for our
Cloudflare R2 bucket. It should NOT receive the file itself. Return this pre-
signed URL and the final public URL to the client.
Step 3: Modify the handleAvatarUpload function in the frontend (app/settings/
page.tsx). It should first call our new API to get the pre-signed URL, then use a
fetch PUT request to upload the raw image file directly to R2 using that URL, and
finally update the user's avatar_url in the user_profiles database table.
```

By following this step, the architecture of the existing application can be upgraded to provide users with complete avatar upload and management functions, while ensuring your server remains fast by offloading the heavy file transfer directly to Cloudflare.

Building a scalable content management architecture

Content management is a frequent requirement in product development. For example, product or marketing teams may need to adjust page text, update documents, or publish announcements. In traditional development processes, any content update requires developers to modify the source code, submit it, and deploy it. This process is inefficient and delays the timely release of content.

Before introducing a dedicated **content management system** (**CMS**), let's first analyze the current state of content management in our application. Taking the behavior tracker app project demonstrated in this chapter as an example, it adopts a typical **hard-coding** approach, where all UI text in the `app/settings/page.tsx` file is directly embedded in React components. Let's ask the AI to find these instances:

```
@app/settings/page.tsx Please identify all display text that is directly hardcoded
into the React components on this page (e.g., 'Settings', 'User Profile',
'Notification Settings') and organize them into a list for me.
```

You will see that the hard-coding method, which directly writes the interface text into the code, is also common in other pages of the application.

Advantages and disadvantages of hard coding

In the early stages of a project, this management approach of hard-coding content directly into components has its merits, as detailed below.

- **The implementation method is simple:** Content is code; no additional infrastructure needs to be built
- **Excellent loading performance:** The text is loaded along with the application code without any additional network request overhead.
- **The system is stable and reliable:** There is no risk of content loading failure, ensuring the stability of the application.
- **Version control consistency:** Content changes and code changes follow the same version control system

However, as the scale of applications expands and the demand for team collaboration increases, its limitations become increasingly prominent:

- **Difficulty in providing international support:** It is difficult to efficiently switch between multiple languages to adapt to users in different regions.
- **Inefficient teamwork:** Non-technical personnel (such as product and operations staff) cannot directly edit the content and must rely on developers

- **Delayed content updates:** Content updates require a complete development and deployment process, making it impossible to quickly respond to copywriting adjustment requests
- **A/B testing is inconvenient:** The inability to quickly iterate on copy and test its effectiveness impacts user experience optimization

To address these challenges, the introduction of a dedicated CMS has become an inevitable choice.

Evolution and selection of CMS architecture

The architectural evolution of modern CMS has undergone multiple stages, with each architecture having its own suitable scenarios.

- **Traditional CMS (such as WordPress):** It adopts a *coupled architecture*, which tightly integrates content management with frontend display. It is easy to set up and deploy, but its scalability, migration, and multi-terminal adaptation capabilities are weak, making it difficult to meet the needs of modern multi-platform applications.
- **Headless CMS (such as Contentful and Strapi):** It adopts a *decoupled architecture*, with the backend focusing on content management and storage, providing content data to the frontend application via RESTful APIs or GraphQL. The frontend technology stack is flexible. While these platforms provide rich, professional interfaces for entering and editing content, they separate the data from the design. Because non-technical teams are filling out structured forms rather than using a 'What You See Is What You Get' visual page builder, previewing the final layout can sometimes be less intuitive.
- **Git-based CMS (such as Keystatic):** A hybrid approach that also decouples content from presentation, but instead of using a database and APIs, it stores all content directly in your code repository (like GitHub) as structured files (such as Markdown). This allows content and code to be version controlled together.
- **Decoupled CMS:** While a Headless CMS has no built-in frontend at all, a Decoupled CMS does come with a frontend delivery system—it is just separated from the backend creation environment. Content creation and publishing are separated, with content being pushed from the repository to a designated platform upon publication. This gives businesses greater flexibility, allowing marketers to create content themselves while developers focus on programming. However, once a publishing system is chosen, content can only be published through that specific system, limiting its ability to distribute across multiple channels compared to a true Headless API.

- **Hybrid CMS:** It combines the advantages of coupled and headless CMS, supporting flexible calls to RESTful APIs while providing visual template editing. This architecture allows marketers to control and optimize the customer experience while enabling developers to bring application updates to market faster, making it suitable for complex enterprise-level needs.

In modern web development, headless CMS has become a mainstream choice due to its flexible architecture, flexible technology stack, and strong multi-platform distribution capabilities. Its advantages are particularly evident in scenarios requiring support for multiple frontend applications and synchronized content updates across mobile and web platforms. Hybrid CMS, on the other hand, is more suitable for enterprise-level applications that need to balance development efficiency with user experience for non-technical teams.

The headless CMS architecture has significant advantages in terms of technical implementation, as detailed below:

- **Flexible technology stack:** Frontend developers can freely choose frameworks such as React, Vue, or Angular to meet the needs of different projects
- **Supports multi-platform distribution:** The same set of content can serve multiple platforms such as Web, mobile, and mini-programs simultaneously, ensuring content consistency and efficient management
- **High development efficiency:** Because content management and frontend development can be carried out in parallel, the coupling between the two is reduced and team collaboration efficiency is significantly improved
- **Significant room for performance optimization:** Developers can perform dedicated performance optimizations on the frontend display without relying on the CMS's built-in rendering logic, thereby improving the user experience

When an application matures into the multi-role team collaboration phase, introducing a dedicated headless CMS becomes highly valuable. For example, Keystatic (`https://keystatic.com/`) is a powerful next step when you outgrow basic setups. It features deep integration with Next.js, supports Git workflows to synchronize content changes with version control, and provides an intuitive visual editing interface so non-technical teams can manage content independently.

However, at our current product growth stage, introducing an entirely new platform like Keystatic would add unnecessary learning overhead and configuration complexity. Adhering to our *frugal full-stack* philosophy, we can achieve the exact same flexibility by reusing the powerful Supabase infrastructure we have already built.

Next, we will demonstrate how to separate volatile content from your code and build a lightweight, highly effective content management system using our existing database through two specific practical solutions.

Practical Implementation: Two Upgrade Paths

Next, we will demonstrate how to integrate content management functionality into existing applications through two specific practical solutions. These two solutions represent a progressive upgrade approach, from simple to complex and from rapid implementation to a complete architecture.

Option 1: Rapid content management upgrade based on database

This solution reuses existing Supabase infrastructure to quickly implement a simple CMS without introducing new tools. To illustrate its necessity, let's take a typical scenario as an example: the product team needs to change the wording of *User Profile* on the **Settings** page to *Personal Information.*

In the traditional development process, developers need to modify the `app/settings/page.tsx` file, submit code changes, and trigger the entire deployment process, which is time-consuming. In the optimized process, product managers can directly modify the text in the backend and have it take effect in real time without the need for developer intervention, greatly improving the efficiency and flexibility of content updates.

The steps to implement this solution are as follows:

1. We can create a lightweight CMS by simply instructing the AI to set up the database table for us:

    ```
    I need to create a lightweight content management table in
    Supabase. Please generate and execute the SQL statement to create a table
    named app_content with the following columns: id (primary key), key (unique
    text), value (text content), category (default 'general'), and standard
    timestamps.
    ```

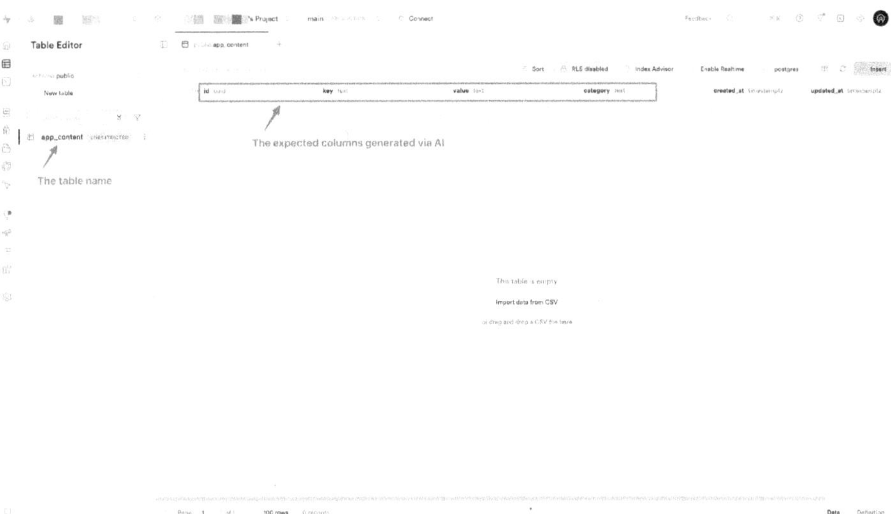

Figure 5.14 – Generating the database table through AI

2. **Add content management API routes:** Based on the existing API architecture, create `app/api/content/route.ts` to implement the CRUD (Create, Read, Update, Delete) interfaces for content.
3. **Build the content management backend interface:** Add administrator-only editing functions to the existing settings page, supporting modification of the content in the `app_content` table.
4. **Dynamically modify frontend components:** Replace hard-coded text with dynamic content retrieved from the database.

Option 2: Implementing progressive content management

If you want to build a truly scalable system while ensuring compatibility with your existing app, we can design a dynamic content-fetching mechanism that is flexible and secure.

We will instruct the AI to build a dynamic data-fetching loop. More importantly, we will ask the AI to keep the original "hardcoded" text as a fail-safe fallback mechanism. This means that if the database encounters an error or you haven't had time to configure the custom copy yet, the page will still display the default text and will never just go blank.

Here are the specific steps:

1. Open your AI assistant in Cursor or TRAE SOLO (for example, press *Ctrl/Cmd + I* in Cursor to open the **Composer** panel). You do not need to manually create any files or folders. Simply send the following instruction to the AI and let it do the heavy lifting for you:

```
First, please create an API route at app/api/content/route.ts. This route
needs to receive a 'category' parameter from the URL and fetch all keys and
values from the app_content data table based on this parameter. Next,
please create a custom React Hook at hooks/useContent.ts. This Hook needs
to call the API we just created to fetch data, handle the loading state
appropriately, and map the fetched data into a Key-Value object to return
to the frontend for use.
```

   The AI will automatically build the communication "bridge" for you. It will generate the API responsible for fetching data from the database, as well as a `useContent` tool (Hook) that packages the network request logic, ready for the frontend to call at any time.

2. Next, we need to connect the logic we just wrote to the actual page. The most critical step here is to use the @ symbol to precisely locate the file and emphasize to the AI that it must keep the "hardcoded text" as our safety airbag.

```
Please modify the @app/settings/page.tsx file. 1. Import the useContent
hook we just created and set the category parameter to 'settings'. 2.
Replace all previously identified hardcoded text on the page with data
dynamically read from the content object.
3. Crucial Requirement (Fail-safe Fallback Mechanism): You must ensure that
the original hardcoded English text remains as a fallback. For example, do
not just write content.page_title; you must write content.page_title ||
"Settings". This ensures that even if there is no corresponding value in
the database, the page will still display the default text normally.
```

Once the AI finishes executing, your page possesses the ability to update dynamically! You can run a quick test:

1. If you preview your live page right now, it will still display the default "Settings" (because there is no data in your database yet, triggering the fail-safe fallback).

2. Now, go to your Supabase `app_content` table and add a new record: set `category` to `settings`, `key` to `page_title`, and enter `User Settings` into the `value` field.
3. Refresh your webpage. You will find that, without modifying a single line of code, the title on the page has instantly changed to *User Settings*.

Through this step-by-step operation, you have not only built a highly flexible content management system but have also perfectly safeguarded the stability of your application.

Summary

In this section, we explored the critical role and evolution of content management in modern applications. We learned how to strategically select appropriate solutions for different stages of our application's life cycle. For the MVP and prototyping stage, we saw the value of starting with simple, hard-coded content to maintain focus and quickly validate core product concepts. As we planned for product growth, we upgraded to a database-driven solution based on Supabase, allowing us to separate volatile text from our code for highly flexible updates. Finally, for the team collaboration phase, we examined how to introduce a professional CMS (such as Keystatic) to empower product and operations teams to manage content independently. By mastering these concepts, we established a scientific strategy for evolving our application's content architecture from a simple MVP to a mature product.

With this habit tracker complete, you have successfully mastered the frugal full-stack. You have learned how to act as the *director*—seamlessly orchestrating frontend interfaces, backend logic, and databases using AI tools to build a complete product. But what if you want to build a product that actually generates revenue? In the next and final chapter—our 'graduation project'—we will level up from a personal utility to a commercial-grade SaaS application. We will build a fully monetized AI Image Generation Platform, learning how to integrate the Replicate API for cutting-edge AI features and Stripe for processing real-world payments. Get ready to turn your digital creation into a real business.

Get this book's PDF version and more

Scan the QR code (or go to `packtpub.com/unlock`). Search for this book by name, confirm the edition, and then follow the steps on the page.

Note: Keep your invoice handy. Purchases made directly from Packt don't require an invoice.

6

Project Practice 2: Building a Commercial-Grade AI Image Generation Platform

This is your graduation exam, and also your coronation ceremony.

In the previous chapters, we've walked together through the entire process from idea to tool mastery, from basic setup to project implementation. Now, it's time to take on the final challenge: building a complex application with real business value.

We're building an image generation platform integrating cutting-edge AI technology, a complete payment system, and a user management system. This project will comprehensively utilize every skill you've learned: from the beautiful interface design of v0.dev to the powerful backend support of Supabase; from calling AI models with Replicate to the professional payment process of Stripe; from advanced integration with MCP to production deployment with Vercel.

After you complete this chapter, you will have fully transitioned from a visionary with an idea into an independent creator and a digital-age entrepreneur.

Technical requirements

The project documents, reports, prompt workflows, and output for this chapter can be found in the book's GitHub repository: `https://github.com/PacktPublishing/Everyone-is-a-Programmer/tree/main/chapters/chapter-06-ai-image-platform`.

Project planning

Before launching any technology project, rigorous product planning is a prerequisite for success. We will clarify the project's business positioning, core functions, and page architecture to ensure that subsequent technical investments precisely serve business objectives.

Product business positioning analysis

This project will be built around a core service called **Replicate**. To understand what Replicate does, imagine you want to shoot a Hollywood blockbuster. You could spend millions of dollars buying state-of-the-art cameras and building a massive studio (this is what developers call 'managing complex GPU infrastructure'). Or you could simply rent a fully equipped studio by the hour, bringing in your script and letting their equipment do the heavy lifting.

Replicate is that rental studio for AI. It is a cloud platform that hosts thousands of cutting-edge, open-source AI models. Running these models normally requires incredibly expensive, specialized computers. Replicate allows developers to bypass this cost by offering a simple API—a secure telephone line where our app can send a text prompt to their massive computers, and their computers send the finished image back. In this project, Replicate will act as our tireless art department, specifically utilizing the Nano Banana model to instantly generate and edit images for our users.

Now that we understand how Replicate acts as our cloud platform for accessing AI, we need to choose our specific tool. Among the thousands of models hosted on Replicate, we chose the Nano Banana model (officially named Gemini 2.5 Flash Image, developed by Google DeepMind). We selected this model because of its exceptional ability to maintain 'character consistency'—meaning it can keep the exact same person, pet, or brand mascot looking identical across multiple different edits. In our project, Nano Banana will serve as the engine for all our core visual functions: generating images from text, editing single uploaded images, fusing multiple images together, and transferring artistic styles.

Based on this, our product positioning is clearly defined as follows: *Designed specifically for creative professionals and content creators, this professional-grade AI image generation and editing tool focuses on character consistency (the ability to keep a specific subject looking identical across multiple images) and advanced image editing capabilities.* This positioning will help us avoid fierce competition in the general-purpose AI painting tool market and focus on serving the specific workflow needs of professional users, thereby building core competitiveness in a niche market.

Core function planning

Based on the above positioning, we have planned the following four core functions that closely address the pain points of our target users

- **Text-to-Image:** As a fundamental function of all image generation tools, the tool allows users to quickly transform creative concepts in their minds into visual images using text prompts. The Replicate platform provides a straightforward and concise API for this purpose.
- **Image-to-Image:** This is the cornerstone of a professional creator's workflow, allowing users to manipulate existing pictures rather than starting from scratch. In our application, this feature is divided into two distinct operating modes:
    - **Single sheet editing:** After users upload a baseline image, they make detailed modifications using text commands (such as `change the background of the product image to a beach` or `adjust the color of the person's clothing to red`)
    - **Multi-image fusion:** After users upload multiple images as references or materials, they combine them with text commands to generate new images that integrate multiple image elements (such as seamlessly placing product image A into scene image B or naturally compositing person image C and pet image D into a group photo)
- **Style transfer:** Leveraging the multi-image processing capabilities of the Nano Banana model, the artistic style of one image (such as Van Gogh's "Starry Night") can be applied to another image (such as a cityscape photo) to create a unique visual effect
- **Image optimization:** This is a crucial commercialization feature. AI-generated raw image files can be too large to be used directly on web pages or marketing materials. This feature will automatically compress and optimize the generated images (e.g., converting them to WebP format) to achieve optimal web loading performance while maintaining high visual quality, which directly impacts user experience and website SEO.

Page architecture design

To support the above functions and guide users through the entire process "from awareness to payment," we will structure the application around the following five core pages:

- **Landing Page:** The product's portal page aims to attract visitors to register through visually impactful product displays and a clear value proposition

- **Generation Workbench:** The core operating area of the product, where users will complete all image generation and editing tasks. The interface design will prioritize intuitiveness and efficiency.
- **Gallery Management:** The user's personal asset library is not only used for storage but also serves as a workspace for users to view, manage, reuse, and share their creative results.
- **User Center:** The user's account management center is used to manage personal information, view remaining points, and upgrade or cancel subscription packages.
- **Pricing Page:** The product's commercial conversion page is used to clearly and intuitively display the value of different paid packages and integrate a seamless payment entry point.

Using TRAE SOLO to quickly draft project documents

Before we begin coding, we will use TRAE SOLO's capabilities to generate the project's PRD and TDD, laying a solid foundation for subsequent development work.

Drafting PRDs using TRAE SOLO

We will first use TRAE SOLO to draft the PRD, and the specific steps are as follows:

1. Open the TRAE app and ensure the switch in the upper left corner of the interface is set to SOLO mode to enable AI's autonomous analysis and document generation capabilities.
2. In the SOLO dialog box, describe your product requirements in detail using natural language, as shown in the example below:

```
I want to develop a commercial AI image generation platform based on the
Replicate API and the Nano Banana model.
The core functions are as follows:
-Text-generated image: Generates an image based on the user's input of text
prompts.
-Image-to-Image: Supports single image editing and multi-image fusion.
- Style transfer: Applying the artistic style of one image to another.
- Image optimization: Automatic compression and format conversion.
- Technology stack: Next.js + TypeScript + Tailwind CSS + Supabase +
Stripe.
- Page architecture: landing page, generation workbench, image library
management, user center, pricing page.
- Business model: Pay-per-use model based on points,
```

Unlike traditional software, calling advanced AI models incurs direct server costs for every single image. To protect our profit margins, we will implement a credits system where 1 credit equals 1 successful image generation. Users can acquire these credits through monthly subscriptions or one-time top-up packages. This approach gives users purchasing flexibility while ensuring our revenue always scales safely alongside our API costs.

```
Target users: creative professionals, content creators, and marketers.
Core value: Provides multi-round image editing capabilities with strong
role consistency.
Please generate a complete PRD based on these requirements.
```

3. View the PRD generation process in real time. SOLO automatically parses these requirements and generates a structured PRD in in the **Document** tool window. The content covers product overview and market positioning, detailed functional requirements specifications, user stories and usage scenarios, technical architecture and integration solutions, and business model and profit strategy.
4. If adjustments or additions to requirements are needed, you can directly communicate with SOLO, as shown in the following example:

```
Add a usage statistics function to the user center page to display the
user's image generation history, points consumption records, and monthly
usage trend charts.
```

SOLO will update the PRD to reflect the new requirements.

Using TRAE SOLO to draft TDD

Next, we will use TRAE SOLO to draft TDD, and the specific steps are as follows:

After the PRD is completed, continue the conversation with SOLO to request the generation of the corresponding TDD, as shown in the following example.

```
Based on the above PRD, please generate a complete technical design document,
focusing on:
-System overall architecture design and module relationship diagram
- Replicate API integration interface design and data flow
-Technical implementation schemes for user authentication and access control
- Backend architecture of the points system and payment process
-Detailed design of image generation and storage
- Database table structure design and relational model
```

```
- Frontend and Backend API definitions
- Deployment architecture and performance optimization strategies
```

SOLO will generate a complete TDD that includes the following key information:

- **System overview:** Project background, technical objectives, and overall architecture description
- **Technology stack selection:** Detailed reasons and trade-off analysis for the technology selection
- **System architecture design:** A high-level design scheme that includes a system relationship diagram
- **Detailed design:** The specific implementation scheme, API definition, and data model design of each submodule
- **Dataflow design:** A complete flowchart from user operations to data persistence
- **Safety design:** Solutions include identity verification, data encryption, and API security
- **Performance design:** Caching strategies, CDN configuration, database optimization
- **Deployment plan:** Production environment configuration, monitoring and alarms, backup strategies

In this way, we can establish a clear and executable technical implementation blueprint, which provides detailed technical guidance for the subsequent coding implementation.

After completing the planning phase, we will enter the technical implementation phase.

10-minute practice: Project architecture design and technology selection

We will leverage AI coding assistants to transform the time-consuming and experience-dependent architecture design process in traditional development into an efficient human-machine collaboration process.

Generating technical architecture using AI assistants

Now that the planning phase is complete and we need to build complex, commercial-grade integrations, we will hand the blueprints over to our construction foreman: Cursor.

As we established in *Chapter 4*, while TRAE SOLO is the best tool for the concept and prototyping stage (going from 0 to 1), Cursor's deep codebase indexing makes it the ultimate tool for the implementation and refinement stage' (going from 1 to N). Open the initial code project folder generated by TRAE SOLO in your Cursor editor, and let's convey the planned product requirements to the AI assistant in a structured manner:

```
I am building a commercial AI image generation platform using the Next.js,
Supabase, Stripe, and Vercel technology stack.
The core requirements are as follows.
1. AI features: Integrates the Replicate API (focusing on the Nano Banana model)
to enable text-to-image generation, single-image editing, and multi-image fusion.
2. User system: Supports email/social account login, and users can manage their
personal image library.
3. Billing system: Users purchase credits to use image generation services, which
requires a complete payment process.
4. Task: Please generate a detailed technical architecture plan and design the
frontend and Backend communication interfaces for the core Replicate API
integration, including the data structures for the task startup interface and the
Webhook callback interface.
use context7
@Web
```

Cursor's AI assistant generates a professional architecture suggestion and interface definition based on best practices for modern full-stack applications.

The `@Web` command instructs Cursor to enable web search functionality, obtain the latest information relevant to the requirements, and integrate it into the context, making the generated answer or code more accurate and timely. Additionally, the prompt `use context7` indicates that **Context7** (the MCP-based real-time document retrieval tool we configured in *Chapter 4*) is enabled. It retrieves the latest documents and code examples that match the current technology stack and specific version from the official source and injects them into the AI's context. This reduces errors caused by outdated APIs or fictitious interfaces and improves the accuracy and usability of the generated results.

Technology stack selection

Combining the AI assistant's suggestions with existing technological foundations, we finalized the project's complete technology stack. In addition to the core components familiar to readers, it also includes several key new tools or frameworks, as shown in *Table 6.1*.

Technology	Roles in the project	Illustrates
Replicate	AI model API services	Provides convenient and unified API calling services for thousands of open-source AI models, such as Nano Banana.
Next.js	React framework	This React-based, open-source framework supports **server-side rendering** (**SSR**) and **static site generation** (**SSG**), improving application performance and SEO.
TypeScript	Programming language	A superset of JavaScript that provides static type checking to enhance code robustness and maintainability.
Tailwind CSS	CSS framework	This CSS framework, primarily composed of utility classes, allows rapid creation of responsive and aesthetically pleasing interfaces by directly combining numerous ready-made style classes within the HTML.

Table 6.1 – Complete Technology Stack

Each component of this technology stack has been carefully selected to maximize the productivity of independent developers, allowing them to focus entirely on building product logic and user experience.

Replicate API design

Next, we need to design how our application will communicate with Replicate. In *Chapter 3*, we compared APIs to a restaurant's waitstaff—they carry requests from customers to the kitchen and bring the finished dishes back.

In a Next.js application, we create these "digital waiters" using API routes. An API route is simply a hidden web address inside our application that allows the frontend and the server to exchange data.

Based on the AI assistant's suggestions, our app needs two API routes to work with Replicate

- **The Task Startup Route (/api/generate-image):** This route starts the image generation process. When a user enters a text prompt, the frontend sends it to this route. The route then forwards the request to Replicate, telling it to begin generating the image.

- **The Webhook Callback Route (/api/webhook/replicate):** Generating AI images takes a few seconds. Instead of making our application wait, we give Replicate a special return address called a webhook. When the image is finished, Replicate sends the result directly to this route, allowing our app to receive and store the completed image.

In short, one route starts the task and the other receives the finished result.

Task startup interface

This interface serves as the entry point for frontend requests, receiving input parameters such as the user's text description (prompt) and the image file to be processed. The server rigorously verifies the user's identity information and points balance to ensure the user has the necessary permissions and sufficient points to execute the operation. After successful verification, the interface calls the Replicate API to initiate an asynchronous image generation task.

To clarify exactly how our frontend and Backend communicate, we need to define the data structures. Think of the **Request Body** as the 'digital order slip' our app hands to the waiter (containing the user's prompt and image choices), and the **Response Body** as the 'receipt' the server hands back (confirming the task has started). For this interface, they are defined as follows:

- **Request Body:** Designed as a JSON object containing multiple fields, with the following format:

  ```
  { "taskType": "text_to_image" | "image_edit" | "image_fusion", "prompt":
  "string", "inputImages": ["string",...], "modelConfig": {...} }
  ```

  Among them, the `taskType` field is used to distinguish different generation modes, prompt is used to store the user's text description, `inputImages` is an array of image URLs, and `modelConfig` stores the specific configuration parameters for the model.

- **Response Body:** It is also a JSON object with the following format

  ```
  { "taskId": "uuid", "predictionId": "string", "status": "processing" }
  ```

  Here, `taskId` is the task record ID created in the Supabase database, and `predictionId` is the unique identifier of the predicted task returned by Replicate. The frontend can use these two IDs to track the execution status of the task.

Webhook callback interface

This is a completely passive server-side interface, responsible only for receiving HTTP POST notifications from the Replicate server. When the image generation task is completed (whether successful or not), Replicate will proactively send a request containing the task result to the pre-configured webhook address.

The interface processing logic follows strict security and business processes: First, it verifies whether the received request truly comes from Replicate (usually verified by signature). This is usually accomplished by verifying a digital 'signature'—a cryptographic code that acts like a 'secret handshake' between Replicate and our server, ensuring malicious hackers cannot send fake completion messages. Once verified, it matches the corresponding task record in the database based on the `predictionId` carried in the request and updates its status; if the task is executed successfully, the interface also needs to complete a series of follow-up operations—downloading the generated image from the Replicate temporary storage server, permanently saving it to our own Supabase storage, and deducting the corresponding points from the user.

The interaction format for frontend and Backend data of this interface is defined as follows:

- **Request Body:** The format is defined by Replicate and includes the following core fields:

```
{ "id": "replicate_prediction_id", "status": "succeeded" | "failed",
"output": ["url",...], "error": "string", "metrics": {...} }
```

  Where `id` is the prediction task ID, `status` indicates the task execution result, `output` is an array of generated image URLs, `error` records the reason for failure, and `metrics` provide performance metrics.

- **Response body:** After the interface is processed, a simple `200 OK HTTP` status code is returned, informing the Replicate server that it has successfully received and processed the notification

This asynchronous design, which separates "task initiation" and "result processing," is the industry standard for building all long-running tasks, such as AI computing, video transcoding, and batch email sending.

Now, we will use another AI tool—v0.dev—to build the frontend interface of the entire application.

10-minute hands-on lesson: Quickly generate a UI using v0.dev

You'll recall that v0.dev is a generative UI tool launched by Vercel that can directly convert natural language descriptions, wireframes, and even design drafts into production-grade, maintainable React and Tailwind CSS code, which is a perfect fit for our technology stack.

Designing a responsive landing page

Open v0.dev, and we will generate a landing page using a precise prompt that includes structure, content, and style requirements:

```
Please create a landing page for my AI image generation SaaS product called Pixel
Alchemy. The page should have a dark, tech-themed theme and use the Inter font.
The page structure should be as follows.
1. Navigation bar: Includes the logo, "Features" and "Pricing" links, as well as
"Login" and "Free Sign-up" buttons. The "Free Sign-up" button should be
highlighted with a background of a gradient from purple to pink.
2. Hero Section: The main title is "Turning your imagination into visual gold,"
with a short subtitle and a similarly styled "Start Creating for Free" CTA button
below.
3. Features area: It adopts a three-column grid layout, with each column
containing a Lucide icon, a feature title (such as "Unlimited Creative Text and
Image Generation", "Amazing Character Consistency", "One-Click Smart Style
Transfer") and a brief descriptive text.
4. Portfolio Showcase: A responsive Masonry (waterfall) image grid displays a
variety of beautifully designed AI-generated images in different styles,
showcasing the tool's powerful capabilities.
```

After submission, v0.dev will generate an adapted UI design in real time. We can then iterate and fine-tune it through subsequent conversations, such as `adjust the rounded corners of all cards to 8px` or `add a shadow effect to the cards when the mouse hovers over them`.

Constructing the image generation workbench

As we learned in *Chapter 2*, v0.dev is our dedicated generative UI tool. It provides a real-time visual preview, allowing us to converse with the AI and instantly see our layout changes without constantly compiling code. We will use v0.dev to perfect the look of our application, and then use its seamless integration to import that code directly into our Cursor project.

The workbench is the core of the product, and its interface design must balance clarity and efficiency. We continued to provide specific requirements to v0.dev:

```
Create an image generation workbench interface using a classic two-column layout.
Left-side control panel: fixed width 320px, background color slightly darker. See
below from top to bottom.
A large, highly variable text input field (Textarea, used to input Prompt);
An image upload area supports dragging and clicking to upload multiple images, and
displays a list of thumbnails of uploaded images, adapting to multi-image fusion
mode;
A drop-down menu for selecting the generation style;
A prominently sized "Generate Image" button.
Right-side display area: Occupying the remaining space, this area displays the
generated results. It needs to handle the following three different states.
Initial state: Displays a placeholder or a prompt message guiding the user through
the process.
In Generating Status: Displays a loading animation (spinner) and text indicating
the estimated remaining time.
Success status: Displays the final generated image, with two buttons below the
image bearing icons: "Download" and "Save to Gallery".
```

This prompt details the structure, size, color, and behavior of the interface under different interactive states. v0.dev can understand it well and generate React component code that includes state management.

Creating the gallery management interface

Finally, for the user's personal gallery page, our prompt is as follows:

```
Create a user gallery page.
1. At the top of the page is a large title "My Creations" and a "Upload New Work"
button.
2. The bottom uses a responsive four-column image grid layout to display all
images generated by the user.
3. Each image is presented as a card element with a slight border and shadow.
4. When the mouse hovers over the image card, a semi-transparent black gradient
overlay appears from the bottom up, containing two white icon buttons: "Download"
and "Delete".
```

After generating and fine-tuning all pages, we used v0.dev's one-click code integration feature. Clicking the **...** button in the upper right corner of the v0.dev design preview page brings up commands to import code via the command line, as shown in *Figure 6.1*.

Figure 6.1. Commands for importing code via command line

Copy this command, open a terminal in your local Cursor editor, paste, and run it. This command will automatically and precisely install the page's React component code, the required `shadcn/ui` dependencies, and the icon library into your Next.js project. In this way, we can complete the application's frontend interface in a very short time, with almost no need to write UI code manually.

10-minute hands-on lesson: Building backend infrastructure with Supabase

After the frontend interface is built, the next step is to provide Backend support. Supabase allows for the declarative and rapid construction of the application's required data, authentication, storage, and real-time communication systems. To initiate this, we feed the following prompt into Cursor:

```
@docs initialize the corresponding Supabase code and database based on my design
document.
```

The AI will automatically generate the required backend code based on our requirements document. Before we walk through the specific code implementation in the upcoming sections, let's first review the structural design the AI has planned out for us.

Database design

Based on Cursor's suggestions and the TDD previously generated by TRAE SOLO, the core data table is planned as shown in *Table 6.2*.

While Cursor will automatically generate the SQL code to build these tables, AI outputs can occasionally vary. Therefore, before executing any code, you must act as the *director* and use the following table as your verification checklist. Ensure that the table names and main fields generated by your AI exactly match this structure; otherwise, the code we write later in this chapter may not connect properly.

Table name	**Main fields**	**Description and relationship**
`user_profiles`	id, user_id, name, avatar_url, preferences, created_at, updated_at	Stores detailed user information and preferences and associates it with the Supabase built-in auth.users table.
`generation_tasks`	id, user_id, task_type, prompt, negative_prompt, status, replicate_id, cost_credits, created_at	Record each generation request initiated by the user and its current status (pending, processing, completed, or failed).
`user_images`	id, user_id, task_id, image_url, thumbnail_url, metadata, created_at	Store the successfully generated final image file and its metadata and associate it with the corresponding generation request.
`Credit_transactions`	id, user_id, amount, type, description, related_id, created_at	Record all credit changes (spending, recharge, bonuses, etc.) for easy auditing and user inquiry.
`orders`	id, user_id, stripe_session_id, amount, status, credits_amount, created_at, updated_at	Stores user order information for purchasing points and integrates with the Stripe payment system
`stripe_subscriptions`	id, user_id, stripe_subscription_id, status, current_period_start, current_period_end	Manage user subscription status and support automatic recharging on a regular basis.

Table 6.2 – Core Data Table

This design, which separates the "generation requests" (`generation_tasks` table) from the "final results" (`user_images` table), is a robust approach to data modeling. It tracks every attempt (success or failure), which is crucial for subsequent debugging and user behavior analysis.

User authentication system

In the Supabase dashboard, click **Authentication** | **Sign In/Providers** to enable email providers. You can also enable social media login methods like Google and GitHub with one click as needed.

Our architecture utilizes Supabase Auth as the primary gatekeeper. The platform is designed to support standard email providers as well as frictionless social media login methods like Google and GitHub. To guarantee data privacy at the foundational level, we rely on Row-Level Security (RLS) policies across all core tables. The core security policy dictates that users can only view and manipulate records where the `user_id` matches their own authenticated UID. This ensures that even if a user bypasses the frontend and directly calls the API, the database itself prevents them from snooping on or tampering with other people's data.

Database views and functions

To simplify data retrieval on the frontend, we created several useful database views.

- `user_stats_view`: Displays summary information such as user generation statistics and points balance
- `monthly_stats_view`: Displays statistics on user generation and points consumption compiled by month
- `credit_consumption_view`: Display users' points consumption patterns
- `generation_type_distribution_view`: Statistically analyze the distribution of different generation types

At the same time, based on our initial prompt, Cursor planned several custom **database functions** to handle complex business logic. If a data table is a *filing cabinet*, a database function is like a *secure automated teller* living directly inside the database. Instead of trusting the frontend website to calculate user credits (which a hacker could manipulate), we use these functions to securely process credit deductions and transaction histories right at the data source. We will look at the specific SQL code Cursor generated for our credit management functions in the implementation steps in the following section.

Real-time functionality

To provide real-time feedback on the progress of time-consuming image generation on the frontend, we will use Supabase Realtime. The frontend **Generation Workbench** page subscribes to changes in the current user's records in the `generation_tasks` table via the Supabase client library. When the Backend Webhook handler updates the `status` field of a task, this change is pushed to the frontend in real time via WebSocket.

This concludes our review of the AI's architectural blueprint. We now have a clear plan for a secure, real-time, and fully functional backend system. In the next section, we will execute this plan and build the database.

Implementation steps

Now, we will translate the above design into actual code and configuration. The following are the detailed implementation steps

Generating the database via cursor

Now, we will translate our database design into actual code. Instead of manually writing hundreds of lines of complex SQL, we will instruct Cursor's Composer to read our TDD and generate the complete migration script.

Open Cursor, press *Ctrl/Cmd + I* to bring up the **Composer** panel, and enter the following prompt:

```
@docs Based on our system design document, please generate a complete PostgreSQL
migration script for
Supabase. I need the following tables created: user_profiles, generation_tasks,
user_images, credit_transactions, orders, and stripe_subscriptions. Include all
appropriate primary keys, UUIDs, and foreign key relationships linking back to
auth.users. After defining the tables, please write the SQL to enable Row-Level
Security (RLS) on all tables, ensuring users can only SELECT, INSERT, UPDATE, or
DELETE their own data where auth.uid() = user_id.
```

Cursor will instantly generate the standard SQL migration script.

Generating Database Views and Credit Functions

To manage and query data more efficiently, we need specific views and functions, particularly for our credit system. Continue in the same Composer chat:

```
Great. Now please generate the SQL to create a view named user_stats_view that
joins the users, tasks, images, and credit_transactions tables to show total
generations and credit balance. Also, create PostgreSQL functions for:
- get_user_credit_balance
- consume_user_credits
- add_user_credits
The get_user_credit_balance function should return the user's current credit
```

```
balance. The consume_user_credits and add_user_credits functions should securely
insert new records into credit_transactions to handle credit deductions and
additions safely.
```

Configuring Supabase storage and triggers

Finally, we need a place to store our generated images and a way to reward new users with free credits.

```
Write the SQL to create a public Supabase Storage bucket named user-images, and
add storage policies so users can only upload and view files in a folder named
after their own
UID. Finally, create a database trigger named on_auth_user_created that
automatically awards 10 free credits to any new user when they register.
```

You can take the SQL scripts Cursor just generated and paste them directly into the Supabase SQL Editor to execute them. By using AI to write the SQL, you guarantee that all syntax, foreign keys, and security policies are perfectly formatted.

Create image generation API routes

We need an API endpoint that receives the user's prompt, checks their credits, and forwards the request to Replicate. Let's have Cursor build this complex logic:

```
Please create a Next.js API route at app/api/generate/route.ts. This route must:
1. Verify the user is authenticated via Supabase.
2. Check if the user has a credit balance > 0 (return a 402 error if not).
3. Check our rate limit function to ensure they haven't exceeded 50 generations
today (return a 429 error if so).
4. Call the Replicate API using the stability-ai/sdxl model with the user's prompt
and an image URL (if it's an image-to-image task).
5. Set up the Replicate webhook to point to ${process.env.APP_URL}/api/webhook/
replicate.
6. Record the pending task in our generation_tasks database table and return the
task ID to the frontend.
```

Create a webhook processor

Because Replicate generates images asynchronously, we need a passive webhook listener to catch the finished image and deduct the user's credits:

```
Now, create the Webhook handler at app/api/webhook/replicate/
route.ts. It needs to receive the POST notification from Replicate. If the status
```

```
is 'succeeded', it must:
1. Download the image URL provided by Replicate.
2. Upload it securely to our Supabase user-images storage bucket.
3. Create a record in the user_images database table.
4. Update the task status to 'completed' in generation_tasks.
5. Call our consume_user_credits database function to deduct 1 credit from the
user. Handle all errors gracefully if the task fails.
```

Completing the code with Cursor

You might have noticed the //TODO: Implement Replicate Webhook signature verification comment in the code above. In traditional development, securing a Webhook requires writing complex cryptographic algorithms. Because we are vibe coding, we will let Cursor do the heavy lifting.

Simply highlight that TODO line in your editor, press *Ctrl/Cmd + K* to bring up Composer, and enter the following prompt: `Please implement the Replicate webhook signature verification using the REPLICATE_WEBHOOK_SIGNING_SECRET from my environment variables. Return a 401 error if the signature is invalid.`

Cursor will instantly replace your comment with the correct security logic, ensuring hackers cannot send fake generation results to your database.

Configure environment variables and install dependencies

Configuring environment variables and installing dependencies are fundamental preparations for project operation. First, create a `.env.local` file in the project root directory to store various environment variables, including the Supabase project URL, anonymous key, service role key, replica API token, Webhook signing key, and the server-side application base URL used to construct webhook callback addresses, among other configuration information. The specific content is as follows.

```
Plaintext
# Supabase configuration
NEXT_PUBLIC_SUPABASE_URL=your_supabase_url
NEXT_PUBLIC_SUPABASE_ANON_KEY=your_supabase_anon_key
SUPABASE_SERVICE_ROLE_KEY=your_supabase_service_role_key

# Replicate configuration
REPLICATE_API_TOKEN=your_replicate_api_token
REPLICATE_WEBHOOK_SIGNING_SECRET=your_replicate_webhook_signing_secret

# Stripe configuration
```

```
STRIPE_SECRET_KEY=your_stripe_secret_key
STRIPE_WEBHOOK_SECRET=your_stripe_webhook_secret

# Application configuration
APP_URL=http://localhost:3000

# Optional public base URL for incoming webhooks during local development
APP_URL=https://your-tunnel.ngrok-free.app
```

Use `NEXT_PUBLIC_APP_URL` for the browser address you open on your own machine. If you want to test Replicate webhooks during local development, you must expose your app through a temporary public tunnel, such as `ngrok`, and set `APP_URL` to that public address. Replicate sends server-to-server webhook requests and cannot reach localhost directly.

For Stripe webhook testing, you have two options. You can expose the same public tunnel and register `/api/webhook/stripe` as a Stripe webhook endpoint, or you can use the Stripe CLI to forward events directly to your local server with stripe listen `--forward-to localhost:3000/api/webhook/stripe`. When using Stripe CLI forwarding, copy the temporary webhook signing secret it prints and use that value for `STRIPE_WEBHOOK_SECRET`.

Next, you need to install the necessary dependencies for the project. You can install packages such as `replicate` and `@supabase/supabase-js` by executing the following bash command, which provides the corresponding functionalities for the project:

```
Bash
npm install replicate @supabase/supabase-js
```

Test API functionality

API functional testing requires verifying that request generation and Webhook function correctly. When testing request generation, tools such as Postman or curl can be used to send a `POST` request to `http://localhost:3000/api/generate`. This request must include Content-Type and Authorization information in the request header, passing parameters such as the prompt word and task type in the request body. An example of the curl command is as follows:

```
Bash
curl -X POST http://localhost:3000/api/generate \
-H "Content-Type: application/json" \
-H "Authorization: Bearer YOUR_JWT_TOKEN" \
-d '{
"prompt": "A cute little cat is sitting in the garden",
```

```
"taskType": "text_to_image"
}'
```

To test the webhook, you need to configure the webhook URL (`https://your-domain.com/api/webhook/replicate`) in the Replicate console. This ensures that notifications are received correctly after the task is completed.

Through the above complete implementation steps, we have successfully built a fully functional backend system, including a complete database infrastructure, a secure points management system, an efficient image generation API, reliable asynchronous task processing, and comprehensive error handling and logging.

10-minute hands-on lesson: Integrating the Replicate API to implement core AI functionality

This section details how to integrate Replicate's AI service into your application to achieve image generation functionality. The core of this process is building a robust, event-driven, asynchronous workflow.

Replicate API key configuration and environment variable management

First, register an account on the Replicate website and generate a new API key on the **API Tokens** page of your account settings. Then, add this key to the `.env.local` file in your project's root directory:

```
Plaintext
REPLICATE_API_TOKEN=your_replicate_token_here
REPLICATE_WEBHOOK_SIGNING_SECRET=your_webhook_secret_here
```

Text-to-image functionality: Integration with multiple AI models

To handle all generation requests, you need to create a Next.js API route: `app/api/generate/route.ts`. The server-side logic flow is as follows:

1. **User authentication**: Utilize Supabase server-side capabilities to verify the **JWT (JSON Web Token)** in the request header to ensure the request originates from a legitimate, logged-in user.
2. **Points check**: Query the `credit_transactions` table in the database to calculate the user's current points balance. If the points are insufficient, return an error immediately.

3. **Call the Replicate API**: Once the user passes the security and points checks, the server officially sends the generation request to the AI. This step packages the user's text prompt, configures the image parameters, and, crucially, provides the Webhook address so Replicate knows exactly where to send the finished artwork. The corresponding code is as follows :

```
TypeScript
const prediction = await this.client.predictions.create({
  version: params.modelVersion ||
"19deaef633fd44776c82edf39fd60e95a7250b8ececf11a725229dc75a81f9ca", // Nano
Banana
  input: {
    prompt: params.prompt,
    negative_prompt: params.negativePrompt,
    width: params.width || 1024,
    height: params.height || 1024,
    num_inference_steps: params.steps || 20,
    guidance_scale: params.guidanceScale || 7.5,
    seed: params.seed,
    ...(params.inputImage && { image: params.inputImage }),
    ...(params.maskImage && { mask: params.maskImage }),
    ...(params.denoisingStrength && { denoising_strength:
params.denoisingStrength })
  },
  ...(getReplicateWebhookUrl()
    ? {
      webhook: getReplicateWebhookUrl()!,
      webhook_events_filter: ['completed'],
    }
    : {}),
});
```

4. **Record tasks in the database**: Store task information in the `generation_tasks` table and set the initial status to processing

The above logic describes the implementation process of the text-to-image function. The process for the image-to-image function is similar; only the input parameters need to be adjusted.

Image generation function: Image editing and fusion

The process for the image-to-image function needs to be slightly adjusted as follows.

1. The frontend first uploads the user-uploaded image to Supabase Storage and obtains the public URL for the image.
2. When calling the API, send the image URL along with the prompt as part of the request body to the backend.
3. In the backend's `replicate.run()` function, the image URL is passed as an input object parameter.

Whether it's text-to-image or image-to-image, Replicate is an asynchronous process, so a dedicated webhook handler is needed to receive and manage callback notifications after the task is completed.

Asynchronous processing: Webhook callbacks and generation state management

Create a Webhook handler `app/api/webhook/replicate/route.ts` to receive and process `POST` notifications from Replicate. Its main responsibilities are as follows:

- **Verify request origin:** Verify the signature of the Webhook request to ensure that the request does indeed come from Replicate
- **Analyze data:** Extract the final state and output of the task from the request body
- **Update database and file transfer:** If successful, download the image from Replicate and upload it to Supabase Storage, creating a record in the `user_images` table; if it fails, update the status to `failed` and log the error message
- **Deduct points:** Demonstrate how to safely deduct user points using a pre-created database function.

```
TypeScript
await supabase.rpc("consume_user_credits", {
p_user_id: task.user_id,
p_amount: -task.cost_credits,
p_type: "consumption",
p_description: `Image generation: ${task.task_type}`,
p_related_id: task.id,
});
```

10-minute hands-on lesson: Implementing a user credits system and usage restrictions

In commercial applications, a reliable credits system is the core foundation for measuring user usage and implementing billing functions. This section will elaborate on how to design and implement a secure and fully functional user credits and usage restriction system.

Credit model design

To meet the needs of different users, we have designed a flexible three-layer credit model:

- **New user registration benefits:** 10 free credits automatically awarded to new users
- **Monthly subscription service:** 100 credits earned for a monthly fee of $10
- **One-time points package:** Users can spend $5 to buy 50 credits

The core measurement rule is simple:

1 credit = 1 successful image generation

Secure credit deduction mechanism

A crucial design decision: we only check the credit balance on the frontend, but we deduct the credit securely in the backend Webhook only after the image is successfully generated. Never trust the client environment with sensitive billing operations.

Implementation steps via cursor

We will direct Cursor to build robust PostgreSQL functions for us, including credit consumption, rate limits, and credit history:

```
@docs We need to implement our User Credits System in Supabase. Please generate
the SQL to do the following:
1. Create a get_user_credit_balance function that calculates a user's total
credits from the credit_transactions table.
2. Create a consume_user_credits function that securely deducts a credit (throws
an error if the balance is insufficient).
3. Create a credit_packages table and insert default rows for a 'Free Trial' (10
credits), 'Credit Pack' (50 credits), and 'Pro Subscription' (500 credits).
4. Create a check_user_rate_limit function that prevents a user from generating
more than 50 images a day.
```

Credit management API routing

To allow the frontend UI to display the user's remaining credits and transaction history, we need a dedicated API route. We'll input the following prompt:

```
Please create a GET route at app/api/credits/route.ts. It should authenticate the
user, fetch their current credit balance, fetch their last 20 credit transactions
(for a history table), and fetch all active credit packages from the database.
Return this data as a clean JSON response.
```

Test the functionality of the points system

After the code implementation is complete, the functionality of each module needs to be verified through the following tests.

Test the credit functions

Before testing the credit functions, it is important to understand the data model. This chapter uses a signed transaction ledger for credit history. In the `credit_transactions` table, positive amounts add credits and negative amounts deduct credits. For example, purchasing 100 credits inserts +100, consuming 1 credit inserts -1, and refunding 1 credit inserts +1. In this implementation, `user_profiles.credits` stores the current balance, while `credit_transactions` stores the audit trail used for reporting and analytics.

> **Note**
>
> This sign convention matters. If you insert every transaction as a positive number, your reports will be wrong and the stored balance will no longer match the transaction history. To avoid this mistake, do not insert ledger rows manually unless you are certain about the sign. Instead, update credits through the database functions, which apply the balance change and record the matching transaction entry in one step.

Execute the following query in the Supabase SQL editor to verify the functions of points query, spending, recharge, and historical query.

```sql
SQL
-- Test points balance query
SELECT get_user_credit_balance('your-user-id-here');

-- Test points consumption
SELECT consume_user_credits(
'your-user-id-here',
```

```
1,
'Test consumption',
'test-task-id'
);

-- Test points recharge
SELECT add_user_credits(
'your-user-id-here',
10,
'Test recharge',
'Test Recharge Description'
);

-- View points history
SELECT * FROM get_user_credit_history('your-user-id-here', 10, 0);
```

Test frequency limit

Execute the following query to verify the user's daily usage statistics and frequency limit logic.

```
SQL
-- Check user usage today
SELECT * FROM user_daily_usage WHERE user_id = 'your-user-id-here';

-- Test frequency limit check
SELECT check_user_rate_limit('your-user-id-here', 50);
```

Verifying the results and troubleshooting

What actually happens when you run this code?

- **When it is right:** The **Results** panel at the bottom of your Supabase SQL Editor will populate with a neat table. You will see the math working—your test user's balance will reflect the added points, and the transaction history will successfully display the records.
- **When something is wrong:** You will likely see a red SQL error message. The most common mistake for beginners here is forgetting to replace the 'your-user-id-here' placeholder text with an actual user ID copied from your `auth.users` table.

How to fix it: If your ID is correct but you are still getting an error, don't panic! Remember the *Sherlock Holmes debugging method* we learned in *Chapter 4*. Simply copy the red error message from Supabase, paste it into your Cursor AI chat, and ask: `I ran my database test and got this error: [paste error]. How do I fix it?` The AI will analyze your codebase and tell you exactly which step you missed.

Through the steps above, we have successfully implemented a complete and secure credits system.

10-minute hands-on lesson: Integrating Stripe to implement a complete payment process

Now, we will integrate commercial-grade payment functionality into the points system. By integrating with Stripe, an industry-standard payment platform, we can build a complete and automated payment loop for the application.

Stripe product and pricing configuration

Configure the sale of *products* in a declarative manner in the Stripe dashboard. This process does not require writing code. The steps are as follows:

1. Log in to your Stripe account and ensure you are in **Test Mode**.
2. Go to the **Products** directory.
3. Create products and services. First, create two subscription products: a "Fan Package" and a "Pro Package." Add `$10` and `$25` per month prices to them, respectively, making sure to select **Recurring** as the price type. Next, create a single-purchase product named "Rewards Pack,'" add a `$5` price to it, and select **One-time** as the price type.
4. Add metadata. This is a core step in linking Stripe products with the app's credits system.

   > **Note**
   >
   > Stripe frequently updates its dashboard UI. If you do not see the "Metadata" option immediately, look for an "Additional options" or "Advanced" toggle. If you still can't find it, use your AI assistant! Simply ask: `Where do I add metadata to a product in the current Stripe dashboard?`

   Configure custom metadata fields for each Price as follows.

   - **Fan package:** key is credits, value is 100

- **Professional package:** key is credits, value is 500
- **Points package:** key is credits, value is 50

This metadata will be read in subsequent payment success webhooks to automatically top up the corresponding credits for the user. Specific configuration information is shown in *Table 6.3*:

Product name	type	Price (USD)	Points awarded	Stripe metadata
Free package	Register now and receive a free gift	0	10	not applicable
Points package	One-time purchase	5	50	{"credits": 50}
Fan package	subscription	$10 per month	100	{"credits": 100}
Professional package	subscription	$25 per month	500	{"credits": 500}

Table 6.3 – Stripe Product Configuration Information

Payment process integration

The payment process implementation here references the best practices in the Next.js + Supabase + Stripe subscription template provided by Vercel. The specific steps are as follows:

1. **Create a checkout session (Server-side):** Create an API route in `app/api/stripe/create-checkout-session/route.ts`. When a user clicks the purchase button, the frontend calls this API and passes the price ID (`price_id`) of the selected product. The backend logic creates or retrieves a customer object for the user in Stripe, then uses the Stripe Node.js library to create a checkout session and return the session ID (`session_id`) to the frontend.
2. **Redirect the user to Stripe checkout page (Client-side):** After obtaining the `session_id`, the frontend uses the `redirectToCheckout` method of the Stripe.js client library to securely redirect the user to the Stripe-hosted checkout page. All sensitive payment information is handled by Stripe, and the application server does not directly access it, greatly simplifying PCI security compliance work.

3. **Handle the payment confirmation (Server-side Webhook):** After payment is complete, you need to receive a payment result notification from Stripe. Configure a webhook endpoint in the Stripe dashboard, pointing to the application's `app/api/webhook/stripe/route.ts` file, and specifically listen for the `checkout.session.completed` event. When Stripe successfully processes the payment, it will send a `POST` request containing event details to this webhook address. The backend then uses this request to provide the user's credits.

Automatic points recharge system

The Stripe Webhook processor is the core of the automatic credits top-up mechanism. When it receives the `checkout.session.completed` event, it strictly executes the following automated logic.

1. **Verify Webhook signature:** As a primary step in ensuring system security, the Webhook signing key obtained from the Stripe dashboard is used to verify the Stripe-Signature in the request header. This ensures the authenticity and integrity of the request.
2. **Parsing event data:** It securely extracts the user's `stripe_customer_id` and the price information of the purchased products from the event object.
3. **Points to be extracted:** It reads the pre-set corresponding credit value from the `metadata.credits` of the price object.
4. **Update database:** When Stripe sends a successful payment notification, we must instantly apply those credits to the user. In your AI coding assistant, with the project open, paste the following prompt:

```
Update app/api/webhook/stripe/route.ts so it verifies the Stripe signature
using the raw request body, handles checkout.session.completed and
checkout.session.expired, updates the matching order, and awards credits
only once.
```

Thus, a fully automated business loop has been formed, from user click to purchase to automatic crediting of points, laying a solid foundation for the commercialization of AI applications. After resolving the payment issue, the next step is to establish effective user communication channels, which are crucial for improving user activity and retention rates.

10-minute hands-on lesson: Building an email marketing system with Resend

Apart from powerful functionality, a successful SaaS product also needs efficient communication with users at critical junctures. To this end, we will integrate Resend to build intelligent and automated email communication systems for applications. Resend is deeply integrated with the open-source project `react.email`, allowing developers to use familiar React component syntax to build well-designed, responsive email templates, and it is well-suited for the Next.js technology stack.

Automating user lifecycle emails

You might notice we haven't provided the raw code for these `pg_cron` tasks or Edge Functions. That is intentional! Setting up database scheduled tasks manually is highly complex. Instead, we are giving you the architectural blueprint. When you are ready to build these, simply open Cursor's Composer and use this logic as your prompt. For example: `Please create a Supabase Edge Function to send a welcome email via Resend, and write the SQL trigger to execute it whenever a new user is added to auth.users.` The AI will handle the heavy lifting, turning this strategy into functioning code.

Automatically sending emails at key points in the user lifecycle can effectively improve user experience and long-term retention rates. To achieve this, we can set up the following three core automated email flows:

- **Registration welcome email:** This is achieved through a Supabase database trigger—when a new record is added to the `auth.users` table, the trigger calls a edge function to send a welcome email via the Resend SDK.
- **User guide email after registration:** Use the built-in `pg_cron` extension in Supabase to create a scheduled task that runs once a day, selects users who have been registered for at least three days, and sends them an email with a guide containing advanced usage tips.
- **Subscription renewal reminder emails:** Use `pg_cron` to create daily tasks that query valid subscriptions about to expire and call edge functions to send reminder emails three days before the renewal date, reducing involuntary churn.

Asynchronous task completion notification email

The core functionality of an application (such as AI image generation) is typically executed asynchronously, requiring users to wait after submitting a task. Email notifications are the best way to ensure users receive results promptly and improve their experience. This logic can be seamlessly integrated into the Replicate Webhook handling route (`/api/webhook/replicate`).

Once a successful generation notification is received and the image is successfully saved to Supabase Storage, before completing all database operations, add a step. In your AI coding assistant, with the project folder open, paste the following prompt:

```
Update the notification workflow so it adds a step that calls the Resend API to
send a notification email. Keep the implementation production-ready, use clear
error handling, and return structured JSON responses.
```

User behavior triggered marketing emails

Email systems can be used to achieve advanced marketing automation, enabling precise targeting by observing user behavior to improve conversion rates. For example, you can set up a low credits reminder and promotion mechanism. When a user's remaining credits fall below a preset threshold (e.g., 5 points), the system will automatically trigger a personalized email.

A new logic for checking the user's remaining credits can be added inside the Supabase Edge Function each time points are successfully deducted. If the credits are below the threshold, another dedicated Edge Function is called to send an email containing personalized copy and promotional offers via Resend to incentivize the user to recharge again.

By integrating Resend, the application is no longer a passively responding tool but a platform that can proactively communicate with users, allowing user experience and business goals to be more closely integrated.

10-minute hands-on lesson: Deploying and configuring a production environment with Vercel

After completing the core functionalities developed locally, the next step is to deploy the application online to serve users worldwide. We will use the Vercel platform to accomplish this, which provides a highly integrated and seamless deployment experience for Next.js.

Environment variable configuration

In the Vercel project's **Environment Variables** settings, add all the keys and configuration information from the local `.env.local` file one by one, including:

```
The Supabase URL, ANON_KEY, and the server's SERVICE_ROLE_KEY;
API_TOKEN for Replicate;
Stripe's SECRET_KEY and WEBHOOK_SECRET;
API_KEY for Resend.
```

By configuring these variables on the Vercel platform, you can ensure that they are securely injected into the application during build and runtime, preventing them from being leaked in public code repositories.

Domain binding and SSL certificates

On the Vercel project's **Domains** settings page, add the purchased custom domain. Based on the DNS records provided by Vercel (usually A or CNAME records), complete the configuration in your domain registrar's backend. After the DNS configuration takes effect, Vercel will automatically apply for, configure, and continuously renew a free **Let's Encrypt SSL** certificate for the domain, enabling HTTPS across the entire site without manual intervention.

Performance optimization

One of Vercel's main advantages is its built-in performance optimization mechanism, allowing developers to achieve good website performance without complex additional configurations. Specifically, the platform automatically accelerates your application through three core features:

- **Global Edge Network:** After deployment is triggered by git push, Vercel builds and deploys the application to an edge network around the world. When a user accesses the application, the content is automatically retrieved from the node with the closest geographical location, significantly reducing network latency.
- **Image optimization:** The Image component built into Next.js is deeply integrated with Vercel Network. When using this component to display images from Supabase Storage, Vercel automatically optimizes the images in real time (such as format conversion and size scaling) and caches them on CDNs around the world.
- **Edge function:** All Next.js API routes (such as `/api/generate-image`, `/api/webhook/*`) and data fetching logic for server components are automatically deployed by Vercel as high-performance edge functions. This means that the backend logic also runs on servers around the world, closer to the user, thereby reducing API response time.

Vercel abstracts away tedious infrastructure maintenance tasks, allowing developers to focus more on product development.

Generating your first AI image

You have successfully deployed your application to the global edge network. Your infrastructure is secure, your database is live, and your payment system is ready. Now, it is time to experience the magic of what you have built from the perspective of your users. Let's run a complete end-to-end test in your live production environment.

1. **Claim Your welcome bonus:** Open your browser and visit your live Vercel domain (e.g.,). Click the "Free Sign-up" button we designed. Register a new account. Thanks to the Supabase database trigger we configured earlier, your account will instantly be credited with 10 free points.
2. **Enter the generation workbench:** Navigate to your *generation workbench*. In the prompt input box, type a creative instruction. Let's try: `A futuristic cyberpunk cat wearing neon goggles, highly detailed, cinematic lighting.`
3. **Watch the engine work:** Click **Generate**. Behind the scenes, your Next.js API securely verifies your points and hands the task to the Nano Banana model via Replicate. You will see the loading state on your screen. Meanwhile, Replicate processes the image and silently sends a webhook back to your server to securely deduct 1 credit.

Within seconds, the completed image will appear on your screen, automatically saved to your Supabase Storage, and visible in your **Gallery** page.

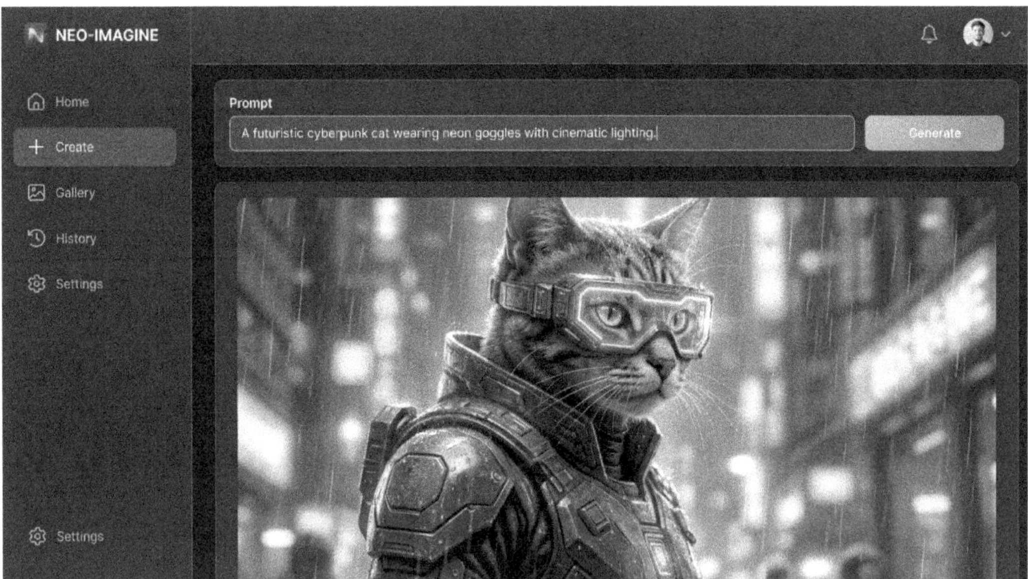

Figure 6.2 – Look at the screen in front of you. Just days ago, this was merely an idea. Now, it is a fully functioning, commercial-grade AI platform.

At this point, our AI image generation station is a fully functional, standalone product.

Summary

Through this chapter, we have not only mastered the entire process of building a complete, commercially viable AI application from scratch, but also gained a deep understanding of how to leverage AI to assist development and how to seamlessly integrate various modern network technology stacks.

Before we close this book, let's reflect on exactly what you accomplished in this final graduation project. You engineered a complete, commercial-grade SaaS product. Specifically, you accomplished the following:

- Used v0.dev and Cursor to rapidly generate a responsive, professional UI
- Integrated the Replicate API to command the powerful Nano Banana model for text-to-image and image-to-image generation
- Engineered a secure, multi-tiered points and billing system using Supabase
- Closed the commercial loop by integrating Stripe for subscriptions and Resend for automated marketing emails
- Deployed the application to a global edge network using Vercel

Parting words to the creators of tomorrow

In the opening pages of this book, we talked about the *execution gap*—the tragedy of brilliant ideas remaining trapped in a notebook, or ending up like a sparse, empty warehouse because of technical barriers. This book was written to tear down that invisible *wall of technology*.

By embracing vibe coding and the frugal full stack, you have proven that the traditional barriers of technical difficulty and capital are dissolving. You no longer need to rely on expensive engineering teams to bring your visions to life. You have crossed the chasm. You are no longer just a dreamer; you are a builder and a creator. The tools are in your hands, the cost of creation is near zero, and the future is unfolding at your fingertips. We cannot wait to see what you build next.

Get This Book's PDF Version and Exclusive Extras

Scan the QR code (or go to `packtpub.com/unlock`). Search for this book by name, confirm the edition, and then follow the steps on the page.

UNLOCK NOW

Note: Keep your invoice handy. Purchases made directly from Packt don't require one.

7

Unlock Your Exclusive Benefits

Your copy of this book includes the following exclusive benefits:

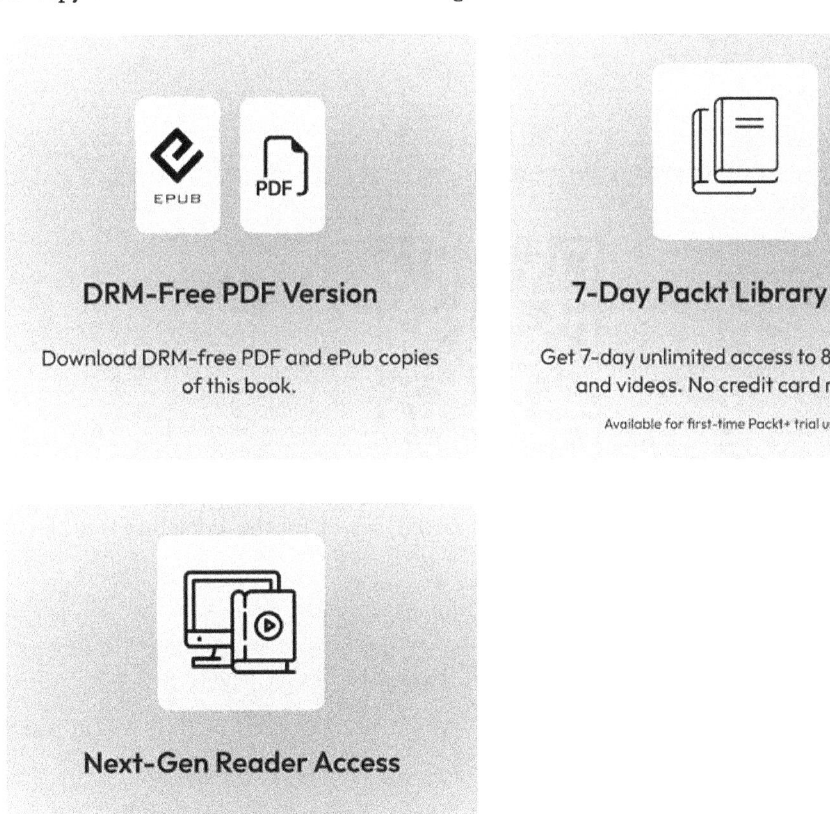

Follow the guide below to unlock them. The process takes only a few minutes and needs to be completed once.

Unlock this Book's Free Benefits in 3 Easy Steps

Step 1

Keep your purchase invoice ready for *Step 3*. If you have a physical copy, scan it using your phone and save it as a PDF, JPG, or PNG.

For more help on finding your invoice, visit `https://www.packtpub.com/en-us/unlock?step=1`.

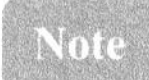

Note: If you bought this book directly from Packt, no invoice is required. After *Step 2*, you can access your exclusive content right away.

Step 2

Scan the QR code or go to `packtpub.com/unlock`.

On the page that opens (similar to *Figure 7.1* on desktop), search for this book by name and select the correct edition.

Unlock Your Book's Free Benefits

Bought a Packt book from Amazon or one of our channel partners? Unlock your free benefits in 3 easy steps.

Find Your Book Sign Up or Sign In Upload Purchase Proof

Need Help?

Search for your book here

1. Find Your Book

Search by title or ISBN

2. Sign up (Free) or Sign In

3. Upload Purchase Proof

Figure 7.1: Packt unlock landing page on desktop

Step 3

After selecting your book, sign in to your Packt account or create one for free. Then upload your invoice (PDF, PNG, or JPG, up to 10 MB). Follow the on-screen instructions to finish the process.

Need Help

If you get stuck and need help, visit `https://www.packtpub.com/unlock-benefits/help` for a detailed FAQ on how to find your invoices and more. This QR code will take you to the help page.

> Note
>
> **Note**: If you are still facing issues, reach out to `customercare@packt.com`.

Other Books You May Enjoy

If you enjoyed this book, you may be interested in these other books by Packt:

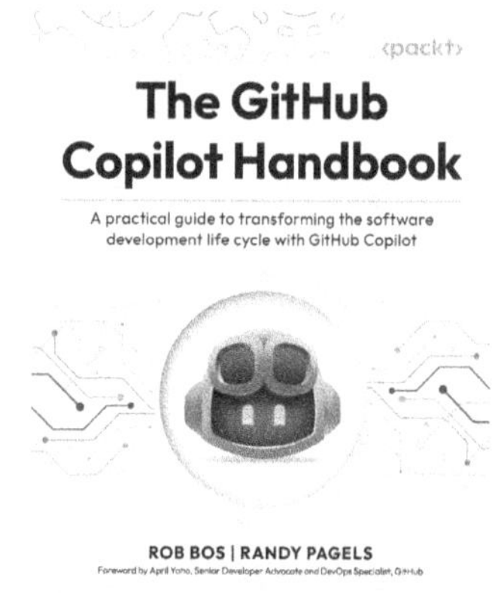

The GitHub Copilot Handbook

Rob Bos, Randy Pagels

ISBN: 978-1-80611-663-8

- Apply GitHub Copilot across the full software development life cycle
- Understand how AI powers the suggestions and chat features
- Boost productivity by automating tests, reviews, and pipeline fixes
- Integrate Copilot into IDEs and GitHub for maximum value
- Roll out Copilot across teams with proven onboarding strategies
- Build a knowledge-sharing culture with Copilot community champions

Supercharged Coding with GenAI

Hila Paz Herszfang, Peter V. Henstock

ISBN: 978-1-83664-529-0

- Work with GitHub Copilot in PyCharm, VS Code, and Jupyter Notebook
- Apply advanced prompting methods with ChatGPT and OpenAI API
- Gain insight into GenAI fundamentals to achieve better outcomes
- Adopt our structured framework to produce high-quality code
- Find out how to select the optimal GenAI tool for solving your specific tasks
- Elevate your use of GenAI tools from debugging to delivery
- Join the next generation of supercharged software engineers

If you're interested in becoming an author for Packt, please visit `authors.packt.com` and apply today. We have worked with thousands of developers and tech professionals, just like you, to help them share their insight with the global tech community. You can make a general application, apply for a specific hot topic that we are recruiting an author for, or submit your own idea.

Share your thoughts

Now you've finished *Everyone Is a Programmer*, we'd love to hear your thoughts! Scan the QR code below to go straight to the Amazon review page for this book and share your feedback or leave a review on the site that you purchased it from.

`https://packt.link/r/1807305597`

Your review is important to us and the tech community and will help us make sure we're delivering excellent quality content.

Index

V

W

www.ingramcontent.com/pod-product-compliance
Lightning Source LLC
LaVergne TN
LVHW081256100826
845148LV00005B/891

* 9 7 8 1 8 0 7 3 0 5 5 9 8 *